Sandblom: Elementary

Carl-Louis Sandblom

Elementary Statistics for Business and Economics

Walter de Gruyter
Berlin · New York 1983

Professor Dr. Carl-Louis Sandblom
Faculty of Commerce and Administration,
Concordia University, Montreal/Canada

CIP-Kurztitelaufnahme der Deutschen Bibliothek

Sandblom, Carl-Louis:
Elementary Statistics for Business
and Economics/Carl-Louis Sandblom.
– Berlin ; New York : de Gruyter, 1983.
ISBN 3-11-008302-7

Library of Congress Cataloging in Publication Data

Sandblom, Carl-Louis, 1942-
Elementary statistics for business and economics.
Includes bibliographies and index.
1. Social sciences – Statistical methods. 2. Statistics. 3. Commercial statistics. 4. Economics – Statistical methods. I. Title.
HA29.S249 1983 519.5 83-11627
ISBN 3-11-008302-7

Printing: Tutte Druckerei GmbH, Salzweg. Binding: Lüderitz & Bauer, Berlin.

Preface

A striking feature of this book is its size. By careful attention to the language, by appropriately using examples to illustrate concepts and methods and by omitting any unnecessary material, I have managed to keep the size to about half of most other similar books, and by so doing I hope to have combined brevity with clarity. Comments from many students have convinced me that the brief approach is pedagogically superior; the short treatment makes it easier for the students to grasp the main points and to follow the logical development of the material covered.

The contents are intended for basic statistics courses (undergraduate as well as graduate) in business administration, public administration, and economics. The book would be appropriate for a two-semester course but could also be used in a more intensive one-semester course. No previous exposure to statistics is assumed and no university level mathematics is required; however, some analytical capacity of the reader would of course be useful.

The exercises at the end of each chapter form an integral part of the book and the student is urged to solve as many of them that he or she feels are necessary for a thorough understanding of the chapter. This problem-solving aspect is absolutely essential; its importance can hardly be overemphasized. Partial answers to some of the exercises are given at the end of the book. Starred (*) or double-starred (**) problems are mathematically more challenging. Some chapter sections are also marked by a star; these can be left out without disrupting continuity.

All diagrams in the text are drawn to scale, using a Hewlett-Packard microcomputer and plotter.

I am grateful to several persons, first of all to the editor, Werner Schuder of Walter de Gruyter & Co. for encouragement, patience and understanding. My assistants, Richard Germain and Kathie Brown and my wife Ulrika helped by reviewing the entire manuscript, pointing out errors and making many helpful suggestions for improvement. In addition, Kathie Brown produced the diagrams. Thanks are also due to Antoinette Gerritse and Anita Beauchamp for efficient and meticulous typing.

I am also grateful to the Literary Executor of the late Sir Ronald A. Fisher,

F. R. S. to Dr. Frank Yates, F. R. S. and to Longman Group Ltd. London, for permission to adapt for Table No. 7 material from their book *Statistical Tables for Biological, Agricultural and Medical Research* (6th edition, 1974).

Carl-Louis Sandblom

Contents

1. Introduction

1.1 What is Statistics?

Statistics is a discipline concerned with collecting, analyzing and interpreting data. There are two basic types of statistical methods, *descriptive* and *inferential.* Descriptive statistics deals with summarizing and describing a given set of data, for display purposes. Chapters 2, 3 and 15 of this book fall into this category. Inferential statistics is concerned with drawing conclusions about a collection of data, based on observations taken from only a small part of the data. Inferential statistics is dealt with in Chapters 8 to 14. The *theory of probability,* treated in Chapters 4 to 7, will provide us with the logical foundation of statistical inference.

Statistical methods have been used for a long time in fields as diverse as economics, genetics, meteorology and physics. With the development of modern facilities for collecting, storing and retrieving large amounts of statistical data, and with the explosive advancement of computer technology, statistics have become more important than ever before. The use of statistics is now widespread in the natural as well as the social sciences; some knowledge of statistics is essential for the professional in industry of government as well as in the public or education sectors.[1] It is the purpose of this book to provide the reader with enough statistical background to enable him or her to function well in our modern society. I hope that in the process some of the mystique surrounding this field will disappear. It is not only desirable to know what can be done using statistical techniques; it is just as important to understand what they cannot do. My goal is to educate a knowledgeable but somewhat skeptical person; no matter how fascinating and powerful modern quantitative techniques may appear, they should only be used to complement (and never to replace) intelligent common sense.

Even though the study of statistics may be a duty, it can still be pleasant. Let me quote Francis Galton[2]: "Some people hate the very name of statistics, but I find them full of beauty and interest."

[1] See e.g. the books by Fairley and Mosteller, and by Baum and Scheuer.
[2] Sir Francis Galton, English biologist and statistician, 1822–1911.

1.2 Historical Background

The theory of probability dates back to the sixteenth and seventeenth centuries in Italy and France. It started as an analysis of games of hazard more than four centuries ago by Cardano[3]. It is in this tradition that probability concepts are often introduced in the connection of drawing cards from a shuffled deck, throwing dice or flipping coins. The theory of probability was then steadily developed, in particular by French and later by Russian mathematicians, into its modern complete and rigorous structure.

The theory of statistics can be said to have originated by Gauss[4] about one and a half centuries ago, as a theory of measurement errors in physics. Another more important development started in biology and genetics, pioneered by Galton, Pearson[5] and Fisher[6].

Most of the material in this book is based on classical results, except for some sections on nonparametric techniques and modern time series analysis. My ambition has been to make it as fresh and appealing to the reader who makes his first acquaintance with it, as it must have been to those who pioneered the field, whether it be fourteen, forty or four-hundred years ago.

1.3 Basic Concepts

For a proper understanding of this book, some very fundamental statistical concepts must be introduced. This is best done by way of a clarifying example.

Example 1.1

Consider a group of a hundred students of a certain university. If their ages are recorded, we obtain a *population* of *quantitative* data. If their continents of birth are recorded (North America, South America, Europe, etc.) we get another population of *qualitative* data. We could get other populations of each type by recording each student's sex, 1983 earnings, mother tongue, height, eye colour, current gross bank deposit holdings, etc.

In general, we define a *population* as a set of all data of some kind.

[3] Hieronymo Cardano, Italian mathematician, 1501–1576.
[4] Karl Friedrich Gauss, German mathematician, 1777–1855.
[5] Karl Pearson, English geneticist and mathematician, 1857–1936.
[6] Sir Ronald Aylmer Fisher, English statistician, 1890–1962.

Suppose now that instead of considering the whole group of a hundred students, we select only a part (subset), say, twenty students. This would be a *sample* taken from our population. We also define the two following concepts:

A *parameter* is a summary description of a population.

A *statistic* is a summary description of a sample.

Example 1.2

Suppose that the average age of our university student population is 21.4 years (it is then a *parameter*), and that the average age of our sample is 21.7 (it is then a *statistic*). As calculating this parameter involves adding a hundred numbers (and dividing the sum by a hundred), we might prefer not to compute the parameter but to use the sample statistic (which requires much less effort to compute). We can then use the value of the sample statistic to *infer* or *estimate* the unknown value of the parameter. Inferential statistics tells us how to do this prediction, and how reliable it will be.

References

Baum, P., and E.M. Scheuer: *Statistics Made Relevant: A Casebook of Real Life Examples*. John Wiley & Sons, New York 1976.

Chou, Y.: *Statistical Analysis*, 2nd edition. Holt, Rinehard and Winston, New York 1975.

Fairley, W.B., and F. Mosteller: *Statistics and Public Policy*. Addison-Wesley, Reading, Mass. 1977.

Hamburg, M.: *Statistical Analysis for Decision Making*, 2nd edition. Harcourt, Brace, Jovanovich, New York 1977.

Harnett, D.L.: *Statistical Methods*, 3rd edition. Addison-Wesley, Reading, Mass. 1982.

Hawkins, C.A., and J.E. Weber: *Statistical Analysis. Applications to Business and Economics*. Harper & Row, New York 1980.

Lapin, L.L.: *Statistics for Modern Business Decisions*, 3rd edition. Harcourt, Brace, Jovanovich, New York 1982.

Mansfield, E.: *Statistics for Business and Economics*, Norton & Company, New York 1980.

Neter, J., W. Wasserman and G.A. Whitmore: *Applied Statistics*, 2nd edition. Allyn and Bacon, Boston, Mass. 1982.

Ott, L.: *An Introduction to Statistical Methods and Data Analysis*, Duxbury Press, North Scituate, Mass. 1977.

Summers, G.W., W.S. Peters and C.P. Armstrong: *Basic Statistics in Business and Economics*, 3rd edition. Wadsworth, Belmont, California 1981.

Wonnacott, T.H., and R.J. Wonnacott: *Introductory Statistics for Business and Economics*, 2nd edition. John Wiley & Sons, New York 1977.

2. Graphical Display Methods

We shall now consider graphical methods to describe and display sets of statistical data. These methods form an important area of descriptive statistics. He or she who believes that "figures speak for themselves" will find that on the contrary, they tend to remain mute. It is the task of the statistician to reveal and describe the message that the figures convey.

In Section 2.1 we discuss and show how the frequency histogram and the frequency polygon are used to display quantitative date. The bar chart for displaying qualitative data is covered in Section 2.2.

2.1 Quantitative Data: The Frequency Histogram and the Frequency Polygon

Example 2.1

Consider the following data, which denote the number of completed years of service for each of a small company's employees:

3, 5, 2, 7, 3, 4, 1, 6, 3, 4, 7.

In this example, the data consists of numerical observations (measurements), and is therefore labelled as *quantitative*.

Definition: Observations or measurements that are recorded as numerical values form *quantitative* data.

Example 2.2

If in Example 2.1 the sex of each of the employees was recorded, we might get:

M, M, F, M, F, M, F, F, F, M, F
("M" for male and "F" for female).

In this example, the data consists of observations that are classifications and is therefore labelled as *qualitative*.

Definition: Observations or measurements that can be naturally classified into categories form *qualitative* data.

In this section we shall be concerned with quantitative data, and defer a discussion of qualitative data till the next section.

For display purposes, we may wish to present the data of Example 2.1 in graphical form, using a years of service *histogram.* We then number the employees from 1 to 11, and indicate this number on the horizontal axis of a diagram. On the vertical axis we put the number of years of service, and for each employee draw a rectangle with a height indicating the number of years of service. This is done in the histogram in Fig. 2/1.

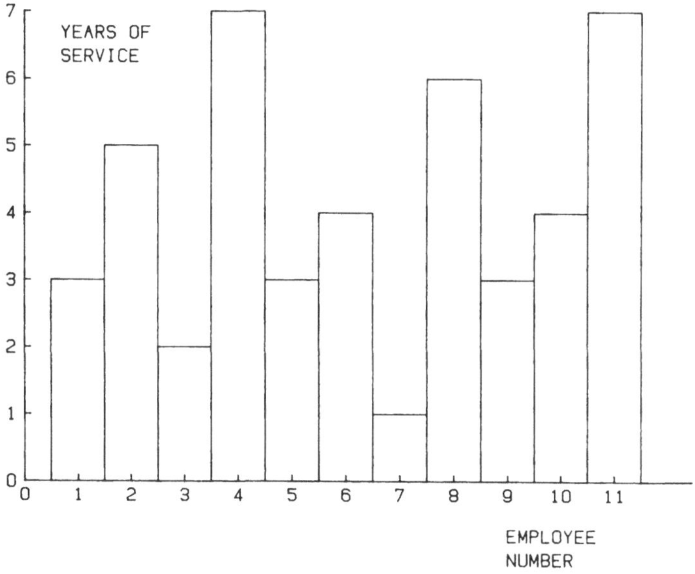

Fig. 2/1: Histogram for Example 2.1.

However, a more useful display of the data (which we describe as *raw data,* because it has not been organized in any way) can be obtained. First we group the observations into suitable *classes* and then indicate the number of observations that fall into each class. Starting at 0 years of service and using a *class interval* (*class width*) of 2 years we would obtain:

Class	Frequency (no. of observations)
0 years – less than 2 years	1
2 years – less than 4 years	4
4 years – less than 6 years	3
6 years – less than 8 years	3
Total	11

Fig. 2/2: Classifying the data of Example 2.1

The number of observations that fall into a category is called the *(absolute) frequency* of that category. We say that we have transformed the *raw data* into *grouped data*. We can now draw a *frequency histogram* based on the classification we have chosen. On the horizontal axis we have indicated the classes, and on the vertical axis the absolute frequencies are given:

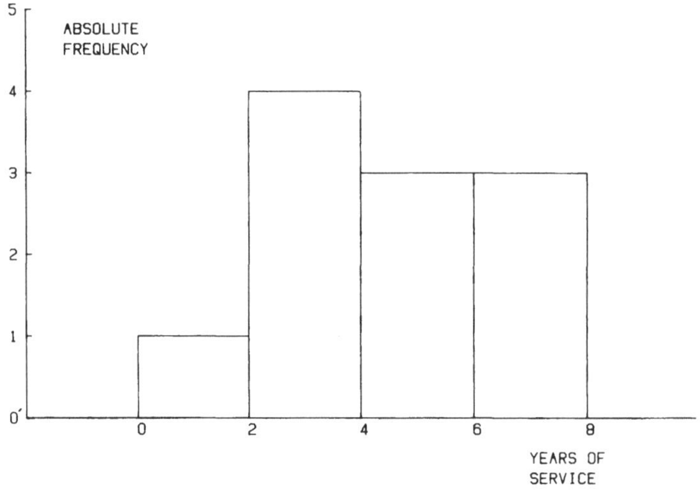

Fig. 2/3: Absolute frequency histogram.

As we see, the frequency histogram is a convenient aid to display the essential features of a data set. The need for such a display becomes more obvious if the data set consists of many observations.

Example 2.3

The age (in years, to one decimal point) and continent of birth for a sample of 100 students at a certain university in North America are given in the following table:

20.9	21.3	18.1	33.7	22.9	20.7	19.1	18.7	21.0	19.2
N.Am.	N.Am.	Eur.	Aus.	N.Am.	Afr.	N.Am.	S.Am.	Asia	N.Am.
18.6	19.6	19.0	21.5	20.8	21.1	28.6	25.3	19.9	20.6
N.Am.	N.Am.	N.Am.	N.Am.	Asia	N.Am.	N.Am.	N.Am.	N.Am.	N.Am.
21.1	18.0	30.2	23.6	24.0	17.9	21.6	27.2	23.4	22.9
N.Am.	N.Am.	Asia	N.Am.	N.Am.	N.Am.	N.Am.	Eur.	Afr.	N.Am.
20.5	23.8	20.9	22.3	25.6	21.8	23.2	19.8	18.7	27.8
N.Am.	Eur.	N.Am.	N.Am.	Eur.	N.Am.	S.Am.	N.Am.	N.Am.	N.Am.
23.3	22.5	25.3	23.8	21.5	26.4	24.1	26.9	22.6	24.5
N.Am.	N.Am.	N.Am.	N.Am.	N.Am.	N.Am.	Asia	N.Am.	N.Am.	Eur.
20.6	27.1	24.2	21.3	24.7	19.8	22.3	17.2	26.2	23.6
N.Am.	Afr.	N.Am.	Asia	Asia	N.Am.	N.Am.	Asia	N.Am.	N.Am.
24.4	22.8	20.3	17.0	23.1	26.7	23.4	26.5	21.4	25.5
Eur.	N.Am.	N.Am.	N.Am.	Afr.	N.Am.	N.Am.	N.Am.	N.Am.	Asia
21.1	25.2	22.2	23.7	25.4	19.0	26.3	22.7	24.8	21.7
N.Am.	S.Am.	N.Am.	Eur.	N.Am.	N.Am.	Aus.	N.Am.	S.Am.	N.Am.
23.5	18.8	22.9	24.0	28.7	26.6	28.2	26.8	19.9	24.6
N.Am.	N.Am.	Afr.	N.Am.	N.Am.	N.Am.	N.Am.	N.Am.	N.Am.	N.Am.
22.9	23.9	21.6	20.8	25.1	22.4	24.3	18.9	23.2	21.3
Asia	N.Am.	N.Am.	Eur.	N.Am.	N.Am.	Asia	N.Am.	N.Am.	N.Am.

Fig. 2/4: Data for Example 2.3

First of all, this data set consists of a qualitative part (the continent of birth), which we disregard in this section. The quantitative part (the age), which we shall now consider, is not in a form easy to digest for the ordinary reader. The data set is too massive for an easy appreciation of its characteristic features. We therefore take this raw data and transform it into grouped data. We select, conveniently, age classes as in the table below and calculate the absolute frequency for each class. We obtain:

Age (years)	Absolute frequency
17.0–18.9	10
19.0–20.9	18
21.0–22.9	26
23.0–24.9	23
25.0–26.9	15
27.0–28.9	6
29.0–30.9	1
31.0–32.9	0
33.0–34.9	1
	Total: 100

Fig. 2/5: Grouped data for Example 2.3

The grouped data can now be displayed in a histogram:

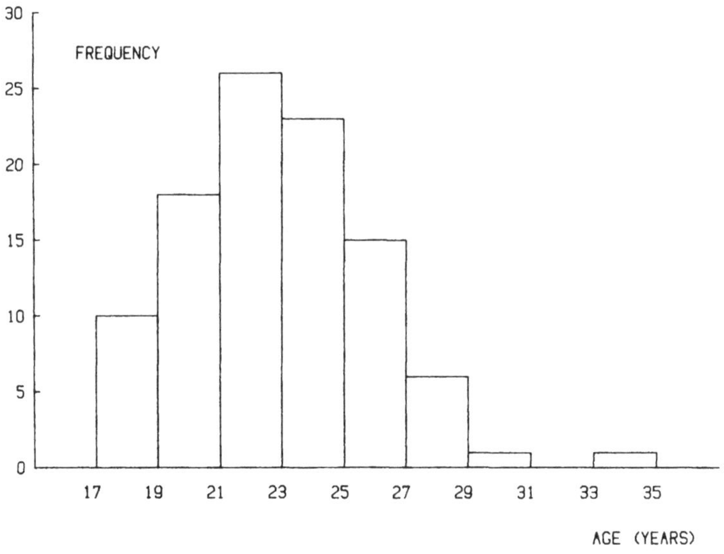

Fig. 2/6: Frequency histogram for Example 2.3, grouped data.

From the histogram in Fig. 2/6 we can easily see the age distribution of the 100 students in the sample. Another useful graphical display device is the *frequency polygon* which is closely related to the frequency histogram:

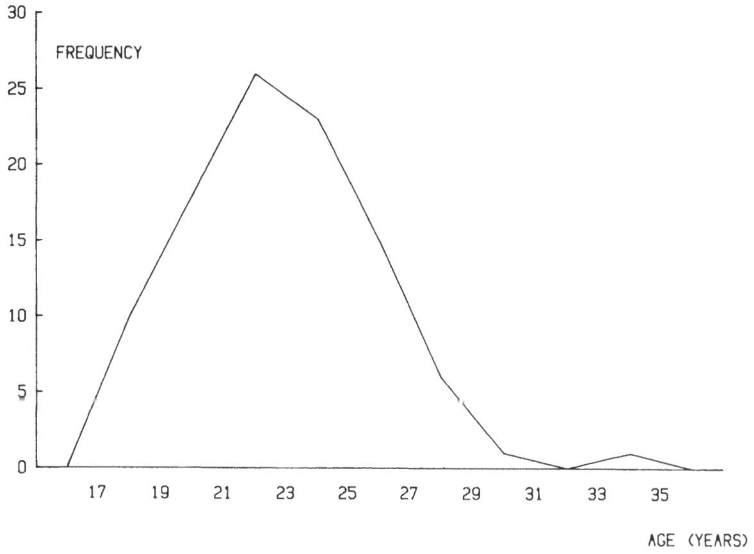

Fig. 2/7: Frequency polygon for Example 2.3, grouped data.

The method for constructing a frequency polygon should be clear from Fig. 2/7. After the data has been grouped into classes and the absolute frequencies determined, a dot is placed at the midpoint of each class, at at height corresponding to the absolute frequency. Then the dots are connected, for visual ease, by straight line segments. One dot is also placed on the horizontal axis at the midpoint of the class intervals outside of the data set, on each side.

We usually denote absolute frequencies by f_i, where i indicates the class. With N being the total number of observations in our data set we must then obviously have:

$$f_1 + f_2 + \ldots + f_k = \sum_{i=1}^{k} f_i = N,$$

where k is the number of classes.

Remark: The class intervals are usually of equal size, and must of course be such that:

a) every observation will fall into some class,
b) no observation belongs to more than one class.

Instead of using the absolute frequencies f_i, we may sometimes wish to use *relative frequencies*, f_i/N, which denote the proportion of observations that fall into the various categories. Relative frequencies are preferable when we compare data sets of different sizes.

Example 2.4

Referring to Example 2.1 and the grouped data shown in Fig. 2/2, we get the following table of relative frequencies. Note that N, the total number of observations, is 11, so that the relative frequencies are obtained from the absolute frequencies by dividing by 11:

Class	Relative frequency
$0 \leqq x < 2$	$1/11 \approx 0.0909$
$2 \leqq x < 4$	$4/11 \approx 0.3636$
$4 \leqq x < 6$	$3/11 \approx 0.2727$
$6 \leqq x < 8$	$3/11 \approx 0.2727$
TOTAL	$1 \approx 0.9999$

Fig. 2/8: Relative frequencies for Example 2.1

Example 2.5

Referring to Example 2.3 and the grouped data shown in Fig. 2/5 we obtain (note that $N = 100$):

Age (years)	i	Absolute frequency, f_i	Relative frequency, f_i/N
17.0–18.9	1	10	0.10
19.0–20.9	2	18	0.18
21.0–22.9	3	26	0.26
23.0–24.9	4	23	0.23
25.0–26.9	5	15	0.15
27.0–28.9	6	6	0.06
29.0–30.9	7	1	0.01
31.0–32.9	8	0	0.00
33.0–34.9	9	1	0.01
TOTAL		100	1.00

Fig. 2/9: Absolute and relative frequencies for Example 2.3

Remark: Relative frequencies f_i/N must always sum up to 1, as we can easily see:

$$\frac{f_1}{N} + \frac{f_2}{N} + \ldots + \frac{f_k}{N} = \frac{f_1 + f_2 + \ldots + f_k}{N} = \frac{N}{N} = 1,$$

because, as we pointed out above,

$$f_1 + f_2 + \ldots + f_k = N.$$

Instead of drawing absolute frequency histograms and absolute frequency polygons, we can draw relative frequency histograms and relative frequency polygons. The only difference is that relative instead of absolute frequencies are used on the vertical axis.

As a closing remark for this section, let us comment on the number of classes to choose. It is common practice to use no less than five (if possible) and no more than twenty classes. The reader will also realize that the number of classes is related to the width of the class intervals (the wider the intervals, the fewer the classes).

Other display methods exist, including *cumulative* frequency histograms and frequency polygons, but we shall omit them here.

2.2 Qualitative Data: The Bar Chart

Frequencies for qualitative data can conveniently be displayed in a *bar chart,* which corresponds to the histogram for quantitative data. The classes will now correspond to the categories into which the measurements must fall.

Example 2.6

The qualitative data set of Example 2.2 can be displayed in the following bar chart:

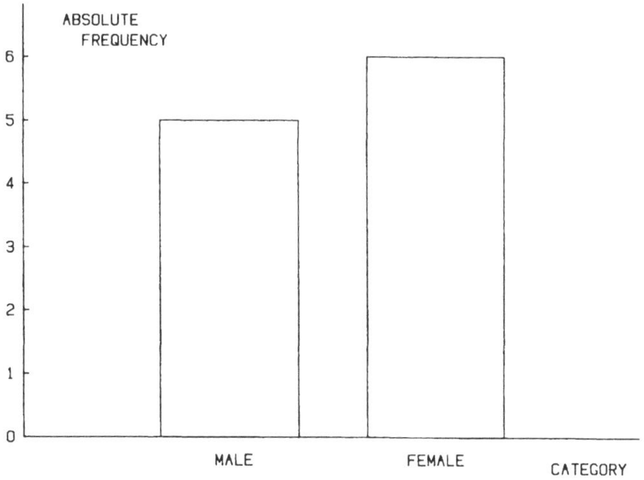

Fig. 2/10: Bar chart for Example 2.6.

Example 2.7

Summarizing the qualitative part of the data of Example 2.3, i.e. the continent of birth, we get the following table:

Continent	Afr.	Asia	Aus.	Eur.	N.Am.	S.Am.
Absolute Frequency	5	10	2	8	71	4
Relative Frequency	0.05	0.10	0.02	0.08	0.71	0.04

Fig. 2/11: Absolute and relative frequencies for Example 2.7

A bar chart using relative frequencies for the data of Example 2.7 would look as follows:

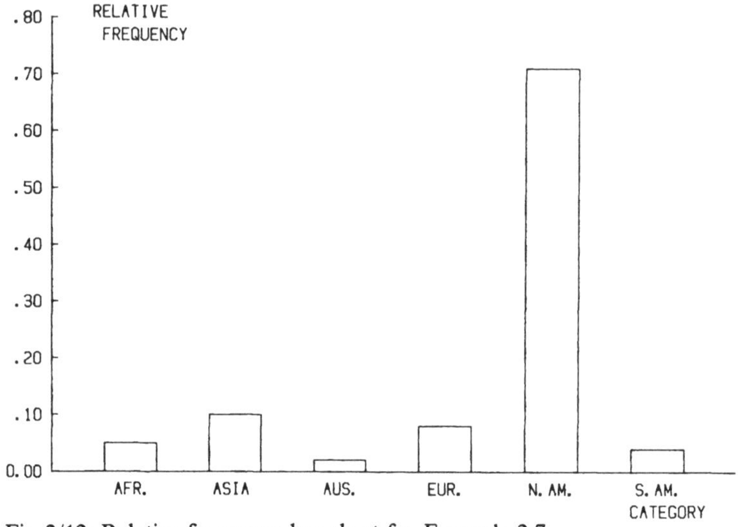

Fig. 2/12: Relative frequency bar chart for Example 2.7.

We end this chapter with an example to indicate how graphical techniques can be used to misrepresent statistical data.

Example 2.8 (How to lie with statistics)

Suppose that the following series of monthly consumer price index data is given:

120 122 118 124 126 130

Graphically, we get:

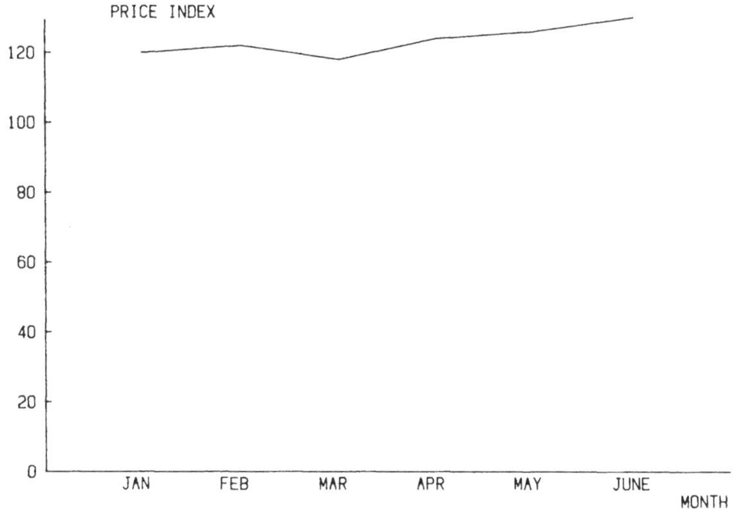

Fig. 2/13: "The consumer price index is stable".

By stretching the vertical axis and only showing the part between 110 and 130 points, and by compressing the horizontal axis we obtain the following picture:

Fig. 2/14: "The consumer price index is rising".

The truth is of course that the price index shows a rising tendency, but that this fact is suppressed in the first figure and exaggerated in the second.

Other display methods for qualitative data exist, including the *pie chart* and pictorial representation, but we shall not go into that here.

References

Coladarci, A., and Th. Coladarci: *Elementary Descriptive Statistics: For Those Who Think They Can't*. Wadsworth, Belmont, California 1981.

Harnett, D. L.: *Statistical Methods,* 3rd edition. Addison-Wesley, Reading, Mass. 1982.

Hawkins, C. A., and J. E. Weber: *Statistical Analysis. Applications to Business and Economics*. Harper & Row, New York 1980.

Huff, D.: *How to Lie with Statistics,* Norton & Company, New York 1954.

Johnson, R., and B. Siskin: *Elementary Statistics for Business*. Duxbury Press, North Scituate, Mass. 1980.

Madsen, R. W., and M. L. Moeschberger: *Statistical Concepts, With Applications to Business and Economics*. Prentice-Hall, Englewood Cliffs, New Yersey 1980.

Mansfield, E.: *Statistics for Business and Economics*. Norton & Company, New York 1980.

Wonnacott, T. H., and R. J. Wonnacott: *Introductory Statistics for Business and Economics,* 2nd edition. John Wiley & Sons, New York 1977.

Exercises

2–1 During the ten-year period 1967–1976, the yearly sales for the I. B. M. Corporation were as follows (billions of U.S. dollars): 5.3, 6.9, 7.2, 7.5, 8.3, 9.5, 11.0, 12.7, 14.4, 16.3.

a) Draw a frequency histogram displaying this data set.
b) Display the data set by a histogram, using the horizontal axis as the time scale, and indicating yearly sales on the vertical axis.

2–2 Below are temperatures (in degrees Fahrenheit) recorded for Montreal during January one particular year. This information must be summarized for the weather bureau.

40	14	18	26	26
38	5	21	27	25
35	0	25	34	27
20	−3	30	33	
15	2	32	29	
17	7	31	31	
18	14	28	30	

a) Group the data using class intervals of ten degrees, and construct a relative frequency histogram.
b) Group the data using class intervals of five degrees, and construct an absolute frequency histogram.
c) Using the classification in (a) above, draw an absolute frequency polygon.

2–3 Using the data and classification from Figure 2/2 in the text, construct:

a) an absolute frequency polygon.
b) a relative frequency polygon.

2–4 The following data shows the monthly beer consumption (in pints) of 110 English university students.

Class interval (pints)	Absolute frequency
25–29	38
30–34	42
35–39	14
40–44	7
45–49	3
50–54	4
55–59	2
Total:	110

a) Construct an absolute frequency histogram.
b) Construct a relative frequency polygon.

2–5 The following are starting salaries (fictitious) of Concordia B. Comm. graduates:

$20,600	17,300	19,100	18,100	18,300	20,200	20,400
20,200	19,800	19,100	18,900	21,500	20,600	19,500
17,900	20,700	18,100	19,400	18,500	19,500	19,400
17,500	19,400	17,600	21,400	18,100	20,400	20,900
18,300	17,000	17,100	18,400	18,300	18,300	17,900
20,200	19,400	20,400	20,500	18,700	17,100	20,300
18,300	17,900	18,400	21,400	17,900	17,300	18,100
18,100	16,400	16,600	18,000	19,400	16,500	18,400
19,100	18,400	20,100	19,300	20,300	17,600	18,100
21,400	18,200	20,000	17,300	18,100	21,400	20,400

a) Construct a frequency histogram using as class intervals $16,000 – 16,999, $17,000 – 17,999, etc.
b) Construct a frequency polygon using as class intervals $16,000 – 16,499, $16,500 – 16,999, etc.

2–6 Using the data of Example 2.3 in the text, construct a frequency histogram using as class intervals 17.0 – 17.9, 18.0–18.9, etc.

2–7 According to Statistics Canada, the following are the November 1979 provincial unemployment rates (unadjusted for seasonal variation):

Newfoundland	Ontario
14.3	6.1
Prince Edward Island	Manitoba
12.0	4.3
Nova Scotia	Saskatchewan
9.6	3.3
New Brunswick	Alberta
9.7	3.3
Quebec	British Columbia
8.8	6.9

Draw a bar chart representing this data.

2–8 Consider the qualitative data set of Example 2.7, displayed in Fig. 2/11 in the text. Construct a relative frequency bar chart for students born outside North America.

3. Measures of Central Location and Dispersion

In the previous chapter we considered different ways of describing and displaying, in graphical form, the essential features of any particular set of statistical data. Now we shall develop, in Section 3.1, different *numerical* measures to describe the central location (or central tendency) of a given quantitative data set. In Section 3.2, we consider different numerical measures of the variability (or dispersion) of data.

The numerical descriptions of central location and dispersion of a statistical population form an important part of descriptive statistics. They also point the way to probability theory, which will be our concern in subsequent chapters.

3.1 Numerical Measures of Central Location

In this section, we shall consider different methods for numerically describing the central location of a given set of quantitative data. By the central location or central tendency of the data we understand the "middle" or "centre" around which the observations tend to cluster in a sense to be made precise below.

Definition: The *arithmetic mean* μ of a data set is the sum of all observations, divided by the number of observations (elements) in the set.
Mathematically, suppose that there are N observations in the set, denoted by $X_1, X_2, \ldots, X_N$. Then we have:

$$\mu = \frac{X_1 + X_2 + \ldots + X_N}{N} = \frac{\sum_{i=1}^{N} X_i}{N}$$

The arithmetic mean is the most frequently used measure of central location. It is often referred to simply as the *mean* or the *average* of a data set (population).

For a sample taken from a given population, we usually denote the number of observations by n (as opposed to N for the population), and denote the *sample mean* by $\bar{X}$:

$$\bar{X} = \frac{X_1 + X_2 + \ldots + X_n}{n} = \frac{\sum_{i=1}^{n} X_i}{n}$$

Example 3.1

Consider the following data: 3, 5, 2, 7, 3, 4, 1, 6, 3, 4, 7. The figures denote the completed years of service for a certain company's employees. (Cf. Example 2.1 of the previous chapter).

The mean completed years of service, μ, will then be:

$$\mu = \frac{3 + 5 + 2 + 7 + \ldots + 3 + 4 + 7}{11} = \frac{45}{11} \approx 4.09$$

Example 3.2

We take a sample consisting of the first four observations of the population in Example 3.1. We get: 3, 5, 2, 7. The sample mean $\bar{X}$ will then be:

$$\bar{X} = \frac{3 + 5 + 2 + 7}{4} = \frac{17}{4} = 4.25$$

Example 3.3

Suppose that we record the annual salaries (in thousands of dollars) of the eleven employees of the company in Example 3.1. The result might be: 13.1, 15.2, 14.7, 19.2, 56.3, 17.1, 12.7, 24.4, 14.5, 16.2, 18.9. The mean annual salary μ will then be:

$$\mu = \frac{13.1 + 15.2 + \ldots + 16.2 + 18.9}{11} = \frac{222.3}{11} \approx 20.21$$

In Example 3.3 we see that one observation (56.3, corresponding to the salary of the company manager) is far above all the others in size. The effect of this observation is to pull up the value of the mean. This is clearly seen if we calculate the mean of the other ten observations, which is 16.6. A measure of central tendency which is not so sensitive to outlying observations (very much larger or very much smaller than the majority) is provided by the *median*.

Definition: The median M of a data set is a number such that half of the observations are as large or larger, and half of the observations are as small or smaller.

If we order the observations in ascending order of magnitude, the median M will be the value of the middle observation, if the total number of observations is odd. For a population with an even number of elements, the median will fall between the two middle observations. In this case, the median is defined to be the average of the two middle observations.

Example 3.4

Rearranging the data set of Example 3.1 in ascending order, we get: 1, 2, 3, 3, 3, 4, 4, 5, 6, 7, 7. The middle observation is now the sixth from the bottom (or the top), which is 4. Therefore the median M is 4.

Example 3.5

From the data set of Example 3.2, we compute the median M which in this case is the average of the two middle observations 3 and 5:

$$M = \frac{3+5}{2} = 4$$

Example 3.6

The median M of the data set in Example 3.3 is 16.2. This should be compared to the mean, $\mu = 20.21$.

Yet another measure of central location is provided by the *mode*.

Definition: The *mode* is the most frequently occurring value in a data set.

Example 3.7

The mode of the data set in Example 3.1 is 3.

It can easily happen that two or more values occur with the same frequency in a population. If this is so, the mode will not be unique.

Example 3.8

As in the data set 3, 5, 2, 7 from Example 3.2 each value occurs once, *each* will be a mode.

From the above example it is clear that the mode is not as useful as the mean or the median for expressing the central location of a population.

Grouped Data

Assume now that we are dealing with grouped data (see the previous chapter), having k classes with absolute frequencies f_i, $i = 1, \ldots, k$, respectively. Let X_i, i

= 1, ..., k, denote the measured value at the midpoint of each class interval no. i. If we approximate each observation in class i by the midpoint of the class, we find that the corresponding approximate value of the arithmetic mean μ is given by:

$$\mu \approx \frac{f_1 X_1 + f_2 X_2 + \ldots + f_k X_k}{N} = \frac{\sum_{i=1}^{k} f_i X_i}{N}$$

Alternatively, we can write:

$$\frac{f_1 X_1 + f_2 X_2 + \ldots + f_k X_k}{N} = X_1 \left(\frac{f_1}{N}\right) + X_2 \left(\frac{f_2}{N}\right) + \ldots + X_k \left(\frac{f_k}{N}\right)$$

$$= \sum_{i=1}^{k} X_i \left(\frac{f_i}{N}\right)$$

so that we have the alternative approximate formula for the arithmetic mean of grouped data:

$$\mu \approx \sum_{i=1}^{k} X_i \left(\frac{f_i}{N}\right)$$

(Remember that $\sum_{i=1}^{k} \frac{f_i}{N} = 1$)

Example 3.9

Refer to the grouped data represented by Fig. 2/2 of the previous chapter (for the raw data see Example 3.1). We have:

Class midpoint, X_i	Absolute frequency, f_i
1	1
3	4
5	3
7	3
	11

The approximate mean for the grouped data will then be:

$$\mu \approx \frac{\sum_{i=1}^{k} f_i X_i}{N} = \frac{f_1 X_1 + f_2 X_2 + f_3 X_3 + f_4 X_4}{N}$$

$$= \frac{1 \cdot 1 + 3 \cdot 4 + 5 \cdot 3 + 7 \cdot 3}{11} = \frac{49}{11} \approx 4.45$$

This value should be compared to the correct value of μ, which we found to be 4.09 (see Example 3.1).

We shall leave out a discussion of the median for grouped data and refer the interested reader to the books by Harnett and by Hawkins and Weber. (See the list of references at the end of this chapter.)

The mode for grouped data is defined as the midpoint of the class with the highest frequency. This class is referred to as the *modal class*. We may of course have populations with more than one mode (and consequently more than one modal class).

Example 3.10

The grouped data of Example 3.9 has mode 3; the class "2 – less than 4 years" is the modal class.

Symmetry and Skewness

We have discussed three different measures of central tendency; the mean, the median and the mode. How are they related to each other? This question is best answered by taking a graphical approach and considering the data sets (populations) by their frequency polygons (which we covered in the previous chapter).

Example 3.11

Consider a population with a relative frequency polygon as in Fig. 3/1.

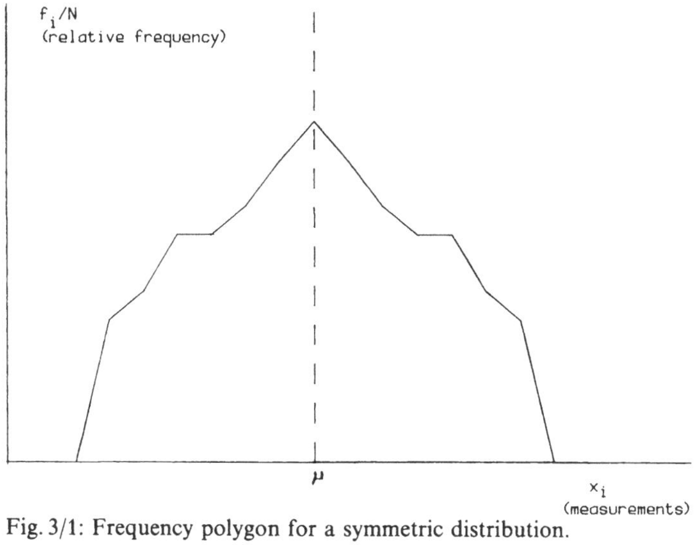

Fig. 3/1: Frequency polygon for a symmetric distribution.

This distribution is symmetric, i.e. if it were rotated 180° around the vertical line (dashed) through its arithmetic mean, it would still look the same. For a symmetric distribution, the mean and the median coincide. In Fig. 3/1, the mode coincides with the mean and the median. There are symmetric distributions, however, for which the mode will *not* coincide with the mean and the median.

Example 3.12

Consider the relative frequency polygon of Fig. 3/2.

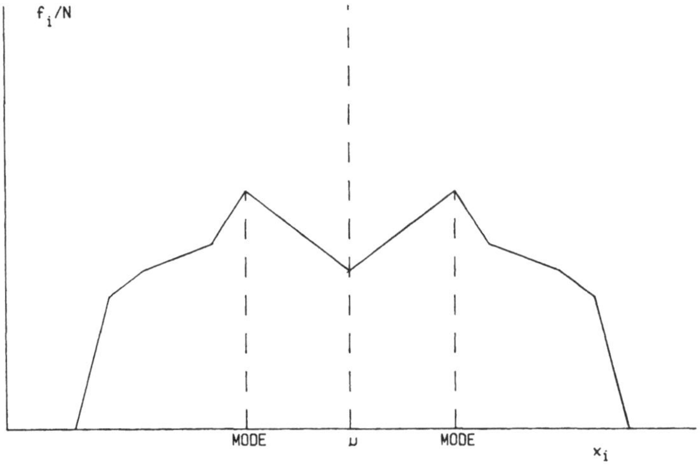

Fig. 3/2: Frequency polygon for a symmetric bimodal distribution.

This distribution is symmetric, but has *two* modes, as indicated, and is therefore called *bimodal.*

For distributions that are not symmetric, the mean and the median will not coincide. Such distributions are said to be *skewed.* If the mean is larger than the median, we say that the distribution is *skewed to the right;* if the mean is smaller than the median, the distribution is said to be *skewed to the left.*

Example 3.13

The distributions in Fig. 3/3 and 3/4 are skewed.

There are numerical measures for skewness, and also for how "peaked" a distribution is (high, narrow peak or low, wide peak). We shall not go into this here; more on the subject can be found in books by Chou and by Hawkins and Weber. (See the list of references at the end of this chapter.)

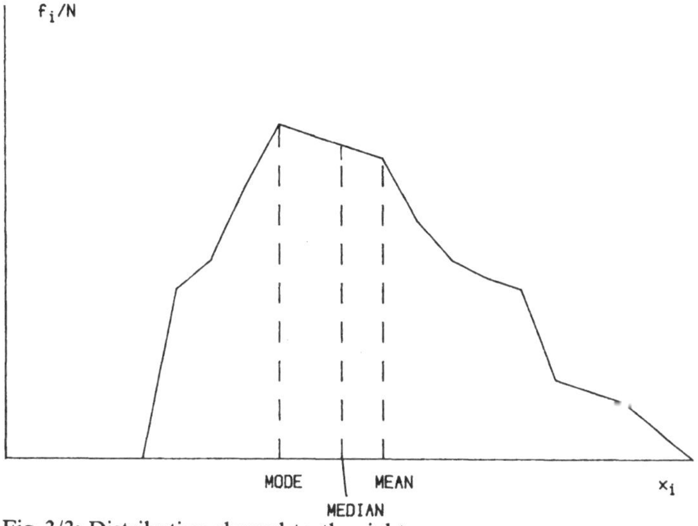

Fig. 3/3: Distribution skewed to the right.

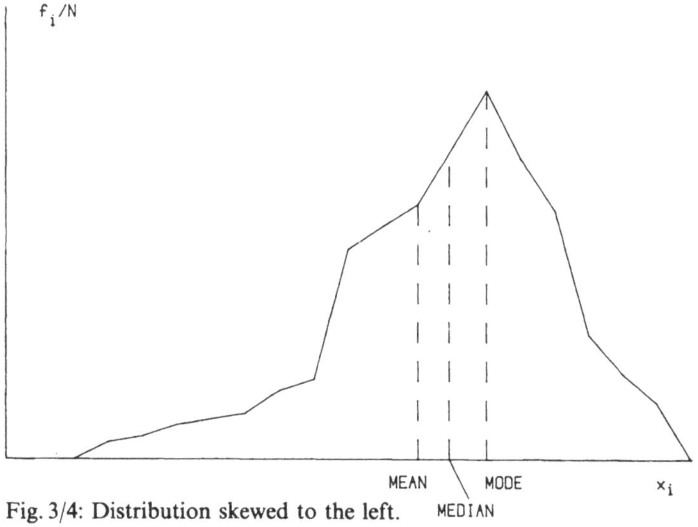

Fig. 3/4: Distribution skewed to the left.

3.2 Numerical Measures of Dispersion

Our aim now is to develop different measures of the dispersion of a given set of quantitative data. Measuring a population's variability, or dispersion, is just as important as finding its centre. One measure of dispersion is the *range*, which is the difference between the largest and the smallest observation values. This will unfortunately ignore all other values that fall in between.

We can give another dispersion measurement based on *quartiles*. The *first quartile* is the value below which 25% of the observations lie; in a similar way we define the *second quartile* (which is the same as the median) and the *third quartile*. (The p'th percentile is the value below which p% of the observations fall.) A dispersion measure based on quartiles is the *interquartile range,* which is the difference between the 3rd and 1st quartiles and represents the middle 50% of the observation values.

We are still looking for a dispersion measure that considers *every* observation. One might try to take the deviations from the mean $X_i - \mu$ and then take the average of these. But we will then always get 0, because:

$$\frac{1}{N}\sum_{i=1}^{N}(X_i-\mu)=\frac{1}{N}\left(\sum_{i=1}^{N}X_i-\sum_{i=1}^{N}\mu\right)$$
$$=\frac{1}{N}\left(N\underbrace{\sum_{i=1}^{N}\frac{X_i}{N}}_{\mu}-N\mu\right)=0$$

Instead, we make the following definition.

Definition: The *population variance,* σ^2, is the mean of the *squared* deviations, i.e.

$$\sigma^2=\frac{(X_1-\mu)^2+(X_2-\mu)^2+\ldots+(X_N-\mu)^2}{N}$$
$$=\frac{\sum_{i=1}^{N}(X_i-\mu)^2}{N}$$

Definition: The *population standard deviation,* σ, is the square root of the variance, i.e.

$$\sigma=\sqrt{\frac{1}{N}\sum_{i=1}^{N}(X_i-\mu)^2}$$

Expanding $(X_i-\mu)^2=X_i^2-2\mu X_i+\mu^2$ we find

$$N\sigma^2=\sum_{i=1}^{N}(X_i-\mu)^2=\sum_{i=1}^{N}(X_i^2-2\mu X_i+\mu^2)$$
$$=\sum_{i=1}^{N}X_i^2-\sum_{i=1}^{N}2\mu X_i+\sum_{i=1}^{N}\mu^2$$
$$=\sum_{i=1}^{N}X_i^2-2\mu\underbrace{\sum_{i=1}^{N}X_i}_{N\mu}+N\mu^2=\sum_{i=1}^{N}X_i^2-2N\mu^2+N\mu^2$$
$$=\sum_{i=1}^{N}X_i^2-N\mu^2$$

so that

$$\sigma^2 = \frac{1}{N}\left(\sum_{i=1}^{N} X_i^2 - N\mu^2\right) \quad \text{or} \quad \sigma^2 = \frac{\sum_{i=1}^{N} X_i^2}{N} - \mu^2$$

This is called the *shortcut* formula for the population variance. Generally, the shortcut expression is numerically easier to use than the definitions, when the variance or the standard deviation of a population is to be calculated.

For a sample with n observations X_i, $i = 1, \ldots, n$ and sample mean $\bar{X} = \frac{1}{N} \cdot \sum_{i=1}^{N} X_i$ we have:

Definition: The *sample variance,* s^2, is given by:

$$s^2 = \frac{\sum_{i=1}^{n} (X_i - \bar{X})^2}{n-1}$$

and the *sample standard deviation,* s, by:

$$s = \sqrt{s^2} = \sqrt{\frac{\sum_{i=1}^{n} (X_i - \bar{X})^2}{n-1}}$$

Remark: The reason why we have $n - 1$ instead of n in the denominator of these two expressions will become clear later on.

In analogy with the population variance case, we obtain the following shortcut expression for the sample variance.

$$s^2 = \frac{1}{n-1}\left(\left(\sum_{i=1}^{n} X_i^2\right) - n\bar{X}^2\right)$$

$$= \frac{1}{n-1}\left(\sum_{i=1}^{n} X_i^2 - \frac{\left(\sum_{i=1}^{n} X_i\right)^2}{n}\right)$$

The shortcut formula for the sample variance is proved in the same fashion as the shortcut formula for the population variance, and is left to the reader as an exercise.

Example 3.14

With our data set of Example 3.1 we organize the calculations as follows (fill in the table *columnwise*):

i	X_i	X_i^2	$X_i - \mu$	$(X_i - \mu)^2$
1	3	9	−1.0909	1.1901
2	5	25	0.9091	0.8265
3	2	4	−2.0909	4.3719
4	7	49	2.9091	8.4629
5	3	9	−1.0909	1.1901
6	4	16	−0.0909	0.0083
7	1	1	−3.0909	9.5537
8	6	36	1.9091	3.6447
9	3	9	−1.0909	1.1901
10	4	16	−0.0909	0.0083
11	7	49	2.9091	8.4629
$\Sigma =$	45	223	0.0001	38.9095

We have $N = 11$ and get, as before, $\mu = \frac{45}{11} \approx 4.0909$

For the population variance, σ^2, we obtain, using the formula from the definition, and the $(X_i - \mu)^2$ column:

$$\sigma^2 = \frac{1}{N} \cdot \sum_{i=1}^{N} (X_i - \mu)^2 \approx \frac{1}{11} \cdot 38.9095 \approx 3.5372$$

or using the shortcut formula:

$$\sigma^2 = \frac{1}{N} \sum_{i=1}^{N} X_i^2 - \mu^2 = \frac{1}{11} \cdot 223 - \left(\frac{45}{11}\right)^2 \approx 3.5372.$$

We see that in this example the shortcut formula is superior from a computational point of view, as only the X_i and X_i^2 columns are needed.

The population standard deviation, σ, is then:

$$\sigma = \sqrt{\sigma^2} \approx \sqrt{3.5372} \approx 1.8807.$$

The range is, of course, $7 - 1 = 6$.

Example 3.15

Considering the data set of the previous example as a *sample* we would get:

$$n = 11, \quad \bar{X} = \frac{45}{11} \approx 4.0909 \quad \text{(the sample mean)}$$

and the sample variance s^2 (shortcut formula):

$$s^2 = \frac{1}{n-1}\left(\sum_{i=1}^{n} X_i^2 - \frac{\left(\sum_{i=1}^{n} X_i\right)^2}{n}\right)$$

$$= \frac{1}{11-1}\left(223 - \frac{(45)^2}{11}\right) \approx \frac{1}{10}(223 - 184.0909) \approx 3.8909$$

and the sample standard deviation, s

$$s = \sqrt{s^2} \approx \sqrt{3.8909} \approx 1.9725\,.$$

Grouped Data

For grouped data, we have, in analogy with the case of the mean, the following formulas:

The population variance, σ^2, for grouped data is approximately given by:

$$\sigma^2 \approx \frac{\sum_{i=1}^{k} f_i (X_i - \mu)^2}{N} = \sum_{i=1}^{k} (X_i - \mu)^2 \left(\frac{f_i}{N}\right).$$

The sample variance, s^2, for grouped data is approximately given by:

$$s^2 \approx \frac{\sum_{i=1}^{k} f_i (X_i - \bar{X})^2}{n-1} = \sum_{i=1}^{k} (X_i - \bar{X})^2 \left(\frac{f_i}{n-1}\right).$$

By taking the square root of the expressions in the above formulas, we obtain approximate expressions for the population standard deviation σ and the sample standard deviation s.

In shortcut form, the formulas are:

$$\sigma^2 \approx \sum_{i=1}^{k} X_i^2 \left(\frac{f_i}{N}\right) - \mu^2$$

$$s^2 \approx \frac{1}{n-1}\left(\sum_{i=1}^{k} f_i X_i^2 - \frac{\left(\sum_{i=1}^{k} f_i X_i\right)^2}{n}\right).$$

Example 3.16

The population variance σ^2 for the data set of Example 3.1, grouped as in Example 3.9, can be calculated approximately using the shortcut formula:

$$\sigma^2 \approx \sum_{i=1}^{k} X_i^2 \left(\frac{f_i}{N}\right) - \mu^2$$

$$= X_1^2\left(\frac{f_1}{N}\right) + X_2^2\left(\frac{f_2}{N}\right) + X_3^2\left(\frac{f_3}{N}\right) + X_4^2\left(\frac{f_4}{N}\right) - \mu^2$$

$$= 1^2\cdot\left(\frac{1}{11}\right) + 3^2\cdot\left(\frac{4}{11}\right) + 5^2\cdot\left(\frac{3}{11}\right) + 7^2\cdot\left(\frac{3}{11}\right) - \left(\frac{45}{11}\right)^2$$

$$= \frac{1}{11}\cdot 259 - \left(\frac{45}{11}\right)^2 \approx 3.70\,.$$

This value should be compared to 3.54, obtained for the raw data.

How can we interpret the population or sample standard deviation σ?

It is a measure of how much the values are "spread out" around the mean. In a sense, it is the average distance of the values from the mean.

In many real-life situations, the data will be *normally distributed* (we shall come to this in Chapter 6) or approximately so; in such a case one can show that about two thirds of the values will be within a distance of one standard deviation from the mean. About 95% of the values will be within two standard deviations from the mean.

References

Chou, Y.: *Statistical Analysis,* 2nd edition, Holt, Rinehart and Winston, New York 1975.

Coladarci, A., and Th. Coladarci: *Elementary Descriptive Statistics: For Those Who Think They Can't.* Wadsworth, Belmont, California 1980.

Daniel, W. W., and J. C. Terrell: *Business Statistics. Basic Concepts and Methodology,* 3rd edition. Houghton Mifflin, Boston 1983.

Harnett, D. L.: *Statistical Methods,* 3rd edition. Addison-Wesley, Reading, Mass. 1982.

Hawkins, C. A., and J. E. Weber: *Statistical Analysis. Applications to Business and Economics.* Harper & Row, New York 1980.

Mansfield, E.: *Statistics for Business and Economics.* Norton & Company, New York 1980.

Mendenhall, W., and J. E. Reinmuth: *Statistics for Management and Economics,* 3rd edition. Duxbury Press, North Scituate, Mass. 1978.

Wonnacott, T. H., and R. J. Wonnacott: *Introductory Statistics for Business and Economics,* 2nd edition. John Wiley & Sons, New York 1977.

Exercises

3–1 Using the data set of Exercise no. 1 of Chapter 2, compute:

a) the arithmetic mean, b) the median.

3–2 Using the data set of Exercise no. 2 of Chapter 2, compute the arithmetic mean.

3–3 Using the data set of Exercise no. 7 of Chapter 2, compute the mean.

3–4 Using the data set of Exercise no. 5 of Chapter 2, compute:

a) the mean,
b) the median,
c) the mode.

3–5 Using the data set of Example 2.3 of Chapter 2, compute:

a) the mean,
b) the median,
c) the mode.

3–6 Using the grouped data resulting from Exercise no. 2a of Chapter 2, compute the mean.

3–7 Using the grouped data resulting from Exercise no. 2b of Chapter 2, compute the mean.

3–8 Using the grouped data of Exercise no. 4 of Chapter 2, compute the mean.

3–9 Based on the grouped data resulting from Exercise no. 5a of Chapter 2, compute the mean and the mode.

3–10 Based on the grouped data resulting from Exercise no. 5b of Chapter 2, compute the mean and the mode.

3–11 Based on the grouped data resulting from Exercise no. 6 of Chapter 2, compute the mean and the mode.

3–12 Using the same data as in Exercise no. 1, compute:

a) the population variance,
b) the sample variance,
c) the population standard deviation,
d) the sample standard deviation,
e) the range.

3–13 Using the same data as in Exercise no. 2, compute:

a) the range,
b) the sample variance,
c) the population standard deviation.

3–14 Using the same data as in Exercise no. 3, compute:

a) the range,
b) the sample standard deviation,
c) the population variance,
d) the sample variance.

3–15 Using the same data as in Exercise no. 4, calculate:

a) the range,
b) the population standard deviation,
c) the sample variance,
d) the population variance.

3–16 Using the same data set as in Exercise no. 5, find:

a) the population variance,
b) the population standard deviation,
c) the sample variance,
d) the sample standard deviation.

3–17 Based on the grouped data used in Exercise no. 6, compute:

a) the population variance,
b) the sample variance.

3–18 Based on the grouped data used in Exercise no. 7, calculate:

a) the population variance,
b) the sample variance,
c) the population standard deviation,
d) the sample standard deviation.

3–19 Based on the grouped data used in Exercise no. 8, find:

a) the sample standard deviation,
b) the sample variance.

3–20 Based on the grouped data used in Exercise no. 9, find:

a) the population variance,
b) the sample standard deviation,
c) the sample variance.

3–21 Based on the grouped data used in Exercise no. 10, compute:

a) the population variance,
b) the population standard deviation,
c) the sample standard deviation,
d) the sample variance.

3–22 Based on the grouped data used in Exercise no. 11, calculate:

a) the sample variance,
b) the sample standard deviation,
c) the population variance,
d) the population standard deviation.

4. Probability

The theory of probability, which is treated in this chapter, forms the foundation for the material in the remainder of this book. Because of the limited mathematical ability assumed on the part of the reader, the treatment is necessarily very basic. We shall only cover enough ground for our needs later on.

In Section 4.1 we introduce basic concepts such as random experiment, simple and composite events and event space. We also consider the tree diagram and give a somewhat pragmatic but usable definition of probability. Some basic set algebra is covered in Section 4.2, stressing the usefulness of the Venn diagram approach. We continue the set algebra in Section 4.3 by defining and giving examples of mutually exclusive and collectively exhaustive events.

The addition law for probabilities is the topic of Section 4.4, and we continue in Section 4.5 by defining and exemplifying conditional probability. This leads us in a natural way to the multiplication law, which is the topic of Section 4.6, and statistical independence, which is treated in Section 4.7.

Section 4.8 is devoted to Bayes' theorem and the revision of probabilities, which are introduced by an example from the marketing area. We conclude the chapter by covering, in Section 4.9, some combinatorial analysis (by some authors referred to as "counting rules"), which we shall need later on.

4.1 Basic Definitions

The *probability* of an *event* (or outcome of an experiment) is a number p, $0 \leqq p \leqq 1$, which measures the likelihood that the event will occur. If p is near 1 the event is very likely to happen; a p near to 0 indicates that the event is unlikely to happen. We think of p as the *proportion of times* that the event will occur, if the experiment is repeated a large number of times; in other words, p is the event's long-run relative frequency of occurrence.

Suppose that we toss a coin to get "head" or "tail". We call this a (*random*) *experiment,* because we can repeat it any number of times (or at least imagine that we could), and before each toss, the outcome "head" or "tail" would be unknown in advance. The outcomes "head" and "tail" are called *events* of the random experiment "toss a coin". The *event* (or *sample*) *space* of a random experiment is the set of all possible events that may occur. Exactly one of the events from the event space will occur. In the "toss a coin" experiment the event space will be {head, tail}. The elements of the event space are sometimes also referred to as *simple* or *elementary* events as opposed to *composite* events, which are combinations of simple events.

Example 4.1

Consider the random experiment "toss a die and record the number of dots showing".

The event space is {1, 2, 3, 4, 5, 6}. {3} is an elementary event, but {odd value} is the composite event (or *event set*) {1, 3, 5}.

Suppose that we toss a coin three times and record the outcome for each toss. By (T, H, H) we mean the event: "tail in the first toss and head in the second and third". This is *not* the same event as (H, H, T): "head in the first and second tosses and tail in the third". There are 8 simple events for the random experiment "toss a coin three times", because there are two possibilities for the first toss. For each of these, there are two possibilities for the second toss, which gives $2 \times 2 = 4$ possibilities for the first two tosses. For each of these four there are two possibilities for the third toss, i.e. $2 \times 2 \times 2 = 8$ possibilities for all three tosses.

We can illustrate the outcome of a random experiment like the above where there are several stages, by a so-called *tree diagram*. See Fig. 4/1 on the next page.

The tree grows from left to right and branches out at the *event forks*.

Suppose now that a random experiment is repeated a large number of times, n, and that an event, e, occurs n_e times ($n_e \leqq n$). We define the *probability of the event e*, P(e), as the value to which $\frac{n_e}{n}$ tends, when n becomes very large:

$$P(e) = \lim_{n \to \infty} \frac{n_e}{n}.$$

Remark: We can not be absolutely sure that $\frac{n_e}{n}$ will tend to some number as n grows, but all empirical evidence tells us that it will.

As we must have $0 \leqq n_e \leqq n$ we get $0 \leqq \frac{n_e}{n} \leqq 1$ and so $0 \leqq P(e) \leqq 1$ for every event. Furthermore, if the event space of a random experiment consists of the elementary events $e_1, e_2, \ldots, e_m$, i.e. the event space $\{e_1, e_2, \ldots, e_m\}$, and each

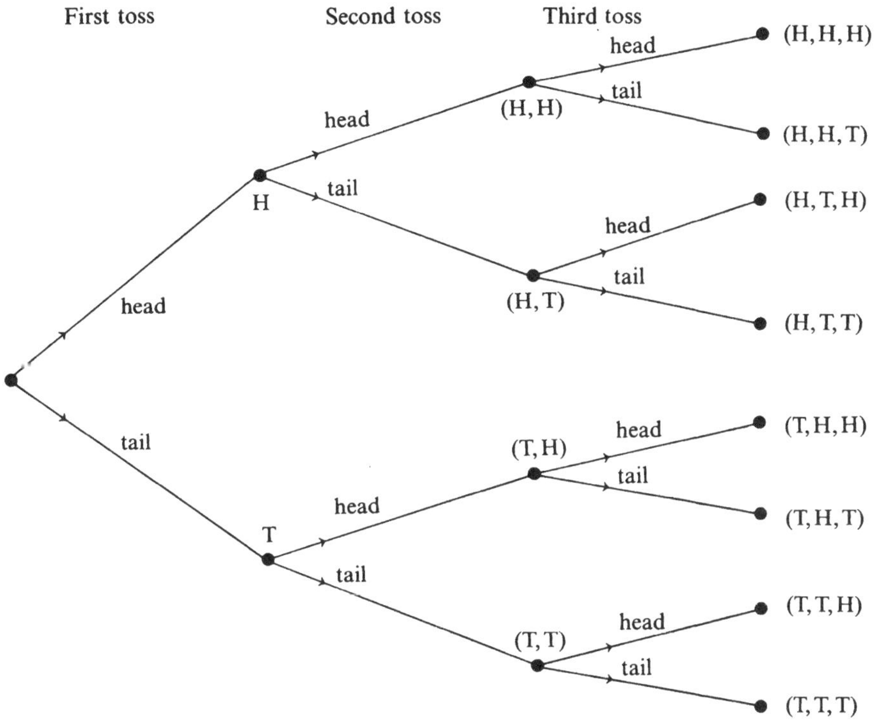

Fig. 4/1: Tree diagram for the experiment "toss a coin three times".

of these events occur $n_1, n_2, \ldots, n_m$ number of times, we must have $n_1 + n_2 + \ldots + n_m = n$. Hence, to calculate $P(e_1) + P(e_2) + \ldots + P(e_m)$, we form $\frac{n_1}{n} + \frac{n_2}{n} + \ldots + \frac{n_m}{n} = \frac{n_1 + n_2 + \ldots + n_m}{n} = \frac{n}{n} = 1$ and so we conclude that $P(e_1) + P(e_2) + \ldots + P(e_m) = 1$ or

$$\sum_{i=1}^{m} P(e_i) = 1 .$$

Example 4.2

Consider the random experiment "toss a coin". The event space is {head, tail}. We find $P(\text{head}) + P(\text{tail}) = 1$.

Example 4.3

Consider the random experiment "draw a card from a shuffled deck of 52 cards".

The event space is {spades, hearts, clubs, diamonds}. We have: P(spades) + P(hearts) + P(clubs) + P(diamonds) = 1. In addition, P(jack of hearts) + P(not jack of hearts) = 1. We also have: P(impossible event) = 0, P(certain event) = 1.

If each of the m elementary events $e_1, \ldots, e_m$ of a random experiment are *equally likely* then putting:

$$P(e_1) = P(e_2) = P(e_3) = \ldots = P(e_m) \quad \text{we get:}$$

$$1 = \sum_{j=1}^{m} P(e_j) = \sum_{j=1}^{m} p = mp \quad \text{i.e.} \quad p = \frac{1}{m}.$$

Example 4.4

For "toss a coin" we get P(head) = 1/2; for "draw a card" we get P(king of spades) = 1/52.

Also, if an event space consists of m equally likely elementary events, and a composite event e consists of r of these elementary events, then $P(e) = \frac{r}{m}$.

Example 4.5

Draw a card. We find: P(clubs) = 13/52 = 1/4, P(face card) = 12/52 = 3/13.

Remark: Sometimes, particularly in betting games, the probability of an event is measured by the *odds* of the event.

Definition: The *odds* of an event with probability p are:

$$\frac{p}{1-p}.$$

For example, if $p = 3/4$, we find the odds:

$$\frac{p}{1-p} = \frac{3/4}{1-3/4} = 3.$$

4.2 Basic Set Algebra

Although the sets in this section can be thought of as event sets, they may also be sets of numbers or other objects.

Definition: The *union* $A \cup B$ ("A union B") of two sets A and B consists of elements belonging to A and/or B, and the *intersection* $A \cap B$ ("A intersection B") consists of elements belonging to both A and B. We can illustrate these concepts in a so-called *Venn diagram*, where the sets A and B correspond to the points inside the respective contours:

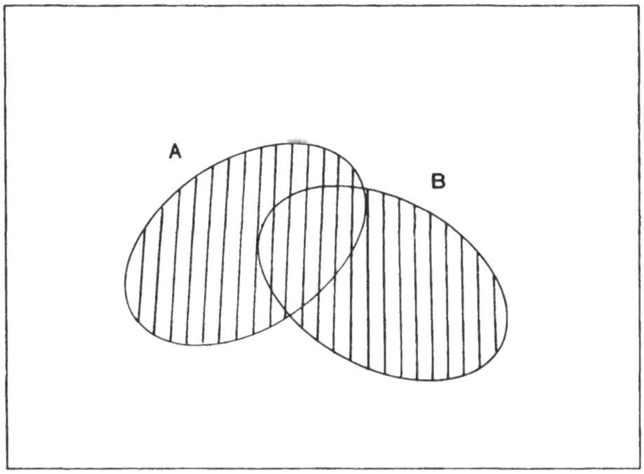

Fig. 4/2: The shaded area is $A \cup B$.

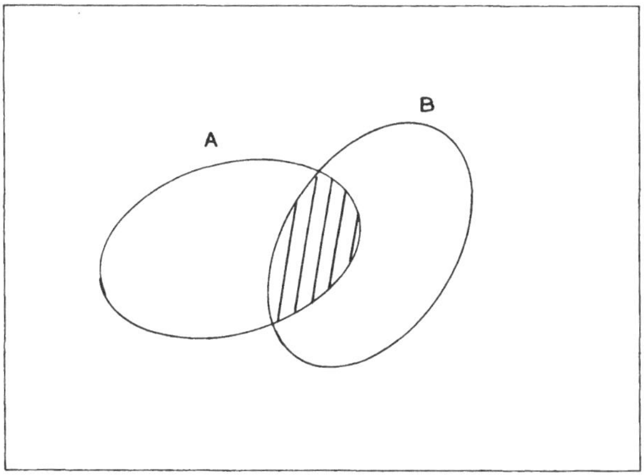

Fig. 4/3: The shaded area is $A \cap B$.

The *complement* $\bar{A}$ (also denoted by C A) of A consists of the elements which do not belong to A:

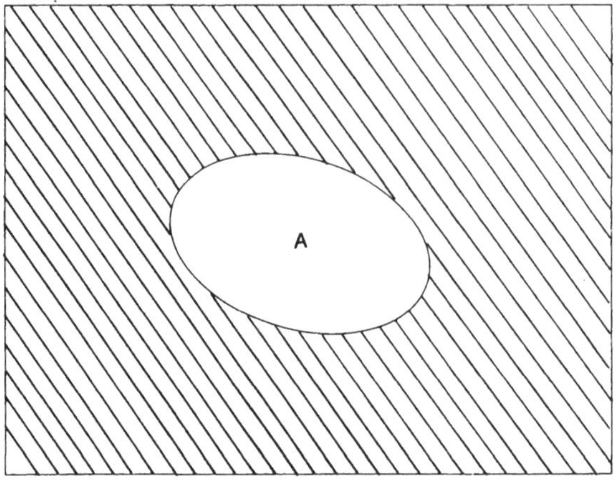

Fig. 4/4: The shaded area is $\bar{A}$.

Remark: In the Venn diagram approach, all points are supposed to be inside the rectangle, which we refer to as the *universal set* E or simply the *universe*.

Example 4.6

Consider the number of dots that a die can show; the universe is $\{1, 2, 3, 4, 5, 6\}$. Then "not less than two" refers to the set $A = \{2, 3, 4, 5, 6\}$, and "less than five" refers to the set $B = \{1, 2, 3, 4\}$.

Now we get:

$$
\begin{aligned}
A \cup B &= \{1, 2, 3, 4, 5, 6\}, \quad \text{i.e. the universe} \\
A \cap B &= \{2, 3, 4\} \\
\bar{A} &= \{1\} \\
\bar{B} &= \{5, 6\} \\
\bar{A} \cup B &= \{1, 2, 3, 4\} \\
\bar{A} \cap B &= \{1\} \\
A \cap \bar{B} &= \{5, 6\} \\
\overline{A \cap B} &= \{1, 5, 6\}.
\end{aligned}
$$

The last set in Example 4.6, $\overline{A \cap B}$, is the complement of $A \cap B$. If $A \cap B$ is empty, we write:

$$A \cap B = \emptyset$$

where $\emptyset$ is called the *empty set*, and we say that A and B are *disjoint*.

One can state and prove several rules of set algebra, e.g.

$$\overline{A \cup B} = \bar{A} \cap \bar{B}$$
$$\overline{A \cap B} = \bar{A} \cup \bar{B}$$
$$\overline{(\bar{A})} = A$$
$$(A \cap B) \cup (A \cap \bar{B}) = A \quad \text{etc.}$$

The Venn diagram is a very useful aid in this context.

4.3 Mutally Exclusive and Collectively Exhaustive Events

Definition: A collection of sets is *mutually exclusive* if each intersection of any two of the sets is empty.

Example 4.7

Consider the following sets:

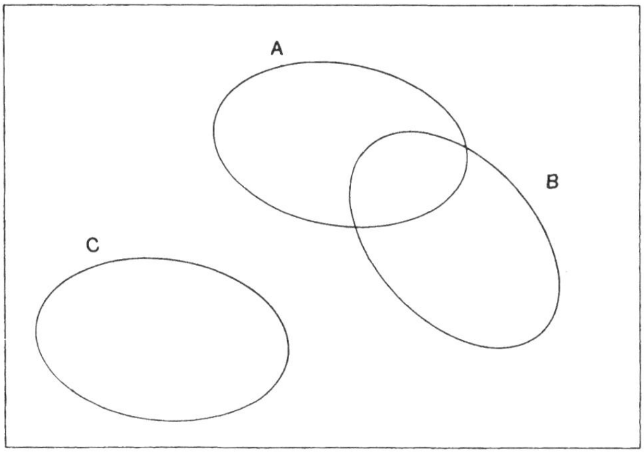

Fig. 4/5: A, B and C are not mutually exclusive.

We see that A and C are mutually exclusive (they are disjoint), and so are B and C. However, even though $A \cap B \cap C$ is empty, A, B and C are *not* mutually exclusive, because $A \cap B$ is not empty.

Example 4.8

Consider the following sets:

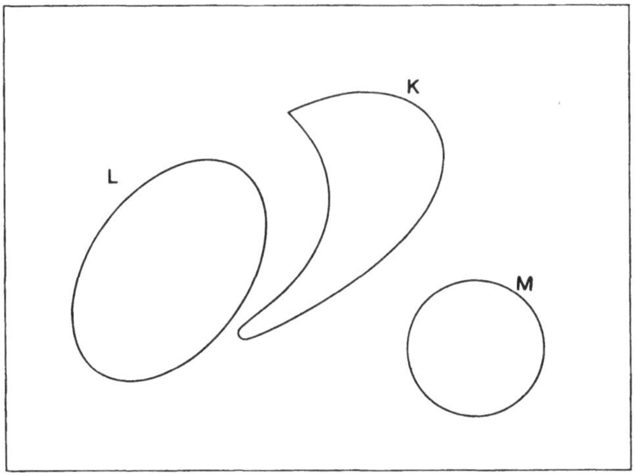

Fig. 4/6: L, K and M are mutually exclusive.

We find:

$$L \cap K = \emptyset$$
$$L \cap M = \emptyset$$
$$K \cap M = \emptyset$$

so that L, K and M are mutually exclusive.

Regarding event sets, we realize that for mutually exclusive events, at most one of them can occur.

Definition: A collection of sets is *collectively exhaustive* if their union equals the universal set.

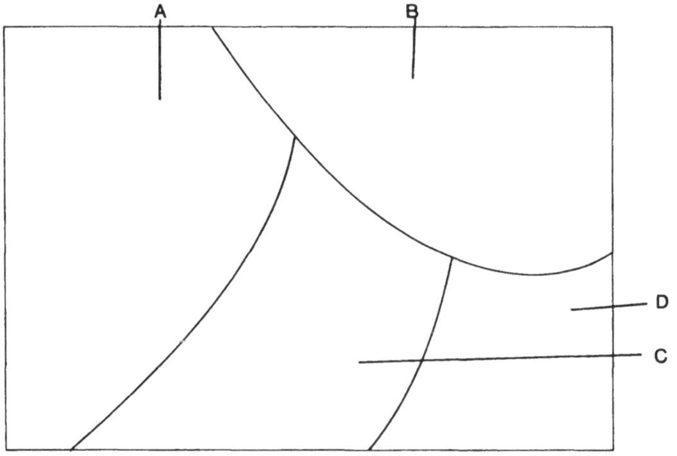

Fig. 4/7: Collectively exhaustive and mutually exclusive sets.

Example 4.9

Consider the following sets in Fig. 4/7 on the previous page.

We find that A, B, C and D are mutually exclusive and also collectively exhaustive.

We shall also deal with sets of numbers, e.g. the set $A = \{x \mid x \leqq 3\}$ is the set of all real numbers x such that x is less than or equal to 3. It is clear that $\bar{A} = \{x \mid x > 3\}$, i.e. the set of all x such that x is greater than 3. If $B = \{x \mid x \geqq 0\}$ (the set of all nonnegative real numbers) then $A \cap B = \{x \mid 0 \leqq x \leqq 3\}$.

4.4 The Addition Law

Theorem: For any events A and B, we have:

$$P(A \cup B) = P(A) + P(B) - P(A \cap B).$$

Instead of proving this theorem, we shall illustrate it by way of an example.

Example 4.10

Consider a couple planning a family of three children. We can draw a tree diagram for this:

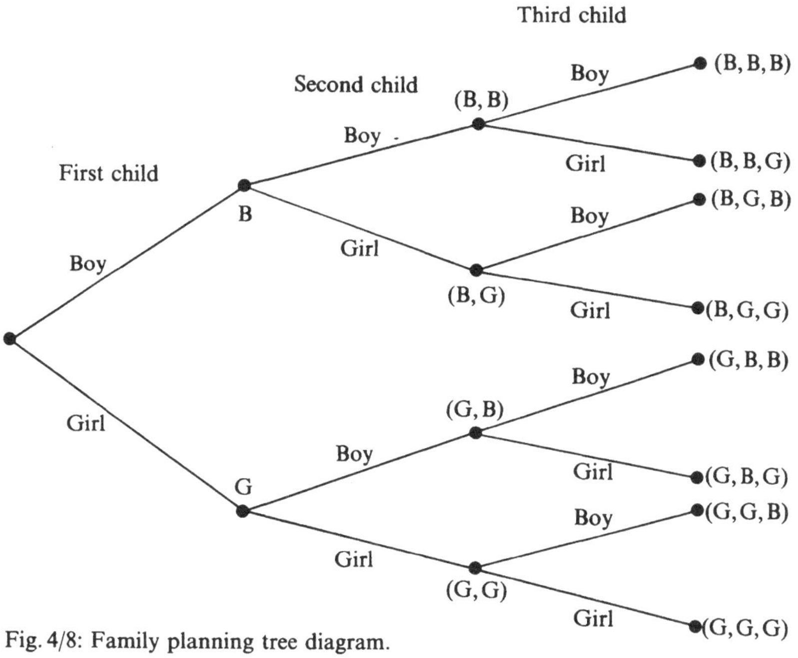

Fig. 4/8: Family planning tree diagram.

We regard the eight events (B, B, B), (B, B, G), ..., (G, G, G) as equally likely; they must therefore have probability 1/8 each.

Let A be the event: "fewer than two boys" and D: "all three the same sex".

Then we can see that:

$$A = \{(B, G, G), (G, B, G), (G, G, B), (G, G, G)\}$$

and $D = \{(B, B, B), (G, G, G)\}$, and it follows that:

$$P(A) = 4/8, \quad P(D) = 2/8.$$

Furthermore:

$$A \cup D = \{(B, B, B), (B, G, G), (G, B, G), (G, G, B), (G, G, G)\}$$

and $A \cap D = \{(G, G, G)\}$, from which we conclude:

$$P(A \cup D) = 5/8, \quad P(A \cap D) = 1/8.$$

Using the addition law $P(A \cup D) = P(A) + P(D) - P(A \cap D)$ we get: $5/8 = 4/8 + 2/8 - 1/8$ as we expected. The $-P(A \cap D)$ is needed because (G, G, G) would otherwise have been counted twice on the right-hand side (being an element of both A and D).

Remark: If E is the universal set, obviously $P(E) = 1$; for the empty set $\emptyset$ we have $P(\emptyset) = 0$. Furthermore, if A and B are disjoint, so that $A \cap B = \emptyset$, then we see that the addition law takes the simple form:

$$P(A \cup B) = P(A) + P(B).$$

Example 4.11

As an event A and its complement $\bar{A}$ are disjoint, we get:

$$P(A \cup \bar{A}) = P(A) + P(\bar{A}).$$

Furthermore, A and $\bar{A}$ are collectively exhaustive, i.e. $A \cup \bar{A} = E$, the universal set, from which we obtain:

$$P(A \cup \bar{A}) = P(E) = 1.$$

Consequently,

$$P(A) + P(\bar{A}) = 1$$

or:

$$P(\bar{A}) = 1 - P(A).$$

This result is often quite useful in applications. E.g., to compute in our Example 4.10 above the probability of the event "both sexes are represented", we realize that this is the complement of D. Then we get:

$$P(\bar{D}) = 1 - P(D) = 1 - 2/8 = 3/4\,.$$

Similarly,

$$P(\text{at least one boy}) = 1 - P(\text{no boy}) = 1 - P(G, G, G) = 1 - 1/8 = 7/8\,.$$

For three or more events, the addition law becomes complicated, except when the events are mutually exclusive. Guided by the result for two disjoint events, one can prove the following:

Theorem: If $A_1, A_2, \ldots, A_n$ are mutually exclusive events, then:

$$P(A_1 \cup A_2 \cup \ldots \cup A_n) = P(A_1) + P(A_2) + \ldots + P(A_n)\,,$$

i.e. $$P\left(\bigcup_{i=1}^{n} A_i\right) = \sum_{i=1}^{n} P(A_i)\,.$$

In the general case, resorting to a Venn diagram and using the above theorem is recommended.

Example 4.12

For three events A, B and C we consider a Venn diagram:

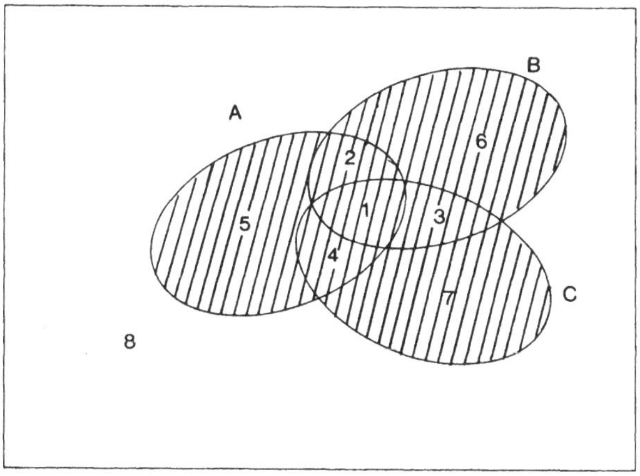

Fig. 4/9: Venn diagram for three events.

By assigning numbers as in the figure to the various regions $1, 2, \ldots, 8$ which are mutually exclusive, and by using the addition law above for mutually exclusive events, we can justify the addition law for three events:

$$P(A \cup B \cup C) = P(A \cup B) + P(A \cup C) + P(B \cup C) - P(A \cap B) - P(A \cap C) - P(B \cap C) + P(A \cap B \cap C).$$

This is left as an exercise for the reader.

4.5 Conditional Probability

Eighty people are asked if they read the newspapers Gazette or Times. The following table gives the result:

	Reads Gazette	Does not read Gazette	Total
Reads Times	5	15	20
Does not read Times	25	35	60
Total	30	50	80

Fig. 4/10: Absolute frequency table for newspaper readers.

From this we can calculate the *joint probability* table by dividing all numbers by 80:

	Read Gazette	Does not read Gazette	
Reads Times	1/16	3/16	1/4
Does not read Times	5/16	7/16	3/4
	3/8	5/8	

Fig. 4/11: Probability table for newspaper readers.

We say that e.g. {Reads Times} $\cap$ {Does not read Gazette} is a *joint* event. The row and column totals are called *marginal* probabilities.

Obviously {Reads Times} = ({Reads Times} $\cap$ {Reads Gazette}) $\cup$ ({Reads Times} $\cap$ {Does not read Gazette}) and because all four joint events are mutually exclusive, we get:

P({Reads Times}) = P({Reads Times} $\cap$ {Reads Gazette}) +
P({Reads Times} $\cap$ {Does not read Gazette}) = 1/16 + 3/16 = 1/4

in accordance with our table.

From the original table we also see that out of the 30 people who read Gazette, there are 5 Times readers; the probability that a Gazette reader is also a Times reader is therefore 5/30 = 1/6. We say that the *conditional* probability of Times reader, given Gazette reader, is 1/6 and we write

$$P(\{\text{Times reader}\} \mid \{\text{Gazette reader}\}) = 1/6 .$$

In general, we have the following:

Definition: For any events A, B, the *conditional probability* $P(A \mid B)$ of A, *given B,* is

$$P(A \mid B) = \frac{P(A \cap B)}{P(B)} .$$

Remark: We must of course assume that $P(B) \neq 0$ in the above expression.

Example 4.13

From our newspaper joint probability table above we can calculate the following conditional probabilities, where "Z" stands for Times reader and "W" denotes Gazette reader:

$$P(Z \mid W) = \frac{P(Z \cap W)}{P(W)} = \frac{1/16}{3/8} = 1/6$$

$$P(Z \mid \bar{W}) = \frac{P(Z \cap \bar{W})}{P(\bar{W})} = \frac{3/16}{5/8} = 3/10$$

$$P(W \mid Z) = \frac{P(W \cap Z)}{P(Z)} = \frac{1/16}{1/4} = 1/4$$

$$P(\bar{W} \mid \bar{Z}) = \frac{P(\bar{W} \cap \bar{Z})}{P(\bar{Z})} = \frac{7/16}{3/4} = 7/12$$

etc.

Example 4.14

Consider the problem of carrying out quality control of manufactured objects. The objects are either "good" or "bad" and are being tested, with result "accept" or "reject". The result is displayed in the table below:

	Accept	Reject	
Good	0.70	0.15	0.85
Bad	0.05	0.10	0.15
	0.75	0.25	1.00

Fig. 4/12: Joint probabilities for quality control

We obtain: $P(\text{good} \mid \text{accept}) = \frac{0.70}{0.75} = \frac{14}{15} \approx 0.93$, which should be compared with $P(\text{good}) = 0.85$ which is what we would get without testing. In other words, only 7 percent of the accepted items are actually bad, whereas 15 percent of the untested items are bad. On the other hand, we see that $P(\text{reject} \mid \text{good}) = \frac{0.15}{0.85} = \frac{3}{17} \approx 0.18$, which represents the "cost" or "waste" for getting the higher quality, as 18 percent of the good items are inadvertently rejected.

4.6 The Multiplication Law

From the definition of conditional probability in the previous section we immediately obtain the *multiplication law:*

Theorem: For any events A and B, the following relationship holds:

$$P(A \cap B) = P(A \mid B) \cdot P(B).$$

Because $A \cap B = B \cap A$ we can also write:

$$P(A \cap B) = P(B \mid A) \cdot P(A).$$

For three events we get $P(A \cap B \cap C) = P(A \mid B \cap C) \cdot P(B \cap C) = P(A \mid B \cap C) \cdot P(B \mid C) \cdot P(C)$.

It is left to the reader as an exercise to show that we also have:

$$P(A \cap B \cap C) = P(A) \cdot P(B \mid A) \cdot P(C \mid A \cap B).$$

If we repeat this procedure we get the *multiplication law for n events:*

Theorem: For any events A_i, $i = 1, \ldots, n$, the following expression is true:

$$P(A_1 \cap A_2 \cap \ldots \cap A_n) = P(A_1) \cdot P(A_2 \mid A_1) \cdot P(A_3 \mid A_1 \cap A_2) \cdot \ldots \cdot P(A_n \mid A_1 \cap A_2 \cap \ldots \cap A_{n-1}).$$

Example 4.15

Draw four cards from a shuffled deck of 52 cards. What is the probability that all four are kings? To calculate this probability we denote by A_j the event "card j is a king". Then we find:

$$P(A_1) = 4/52, \qquad P(A_2|A_1) = 3/51,$$
$$P(A_3|A_1 \cap A_2) = 2/50, \quad P(A_4|A_1 \cap A_2 \cap A_3) = 1/49.$$

Consequently, $P(\text{all four are kings}) = \dfrac{4\cdot 3\cdot 2\cdot 1}{52\cdot 51\cdot 50\cdot 49} = \dfrac{1}{270725} = 0.00000369$ $= 3.69\cdot 10^{-6}$.

4.7 Statistical Independence

Definition: The events A and B are said to be *statistically independent* if $P(A \cap B) = P(A)\cdot P(B)$.

Remark: We see that the definition of statistically independent events leads to the multiplication law for such events.

Let us consider the conditional probability of A, given B, for statistically independent events:

$$P(A|B) = \frac{P(A \cap B)}{P(B)} = \frac{P(A)\cdot P(B)}{P(B)} = P(A).$$

Similarly, we find:

$$P(B|A) = \frac{P(B \cap A)}{P(A)} = \frac{P(B)\cdot P(A)}{P(A)} = P(B).$$

Summarizing, we get the following:

Theorem: It the events A and B are statistically independent, then we have:

$$P(A|B) = P(A) \quad \text{and} \quad P(B|A) = P(B).$$

In other words the probability of one of the events is not dependent on whether the other event has occured or not.

Example 4.16

In our newspaper example we had $P(Z|W) = 1/6 \neq 1/4 = P(Z)$ so that Z and W are *statistically dependent*.

For several events $A_1, \ldots, A_n$ we talk of *collective* statistical independence, if each of the events is statistically independent of every intersection of combinations of the others. For collectively statistically independent events we get the simplified *multiplication law:*

Theorem: For any collectively statistically independent events A_i, $i = 1, \ldots, n$ we have:

$$P(A_1 \cap A_2 \cap \ldots \cap A_n) = P(A_1) \cdot P(A_2) \cdot \ldots \cdot P(A_n)$$

which we can write:

$$P\left(\bigcap_{j=1}^{n} A_j\right) = \prod_{j=1}^{n} P(A_j).$$

Remark: Some authors *define* statistical independence by the relation $P(A|B) = P(A)$. They can then prove, as a *theorem,* the relation $P(A \cap B) = P(A) \cdot P(B)$. As both definitions are equivalent, it does not matter which approach is taken; however, one can argue that our approach is the more elegant of the two.

4.8 Bayes' Theorem

Example 4.17

A firm is about to launch a new product on the market. Depending on the sales, the firm estimates that the product will be a *success* (with a probability of 0.40) or a *failure* (with a probability of 0.60). To obtain some more information, a market research survey is carried out. For a successful product, there is a 0.70 chance that the survey will give a *favourable* indication, a 0.20 chance of a *neutral* indication and 0.10 chance of an *unfavourable* indication. For an unsuccessful product, the corresponding figures are 0.10, 0.30 and 0.60, respectively. Suppose that the survey gives a favourable indication. What is then the probability of success?

Solution: Let us denote the event "success" by S, the event "failure" by F and the events "favourable", "neutral" and "unfavourable" by A, B and C respectively. The information we have is the following:

$$P(S) = 0.40, \quad P(F) = 0.60,$$

$$P(A|S) = 0.70, \quad P(B|S) = 0.20, \quad P(C|S) = 0.10,$$
$$P(A|F) = 0.10, \quad P(B|F) = 0.30, \quad P(C|F) = 0.60.$$

However, we wish to calculate $P(S|A)$.

We get:

$$P(S|A) = \frac{P(S \cap A)}{P(A)} = \frac{P(A|S) \cdot P(S)}{P(A)}.$$

In this expression, only $P(A)$ is unknown, and needs to be calculated. How should this be done? A clue to the solution of this problem lies in the fact that S and F are mutually exclusive and collectively exhaustive.
Using set algebra we then see that:

$$A = (A \cap S) \cup (A \cap F),$$

where $A \cap S$ and $A \cap F$ are mutually exclusive.

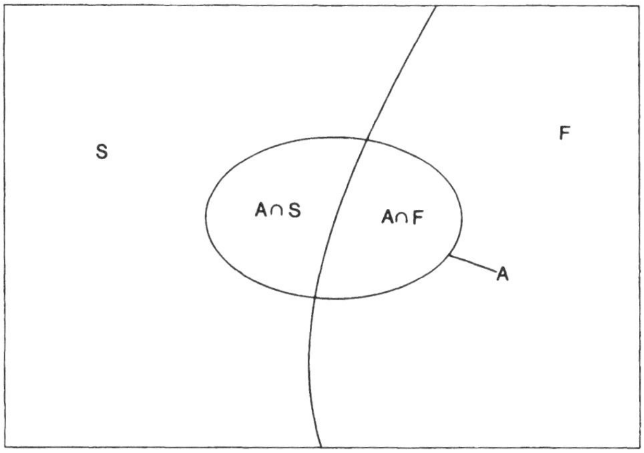

Fig. 4/13: $A \cap S$ and $A \cap F$ are mutually exclusive.

Therefore, we can write:

$$\begin{aligned} P(A) &= P(A \cap S) + P(A \cap F) \\ &= P(A|S) \cdot P(S) + P(A|F) \cdot P(F). \end{aligned}$$

We see that in the above expression, all entering probabilities are known. Inserting this expression for $P(A)$ in the previous formula for $P(S|A)$, we find:

$$\begin{aligned} P(S|A) &= \frac{P(A|S) \cdot P(S)}{P(A)} = \frac{P(A|S) \cdot P(S)}{P(A|S) \cdot P(S) + P(A|F) \cdot P(F)} \\ &= \frac{0.7 \cdot 0.4}{0.7 \cdot 0.4 + 0.1 \cdot 0.6} = \frac{14}{17} \approx 0.82. \end{aligned}$$

In this example we have developed and used a special case of Bayes' theorem[1], which we shall now give in the general case:

Bayes' Theorem

Suppose that the events $A_1, A_2, \ldots, A_n$ are mutually exclusive and collectively exhaustive. Then, for any event B and any A_j we have:

$$P(A_j \mid B) = \frac{P(B \mid A_j) \cdot P(A_j)}{\sum_{i=1}^{n} P(B \mid A_i) \cdot P(A_i)} .$$

Remark: In the context of Bayes' theorem, the events A_i, $i = 1, \ldots, n$ are often referred to as *states of nature* or *hypotheses.*

Exercise: Prove Bayes' theorem by using the fact that $B \cap A_i$, $i = 1, \ldots, n$ are mutually exclusive and have their union equal to B. This fact is used in conjunction with the formula:

$$P(A_j \mid B) = \frac{P(A_j \cap B)}{P(B)} = \frac{P(B \mid A_j) \cdot P(A_j)}{P(B)} .$$

In Bayes' theorem, the probabilities $P(A_j)$ are called *prior* probabilities, whereas $P(A_j \mid B)$ are referred to as *posterior* probabilities.

In our example above, we saw that the prior probability of success was 0.40, which corresponded to the posterior probability of 0.82, given the information that the survey gave a favourable indication. The extra information provided by the survey enabled us to *revise* or *update* the prior probability. As an end of the chapter exercise, the reader will be asked to revise more probabilities from this example.

Bayes' theorem lies at the foundation of a whole branch of modern statistics, called *Bayesian statistics.* In this setting, the prior probabilities are often more of less informed guesses of the statistician or decision maker, and are then usually called *subjective* probabilities. Additional information is then collected, providing a basis for the revision of the subjective probabilities.

4.9 Combinatorial Analysis

We have already been using the following principle, when we dealt with tree diagrams:

[1] From the English clergyman, Thomas Bayes, 1702–1761.

Multiplication Principle

If an experiment A has N possible outcomes and an experiment B has M possible outcomes, then there are $N \times M$ possible outcomes of the combined experiment A and B.

Let us now consider a problem where we use this principle.

Example 4.18

Four political candidates are to be ranked, in order. How many possible ranking lists are there?

Solution: There are four possibilities for the top position. For each of these possibilities, there are three choices for the second, i.e. $4 \times 3 = 12$ possibilities for the top two positions on the list. For each of these, there are two possibilities for the third position. After that, there is only one candidate left for the bottom position. Summarizing, there are $4! = 4 \times 3 \times 2 \times 1 = 24$ possible ranking lists.

In general, N elements can be ordered in $N! = N \times (N-1) \times (N-2) \times \ldots \times 2 \times 1$ ways. We say that N! ("N-factorial") is the number of *permutations* of N objects.
We have:

N	0	1	2	3	4	5	6	7	...
N!	1	1	2	6	24	120	720	5040	...

Remark: We define $0! = 1$ which may appear strange, but the reason will become clear below.

Example 4.19

Suppose that we now wish to establish a ranking list of four politicans selected out of eleven. How many such ranking lists are there?

Solution: There are eleven choices for the top position; for each of these there are ten for the second; for each of these there are nine for the third; finally there are eight for the bottom fourth. That is, there are $11 \times 10 \times 9 \times 8 = 7920$ ranking lists.

We can write $11 \times 10 \times 9 \times 8 = \dfrac{11 \times 10 \times 9 \times 8 \times 7 \times 6 \times \ldots \times 2 \times 1}{7 \times 6 \times \ldots \times 2 \times 1} = \dfrac{11!}{7!}$ $= \dfrac{11!}{(11-4)!}$.

In general, there are $\frac{N!}{(N-n)!}$ possible ranking lists of n elements, selected out of N. We call it the number of *permutations of n objects chosen from N.*

Remark: With $n = N$ we get $\frac{N!}{(N-N)!} = \frac{N!}{0!} = N!$, and we are back to the first case.

Example 4.20

Consider the problem of forming a committee of four politicians selected out of eleven. This time we are not concerned about the order in which the four are selected or ranked. How many such committees are there?

Solution: Denote the number of possible committees by $\binom{11}{4}$ ("eleven over four"). The members of each such committee can be ranked in 4! ways. In other words, there are $\binom{11}{4} \times 4!$ possible ranking lists of four politicians selected out of eleven. But we have already calculated this number, and found it to be $\frac{11!}{7!}$. That is, $\binom{11}{4} \times 4! = \frac{11!}{7!}$. from which we obtain

$$\binom{11}{4} = \frac{11!}{4!\,7!} = \frac{11 \times 10 \times 9 \times 8}{4 \times 3 \times 2 \times 1} = 330\,.$$

In general, there are $\frac{N!}{n!(N-n)!}$ ways of selecting n elements out of N, without considering order. We say that this is the number of *combinations of n objects chosen from N* and denote it by $\binom{N}{n}$. We have:

$$\binom{N}{n} = \frac{N!}{n!(N-n)!}\,.$$

Example 4.21

Out of eight items, three are defective (but we do not know which). If five of these items are selected at random, what is the probability that we obtain:

a) no defective,
b) exactly one defective,

c) at most one defective,
d) all three of the defectives?

Solution: There are $\binom{8}{5}$ ways to select the items, all equally likely.

a) There is only one way of getting no defective, so the probability is:

$$\frac{1}{\binom{8}{5}} = \frac{1}{\frac{8!}{5!(8-5)!}} = \frac{5!\,3!}{8!} = \frac{3\cdot 2}{8\cdot 7\cdot 6} = \frac{1}{56} \approx 0.0179\,.$$

b) There are $\binom{3}{1}\cdot\binom{5}{4}$, i.e. fifteen ways to select exactly one defective. The probability is therefore:

$$\frac{\binom{3}{1}\cdot\binom{5}{4}}{\binom{8}{5}} = \frac{15}{56} \approx 0.268\,.$$

c) This is the sum of the probabilities in (a) and (b), i.e.

$$\frac{1}{56} + \frac{15}{56} = \frac{2}{7} \approx 0.286\,.$$

d) There are $\binom{3}{3}\cdot\binom{5}{2} = \frac{5!}{3!\,2!} = 10$ ways to select all three of the defectives so the probability is:

$$\frac{10}{56} = \frac{5}{28} \approx 0.179\,.$$

References

Feller, W.: *An Introduction to Probability Theory and Its Applications,* Vol. 1, 3rd edition. John Wiley & Sons, New York 1968.
Harnett, D. L.: *Statistical Methods,* 3rd edition. Addison-Wesley, Reading, Mass. 1982.
Hawkins, C. A., and J. E. Weber: *Statistical Analysis. Applications to Business and Economics.* Harper & Row, New York 1980.
Mansfield, E.: *Statistics for Business and Economics.* Norton & Company, New York 1980.
Mendenhall, W.: *Introduction to Probability and Statistics,* 5th edition. Duxbury Press, North Scituate, Mass. 1979.
Ross, S. M.: *A First Course in Probability.* Macmillan, New York 1976.

Wonnacott, T.H., and R.J. Wonnacott: *Introductory Statistics for Business and Economics,* 2nd edition. John Wiley & Sons, New York 1977.

Exercises

4–1 For two events A and B, the following probabilities are given:

$$P(A) = 0.4, \quad P(B) = 0.5, \quad P(A \cap B) = 0.3 .$$

Find $P(A \cup B)$.

4–2 Take a well made coin and flip it a hundred times, recording the outcomes. Graph the result on a diagram, where the number of tosses (on the horizontal axis) is plotted against the relative frequency of "head" on the vertical axis. After a sufficient number of flips, the frequency should begin to stabilize at about 0.5.

4–3 For three events A, B and C we have:

$$P(A) = 0.33, \quad P(B) = 0.32, \quad P(C) = 0.33,$$
$$P(A \cap B) = 0.07, \quad P(A \cap C) = 0.03, \quad P(A \cap B \cap C) = 0.02.$$

Calculate:

a) $P(A \cup B)$
b) $P(A \cup C)$
c) $P((A \cap B) \cup C)$
d) $P(B \cup (A \cap C))$.

4–4 A print shop has three presses, A, B and C. Each press is shut down for repair 7 percent of the time. The probability of any press being shut down for repair is not influenced by the operating condition of the other two. Determine the probability that:

a) A or B or are both shut down.
b) No press is shut down
c) A and B are shut down but C is not
d) All three presses are shut down
e) A is shut down but B and C are not.

4–5 Given the set-up of Exercise 4 above, calculate the probability that:

a) Exactly one press is shut down
b) Exactly two presses are shut down
c) At least one press is shut down
d) At least two presses are shut down
e) At most two presses are shut down.

4–6 A certain firm runs a risk of 3% of bankruptcy in any particular year. If it is declared bankrupt in any year, it will cease to exist. What is the probability that after four years it has not gone bankrupt, i.e. still exists?

4–7 A food processing firm has an inspector who accepts or rejects incoming shipments after examining a few sample items from the supply. We know from the past that the inspector accepts 97% of all good shipments. 6% of all shipments are of poor quality and the inspector accepts 92% of all shipments. On the assumption that a shipment is either good or poor, calculate the probability that:

a) A shipment is rejected
b) A shipment is good
c) A shipment is good and accepted
d) A shipment is poor and accepted.

4–8 Airplanes are designed with backup systems for many of the functions vital to the safety of the people on board. Suppose that the brakes consist of three major components. As long as at least two of the three components are functioning, the braking system will work. The three components of the system are denoted by X, Y and Z, respectively. The probabilities that the components will be damaged during a landing are 4.1 percent for component X, 2.2 percent for component Y, and 1.3 percent for component Z. The components are subject to different stresses. Accordingly, the probability of any one component being damaged does not influence the probability that damage has been suffered by any of the other two.

Using a Venn diagram approach, calculate the probability that the braking system will malfunction.

4–9 Given the set-up of Exercise 7 above, find the probabilities for the following events:

a) A shipment is rejected, given that it is good
b) A shipment is accepted, given that it is good
c) A shipment is accepted, given that it is poor
d) A shipment is rejected, given that it is poor.

4–10 Prove that if the events A and B are statistically independent, then so are:

a) A and $\bar{B}$
b) $\bar{A}$ and $\bar{B}$.

4–11 Prove that if $P(A) = 0$, then the events A and B are statistically independent for all B. (Hint: Prove and use the fact that $P(A \cap B) \leqq P(A)$).

4–12 Two companies X and Y are bidding for a contract. X stands a chance of 1/3 of getting the contract, and Y stands a chance of 2/3 of getting the contract. If X gets the contract, the probability that the work will be completed on time is 2/5; if Y gets the contract, the work will be completed on time with probability 4/5. What is the probability that the work will be completed on time?

4–13 Prove Bonferroni's inequality: For any events A and B, we have:

$$P(A \cap B) \geqq P(A) + P(B) - 1 .$$

4–14 In the U.S.A. the date 06-05-1980 is interpreted as 5 June 1980, whereas in other parts of the world it means 6 May 1980. 13-05-1980 (or 05-13-1980) could on the other hand not be confused. Given that any day of the 365-day year is equally likely to appear as a date, what is the probability that confusion will arise?

4–15 According to a well known peace researcher, data suggest that the outbreak of wars is a random phenomenon. Specifically, the probability of outbreak of a major (world-wide) war is 2% in any given year. If these assumptions are correct, what is the probability that no major war will break out during the next thirty years?

4–16 Two New York journalists have stated that if the probability of successfully intercepting an attacking enemy airplane were 0.15 at each of five defense stations, and if the enemy airplane had to pass all five stations before reaching its target, the probability of intercepting the airplane before it reaches its target would be 0.75.

a) Is this reasoning correct?
b) If not, what is the correct probability?

4–17 A shipment contains 120 items of which 7 are defective. To decide if the shipment should be accepted, one item out of the 120 is selected at random. Then another is selected at random, without replacing the first. If neither of the two items selected is defective, the shipment is accepted; otherwise it is rejected. What is the probability that the shipment is rejected?

4–18 Consider the following joint probability table for the sex and marital status of a certain group of people:

	Single	Married	Divorced
Male	0.25	0.15	0.05
Female	0.20	0.25	0.10

A person is selected at random. Calculate the following probabilities:

a) P(male | married)
b) P(divorced | female)
c) P(single | male)
d) P(female | divorced).

4–19 Draw two cards from a shuffled deck of 52 cards. What is the probability that exactly one of them is a face card?

4–20 A sample of 400 male and 400 female students was selected from a university Commerce programme. The sample reflects the same ratio of males and females as the entire programme. It was found that of the males selected 14.5 percent had failed a course, whereas only 10.75 percent of the females had a recorded failure.

a) Prepare a two by two table showing all the four joint probabilities, i.e. the probability that a student selected at random is a male and fails; that the student is a male and passes; that the student is a female and passes; that the student is a female and fails.
b) What is the probability that if a student fails, that particular student is a male?

c) Use the multiplication law of probability to determine whether failing is independent of sex.

4–21 Compute, using the set-up of Example 4.17 in the text, the following probabilities:

a) P(S | B)
b) P(S | C)
c) P(F | A)
d) P(F | B)
e) P(F | C).

4–22 A computer service firm specializing in information services is opening a new branch and estimates that the demand for its information services will be either high (with a probability of 0.3) or low (with a probability of 0.7). A demand forecast is bought from a market research institute giving either a favourable or an unfavourable report. Assume the following: The probability that the research institute gives a favourable report for a high demand outcome is 0.8, and the probability that the report is unfavourable is 0.9 for a low demand outcome. Revise the probabilities, given that the report is either favourable or unfavourable.

4–23 An insurance company classifies motorcar drivers into one of three categories, "high", "average" and "low" risks. The percentage of drivers in each category is 20, 50 and 30, respectively. Records indicate that the probability that a high, average and low risk dricer is involved in a road accident in any given year is 0.40, 0.15 and 0.05, respectively. What is the proportion of drivers involved in a road accident in any given year?

4–24 A coin is altered so that a head is three times as likely as a tail. If the coin is flipped six times, what is the probability of getting

a) no tails
b) no heads
c) exactly two heads
d) two or more heads
e) five or six tails?

4–25 A group of ten people contains six women. Out of the ten, eight are married persons. Half of the married people are men. From the ten, a random sample of four people is selected. What is the probability that of the selected people:

a) all four are married
b) all four are women
c) all four are married men
d) all four are married women
e) all four are single?

4–26 Throw a die five times. What is the probability of getting "four" three times out of the five?

4–27 Prove that:

$$\binom{N}{n} + \binom{N}{n+1} = \binom{N+1}{n+1}$$

4–28 Show that:

$$\binom{N}{n} = \binom{N}{N-n}$$

4–29 Prove that:

$$\binom{N}{n} \cdot \binom{N-n}{m} = \binom{N}{m} \cdot \binom{N-m}{n}$$

*4–30 Prove that:

$$\binom{N}{0} + \binom{N}{1} + \ldots + \binom{N}{N} = 2^N$$

**4–31 Prove the *binomial theorem:* For any real numbers x and y

$$(x+y)^n = \sum_{i=0}^{n} \binom{n}{i} x^i y^{n-i}$$

*4–32 Prove that:

$$\binom{N}{0}^2 + \binom{N}{1}^2 + \ldots + \binom{N}{N}^2 = \binom{2N}{N}$$

4–33 A batch of 8 fuses contains 6 good and 2 bad ones. Pick at random one of the 8 fuses and then a second one from the 7 remaining, without replacing the first. What is the probability that:

a) the first fuse is good
b) both are bad
c) the second is bad
d) the first is good and the second is bad?

4–34 In how many of the numbers 0000, 0001, 0002, ..., 9999 will

a) the digit 4 not appear
b) the digit 5 appear
c) the digit 6 appear exactly once
d) the digit 7 appear exactly twice
e) the digit 8 appear at least twice?

4–35 There are seven men and four women on a board of directors. In how many ways can a committee of three people be formed among the board members, if

a) two men and a woman should be on the committee?
b) one man and two women should be on the committee?

5. Discrete Random Variables

The definitions and results of probability theory are now used to introduce the concepts of random variables and probability distributions. Several different distributions are covered, and some of their applications are discussed.

In Section 5.1 we introduce the notion of random variables, discrete as well as continuous, and give a few examples. Section 5.2 is devoted to the fundamental constructs expected value and variance, and some rules for their computation, with numerical illustrations. Chebyshev's inequality is also briefly covered.

The following sections provide a catalogue of the most important discrete probability distributions which we shall need later on. Section 5.3 deals with the binomial distribution, and we also define the Bernoulli process and the cumulative probability distribution function. In Section 5.4 the hypergeometric distribution is described, with examples, and sampling with and without replacement is discussed. Section 5.5 treats the Poisson distribution, its use as an approximation of the binomial distribution, and its connection to queueing theory via the Poisson process. Section 5.6, finally, gives a very short exposition of the geometric distribution.

5.1 Random Variables

Example 5.1

Toss a coin three times and count the number of heads obtained. We will get either 0, 1, 2, or 3 depending on the outcome of the random experiment "toss a coin three times". The number of heads in three tosses is a *random variable,* which is a numerical variable with its value determined by the outcome of a random experiment. In our example, the random variable can only assume *discrete* values (we can enumerate or count them) and is therefore called a *discrete random variable.*

On the other hand, if we record the annual incomes of a group of people, we could get any value (between certain limits) on a continuous scale, and we say that we have a *continuous random variable.* Because any value on the scale, between the limits, could occur, we realize that any particular single value must have a probability of zero. We shall defer a detailed discussion of continuous random variables to the next chapter and now devote our attention to discrete random variables.

We saw in the previous chapter that the possible outcomes for the random experiment "toss a coin three times" were: (H,H,H), (H,H,T), (H,T,H), (H,T,T), (T,H,H), (T,H,T), (T,T,H), (T,T,T), each with a probability of 1/8.

If we define the random variable X as the number of heads in three tosses, we know that the possible values of X are 0, 1, 2, 3. We can also find the probabilities for the events $X = j$, for $j = 0, 1, 2, 3$:

$$\begin{aligned}
P(X = 0) &= P((T,T,T)) = 1/8 \\
P(X = 1) &= P((H,T,T), (T,H,T), (T,T,H)) = 3/8 \\
P(X = 2) &= P((H,H,T), (H,T,H), (T,H,H)) = 3/8 \\
P(X = 3) &= P((H,H,H)) = 1/8
\end{aligned}$$

For the random variable X, we have now calculated the values of its *probability distribution function* $p_X(j) = P(X = j)$. We shall also write p(j) when there can be no confusion which random variable we are referring to.

We can graphically portray the probability distribution function of our random variable:

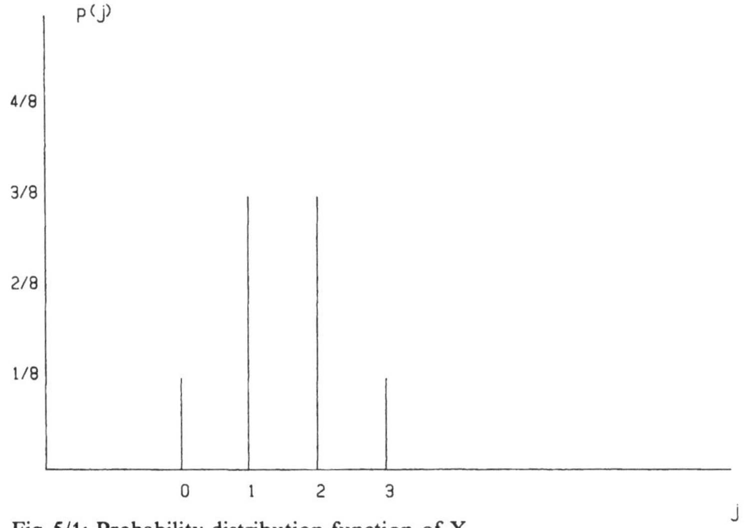

Fig. 5/1: Probability distribution function of X.

This random variable belongs to the so-called *binomial* family of random variables, to be treated in some detail in Section 5.3.

Because the values of the probability distribution function denote probabilities, we find:

a) $0 \leqq p(j) \leqq 1$, for all j , b) $\sum_j p(j) = 1$.

(b) follows, because the events $\{X = j\}$ are mutually exclusive and collectively exhaustive.

Below we give two more examples of discrete random variables.

Example 5.2

Throw two dice u, v and count the total number Y of dots showing, i. e. $Y = u + v$. This is a discrete random variable Y taking the possible values $Y = 2, 3, \ldots, 12$. We can calculate its probability distribution function p:

$$
\begin{aligned}
p(2) &= P(Y = 2) = P((1,1)) = 1/36\\
p(3) &= P(Y = 3) = P((1,2),(2,1)) = 2/36\\
p(4) &= P(Y = 4) = P((1,3),(2,2),(3,1)) = 3/36\\
p(5) &= P(Y = 5) = P((1,4),(2,3),(3,2),(4,1)) = 4/36\\
p(6) &= P(Y = 6) = P((1,5),(2,4),(3,3),(4,2),(5,1)) = 5/36\\
p(7) &= P(Y = 7) = P((1,6),(2,5),(3,4),(4,3),(5,2),(6,1)) = 6/36\\
p(8) &= P(Y = 8) = P((2,6),(3,5),(4,4),(5,3),(6,2)) = 5/36\\
p(9) &= P(Y = 9) = P((3,6),(4,5),(5,4),(6,3)) = 4/36\\
p(10) &= P(Y = 10) = P((4,6),(5,5),(6,4)) = 3/36\\
p(11) &= P(Y = 11) = P((5,6),(6,5)) = 2/36\\
p(12) &= P(Y = 12) = P((6,6)) = 1/36
\end{aligned}
$$

Graphically, this distribution looks as follows:

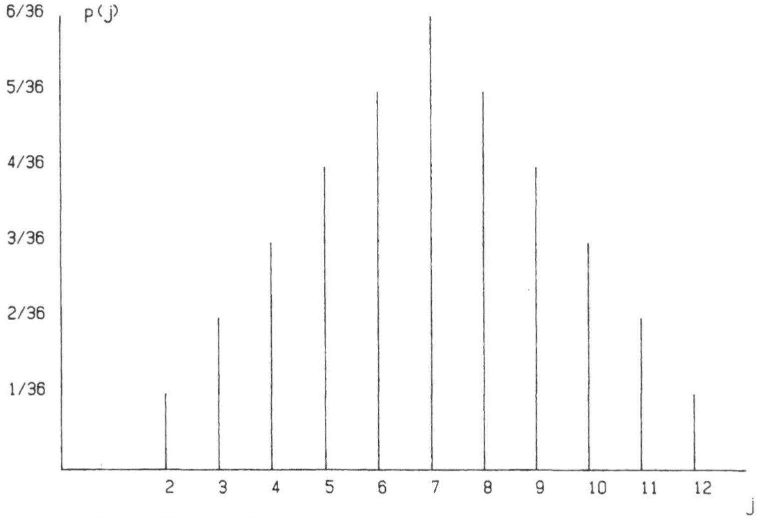

Fig. 5/2: Probability distribution function of Y.

Example 5.3

Let Z be the number of customers waiting to be served in a particular post office at 11:30 hours on any Monday which is not a holiday. Although the probability distribution for Z cannot be determined a priori, as for X and Y in the two previous examples, we could estimate it (approximately) by empirical observation. We might then obtain something like:

$$
\begin{aligned}
p(0) &= 0.4493\\
p(1) &= 0.3595\\
p(2) &= 0.1438\\
p(3) &= 0.0383\\
p(4) &= 0.0077\\
p(5) &= 0.0012\\
p(6) &= 0.0002\\
p(j) &= 0 \quad \text{for} \quad j \geqq 7
\end{aligned}
$$

Graphically, the distribution of Z has the following shape:

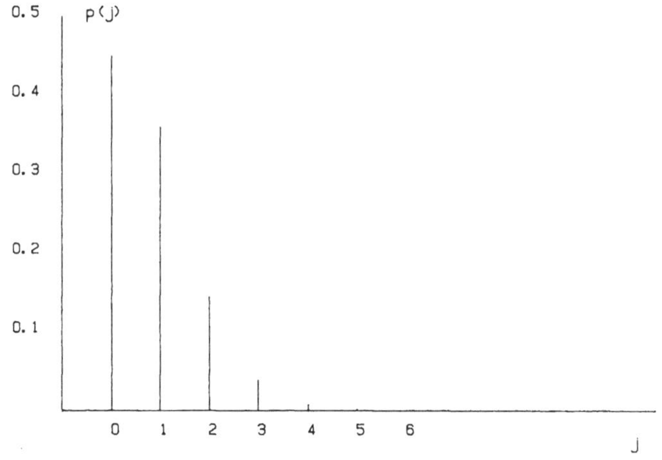

Fig. 5/3: Probability distribution function of Z.

This random variable is of the so-called *Poisson* type, which we shall consider in Section 5.5.

5.2 Expected Value and Variance

Although the probability distribution completely characterizes a random variable, we may wish to provide some more concise information. This information is provided by the *expected value* and the *variance* of a random variable. Below we shall point out the relation between these concepts and the corresponding concepts for given data sets, as treated in Chapter 3.

Definition: The *expected value,* E(X), of a discrete random variable X is:

$$E(X) = \sum_{x} x \cdot P(X = x) = \sum_{x} x \cdot p_X(x)$$

where the summation is taken over all possible values for X. Sometimes we refer to E(X) as the *mean* μ of X. If can be thought of as a weighted average of X, with p(x) as the weights. More specifically, we note that this definition of μ resembles very closely the expression in Chapter 3 for the mean of grouped data. There the weights were the relative frequencies f_i/N, whereas here the weights are the probabilities p(x). This correspondence is quite natural; remember that we defined the probability of an event as the limit of its relative frequency, when the number of experiments grows infinitely large.

Example 5.4

A certain firm is faced with a weekly demand of d thousand items of one of its products. The probability distribution function of d is a follows:

Demand d (thousand items)	Probability
3	0.1
4	0.2
5	0.3
6	0.3
7	0.1

Graphically, this distribution looks as follows:

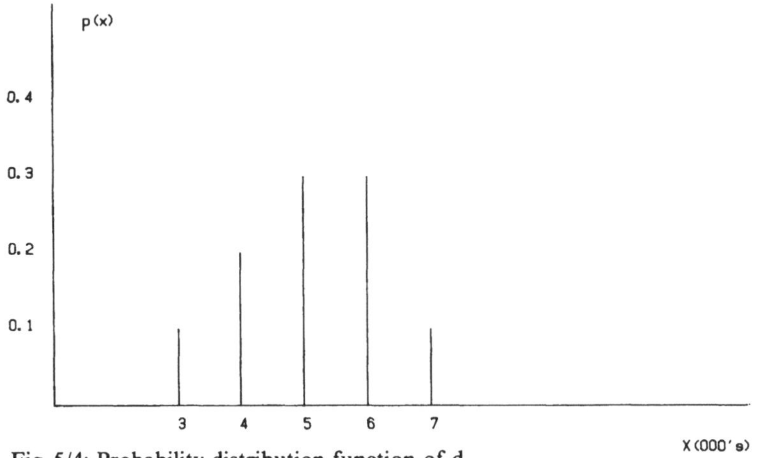

Fig. 5/4: Probability distribution function of d.

We compute the expected weekly demand:

$E(d) = 3 \cdot 0.1 + 4 \cdot 0.2 + 5 \cdot 0.3 + 6 \cdot 0.3 + 7 \cdot 0.1 = 5.1$ thousand items.

This means that over many weeks, the average demand d will approach 5,100 items per week.

Example 5.5

Having calculated the probability distribution for the number of heads, X, after three tosses of a coin, we can calculate E(X):

$$E(X) = \sum_j j \cdot p(j) = 0 \cdot 1/8 + 1 \cdot 3/8 + 2 \cdot 3/8 + 3 \cdot 1/8 = 3/2.$$

Example 5.6

Consider again the firm from Example 5.4 above. Suppose that the items sell at \$2 each, and that the firm must not run out of stock. It must then obtain seven thousand items weekly. Assume furthermore that the items are obtained at a cost of \$1 each. Weekly profits Y will then be: $Y = 2d - 7$ thousand dollars. We find:

Demand (thousand items)	Profit (thousand dollars)	Probability
3	−1	0.1
4	1	0.2
5	3	0.3
6	5	0.3
7	7	0.1

The expected weekly profits can now be calculated; they are:

$E(Y) = -1 \cdot 0.1 + 1 \cdot 0.2 + 3 \cdot 0.3 + 5 \cdot 0.3 + 7 \cdot 0.1 = 3.2$ thousand dollars.

In general, if g is a function of the random variable X, one can easily show the following formula:

$$E(g(X)) = \sum_x g(x) \cdot p_X(x)$$

This expression is often referred to as "the law of the unconscious statistician". Apparently, "unconscious" statisticians have used it, erroneously thinking that it was the definition of $E(g(X))$.

In our Example 5.6, we had $Y = g(d) = 2d - 7$.

Theorem: For any constants a, b we have

$$E(a + bX) = a + bE(X).$$

(We say that E is a *linear operator.*)

The proof of this theorem is a straightforward application of the law of the unconscious statistician.

Example 5.7

The profits for our firm were $2d - 7$, and $E(d) = 5.1$. Consequently, $E(2d - 7) = 2E(d) - 7 = 10.2 - 7 = 3.2$ in accordance with the result in Example 5.6.

We shall now come to the second important measure of a random variable, *variance*.

Definition: The *variance* $V(X)$ (or $Var(X)$ or σ^2) of a discrete random variable X is:

$$V(X) = E([X - E(X)]^2) = E([X - \mu]^2).$$

Using the formula $E(g(X)) = \sum_x g(x) \cdot p(x)$ (the law of the unconscious statistician) we get, with $g(X) = (X - \mu)^2$, an expression for computing the variance:

$$V(X) = \sum_x (x - \mu)^2 p(x).$$

We note that this expression for σ^2 very closely resembles the expression in Chapter 3 for the population variance of grouped data. There the weights were the relative frequencies f_i/N; here they are the probabilities $p(x)$.

For practical purposes, the variance $V(X)$ is often calculated by the useful formula $V(X) = E(X^2) - \mu^2$, which we can easily derive:

$$\begin{aligned} V(X) &= E([X-\mu]^2) = E(X^2 - 2\mu X + \mu^2) \\ &= E(X)^2 - 2\mu \underbrace{E(X)}_{\mu} + \mu^2 = E(X^2) - \mu^2 = E(X^2) - (E(X))^2 . \end{aligned}$$

It reminds us of the shortcut formula of Chapter 3 for calculating the population variance of a numerical data set.

Example 5.8

Toss a die and let X be the number of dots showing. Let us find the variance $V(X)$. We already know that $E(X) = 7/2$, so we get:

$$\begin{aligned} V(X) = \sum_x (x-\mu)^2 p(x) &= (1-7/2)^2 \cdot 1/6 \\ &+ (2-7/2)^2 \cdot 1/6 + (3-7/2)^2 \cdot 1/6 \\ &+ (4-7/2)^2 \cdot 1/6 + (5-7/2)^2 \cdot 1/6 \\ &+ (6-7/2)^2 \cdot 1/6 = (25/4 + 9/4 + 1/4 + 1/4 \\ &+ 9/4) + 25/4) \cdot 1/6 = 35/12 = 2\tfrac{11}{12} \approx 2.917 \end{aligned}$$

Alternatively, employing the useful formula for computing the variance, we first calculate:

$$\begin{aligned} E(X^2) = \sum_x x^2 p(x) &= 1 \cdot 1/6 + 4 \cdot 1/6 + 9 \cdot 1/6 + 16 \cdot 1/6 + 25 \cdot 1/6 \\ &+ 36 \cdot 1/6 \\ &= (1 + 4 + 9 + 16 + 25 + 36) \cdot 1/6 = 91/6, \end{aligned}$$

so that:

$$\begin{aligned} V(X) &= E(X^2) - (E(X))^2 = 91/6 - 49/4 = 182/12 - 147/12 \\ &= 35/12 = 2\tfrac{11}{12} \approx 2.917, \quad \text{as before.} \end{aligned}$$

Example 5.9

With X = number of heads after three tosses of a coin, we found $E(X) = 3/2$ so that:

$$\begin{aligned} V(X) = \sum_x (x-\mu)^2 p(x) &= (0-3/2)^2 \cdot 1/8 + (1-3/2)^2 \cdot 3/8 \\ &+ (2-3/2)^2 \cdot 3/8 + (3-3/2)^2 \cdot 1/8 \\ &= (9/4 + 1/4 \cdot 3 + 1/4 \cdot 3 + 9/4) \cdot 1/8 = 6/8 = 3/4. \end{aligned}$$

Alternatively,

$$E(X^2) = \sum_x x^2 p(x) = 0\cdot 1/8 + 1\cdot 3/8 + 4\cdot 3/8 + 9\cdot 1/8$$
$$= (3 + 12 + 9)\cdot 1/8 = 3, \quad \text{so that:}$$
$$V(X) = E(X^2) - (E(X))^2 = 3 - (3/2)^2 = (12 - 9)/4 = 3/4.$$

Unlike the expectation operator E, the variance operator V is not linear, as we see from the following theorem.

Theorem: For any constants a, b, we have:

$$V(a + bX) = b^2 V(X).$$

Proof:

$$V(a + bX) = E((a + bX)^2) - (E(a + bX))^2 = E(a^2 + 2abX + b^2X^2)$$
$$- (a + bE(X))^2 = a^2 + 2abE(X) + b^2E(X^2) - a^2$$
$$- 2ab\mu - b^2\mu^2 = b^2(E(X^2) - \mu^2) = b^2 V(X).$$

Example 5.10

From our previous Examples 5.4 and 5.6 about a firm's weekly demand d and profit $2d - 7$, we get:

$$E(d^2) = 9\cdot 0.1 + 16\cdot 0.2 + 25\cdot 0.3 + 36\cdot 0.3 + 49\cdot 0.1$$
$$= 0.9 + 3.2 + 7.5 + 10.8 + 4.9 = 27.3;$$

hence:

$$V(d) = E(d^2) - \mu^2 = 27.3 - (5.1)^2 = 27.3 - 26.01 = 1.29.$$

From this we can calculate the variance of the weekly profits, $2d - 7$ using the above theorem:

$$V(2d - 7) = 4V(d) = 5.16.$$

Definition: The *standard deviation* σ of a random variable X with variance V(X) is given by $\sigma = \sqrt{V(X)}$ (other notations are D(X), SD(X)).

Again we point out the connection with the corresponding concept for data sets, the population standard deviation, in Chapter 3.

Example 5.11

The standard deviation of the weekly demand faced by our firm above is $\sqrt{1.29} \approx 1.14$.

As a last item of this section, let us see how knowledge about the variance of a random variable can be used. Specifically, a large variance indicates that large deviations from the expected value are not unlikely to happen. Conversely, a small variance will give us a high probability that a random variable will be close to its mean. This is made explicit in the following theorem:

Chebyshev's[1] Inequality

For any discrete random variable X with mean μ and variance σ^2, we have the following inequality:

$$P(\mu - k\sigma < X < \mu + k\sigma) \geqq 1 - \frac{1}{k^2}$$

for any number $k > 0$.

Remark 1: The event $\{\mu - k\sigma < X < \mu + k\sigma\}$ can also be written as:

$$\{|X - \mu| < k\sigma\}$$

and can be expressed in words as "X assumes a value within k standard deviations of its mean".

Remark 2: We can give the following equivalent formulation of Chebyshev's inequality:

$$P(|X - \mu| \geqq k\sigma) \leqq \frac{1}{k^2}.$$

Remark 3: The inequality is true but uninteresting if $0 < k \leqq 1$.

The proof of Chebyshev's inequality is left as an exercise for the reader. (*Hint:* Write σ^2 as:

$$\begin{aligned}\sigma^2 &= E((X - \mu)^2) = \sum_x (x - \mu)^2 p(x)\\ &= \sum_{\substack{\text{All x}\\ \text{such that}\\ |x-\mu| < k\sigma}} (x - \mu)^2 p(x) + \sum_{\substack{\text{All x}\\ \text{such that}\\ |x-\mu| \geqq k\sigma}} (x - \mu)^2 p(x)\\ &\geqq \sum_{\substack{\text{All x}\\ \text{such that}\\ |x-\mu| \geqq k\sigma}} (x - \mu)^2 p(x)).\end{aligned}$$

[1] Pafnuty Lvovich Chebyshev, Russian mathematician, 1821–1894.

As an application of Chebyshev's inequality we consider our firm of Examples 5.4, 5.6, 5.10 and 5.11. With $\mu = 5.1$ and $\sigma = 1.14$ we find, for instance:

$$P(|d - 5.1| < 2.28) \geqq 3/4$$

(use $k = 2$), and:

$$P(|d - 5.1| \geqq 1.71) \leqq 4/9$$

(use $k = 3/2$).

We shall now turn our attention to some specific probability distributions, that are of great value in real life applications.

5.3 The Binomial Distribution

If any particular name should be associated with the binomial distribution, it would be that of Jacques Bernoulli[2], although earlier mathematicians like Galilei had considered and solved problems related to this distribution.

We begin the exposition by an example.

Example 5.12

Toss a coin, with $P(\text{head}) = p$ wich is not necessarily $1/2$, n times, and count the number of heads, X. We have looked at this problem before, for $n = 3$ and $p = 1/2$. We know that for n tosses there are 2^n possible outcomes. How do we find $P(X = j)$, $j = 0, 1, \ldots, n$? For $j = 0$ (no heads) the answer is simple: $P(X = 0) = P(\text{no heads}) = P(\text{all tails}) = (1 - p)^n$, and similarly, for $j = n$, $P(X = n) = p^n$. The probability of getting first j heads in a row, and then $n - j$ tails is clearly:

$$\underbrace{p \cdot p \cdot \ldots \cdot p}_{\substack{j \\ \text{terms}}} \cdot \underbrace{(1 - p) \cdot (1 - p) \cdot \ldots \cdot (1 - p)}_{\substack{n - j \\ \text{terms}}} = p^j \cdot (1 - p)^{n-j}.$$

We realize that this expression is also the probability of obtaining j heads and $n - j$ tails, in any order.

But how many possible ways are there to get j heads and $n - j$ tails, if we do not consider order? The answer is that it is the same as the number of combinations of j objects chosen from n. In other words, there are $\binom{n}{j} = \frac{n!}{j! \cdot (n - j)!}$ possible ways, each having the same probability $p^j \cdot (1 - p)^{n-j}$. Consequently, $p_X(j) = P(X = j) = \binom{n}{j} p^j (1 - p)^{n-j}$.

[2] Jacques Bernoulli, Swiss mathematician, 1654–1705.

A random variable having this probability distribution function is said to have a *binomial distribution*, and we write 'X is Bin (n, p)'. We say that n and p are the *parameters* of the distribution. n is the number of *trials* and p is the probability of *success* in each trial. The binomial distribution is very important and is applicable to many real life situations.

Example 5.13

In a group of 45 university students taking a particular course, each student has probability $p = 0.8$ to obtain a passing mark in the course. The number of passing students, X, is then Bin (45, 0.8), so that P(exactly 40 pass) $= \binom{45}{40} \cdot 0.8^{40} \cdot 0.2^5 \approx 0.05197$.

Example 5.14

High tensile steel bolts are tested; each bolt has $p = 0.05$ of being bad. If ten bolts are tested, what is P(3 or less are bad)?

We know that the number of bad bolts, X, is Bin (10, 0.05) so that

$$p(3 \text{ or less are bad}) = \sum_{j=0}^{3} \binom{10}{j} 0.05^j 0.95^{10-j} = 0.5987 + 0.3151$$

$+ 0.0746 + 0.0105 = 0.9989$

Below we shall show the graphical image of the distribution of some binomial variables, with different values of the n and p parameters.

Example 5.15

The Bin (4, 0.3) distribution looks as follows:

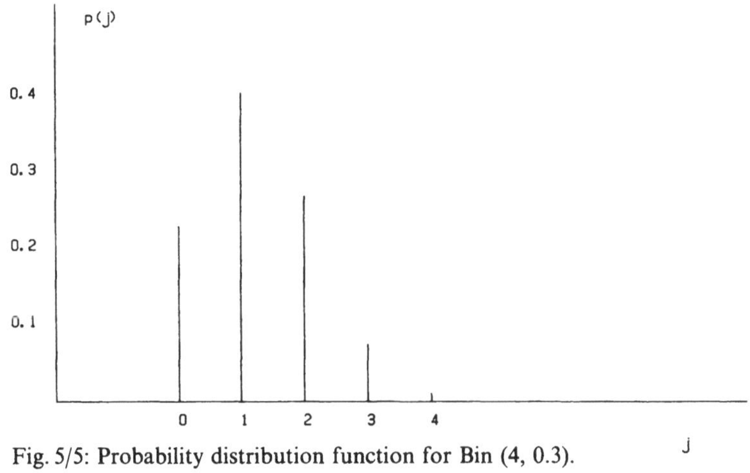

Fig. 5/5: Probability distribution function for Bin (4, 0.3).

In general, for $p < 0.5$, Bin (n, p) is skewed to the right.

Example 5.16

The Bin (6, 0.5) distribution looks as follows:

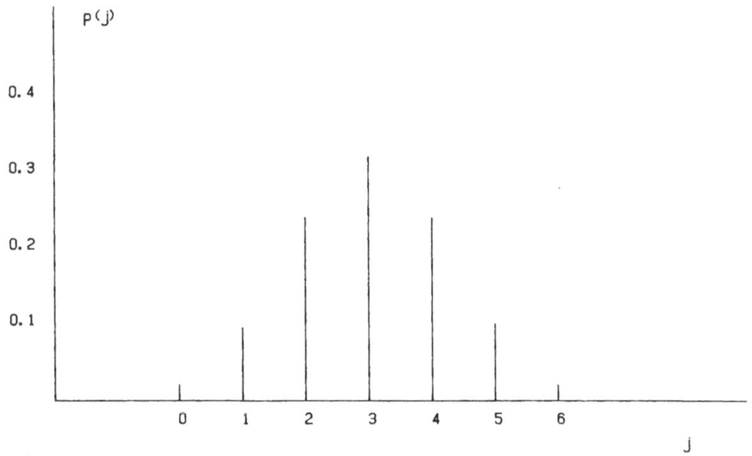

Fig. 5/6: Probability distribution function for Bin (6, 0.5).

In general, for $p = 0.5$, Bin (n, p) is symmetric.

Example 5.17

The Bin (11, 0.6) distribution looks as follows:

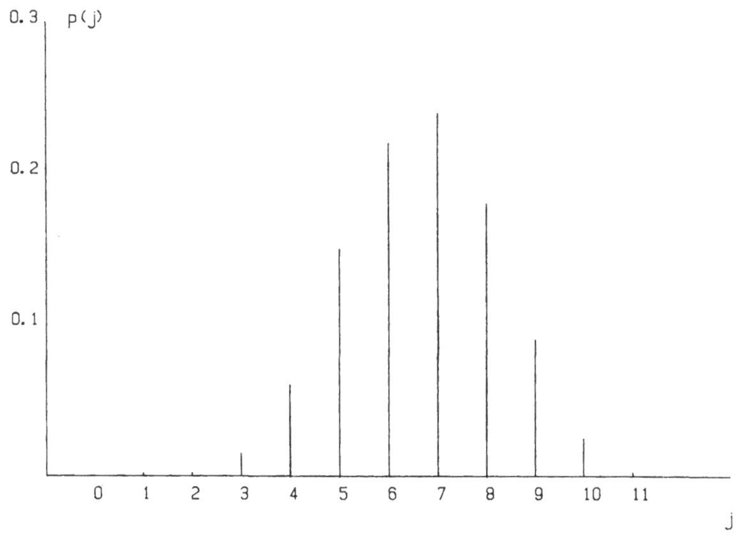

Fig. 5/7: Probability distribution function for Bin (11, 0.6).

In general, for $p > 0.5$, Bin (n, p) is skewed to the left.

The binomial distribution is closely connected to *Bernoulli processes,* where the experimental setting is that of repeated independent trials for which there are only two possible outcomes for each trial (usually labelled *success* and *failure*) and the probability of each outcome remains the same for all the trials.

In the "toss a coin" experiment, "head" might be labelled as success; for the "throw a die" experiment, "four" could serve as success.

For a Bin (n, p) random variable X we shall sometimes talk about the *proportion of successes,* X/n. Sometimes we also make use of the notation $q = 1 - p$.

Theorem: If X is Bin (n, p), then we have:

$$E(X) = np, \; V(X) = np(1-p) = npq.$$

Remark: For the proportion of successes, we get:

$$E(X/n) = p, \quad V(X/n) = \frac{p(1-p)}{n} = \frac{pq}{n}.$$

It is easy to show that this follows from the above theorem.

Example 5.18

For the high tensile steel bolts of Example 5.14, X is Bin (10, 0.05) so that:

$$E(X) = 10 \cdot 0.05 = 0.5,$$
$$V(X) = 10 \cdot 0.05 \cdot 0.95 = 0.475,$$
$$\sigma(X) \approx 0.689.$$

We shall now end this section by introducing a concept that will be of much use later on.

Definition: For any discrete random variable X the *cumulative probability distribution function* $F_X(x)$ is defined by: $F_X(x) = P(X \leqq x)$. When there is no risk of confusion, we shall sometimes write F(x) instead of FX(x). It is sometimes simply referred to as the cumulative distribution function.

Example 5.19

From our steel bolt example, we see that $F_X(3) = P(X \leqq 3) = 0.9989$.

Example 5.20

The cumulative probability distribution function of the variable Bin (4, 0.3) of Example 5.15 has the following shape:

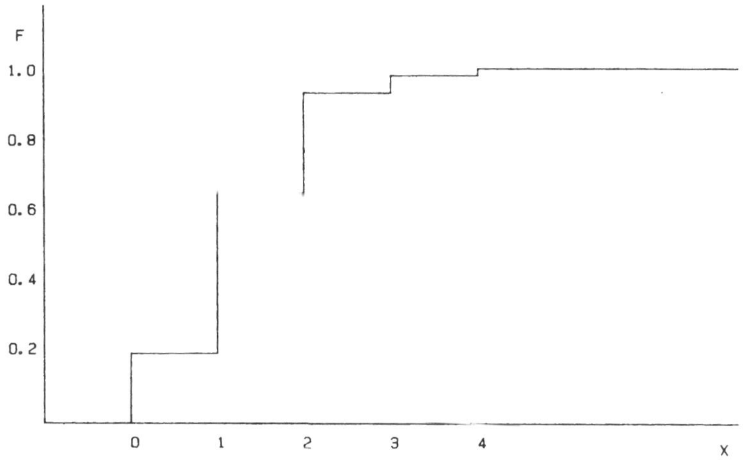

Fig. 5/8: Cumulative probability distribution function for Bin (4, 0.3).

5.4 The Hypergeometric Distribution

In this section we shall introduce a random variable distribution which arises in the context of sampling *without replacement.*

Example 5.21

Consider a population of N objects, r of which are red and b of which are black, so that $N = r + b$. From the N objects, n are randomly selected, one after the other, *without replacement.* If among the n selected, x happen to be red, then $n - x$ must be black. From Section 4.9 on combinatorial analysis, we know that there are $\binom{r}{x} \cdot \binom{b}{n-x}$ ways in which this could happen; furthermore, the n objects can be taken from the N in $\binom{N}{n}$ ways. Thus, if X is the random variable denoting the number of red objects obtained, we get the probability of obtaining precisely x red objects:

$$P(X = x) = \frac{\binom{r}{x} \cdot \binom{b}{n-x}}{\binom{r+b}{n}} = \frac{\binom{r}{x} \cdot \binom{N-r}{n-x}}{\binom{N}{n}}, x = 0, 1, \ldots, n.$$

We call this the *hypergeometric distribution.*

Example 5.22

With $N = 10, r = 3, b = 7, n = 6$, we get the probability of obtaining $X = 2$ red objects:

$$P(X = 2) = \frac{\binom{3}{2} \cdot \binom{7}{4}}{\binom{10}{6}} = \frac{\frac{3!}{2!\,1!} \cdot \frac{7!}{4!\,3!}}{\frac{10!}{6!\,4!}} = \frac{3 \cdot \frac{7 \cdot 6 \cdot 5}{6}}{\frac{10 \cdot 9 \cdot 8 \cdot 7}{24}} = \frac{5}{10} = \frac{1}{2}.$$

Remark: If the n objects had been selected *with replacement,* then n times an object would have been selected, inspected (to be found red or black) and thereafter replaced. X would then be a Bin $\left(n, \frac{r}{N}\right)$ variable, which in our Example 5.22 above would be Bin (6, 0.3). For this distribution we find:

$$P(X = 2) = 0.3241 .$$

This differs significantly from $P = 1/2$ obtained in Example 5.22. Intuitively, though, we expect the probabilities to be approximately the same if N (the population size) is large and n (the sample size) is small relative to N.

Example 5.23

With $N = 100, r = 5$ and $n = 3$, the hypergeometric probability distribution function looks as follows:

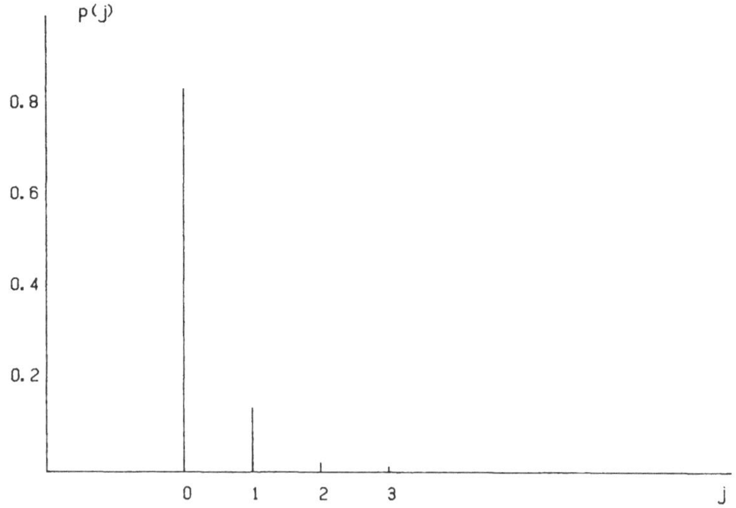

Fig. 5/9: Probability distribution function for a hypergeometric variable.

Regarding the mean and the variance for the hypergeometric distribution, one can show the following theorem:

Theorem: If X is a random variable with a hypergeometric distribution and with notation as above, we have:

$$E(X) = n \cdot \frac{r}{N}, \quad V(X) = \frac{N-n}{N-1} \cdot n \cdot \frac{r(N-r)}{N^2}.$$

Remark: Note how these expressions resemble those for the binomial distribution, with r/N playing the role of p. For large N (and small n/N), the hypergeometric distribution is closely approximated by the binomial distribution. In this context, the expression $\sqrt{\frac{N-n}{N-1}}$ used in the calculation of the standard deviation, is called the *finite population correction factor*.

Example 5.24

From our Example 5.22 above, we get:

$$E(X) = n \cdot \frac{r}{N} = 6 \cdot \frac{3}{10} = 9/5 = 1.8$$

$$V(X) = \frac{N-n}{N-1} \cdot n \cdot \frac{r(N-r)}{N^2} = \frac{10-6}{10-1} \cdot 6 \cdot \frac{3 \cdot (10-3)}{100}$$

$$= \frac{4}{9} \cdot 6 \cdot \frac{3 \cdot 7}{100} = \frac{14}{25} = 0.56.$$

In conclusion, let us repeat that sampling *with* replacement gives rise to the *binomial* distribution; sampling *without* replacement generates the *hypergeometric* distribution. For a large population and small sample, the two distributions are approximately the same (as one would expect).

5.5 The Poisson Distribution

We shall now come to another important distribution, introduced by Poisson[3] in a book which he published in 1837.

Example 5.25

A department store has 1000 customer accounts. Past experience shows that every year 0.7% of the accounts default, causing the store considerable administrative and financial difficulties. The store is therefore interested to know something about the distribution of the number of defaulting accounts. Specifically, what is the expected number of defaulting accounts, and what is the probability that, for example, at most 11 accounts will default in a given year?

To solve this problem, we realize that X, the number of defaulting accounts in a given year, is Bin (1000, 0.007), so that $E(X) = 1000 \cdot 0.007 = 7$ which answers our first question. The probability $P(X \leqq 11)$, on the other hand, is not easy to calculate. We know that it is given by:

$$P(X \leqq 11) = \sum_{j=0}^{11} \binom{1000}{j} \cdot 0.007^{j} \cdot 0.993^{1000-j}.$$

However, we would prefer not to have to calculate $\binom{1000}{9} \cdot 0.007^{9} \cdot 0.993^{991}$ and similar expressions. It turns out that the *Poisson-distribution* will solve our problem.

Definition: A discrete random variable X with probability distribution function:

$$p(x) = P(X = x) = e^{-\lambda} \cdot \frac{\lambda^{x}}{x!}, \quad x = 0, 1, 2, \ldots$$

is said to be *Poisson-distributed* with paramcter λ; we say that X is $P(\lambda)$. (P here stands for Poisson).

[3] Siméon Denis Poisson, French mathematician and physicist, 1781–1840.

Example 5.26

The random variable Z of Example 5.3 (shown graphically in Fig. 5/3) is P(0.8), that is, Poisson-distributed with parameter 0.8.

Example 5.27

The P(2.9) distribution looks as follows:

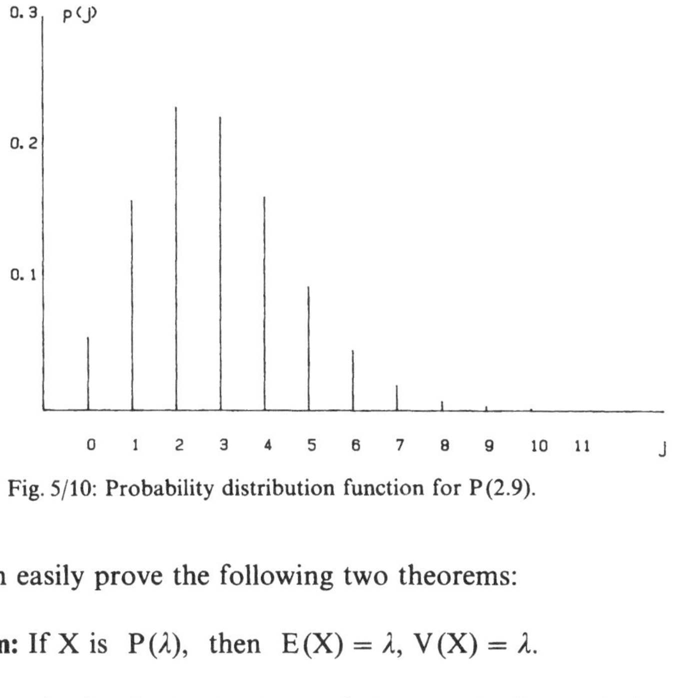

Fig. 5/10: Probability distribution function for P(2.9).

One can easily prove the following two theorems:

Theorem: If X is $P(\lambda)$, then $E(X) = \lambda$, $V(X) = \lambda$.

Theorem: If X is Bin (n, p) where n is large and p is small, then X is approximately P(np).

Remark: The larger the n and the smaller the p, the better is the approximation. If $n \geqq 20$ and $p \leqq 0.1$, the Poisson approximation is generally used, and the numerical error is only a fraction of a percent. Also, most statistical tables do not give the binomial distribution for n larger than 20, so that the approximation by the Poisson distribution then becomes necessary.

Example 5.28

In our Example 5.25 above, we had $n = 1000$ and $p = 0.007$, so that X is very closely $P(1000 \cdot 0.007) = P(7)$. We obtain $E(X) = 7$ from the formula for computing the expected value of a Poisson variable. This is in accordance with our previous results. From a Poisson-table we also find:

$$P(X \leqq 11) = 0.947\,.$$

In general, the Poisson distribution applies to situations where a certain event has a very low individual probability of occurring, but the number of experiments is very large. For instance, consider the number of traffic accidents on a particular stretch of a busy road. For each vehicle passing this stretch, the probability that it will be involved in an accident is low; however, the number of vehicles passing is large. It turns out that the number of road accidents in such a case is Poisson distributed. Similarly, the number of misprints on a book page, and the number of imperfections per meter of a carpet may be Poisson distributed. Another case is given in the following example:

Example 5.29

Consider incoming telephone calls to a switchboard. We assume that the calls satisfy the following condition. For any time points t_1, t_2 and t_3 such that $t_1 < t_2 < t_3$, the number of calls in the time intervals (t_1, t_2) and (t_2, t_3) are statistically independent. Also, we assume that the chance of two or more calls arriving at almost the same time is negligible. If λ is the average number of calls per minute, one can then show that the number X of incoming calls during a particular time interval, of length t minutes, is Poisson distributed with parameter λt, i.e. $P(\lambda t)$. We say that the incoming calls represent a *Poisson process* with *rate* or *intensity* λ. The Poisson process plays an important role in *queueing theory,* the analysis of queueing systems, which is a branch of operations research. In this context, the *exponential* distribution arises, a continuous random variable which we shall describe in the next chapter.

*5.6 The Geometric Distribution

Let us very briefly consider the following example:

Example 5.30

Consider a coin such that $P(\text{head}) = p$ (and consequently $P(\text{tail}) = 1 - p = q$), where p is not necessarily 1/2. Flip it repeatedly until "head" is obtained for the first time. The number X of flips required is a random variable with a *geometric* distribution which is a special case of the so-called *negative binomial* or *Pascal*[4] distribution.

[4] Blaise Pascal, French mathematician and philosopher, 1623–1662.

Definition: A discrete random variable X with probability distribution function:

$$p(x) = P(X = x) = (1 - p)^{x-1} \cdot p = q^{x-1} \cdot p, \quad x = 1, 2, \ldots$$

is said to have a *geometric* distribution.

Example 5.31

For $p = 0.4$, the geometric distribution looks as follows:

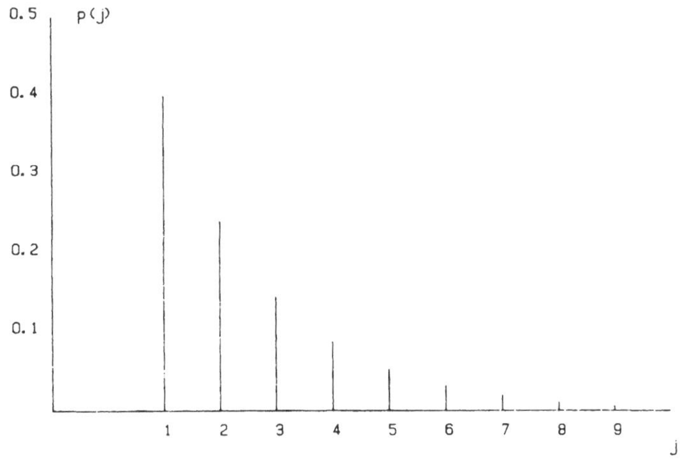

Fig. 5/11: Probability distribution function for a geometric variable with $p = 0.4$.

One can show the following theorem:

Theorem: If X has a geometric distribution then:

$$E(X) = \frac{1}{p}, \quad V(X) = \frac{q}{p^2}.$$

Applications of the geometric distribution include, for a firm with a bankruptcy probability p per year, the number of years till bankruptcy; for job interviewing, where an applicant is acceptable with probability p, the number of interviews until an acceptable candidate is found; for oil drilling the number of drillings until oil is found.

References

Feller, W.: *An Introduction to Probability Theory and Its Applications,* Vol. 1, 3rd edition. John Wiley & Sons, New York 1968

Harnett, D. L.: *Statistical Methods,* 3rd edition. Addison-Wesley, Reading, Mass. 1982.

Hawkins, C. A., and J. E. Weber: *Statistical Analysis. Applications to Business and Economics.* Harper & Row, New York 1980.

Mansfield, E.: *Statistics for Business and Economics.* Norton & Company, New York 1980.

Mendenhall, W., and J. E. Reinmuth: *Statistics for Management and Economics,* 3rd edition. Duxbury Press, North Scituate, Mass. 1978.

Ross, S. M.: *A First Course in Probability.* Macmillan, New York 1976.

Wonnacott, T. H., and R. J. Wonnacott: *Introductory Statistics for Business and Economics,* 2nd edition. John Wiley & Sons, New York 1977.

Exercises

5–1 The annual production of rice in the small country of Halland can be considered as a random variable, distributed according to the following table:

Probability	0.1	0.1	0.2	0.3	0.2	0.1
Rice Production (million tons)	4	6	7	8	9	10

a) Graph the probability distribution function.
b) Find the expected value, variance and standard deviation of the random variable.

5–2 At an opinion poll on a certain issue, the answers were 25 percent "yes", 50 percent "no" and the rest "no opinion". For a random sample of three people, define the number of "yes" answers as a random variable.

a) Determine the probability distribution function of this random variable.
b) Find the expected value, variance, and standard deviation of this random variable.

5–3 An unbalanced coin, with P(head) = 0.6, is flipped twice. The number of tails obtained is a random variable.

a) Determine the probability distribution function of this random variable.
b) Find the expected value, variance and standard deviation of this random variable.

5–4 X is a discrete random variable with expected value μ. Show that for any number a the following relationship holds:

$$E((X-a)^2) = V(X) + (\mu - a)^2 .$$

5–5 X is a discrete random variable. Show that if X is nonnegative, then the same holds for its expected value.

5–6 X is a discrete random variable. Show that if its variance is zero, the random variable is constant.

5–7 The management of a company wants to find out if its employees are satisfied with their working conditions. Assuming that 30% of the employees are dissatisfied, and that 15 of them are selected at random and interviewed, what is the probability that dissatisfaction is expressed by:

a) at most four employees
b) exactly five employees
c) a majority (i.e. eight or more) of the fifteen?

5–8 An investor is considering three types of commercial paper, A, B and C. The interest rate on paper C is fixed and given (12%), but the effective interest rates on papers A and B vary. Assume that the average rates turn out as in the table below, with probabilities as indicated:

A		B	
Interest	Probability	Interest	Probability
8%	0.1	10%	0.1
10%	0.1	11%	0.2
12%	0.2	12%	0.1
14%	0.3	13%	0.1
16%	0.2	14%	0.3
18%	0.1	15%	0.2

a) If the investor seeks to maximize the expected interest rate, which paper should he choose?
b) If the investor is risk averse, so that instead of maximizing E(X), where X is the interest rate, he wishes to maximize $E(X) - 1/2\sqrt{V(X)}$, which paper will he select?
c) If the investor has a stronger aversion to risk than in (b) above, so that he wishes to maximize $E(X) - \sqrt{V(X)}$, which paper will be favoured?

5–9 A random variable X has a Bin (6, 0.4) distribution. Calculate the following probabilities:

a) $P(X = 0)$
b) $P(X \leqq 1)$
c) $P(X = 7)$
d) $P(X \geqq 5)$.

5–10 A random variable Y has a Bin (10, 0.65) distribution. Determine the following probabilites:

a) $P(X = 8)$
b) $P(4 \leqq X \leqq 7)$
c) $P(4 < X < 7)$
d) $P(X \geqq 9)$.

5–11 A random variable X has a Bin (12, 0.1) distribution.

a) Compute E(X), V(X), σ
b) Determine $P(X \geqq 8)$
c) Determine $P(X = 0)$
d) Find $P(X = -2)$.

5–12 Prove the formulas for the expected value and variance of the binomial distribution.

5–13 A random variable Z has a P(1.9) distribution.

a) Determine E(Z), V(Z), σ
b) What is $P(Z \leqq 2)$?
c) What is $P(Z = 4)$?
d) Find $P(Z \geqq 3)$.

5–14 The random variable X is P(4) distributed. Find the following probabilities:

a) $P(X = 0)$
b) $P(X \geqq 1)$
c) $P(X = 6)$
d) $P(2 < X \leqq 4)$.

*5–15 Prove the formulas for the expected value and variance of the Poisson distribution.

5–16 A random variable Y is hypergeometrically distributed with $N = 14$, $n = 5$ and $r = 10$.

a) Determine E(Y), V(Y), σ
b) What is $P(Y = 0)$?
c) What is $P(Y \leqq 2)$?
d) Find $P(Y = 6)$.

5–17 A random variable Z has a hypergeometric distribution with $N = 8$, $n = 3$ and $r = 7$. Determine the following probabilities:

a) $P(Z \geqq 4)$
b) $P(Z = 2)$
c) $P(Z > 0)$
d) $P(Z = 0)$.

5–18 Prove the formulas for the expected value and variance of the hypergeometric distribution.

5–19 An investor holds a property which will be sold with a probability of 1/5 within a year, generating a profit of $10,000. If the property is not sold within a year, a loss of $2,000 will result.

a) What is the expected value of this venture?
b) What probability (if not 1/5) will make the expected value exactly zero?

5–20 The mayor of a small town believes that 50% of the town's population favour fluoridation of the drinking water. One day, the mayor asks his secretary to randomly telephone 100 town residents and ask their opinion regarding fluoridation. Given that the mayor's original assumption is correct, find the probability that at least 50 but not more than 55 indicate that they do not favour fluoridation.

5–21 An advertising agency estimates that 65% of all listeners to a certain advertisement song will associate it with the product it advertises. If 200 listeners are questioned, what is the probability that no more than 140 will associate the product with the song?

5–22 In a country, 75% of the population has been vaccinated against smallpox. Attempting to find the reason why a quarter of the population failed to be vaccinated, a research team is interviewing a number of citizens.

a) If the team interviews ten citizens, randomly selected, what is the probability that at least eight of them have been vaccinated?
b) If seven randomly selected citizens are interviewed, what is the probability that exactly four or five of them have not been vaccinated?
c) To obtain in a random sample an expected value of at least 30 citizens who have not been vaccinated, how large must the sample at least be?
d) The Ministry of Health calls a region "seriously vulnerable" if the number of not vaccinated people in the region is two or more standard deviations above the national average. If a certain region contains 3,500 people, how many non-vaccinated people could the region at most contain, without being labelled "seriously vulnerable"?

5–23 A machine produces 50 items a day, out of which 5 are defective. A random sample of 20 of the day's 50 items is taken.

a) If the items are chosen one at a time, tested and then replaced (defective or not) what is the probability of obtaining at most two defective items?
b) If the items are chosen one at a time, tested and destroyed by the test procedure, what is the probability of obtaining at most two defective items?
c) For each of (a) and (b) above, calculate the expected number of defective items in the sample.

5–24 A salesman receives $100 for each successful sale. He works 210 days a year, seeing 4 clients per working day. He spends 50 minutes with each client and is successful with two thirds.

a) Find the probability that on a particular day exactly one sale is successful.
b) If the salesman's costs are $0.40 per minute spent with a client, what is the salesman's annual expected net income?
c) What is the expected number of working days per year, during which no successful sale is made?
d) Will the expected net income increase if the salesman spends 40 minutes with each of 5 clients per working day?

5–25 25% of the trainees at a certain corporation will stay with it for at least a year. A group of five trainees has just been employed. Assuming that the staying times for the trainees are statistically independent, the corporation is interested to know the number of trainees that will still be with the corporation a year later.

a) Find the probability distribution for this number.
b) Calculate the mean, variance and standard deviation of this number.
c) What is the probability that this number is greater than one?

5–26 In a certain city, the number of murders per month is a Poisson distributed random variable, with parameter 5.4.

a) What is the probability of no murder, in a particular month?
b) What is the expected number of murders per month?
c) During three consecutive months, there were 8, 7 and 9 murders, respectively. Somebody pointed out that this indicated that the murder rate had gone up. She said, that the probability of at least this many murders would be very small. What is this probability?

5–27 A salesman has found that the probability of a sale is 0.12 at each call. If the salesman makes thirty calls, what is

a) the expected number of sales?
b) the probability of at most five sales?
c) the probability of at most eight sales?
d) the probability of at least four sales?
e) the probability of exactly three sales?

5–28 A batch of 100 manufactured objects contains 5 defective objects. Three objects are selected at random.

a) Assuming that the objects are taken *with* replacement, determine the probability distribution corresponding to obtaining 0, 1, 2 and 3 defectives in the sample.
b) Compute the mean and the variance of the distribution in (a).
c) Repeat (a) and (b) above for the case that the objects were taken *without* replacement.
d) Repeat (a) and (b) above, using the Poisson distribution to approximate the probabilities.

5–29 A customer for a $ 50,000 fire insurance policy possesses a home, which according to experience may sustain a total loss in a given year with probability .001 and 50% loss with probability .01.

a) Ignoring all other possible losses, what annual premium should the insurance company charge for a policy in order to exactly break even?
b) Find the variance of the random variable defined above as "loss".

5–30 On an ordinary telephone it takes 0.5 second to dial "one"; for the other digits the time increases by 0.1 second per digit. Hence, it takes $0.4 + 0.1j$ seconds to dial the digit j, $j \geqq 1$, and 1.4 seconds to dial zero. The local numbers include the numbers 10,000–28,999. Find the expected time for dialling a local number, if all local numbers are equally likely to occur.

5–31 It is said that the French nobleman and mathematician de Méré had empirically noticed that it was to his advantage to bet (on equal bets) that in four tosses of a die he would get "six" at least once.

a) What is this probability?
b) If the bet is $100 against $100, what is the expected outcome for de Méré, for a bet?

5–32 A bank is recruiting a teller for a new branch office, and is interviewing applicants. The candidates are interviewed one after the other, and for each interview, there is a 30% chance that the candidate is found acceptable, in which case he/she is employed and the recruitment stops.

a) If the opportunity cost for the bank is assessed at $60 per interview, what is the expected cost for the recruiting?
b) What is the probability that after four interviews still no acceptable candidate has been found?

5–33 The random variable X has a geometric distribution with $p = 0.8$.

a) Determine $E(X)$, $V(X)$, σ
b) Find $P(X = 0)$
c) What is $P(X = 2)$?
d) Calculate $P(X \geqq 3)$.

*5–34 Prove the formulas for the expected value and variance of the geometric distribution.

6. Continuous Random Variables

In this chapter we continue to consider random variables, concentrating on continuous random variables. Several different distributions and their respective properties are discussed, and some of their applications mentioned.

In Section 6.1 we introduce the concept of the cumulative distribution function, for discrete as well as continuous random variables, and discuss some of its properties. The reader is then exposed to the probability density function, which we use to define continuous random variables. Some general results for events involving continuous random variables are covered, and the uniform distribution is used in an example. We end the section by bringing expected value and variance into the picture.

The following sections provide a catalogue of the most important continuous probability distributions which we shall need later on. Section 6.2 deals with the normal distribution. We show how any normal distribution can be transformed into the standard normal distribution, and compute probabilities involving normal variables. Several examples serve as illustrations. In Section 6.3 the exponential distribution is described, with examples, and the connections with the Poisson process and the Poisson distribution are stressed. Section 6.4 shows how the de Moivre theorem can be used to approximate the binomial distribution by the normal. In Section 6.5, 6.6 and 6.7, we define and describe the t, chi-square and F distributions, respectively. As these will be used much more later on, no examples are provided here.

6.1 The Cumulative Distribution Function and the Density Function

Extending a concept introduced earlier for discrete random variables we get the following:

Definition: For any random variable X (discrete or continuous), its *cumulative distribution function* $F_X(x)$ or simply $F(x)$ is given by

$$F_X(x) = P(X \leqq x).$$

Example 6.1

We have seen before that if X is the number of heads in three tosses of a fair coin, then $P(X = j)$ is 1/8, 3/8, 3/8, 1/8 for $j = 0, 1, 2, 3$, respectively. The cumulative distribution function F(x) for this variable will then be:

$$F(x) = \begin{cases} 0, & x < 0 \\ 1/8, & 0 \leqq x < 1 \\ 4/8, & 1 \leqq x < 2 \\ 7/8, & 2 \leqq x < 3 \\ 1 & x \geqq 3. \end{cases}$$

Graphically, F(x) looks as follows:

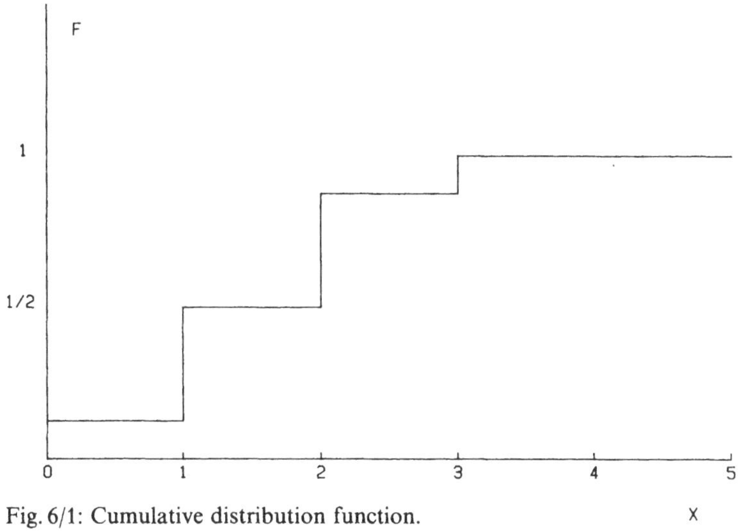

Fig. 6/1: Cumulative distribution function.

From the definition of F(x) the following results are obvious:

Theorem: For any cumulative distribution function F, we have:

1) $0 \leqq F(x) \leqq 1$
2) F(x) increases with x
3) $F(x) \to 0,\ x \to -\infty$
4) $F(x) \to 1,\ x \to +\infty$.

Furthermore, for any $a < b$ we find:

$$\{X \leqq b\} = \{X \leqq a\} \cup \{a < X \leqq b\}$$

where the two sets on the right-hand side are disjoint (mutually exclusive).

Consequently, by the addition law for mutually exclusive events:

$$P(X \leqq b) = P(X \leqq a) + P(a < X \leqq b)$$

or $$F(b) = F(a) + P(a < X \leqq b)$$

or $$P(a < X \leqq b) = F(b) - F(a).$$

This result is of major importance and will be used frequently later on.

For instance, in our example above, we see:

$$P(1 < X \leqq 2) = F(2) - F(1) = 7/8 - 4/8 = 3/8$$ or alternetively
$$P(1 < X \leqq 2) = P(X = 2) = 3/8,$$

as we expected.

Earlier we have indicated the difference between discrete and continuous random variables. We can now be specific:

Definition: A random variable X is *continuous* if there exists a function $f_X(x)$ such that:

$$F_X(x) = \int_{-\infty}^{t} f_X(t)dt.$$

The function $f_X(x)$ (or simply $f(x)$) is called the *probability density function* (or simply the *density function*) for X.

It follows that for continuous random variables, *probabilities* correspond to *areas* under the density function, as illustrated in the following figure:

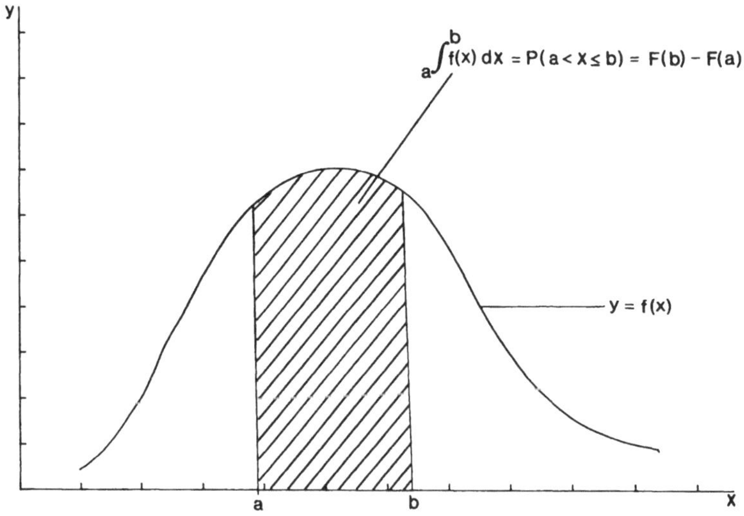

Fig. 6/2: A probability as an area under the density function.

It is also clear that $\int_{-\infty}^{+\infty} f(t)dt = 1$ for any density function (cf. item 4 in our Theorem) so that the total area under a density function is always 1.

Example 6.2

Suppose that a paper machine produces paper rolls that are of a width of between 180 and 182 cm. Assume that the width is a continuous random variable X with the following probability density function:

$$f(x) = \begin{cases} 0, & x < 180 \\ 1/2, & 180 \leqq x \leqq 182 \\ 0, & x > 182. \end{cases}$$

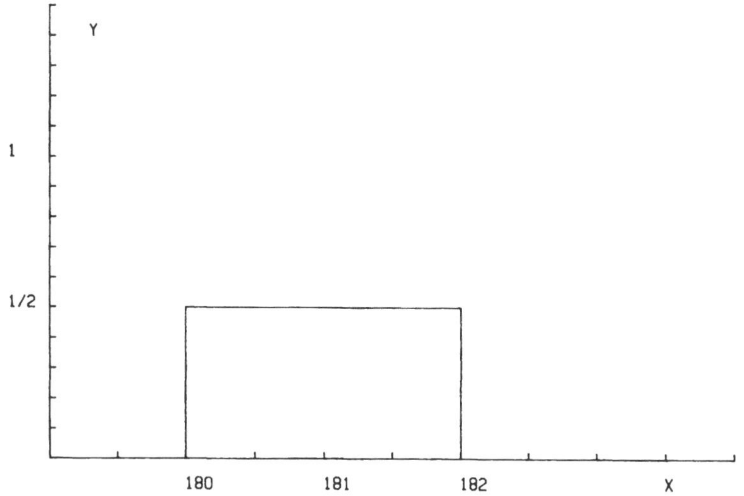

Fig. 6/3: Density function for the width of paper rolls.

Find $P(181.1 < X \leqq 181.8)$!

Solution: The probability we are looking for corresponds to the area under the density function between 181.1 and 181.8:

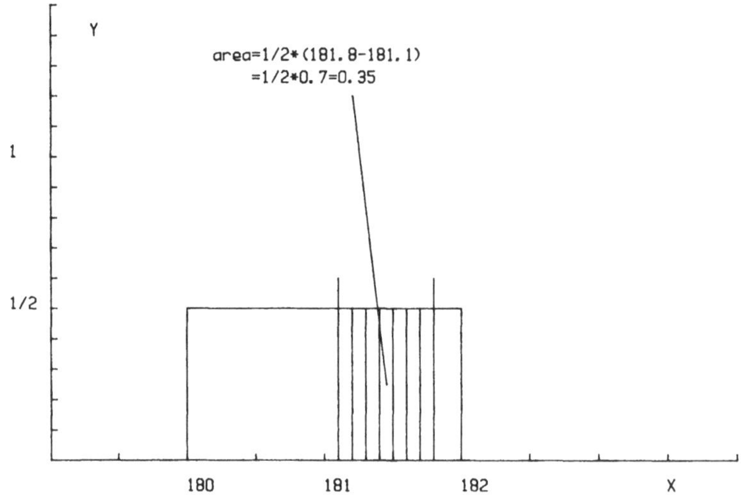

Fig. 6/4: Area corresponding to the probability asked for.

This area is 0.35, so that our probablity is 0.35.

It is obvious that for continuous random variables, probabilities for single points are zero (we have to have an *interval* to get a non-zero probability, i.e. area). Accordingly, we find that the following four events:

$$(a < X \leqq b)$$
$$(a \leqq X \leqq b)$$
$$(a \leqq X < b)$$
$$(a < X < b)$$

all have the *same* probability:

$$\int_a^b f(x)dx = F(b) - F(a).$$

We can also see that for "small" ε, we have:

$$P(a \leqq X \leqq a + \varepsilon) \approx \varepsilon \cdot f(a).$$

(cf. Fig. 6/5 on the next page.)

Guided by the discrete case, one makes the following definitions:

Definition: The *expected value* $E(X)$ (or μ) of a continuous random variable X with density function $f(x)$ is given by:

$$E(X) = \int_{-\infty}^{\infty} x f(x) dx.$$

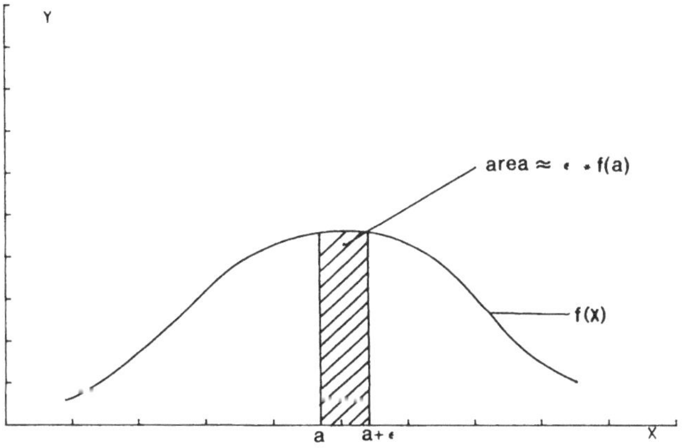

Fig. 6/5: The probability for a small interval of length ε.

Remark: It may happen that the expected value does not exist[1].

Definition: The variance V(X) (or σ^2) of a continuous random variable X with expected value μ is given by:

$$V(X) = E((X - \mu)^2).$$

Remark: It may happen that the variance does not exist.

Example 6.3

One can show, that for the general uniform distribution X with density function

$$f(x) = \begin{cases} \frac{1}{b-a} \text{ if } a \leqq x \leqq b \\ 0 \text{ otherwise} \end{cases}$$

the expected value is

$$E(X) = \frac{a+b}{2}$$

and the variance is

$$V(X) = \frac{(b-a)^2}{12}.$$

[1] This happens, for instance, for the so-called Cauchy distribution. We shall not go into the details.

In analogy with the discrete case, one can show that the variance can be computed by:

$$V(X) = \int_{-\infty}^{\infty} (x - \mu)^2 f(x)\,dx$$

or by:

$$V(X) = E(X^2) - \mu^2 .$$

One can also show the following:

Theorem: If X is a continuous random variable and a and b any constants, we have:

$$E(a + bX) = a + bE(X)$$
$$V(a + bX) = b^2 V(X) .$$

Remark: Exactly the same results hold for discrete random variables, as we saw in the previous chapter. Here we have to assume, of course, that the expected values and the variances *exist*.

6.2 The Normal Distribution

We shall now come to the most important of all probability distributions:

Definition: A random variable X with the probability density function:

$$f(x) = \frac{1}{\sigma\sqrt{2\pi}} e^{-\frac{(x-\mu)^2}{2\sigma^2}}$$

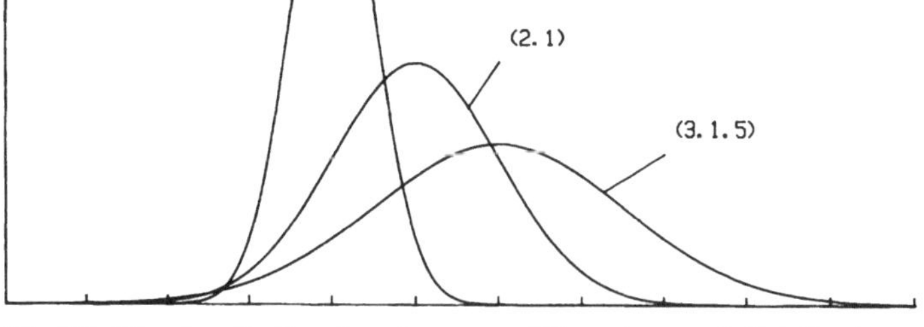

Fig. 6/6: The density function for some different normal distributions.

is said to be *normally distributed* with parameters μ and $\sigma > 0$; we say that X is $N(\mu, \sigma)$, where N here stands for normal.

The normal distribution is sometimes also called the *Gaussian* distribution (after Gauss). One can show the following result.

Theorem: If X is $N(\mu, \sigma)$, then $E(X) = \mu$, $V(X) = \sigma^2$.

In Fig. 6/6 on the previous page below, we show the density functions of some normal distributions, with different μ and σ.

Definition: A random variable Z which is N(0, 1) is called *standard normal.* Thus, a standard normal variable has mean 0 and variance 1.

The density function f(x) of a standard normal variable Z is:

$$f(x) = \frac{1}{\sqrt{2\pi}} e^{-x^2/2}$$

and is called the *normal curve* (or sometimes also the *bell curve* because of its shape):

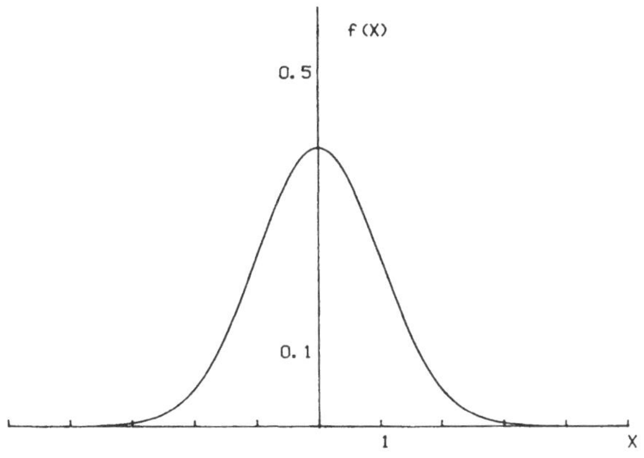

Fig. 6/7: The normal curve.

It is symmetric around the vertical axis.

The cumulative probability distribution function F(x) of Z is:

$$\int_{-\infty}^{x} \frac{1}{\sqrt{2\pi}} e^{-t^2/2}\,dt = \underbrace{\int_{-\infty}^{0} \frac{1}{\sqrt{2\pi}} e^{-t^2/2}\,dt}_{1/2} + \int_{0}^{x} \frac{1}{\sqrt{2\pi}} e^{-t^2/2}\,dt$$

$$= \frac{1}{2} + \int_{0}^{x} \frac{1}{\sqrt{2\pi}} e^{-t^2/2}\,dt\,.$$

The function $\int_{0}^{x} \frac{1}{\sqrt{2\pi}} e^{-t^2/2}\,dt$ is tabulated as "area under the normal curve":

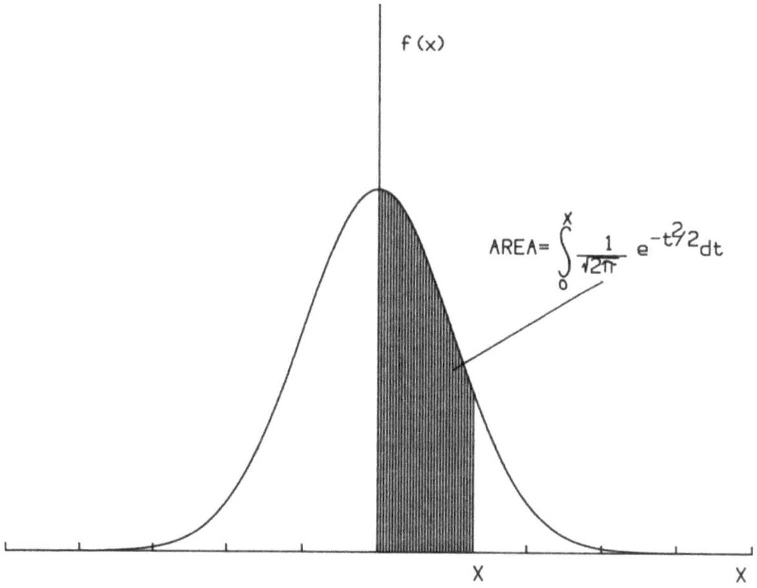

Fig. 6/8: An area under the normal curve.

Example 6.4

If Z is a standard normal variable, then:

$$P(0 \leqq Z \leqq 1.37) = 0.4147\,.$$

Example 6.5

$$P(0 < Z < 0.21) = 0.0832\,.$$

Example 6.6

$$P(0 < Z \leqq 3.04) = 0.4988\,.$$

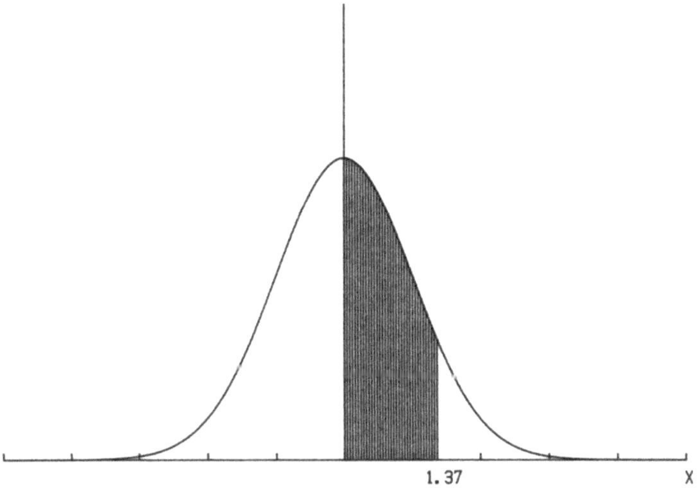

Fig. 6/9: Area under the normal curve for Example 6.4.

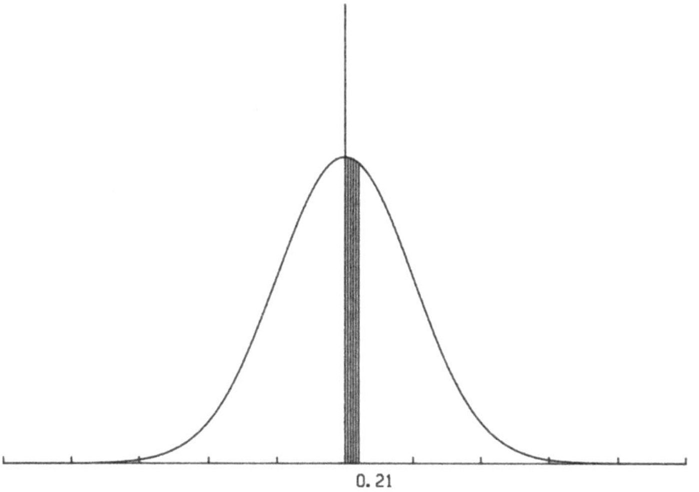

Fig. 6/10: Area under the normal curve for Example 6.5.

Example 6.7

$$P(Z \leqq 0.43) = 1/2 + 0.1664 = 0.6664\,.$$

Example 6.8

$$\begin{aligned} P(Z \leqq -0.26) &= P(Z \geqq 0.26) = 1/2 - P(0 \leqq Z \leqq 0.26) \\ &= 1/2 - 0.1026 = 0.3974\,. \end{aligned}$$

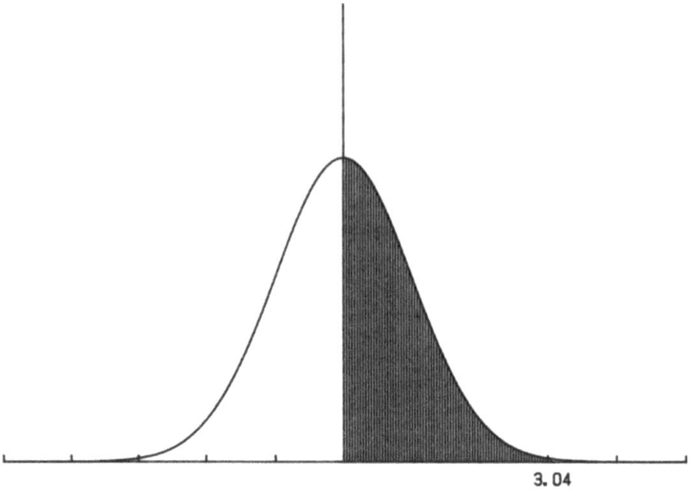

Fig. 6/11: Area under the normal curve for Example 6.6.

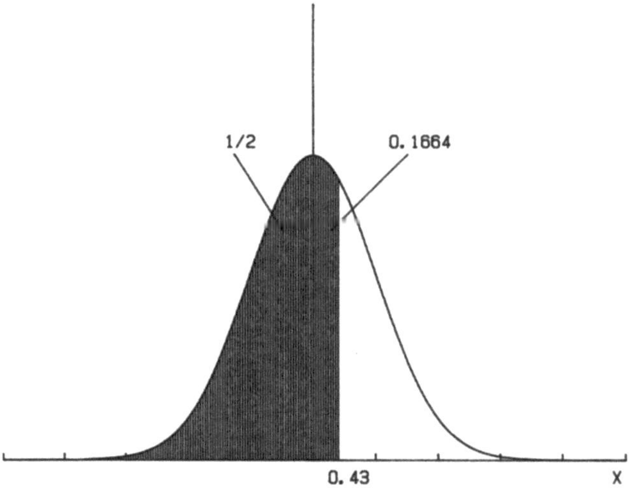

Fig. 6/12: Area under the normal curve for Example 6.7.

Example 6.9

$P(-1.07 \leqq Z \leqq 0.75) = P(-1.07 \leqq Z \leqq 0) + P(0 \leqq Z \leqq 0.75)$
$= P(0 \leqq Z \leqq 1.07) + P(0 \leqq Z \leqq 0.75) = 0.3577 + 0.2734 = 0.6311.$

We can now deal with *standard* normal, i.e. $N(0, 1)$ variables, but what about the *general* normal variable, i.e. $N(\mu, \sigma)$?

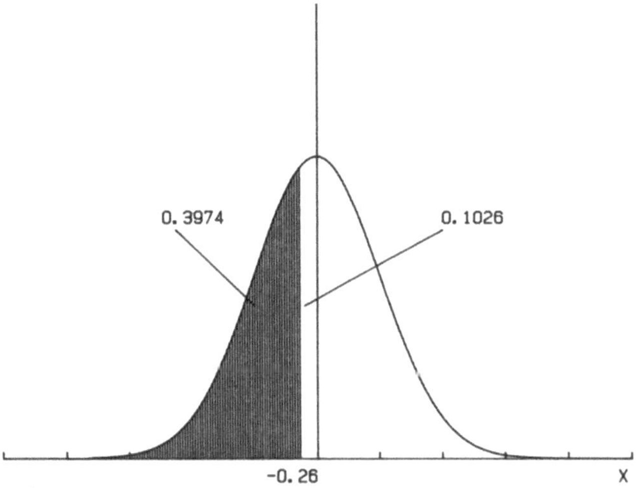

Fig. 6/13: Area under the normal curve for Example 6.8.

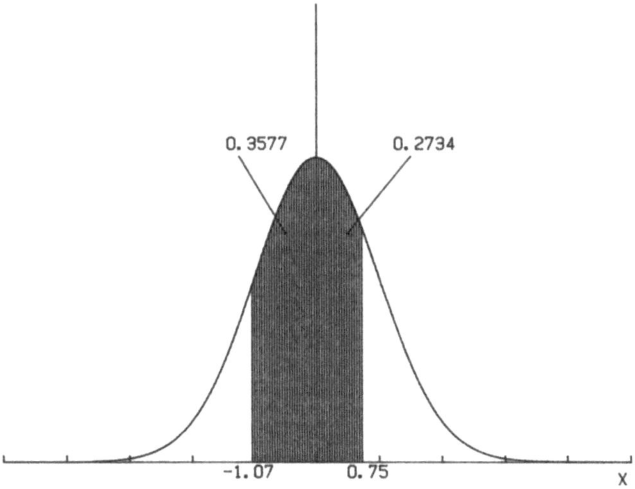

Fig. 6/14: Area under the normal curve for Example 6.9.

The following theorem gives a clue how to answer this question.

Theorem: For any constants a, b, μ, σ (with $\sigma > 0$, $a \neq 0$) we have:
If X is $N(\mu, \sigma)$ then $aX + b$ is $N(a\mu + b, |a| \cdot \sigma)$.

Remark: $|a|$ denotes the *absolute value* of a, defined by:

$$|a| = \begin{cases} a & \text{for } a \geqq 0 \\ -a & \text{for } a < 0 . \end{cases}$$

For example, $|1.3| = 1.3$, $|-2.7| = 2.7$, $|0| = 0$.

From the theorem we now get the following important result:

If X is $N(\mu, \sigma)$, then $Y = \dfrac{X-\mu}{\sigma}$ is $N(0, 1)$.

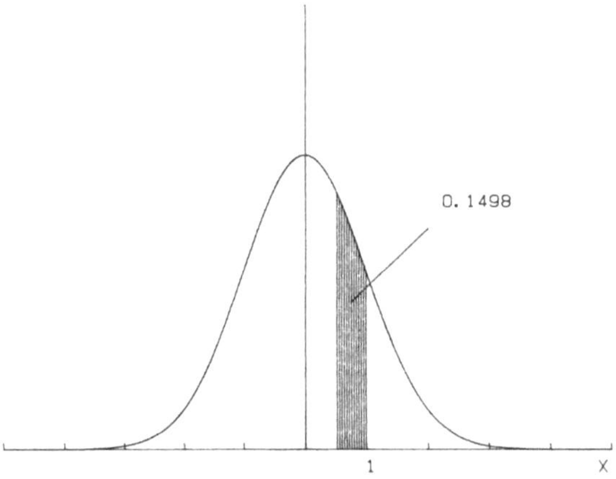

Fig. 6/15: Area under the normal curve for Example 6.10.

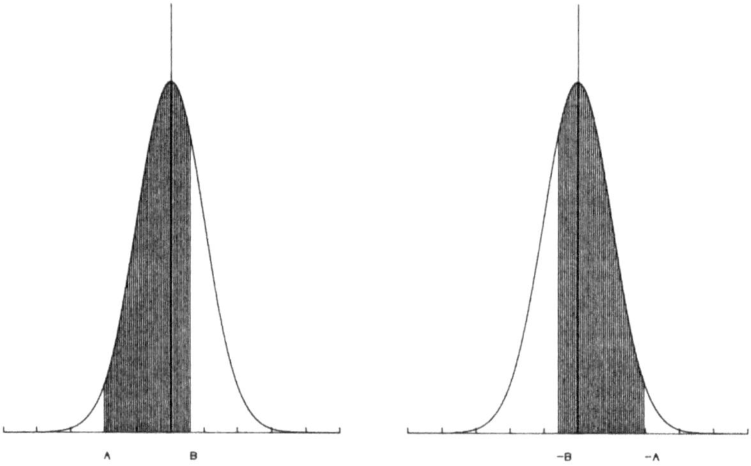

Fig. 6/16: Symmetry of the standard normal distribution.

This result follows from the theorem, because:

$$Y = \frac{1}{\sigma}X - \frac{\mu}{\sigma} \text{ is } N\left(\frac{1}{\sigma}\mu - \frac{\mu}{\sigma}, \left|\frac{1}{\sigma}\right| \cdot \sigma\right), \text{ i.e. } N(0, 1).$$

Example 6.10

Find $P(2 \leqq X \leqq 3)$ where X is $N(1, 2)$.

Solution: We want to work with $\frac{X-1}{2}$, which is $N(0, 1)$.

We get:

$$\begin{aligned} P(2 \leqq X \leqq 3) &= P(2-1 \leqq X-1 \leqq 3-1) \\ &= P\left(\frac{2-1}{2} \leqq \frac{X-1}{2} \leqq \frac{3-1}{2}\right) \\ &= P\left(\frac{1}{2} \leqq \frac{X-1}{2} \leqq 1\right) \\ &= P\left(0 \leqq \frac{X-1}{2} \leqq 1\right) - P\left(0 \leqq \frac{X-1}{2} \leqq \frac{1}{2}\right) \\ &= 0.3413 - 0.1915 = 0.1498\,. \end{aligned}$$

Remark: Because of the symmetry around the vertical axis of the standard normal distribution, we have the following useful result (cf. Fig. 6/16):

$$P(a \leqq Z \leqq b) = P(-b \leqq Z \leqq -a)\,.$$

6.3 The Exponential Distribution

In Section 5.5 on the Poisson distribution we introduced the Poisson process, which arises in queueing situations, where arriving customers form a waiting line at a service station:

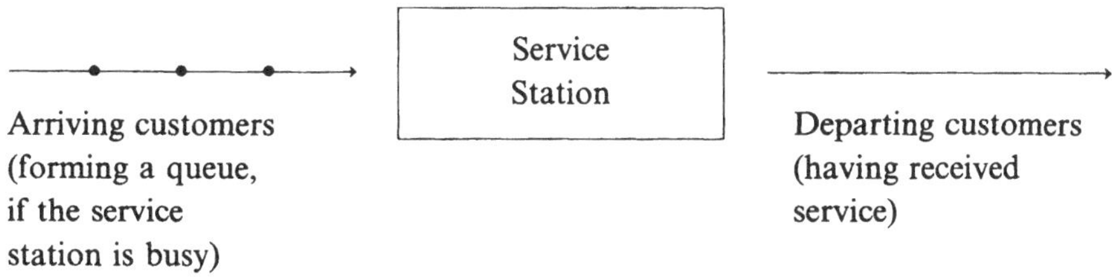

Fig. 6/17: Queueing situation

We saw that the number X of customer arrivals, during a given time interval of length t, is Poisson-distributed with parameter λt. λ denotes the average (expected) number of arrivals per time unit, which is called the *arrival rate*.

Letting Y denote the length of the time interval between two consecutive arrivals (so that Y is a continuous random variable), we may ask what the distribution of Y is.

It turns out that it has a so-called *exponential* distribution, with *parameter* λ:

Definition: A continuous random variable Y with probability density function

$$f_Y(x) = \lambda e^{-\lambda x} (x \geqq 0)$$

is said to be *exponentially* distributed with parameter λ (which of course must be positive). We say that Y is $\mathrm{Exp}(\lambda)$.

We see that the density function of an exponential variable has a y-axis intercept of λ:

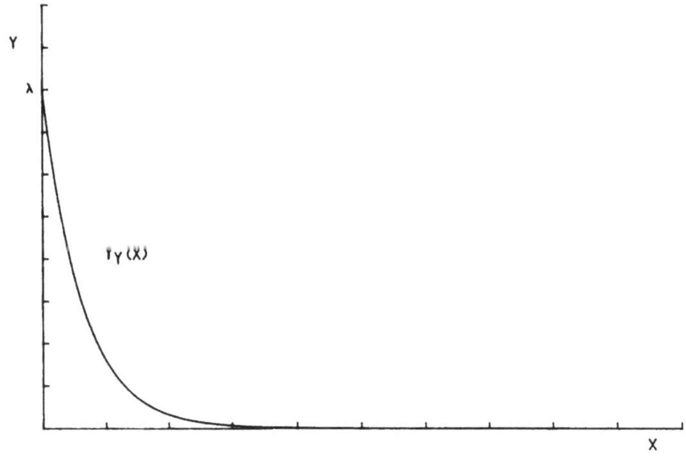

Fig. 6/18: Density function for the exponential distribution.

One can show the following two theorems:

Theorem: If Y is $\mathrm{Exp}(\lambda)$, the $E(Y) = \frac{1}{\lambda}$, $V(Y) = \frac{1}{\lambda^2}$.

The cumulative distribution function of the exponential distribution has a simple form:

Theorem: If Y is $\mathrm{Exp}(\lambda)$, then $F_Y(x) = 1 - e^{-\lambda x}$.

Example 6.11

Customers arrive at a certain post office at the rate of 8 per hour; the arrivals form a Poisson process. What is

a) the expected interarrival time?
b) the probability of at least 20 minutes between two consecutive arrivals?
c) at most 10 minutes?
d) between 5 and 15 minutes?

Solution: Letting Y denote the interarrival time, we know that Y is Exp(8).

a) Hence, $E(Y) = 1/8$ hours $= 7.5$ minutes which is the expected interarrival time.

b) $P(Y \geqq 20 \text{ minutes}) = P(Y \geqq 1/3 \text{ hour}) = 1 - P(Y < 1/3) = 1 - F_Y(1/3) = 1 - (1 - e^{-8 \cdot 1/3}) = e^{-8/3} \approx e^{-2.67} \approx 0.069.$

c) $P(Y \leqq 1/6) = F_Y(1/6) = 1 - e^{-8 \cdot 1/4} \approx 1 - e^{-1.33} \approx 1 - 0.264 = 0.736.$

d) $P(1/12 \leqq Y \leqq 1/4) = F_Y(1/4) - F_Y(1/12) = 1 - e^{-8 \cdot 1/4} - (1 - e^{-8 \cdot 1/12}) \approx e^{-0.67} - e^{-2} \approx 0.513 - 0.135 = 0.378.$

6.4 Approximating the Binomial Distribution by the Normal Distribution

In Section 5.5 on the Poisson distribution we saw that a Bin(n, p) variable could be well approximated by a $P(n \cdot p)$ variable, provided that n is large and p is small. But what if p is not small, say if it is around 1/2? In this case (for large n) it turns out that the *normal* distribution gives a good approximation, thanks to the following theorem by de Moivre[2] (1733):

Theorem: If X is Bin(n, p), then $\dfrac{X - np}{\sqrt{npq}}$ is approximately N(0, 1) for large n.

Example 6.12

Assume that X is Bin(400, 1/2) and that we wish to find $P(181 \leqq X \leqq 210)$. As we usually do not have binomial tables for $n > 30$, we wish to use an approximation method.

As $E(X) = 400 \cdot 1/2 = 200$ and $\sigma = \sqrt{400 \cdot 1/2 \cdot (1 - 1/2)} = \sqrt{100} = 10$, we write

[2] Abraham de Moivre, French mathematician, 1667–1754.

$$P(180 < X \leqq 210) = P\left(\frac{180-200}{10} < \frac{X-200}{10} \leqq \frac{210-200}{10}\right)$$
$$= P\left(-2 < \frac{X-200}{10} \leqq 1\right).$$

According to the de Moivre theorem, $\frac{X-200}{10}$ is closely approximated by a standard normal variable Z. We find:

$P(-2 < Z \leqq 1) = P(-2 \leqq Z \leqq 0) + P(0 \leqq Z \leqq 1)$
$= 0.4772 + 0.3413 = 0.8185$, so that $P(180 < X \leqq 210) \approx 0.8185$.

We can do it better, using a so-called *continuity correction.*
The idea will be clear from the following figure:

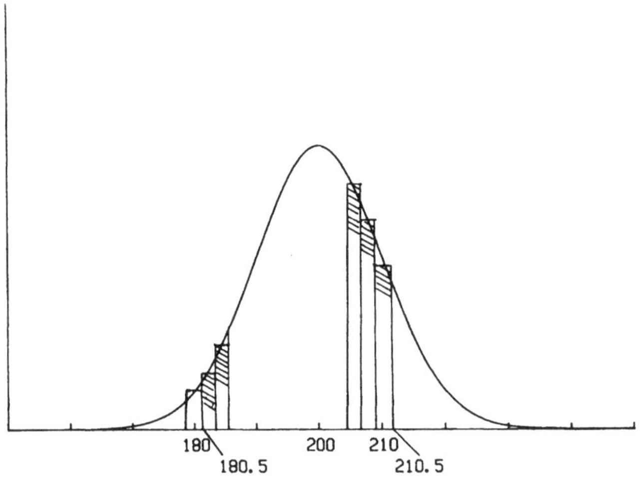

Fig. 6/19: Normal approximation of the binomial distribution using continuity correction.

Now we get:

$P(180 < X \leqq 210) = P(180.5 < X \leqq 210.5) \approx P(-1.95 < Z \leqq 1.05)$
$= 0.4744 + 0.3531 = 0.8275$.

In general, if $npq > 15$, the approximation error is less than half a percent.

Remark: Remember that if $n \geqq 20$ and $p \leqq 0.1$, the Bin(n, p) distribution is well approximated by the $P(n \cdot p)$ (see Section 5.5).

6.5 The t Distribution

A distribution which we shall be using frequently in the following chapters is the *t distribution,* often referred to as the *Student's t distribution.* W. S. Gosset[3], who derived this distribution in 1908, used the pseudonym "Student" as his employer, Guinness Brewery, did not allow him to publish his results under his own name.

Definition: A continuous random variable X is said to have a *t distribution* with n *degrees of freedom,* if its density function f(x) is:

$$f(x) = \frac{\gamma_n}{\left(1 + \frac{x^2}{n}\right)^{\frac{n+1}{2}}}$$

where the constant γ_n depends on n only (and not on x), $n = 1, 2, 3, \ldots$. We say that X is t(n).

One can show the following result.

Theorem: If X is t(n), then:

$$E(X) = 0 \qquad \text{for} \quad n \geqq 2,$$

$$V(X) = \frac{n}{n-2} \qquad \text{for} \quad n \geqq 3.$$

Remark: For $n = 1$ the expected value does not exist, and for $n = 1$ or 2 the variance does not exist.

As we can see, the t distribution is bell-shaped and symmetric around the vertical axis. It is very similar to the normal distribution, but has "fatter" tails (see Fig. 6/20 on the next page).

After considering the shape of the density functions in Fig. 6/20, the following theorem should be no surprise:

Theorem: The density function of the t distribution approaches that of the standard normal distribution as the number of degrees of freedom increases. Symbolically, we can wwrite:

$$t(\infty) = N(0, 1).$$

[3] William Sealy Gosset, English statistician and chemist, 1876–1937.

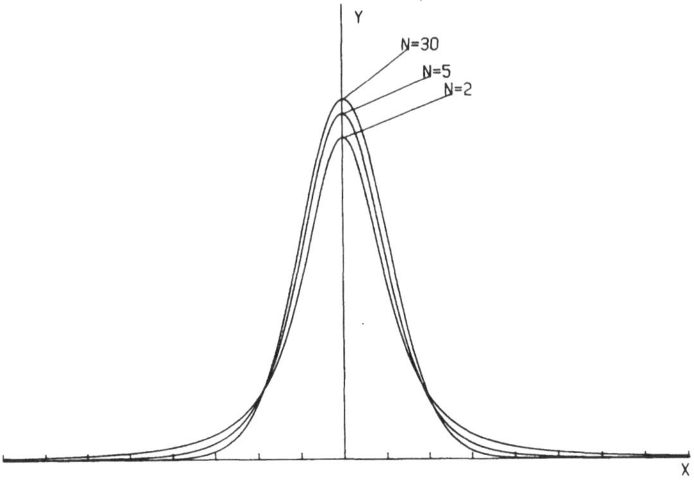

Fig. 6/20: The density function for the t distribution.

As a rule, for $n \geqq 30$, the standard normal distribution is used as an approximation of the t distribution. For this reason, tables of the t distribution usually do not give n greater than 30.

The t distribution will be further discussed in Chapters 8 and 9, where examples will be given.

6.6 The Chi-square Distribution

In addition to the t distribution, we shall encounter the *chi-square* (or χ^2) *distribution* (from the letter chi, χ, of the Greek alphabet). (Although this distribution was developed by F. R. Helmert[4] around 1875, its name derives from K. Pearson who introduced it in 1900.)

Definition: A continuous random variable X is said to have a *chi-square distribution* with n *degrees of freedom,* if its density function f(x) is:

$$f(x) = \alpha_n x^{\frac{n-2}{2}} e^{-\frac{x_2}{2}}, \quad x > 0$$

where the constant α_n depends on n only (and not on x), $n = 1, 2, 3, \ldots$. We say that X is $\chi^2(n)$.

One can show the following result:

[4] Friedrich Robert Helmert, German mathematician, 1843–1917.

Theorem: If X is $\chi^2(n)$, then:

$$E(X) = n, \quad V(X) = 2n.$$

In the figure below, we show the density function for some different values of n:

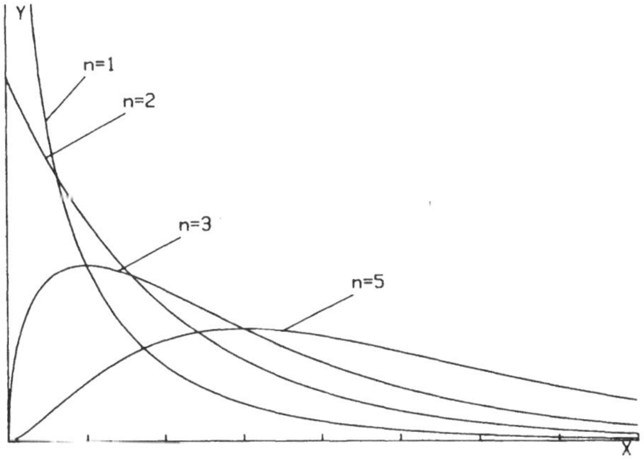

Fig. 6/21: The density function for the chi-square distribution.

We shall return to the chi-square distribution in Chapters 7, 8, 9 and 10, where examples will be given.

6.7 The F Distribution

The F distribution is named after R.A. Fisher who developed it in 1922. It is fundamental for the *analysis of variance* to be considered in Chapter 11.

Definition: A continuous random variable X is said to have an *F distribution* with n_1 *numerator degrees of freedom* and n_2 *denominator degrees of freedom*, if its density function f(x) is:

$$f(x) = \beta_{n_1, n_2} \cdot \frac{x^{\frac{n_1 - 2}{2}}}{(n_1 x + n_2)^{\frac{n_1 + n_2}{2}}}, \quad x > 0$$

where the constant β_{n_1, n_2} depends on n_1 and n_2 only (and not on x), $n_1 = 1, 2, 3, \ldots$, $n_2 = 1, 2, 3, \ldots$. We say that X is $F(n_1, n_2)$.

One can show the following two results:

Theorem: If X is $F(n_1, n_2)$, then:

$$E(X) = \frac{n_2}{n_2 - 2} \quad \text{for} \quad n_2 \geqq 3$$

$$V(X) = \frac{2n_2^2(n_1 + n_2 - 2)}{n_1(n_2 - 2)^2(n_2 - 4)} \quad \text{for} \quad n_2 \geqq 5.$$

Remark: For $n_2 < 3$ the expected value does not exist, and for $n_2 < 5$ the variance does not exist.

Theorem: If X is $F(n_1, n_2)$, then 1/X is $F(n_2, n_1)$.

Remark: We call this the *reciprocal property* of the F distribution. As we shall see later on, it allows us to economize on tables for F.

In the figure below, we show the density function for some different values of n_1 and n_2.

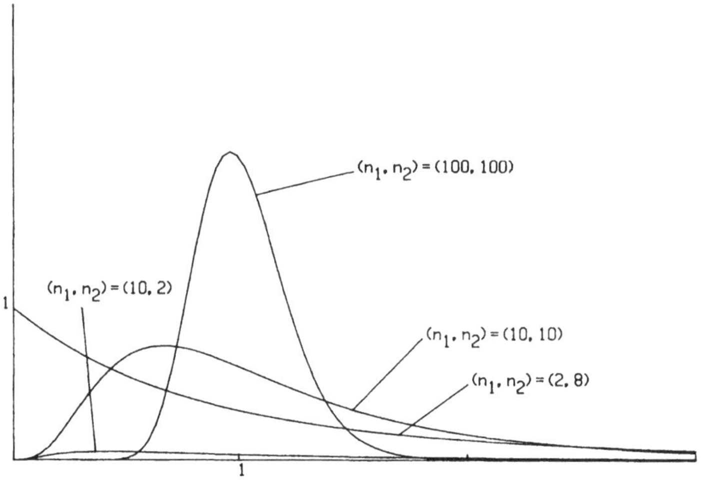

Fig. 6/22: The density function for the F distribution.

We shall return to the F distribution in Chapters 7, 9, 11 and 12, where examples are given.

References

Chou, Y.: *Statistical Analysis*, 2nd edition. Holt, Rinehart and Winston, New York 1975.
Feller, W.: *An Introduction to Probability Theory and Its Applications*, Vol. 1, 3rd edition. John Wiley & Sons, New York 1968.

Harnett, D. L.: *Statistical Methods,* 3rd edition. Addison-Wesley, Reading, Mass. 1982.
Hawkins, C. A., and J. E. Weber: *Statistical Analysis. Applications to Business and Economics.* Harper & Row, New York 1980.
Mansfield, E.: *Statistics for Business and Economics.* Norton & Company, New York 1980.
Ross, S. M.: *A First Course in Probability.* Macmillan, New York 1976.
Wonnacott, T. H., and R. J. Wonnacott: *Introductory Statistics for Business and Economics,* 2nd edition. John Wiley & Sons, New York 1977.

Exercises

6–1 The waiting time for a car at a certain red traffic light can be considered distributed uniformly between 0 and 1.5 minutes.

a) What is the expected waiting time for a car that has to stop at the red light?
b) What is the standard deviation of this waiting time?

*6–2 A uniformly distributed random variable X has the density function

$$f(x) = \begin{cases} \dfrac{1}{b-a} & \text{for} \quad a \leqq x \leqq b \\ 0 & \text{otherwise} \end{cases}$$

a) Prove that $E(X) = \dfrac{a+b}{2}$

b) Prove that $V(X) = \dfrac{(b-a)^2}{12}$.

6–3 A lumber yard delivers timber logs of many different lengths $a_i, a_1 < a_2 < \ldots < a_N$. The timber can be considered uniformly distributed in length. A log with length x such that $a_i \leqq x < a_{i+1}$ is trimmed to length a_i by cutting off the *excess* $x - a_i$. Let $a_i = 1 + 0.01 \cdot (i-1)$ (in meters) for $i = 1, 2, .., N$. If 10,000 logs are cut per day, what is

a) The expected amount of waste per day?
b) The standard deviation of this waste?

*6–4 Show that

$$V(X) = E(X^2) - (E(X))^2$$

for any continuous random variable X for which E(X) and V(X) exist.

*6–5 Show that for all constants a and b,

a) $E(a + bX) = a + bE(X)$,
b) $V(a + bX) = b^2 V(X)$

for any continuous random variable X for which E(X) and V(X) exist.

**6–6 Show that

$$\lim_{x \to +\infty} \int_{-\infty}^{x} \frac{1}{\sqrt{2\pi}} e^{-t^2/2} dt = 1 .$$

**6–7 Show that if X is a normal distribution $N(\mu, \sigma)$, then

a) E(X) exists and is μ
b) V(X) exists and is σ^2.

6–8 The continuous random variable Z has a standard normal distribution. Calculate the following probabilities:

a) $P(Z \leqq 2.34)$
b) $P(Z > 0.59)$
c) $P(-2.43 < Z \leqq 2.44)$.

6–9 Solve Exercise 8 above, replacing Z by a normally distributed variable X which is N(3.13, 0.412).

6–10 The service lives of Sultania super lightbulbs are normally distributed with a mean of 1200 hours and a standard deviation of 36 hours.

a) What percentage of the bulbs will have a service life of between 1200 and 1254 hours?
b) What percentage of the bulbs will have a service life of between 1182 and 1200 hours?
c) What percentage of the bulbs will have a service life of between 1176 and 1230 hours?
d) What percentage of the bulbs will have a service life of between 1230 and 1254 hours?

6–11 The service lives of Sultania super lightbulbs are normally distributed with a mean of 1200 hours and a standard deviation of 36 hours.

a) What percentage of the bulbs will last for longer than 1272 hours?
b) What percentage of the bulbs will last for less than 1146 hours?
c) The 10 percent of the bulbs with the longest service life will last for longer than how many hours?
d) The 20 percent of the bulbs with the shortest service life will last for less than how many hours?

6–12 The length X of a metal rod produced by a manufacturing process is normally distributed with a mean of 14 cm and a standard deviation of 0.2 mm. A rod is considered defective if $X < 13.98$ cm or if $X > 14.02$ cm. In a random sample of 15 rods, what is the probability that there will be

a) less than four defectives?
b) four or five defectives?
c) more than five defectives?

6–13 The average income a student earns per week doing part-time work is $100 with a standard deviation of $10.

a) What is the probability that *a* student earns more than $105.20 per week?
b) If a random sample of 25 students is taken, what is the probability that *all* earn more than $105.20 per week?

6–14 The mileage obtained from Goodbye radial tires can be considered N(20, 5), measured in thousands of miles.

a) What percentage of tires last less than 22,000 miles?
b) Find the probability that a tire will give more than 14,000 miles.
c) What is the mileage that is exceeded by only 1 percent of the tires?

6–15 The Health Ministry of a certain country prescribes that street noise levels must not exceed 42 decibels.

a) In a certain city centre the noise level is normally distributed with a mean of 48 and a standard deviation of 7.2 decibels. What proportion of the city centre has a noise level that is unacceptable?
b) In a certain residential town district the noise level is normally distributed with a mean of 34 and a standard deviation of 6.4 decibels. What percentage of the locations in the residential town district have a noise level that is unacceptable?

6–16 A firm's monthly revenues are N(300, 40) thousand dollars, whereas monthly total costs are $250,000.

a) What is the average monthly profit?
b) What is the probability of making a loss in a given month?

**6–17 Show that if Y is a continuous random variable with density function:

$$f(x) = \begin{cases} \lambda e^{-\lambda x} & \text{if } x > 0 \\ 0 & \text{otherwise} \end{cases}$$

where $\lambda > 0$ is a given constant, then

a) E(Y) exists and is $1/\lambda$
b) V(Y) exists and is $1/_{\lambda}2$

c) $F(x) = \begin{cases} 1 - e^{-\lambda x} & x \geqq 0 \\ 0 & \text{otherwise.} \end{cases}$

6–18 A small resort hotel is located on a small island in the middle of the Pacific Ocean. A major disaster occurrs in the form of a hotel fire. A rescue service is set up to bring survivors to the hospitals on the mainland. The average elapsed time between arrivals of the injured people at a mainland hospital is believed to be 50 minutes.

What is the probability that the time between the previous and the next arrival will be

a) at most 75 minutes?
b) at least 75 minutes?
c) between 60 and 75 minutes?

6–19 Jobs arrive at a computer centre at an average of two every 50 seconds.

a) Calculate the average elapse of time between each single arrival.
b) What is the probability that the time between the previous job's arrival and the next job's will be at most 75 seconds?
c) Given the information above, what is the probability that at least three jobs will arrive in a two-minute interval?

6–20 The length of time between arrivals of helicopters at a disaster area and the length of service time required to provide preliminary aid and load patients are two random variables that play an important role in planning a system for the provision of this service.

a) What kind of probability distribution is most likely to describe the occurrence of these two variables?
b) If the mean time between arrivals for the wounded at a disaster point is 5 minutes, what is the probability that the time that elapses between any two arrivals of the helicopter is less than 2 minutes?
c) What is the probability that the next three successive interarrival times are each less than 2 minutes?
d) What is the probability that any interarrival time will exceed 10 minutes?

6–21 The probability distribution of the waiting time for incoming telephone calls at a switchboard is exponential with an average of 30 seconds.

a) What is the probability that an individual has to wait more than one minute before being served?
b) What is the probability that an individual has to wait less than 12 seconds before being served?
c) What is the probability than an individual waits between one and two minutes before being served?

6–22 A random variable X is binomially distributed with $n = 30$ and $p = 0.5$. Using the normal distribution as an approximation to the binomial, compute the probability $P(10 \leqq X \leqq 13)$,

a) without continuity correction.
b) with continuity correction.

6–23 A census has determined that eighteen percent of a University's commerce students would like to see a third course in statistics made compulsory in the B.Comm. curriculum. A random sample of 175 commerce students is selected. What is the probability that in the sample:

a) less than twenty-five students favour the third course?
b) at least thirty students favour the third course?

c) at least thirty-four and at most thirty-seven students favour the third course?
d) exactly thirty-two students favour the third course?

6–24 An oil company is drilling for oil; for each hole drilled, the probability is 0.5 that oil will be found; the outcomes for different holes are independent. 25 holes are drilled. Find the probability that fewer than 10 holes give oil,

a) exactly, by using a binomial distribution table;
b) by using the normal approximation *without* continuity correction;
c) as b) but *with* continuity correction.

**6–25 Show that for a continuous random variable X which is t-distributed with n degrees of freedom,

a) E(X) exists and is 0 for $n \geqq 2$;

b) V(X) exists and is $\frac{n}{n-2}$ for $n \geqq 3$.

**6–26 Show that for a continuous random variable Y which is chi-square distributed with n degrees of freedom,

a) E(X) exists and is n
b) V(X) exists and is 2n.

**6–27 Show that if X is $F(n_1, n_2)$, then

a) E(X) exists and is $\frac{n_2}{n_2 - 2}$ if $n \geqq 3$

b) V(X) exists and is $\frac{2n_2^2(n_1 + n_2 - 2)}{n_1(n_2 - 2)^2(n_2 - 4)}$ if $n \geqq 5$.

**6–28 Show that if X is $F(n_1, n_2)$, then the variable

$\frac{1}{X}$ is $F(n_2, n_1)$.

7. Sampling and Sampling Distributions

We will now discuss the very important statistical concept of sampling, and lay the foundation for statistical estimation and inference, which will be dealt with in subsequent chapters.

In Section 7.1 we introduce the idea of sampling and consider some reasons for and against sampling. Section 7.2 is devoted to a description of some of the most common sampling designs. Section 7.3 describes in some more detail the simple random sampling design and shows how a simple random sample may be generated using a random number table. In Section 7.4 we look at the expected value and the variance of sums and products of random variables, and also state a few so-called *addition theorems* and other results, relating some of the most commonly occurring statistical distributions to each other. In Section 7.5 we consider the mean, variance and distribution of the sample mean, and Section 7.6, on the central limit theorem, ends the chapter.

7.1 Sampling

An important aspect of a statistical investigation is the selection of observations that will be studied. The whole population under consideration is often not studied, but rather a suitably large part of it, which we call a *sample*. The procedure by which this sample is selected is called *sampling*.

Example 7.1

The public telephone company of a large city is considering a technical modification of the telephone system. It is therefore desirable to obtain some information about how often the average subscriber uses the telephone system, particularly during peak-hours. Although it would be theoretically possible to survey each of the more than a hundred thousand telephone subscribers, the company is likely to restrict its survey to a small sample of at most a few hundred subscribers.

From the above example it is clear that compelling reasons for investigating a sample, rather than the whole underlying population, may be of a time and cost nature. In the telephone example, it would presumably be either too time consuming or too costly (or maybe both) to survey the whole population. The advantage in obtaining the data for a statistical analysis more quickly and cheaply by sampling must be weighed against the disadvantage of some uncertainty regarding the reliability of the sample data.

In addition to time and/or cost considerations, reasons for observing a sample instead of the whole population can also be of another nature. For instance, the observation may involve destroying the items (testing mechanical components for breaking strength, measuring the life length of electrical bulbs, etc.), in which case sampling becomes a necessity.

Also, a sample survey may give higher quality data than a survey of the whole population would; e.g. the U.S. Bureau of the Census makes sample surveys to check the accuracy of population censuses. Finally, if the population is infinitely large (as in the case of experiments that could be repeated any number of times), we must sample.

Obviously it is of crucial importance for any statistical investigation that the characteristics of the population are reflected in the sample. If this is the case, we say that the sample is *representative.*

If a sample is not representative, the sample statistics will differ from the corresponding population parameters to a greater or lesser extent. The errors of misrepresentation are of essentially two different kinds, *sampling errors* and *nonsampling errors.*

By *sampling error* we refer to the difference between a sample statistic and its corresponding population parameter, that occurs because of the chance (random) selection of units to form the sample. In other words, sampling errors are of a random nature and can never be eliminated (unless the sample consists of the whole population). However, we may be able to say something about their statistical distribution.

Nonsampling errors, on the other hand, arise because of imperfections in the sample selection procedure and because of mistakes in analyzing and reporting the data. Nonsampling errors may also be due to *response bias,* when the observations do not accurately reflect what is being measured. This may occur, for instance, when the data are gathered by questionnaires that are poorly worded, so that respondents can misunderstand the questions. Respondents might also consciously provide false information (regarding, say, criminal activities or sex habits).

7.2 Sampling Designs

The theory of sampling is extensive, and we shall just touch on some basic ideas. There are two major types of sampling designs, *probability* and *nonprobability* sampling. In probability sampling, a random mechanism is used to select the sample. Each element of the population must have a nonzero chance of selection. Some probability sampling designs will now be briefly described.

Simple Random Sampling

Refer to Example 7.1 about telephone subscribers. The *sampling frame* is a list of elements from which the sample is drawn. In our example, we would probably choose the latest telephone directory issued. But what about new subscribers, subscribers who have left, and unlisted subscribers?

Errors will arise if those that are not listed in the sampling frame are different as a group from the whole population.

The simple random sampling design involves straightforward selection from the sampling frame using a random generator. It is perhaps being used more than before, as we now have computers.

Before we draw the sample, we must decide on the size of it. This depends on time and cost considerations, as well as statistical aspects. We shall defer the problem of how to determine the sample size till Chapter 8. We shall see later, that the sample only needs to grow proportionately to the *square root* of the size of the population, for confidence intervals to remain constant. Also, any a priori knowledge of the statistical distribution of the population is of help in deciding on the size of the sample.

Complex Random Sampling designs can often yield better results than simple random sampling, if some prior knowledge about the population is available. Of the complex random sampling designs, we shall describe *systematic, stratified, cluster* and *double* sampling.

Systematic Sampling

This design involves the selection of every k-th element from the sampling frame, where k is a predetermined number chosen by the statistician. If there is some periodicity in the sampling frame, this method can obviously give misleading results. Randomizing the sampling frame or changing the value of k might help in such cases.

Stratified Sampling

This design groups the elements of a population into mutually exclusive, relatively homogeneous groups (*strata*) prior to sampling. The stratification offers almost always statistically more efficient results than simple random sampling.

Cluster Sampling

In this design, the entire population is first divided into many (small) groups or *clusters;* then a random sample of clusters is taken. A common form of cluster sampling is *area sampling,* when the clusters can be identified with geographical areas. The design of clusters is obviously crucial. While the statistical efficiency might be low, the design is very attractive from an economical efficiency point of view.

Double Sampling

In a double sampling, or more generally a *multi-stage* sampling design, a sample is first taken. From this sample, a *subsample* is drawn, etc.

Nonprobability Sampling Designs

Time and cost requirements may force the researcher to abandon the use of probability sampling, or maybe no sampling frame is available. In the *purposive sampling* design we deliberately try to make the sample representative. In *judgmental* (also called *expert choice*) sampling, the researcher uses his/her own judgement in selecting the sample. In *quota sampling* the sample is selected so that its composition (for people e. g. according to sex, religion, marital status, education, income) matches that of the population. This design is widely used.

The reader who wishes to learn more about sampling is referred to the books by Kish and by Scheaffer et al which appear in the reference list at the end of this chapter.

7.3 Simple Random Sampling

We shall now look more closely into the simple random sampling design. We recall that a sampling frame is used to draw the sample, and that in our telephone subscriber example, discrepancies between the frame and the population were difficult to eliminate completely. Similar discrepancies apply to practically every real-world population and sampling frame, and it is up to the statistician to take whatever corrective action that may be necessary and possible.

To illustrate the use of a random number table, we shall use the following excerpt from the table of 5-digit random numbers which appears at the end of this book:

Row no. \ Column no.	1	2	3	4	5	6	7
1	63780	59264	31841	65537	27808	57533	62286
2	57436	83070	43862	05447	59025	09380	76080
3	03531	78198	07166	28944	81387	86641	67296
4	86360	96353	67113	53494	76398	45768	21271
5	84825	30378	82162	54754	59021	03167	29355
6	78202	47595	85198	80248	83648	09678	66001
7	44386	64519	68091	42821	97959	38359	60092
8	96459	60821	72667	46910	88184	02291	38869
9	51474	03208	43832	45229	12941	22506	25694
10	86982	09159	13251	67444	22479	38877	90734
11	46247	37766	17547	66966	16309	67889	51071
12	48567	53051	30263	92836	24091	06778	26284
13	06681	65697	68203	16472	00870	76850	52345
14	02338	14956	67813	52583	64112	14975	84860
15	12755	95321	68154	61345	21857	56210	47076

Fig. 7/1: A small random number table

Example 7.2

Consider the following population of seventy annual salaries (cf. Exercise no. 5 at the end of Chapter 2):

\$20,600	17,300	19,100	18,100	18,300	20,200	20,400
20,200	19,800	19,100	18,900	21,500	20,600	19,500
17,900	20,700	18,100	19,400	18,500	19,500	19,400
17,500	19,400	17,600	21,400	18,100	20,400	20,900
18,300	17,000	17,100	18,400	18,300	18,300	17,900
20,200	19,400	20,400	20,500	18,700	17,100	20,300
18,300	17,900	18,400	21,400	17,900	17,300	18,100
18,100	16,400	16,600	18,000	19,400	16,500	18,400
19,100	18,400	20,100	19,300	20,300	17,600	18,100
21,400	18,200	20,000	17,300	18,100	21,400	20,400

If we think of this population as ordered, reading columnwise, and starting with the leftmost column, observation no. 2 would be \$20,200, observation no. 24 \$17,600 and observation no. 41 \$18,300.

Let us now take a random sample of $n = 6$ observations from the population of $N = 70$ data points. We must then find six random numbers i, $1 \leqq i \leqq 70$, and choose to start in row no. 2, column no. 5 of the random number table in Figure 7/1 and proceed downwards, taking the first two digits of each five-digit random number, deleting numbers greater than 70. We get: 59, ~~81~~, ~~76~~, ~~59~~, ~~83~~, ~~97~~, ~~88~~, 12, 22, 16, 24, ~~00~~, 64.

We deleted 59 as it had already occurred, and 00, because no salary received this order number. If the corresponding salaries are recorded we get:

random number	X_i ($1,000's)	X_i^2
59	17.6	309.76
12	19.8	392.04
22	19.1	364.81
16	19.4	376.36
24	17.6	309.76
64	20.9	436.81
TOTAL:	114.4	2,189.54

From this sample of $n = 6$ we now calculate the sample mean $\bar{X}$ and the sample standard deviation s:

$$\bar{X} = \frac{1}{n}\sum X_i = \frac{1}{6}\cdot 114.4 = 19.067$$

$$s^2 = \frac{1}{n-1}\left(\sum X_i^2 - \frac{1}{n}\left(\sum X_i\right)^2\right)$$

$$= \frac{1}{6-1}\left(2{,}189.54 - \frac{1}{6}\cdot 13{,}087.36\right)$$

$$= \frac{1}{5}\cdot 8.3134 = 1.66268 \quad \text{so that} \quad s \approx 1.289\,.$$

We compare our sample results with those for the population: $\mu = 18.953$ and $\sigma \approx 1.473$. Our results are reasonably close. Generally speaking, the statistics get better (closer to the parameters) the larger the sample. We shall be more specific on this later on.

7.4 Sums and Products of Random Variables

If X and Y are two random variables, their *sum* $X + Y$ will also be a random variable; and so will their *product* $X \cdot Y$. In the following we shall be dealing with sums and products of random variables, and are therefore interested to know the distributions of sums and products. We start with a useful result which is not difficult to show:

Theorem: $E(X+Y) = E(X) + E(Y)$.

For several random variables, X_i, $i = 1, \ldots, n$, one then gets:

$$E(X_1 + X_2 + \ldots + X_n) = E(X_1) + E(X_2) + \ldots + E(X_n)$$

or:

$$E\left(\sum_{i=1}^{n} X_i\right) = \sum_{i=1}^{n} E(X_i).$$

For the variance of a sum, we need the concept of independence for random variables:

Definition: The random variables X and Y are *independent* if

$$P((X \leqq x) \cap (Y \leqq y)) = P(X \leqq x) \cdot P(Y \leqq y)$$

for all x and y, i.e. if the events $(X \leqq x)$ and $(Y \leqq y)$ are statistically independent for all values of x and y.

One can show the following result.

Theorem: If X and Y are independent random variables, then we have:

$$V(X+Y) = V(X) + V(Y).$$

Remark: $V(X-Y) = V(X) + V(-Y) = V(X) + (-1)^2 V(Y) = V(X) + V(Y)$.

For several independent random variables, X_i, $i = 1, \ldots, n$, one then gets:

$$V(X_1 + X_2 + \ldots + X_n) = V(X_1) + V(X_2) + \ldots + V(X_n)$$

or:

$$V\left(\sum_{i=1}^{n} X_i\right) = \sum_{i=1}^{n} V(X_i).$$

In general, when X and Y are not necessarily independent, we have the following result:

$$V(X+Y) = V(X) + V(Y) + 2\,\mathrm{Cov}(X, Y),$$

where the *covariance* Cov(X, Y) of X and Y is defined by:

$$\mathrm{Cov}(X, Y) = E\{(X - E(X))\cdot(Y - E(Y))\}.$$

If Cov(X, Y) = 0, we say that X and Y are *uncorrelated.*

Remark: Closely related to the covariance is the *correlation coefficient* $\varrho(X, Y)$ or ϱ, which is defined by:

$$\varrho = \frac{\mathrm{Cov}(X, Y)}{\sqrt{V(X)\cdot V(Y)}}.$$

One can easily show that independent variables are uncorrelated.
The following two theorems can easily be proved:

Theorem: $\mathrm{Cov}(X, Y) = E(X\cdot Y) - E(X)\cdot E(Y)$.

Theorem: If X and Y are uncorrelated random variables, we have:

$$E(X\cdot Y) = E(X)\cdot E(Y).$$

Let us now briefly see what happens if we add random variables belonging to the same class of distributions. We get the following theorems:

Theorem: If X is $\mathrm{Bin}(n_1, p)$ and Y is $\mathrm{Bin}(n_2, p)$, and if X and Y are independent, then we have:

$$X + Y \quad \text{is} \quad \mathrm{Bin}(n_1 + n_2, p).$$

Theorem: If X is $P(\lambda_1)$ and Y is $P(\lambda_2)$, and if X and Y are independent, then we have:

$$X + Y \quad \text{is} \quad P(\lambda_1 + \lambda_2).$$

Theorem: If X is $N(\mu_1, \sigma_1)$ and Y is $N(\mu_2, \sigma_2)$, and if X and Y are independent, then we have:

$$X + Y \quad \text{is} \quad N(\mu_1 + \mu_2, \sqrt{\sigma_1^2 + \sigma_2^2})$$
$$X - Y \quad \text{is} \quad N(\mu_1 - \mu_2, \sqrt{\sigma_1^2 + \sigma_2^2}).$$

Remark: Results like these do *not* hold in general; for instance, the sum of two independent uniform variables is *not* uniform. Similarly, the sum of two independent geometric variables is *not* geometric.

We shall now list some results which indicate how the normal, the t, the chi-square and the F distributions are related.

Theorem: If $X_i, i = 1, \ldots, n$, are independent, $N(0, 1)$ random variables, then $\sum_{i=1}^{n} X_i^2$ is $\chi^2(n)$.

Remark 1: For $n = 1$ we can write symbolically:

$$(N(0, 1))^2 = \chi^2(1).$$

Remark 2: From the theorem it is not difficult to show that if X_1 is $\chi^2(n_1)$ and X_2 is $\chi^2(n_2)$, and if they are independent, then

$$X_1 + X_2 \quad \text{is} \quad \chi^2(n_1 + n_2).$$

The following theorem was first shown by Gosset (who was the person behind the Student's t distribution; cf. Section 6.5).

Theorem: If X is N(0, 1), Y is $\chi^2(n)$, and if X and Y are independent, then we have:

$$\frac{X}{\sqrt{Y/n}} \quad \text{is} \quad t(n).$$

Gosset's theorem is used to establish important results in sampling theory.

We shall now come to a theorem due to Fisher.

Theorem: If X_1 is $\chi^2(n_1)$, X_2 is $\chi^2(n_2)$, and if X_1 and X_2 are independent, then we have:

$$\frac{X_1/n_1}{X_2/n_2} \quad \text{is} \quad F(n_1, n_2).$$

Combining Gosset's and Fisher's theorems, one gets the following useful result:

Theorem: If X is a t(n) random variable, then X^2 is F(1, n). Symbolically:

$$(t(n))^2 = F(1, n).$$

7.5 Sampling Distributions

Suppose that a random sample of size n is taken from a certain population, and that the sample mean $\bar{X} = \frac{1}{n} \sum_{i=1}^{n} X_i$ is calculated. We realize that the X_i's are random variables (because the i-th element is selected at random), so that $\bar{X}$

itself is also a random variable. We are interested to know the distribution of $\bar{X}$, and start by considering its expected value and variance. Assuming that the population mean and variance are μ and σ^2 respectively, we must have: $E(X_i) = \mu$, $V(X_i) = \sigma^2$. Therefore we get:

$$E(\bar{X}) = E\left(\frac{1}{n}\sum_{i=1}^{n} X_i\right) = \frac{1}{n} E\left(\sum_{i=1}^{n} X_i\right)$$

$$= \frac{1}{n}\sum_{i=1}^{n} E(X_i) = \frac{1}{n}\cdot\sum_{i=1}^{n}\mu = \frac{1}{n}\cdot n\mu = \mu.$$

Similarly, as the X_i's are independent, we get:

$$V(\bar{X}) = V\left(\frac{1}{n}\sum_{i=1}^{n} X_i\right) = \frac{1}{n^2} V\left(\sum_{i=1}^{n} X_i\right)$$

$$= \frac{1}{n^2}\sum_{i=1}^{n} V(X_i) = \frac{1}{n^2}\cdot\sum_{i=1}^{n}\sigma^2 = \frac{1}{n^2}\cdot n\sigma^2 = \frac{\sigma^2}{n}.$$

Summarizing, for the sample statistic $\bar{X}$ we have computed the expected value $E(\bar{X}) = \mu_{\bar{X}}$ and the standard deviation $\sqrt{V(\bar{X})} = \sigma_{\bar{X}}$:

$$\mu_{\bar{X}} = \mu$$

$$\sigma_{\bar{X}} = \frac{\sigma}{\sqrt{n}}.$$

$\sigma_{\bar{X}}$ is usually referred to as the *standard error* (of the mean). We see that the standard error decreases with increasing n (this is often called the "averaging out" effect).

Remark: It is important not to confuse μ_{X_i} and σ_{X_i} (i.e., the expectation and the standard deviation of a single observation X_i) with $\mu_{\bar{X}}$ and $\sigma_{\bar{X}}$ (i.e. the expectation and the standard error of the *sample mean*). For the first of these (the expectation) the mistake is not serious, as they are both equal to μ; but in the second, they differ $\left(\sigma_{X_i} = \sigma;\ \sigma_{\bar{X}} = \frac{\sigma}{\sqrt{n}}\right)$.

Can we say anything about the *distribution* of $\bar{X}$? If X_i are $N(\mu, \sigma)$ we can, and the following theorem is useful:

Theorem: Assume that X_i, $i = 1, \ldots, n$ are $N(\mu, \sigma)$ independent random variables. Then the mean $\bar{X} = \frac{1}{n}\sum_{i=1}^{n} X_i$ is $N\left(\mu, \frac{\sigma}{\sqrt{n}}\right)$.

Remark: We have already shown what the expected value and standard deviation must be; the important result here is that if X_i is normally distributed, then so is $\bar{X}$.

Example 7.3

A small firm's monthly net profits are $N(8, 10)$ – distributed, measured in thousand dollars. We assume that profits in different months are independent. What is the probability that the monthly average profit is less than $3000 over

a) a two-month period;
b) a three-month period?

What is the probability of running a loss over

c) a one-month period;
d) a six-month period;
e) a twelve-month period?

Solution: Number the months by $i = 1, 2, \ldots$. We know that X_i is $N(8, 10)$ and independent so that $\bar{X}$ is $N\left(8, \frac{10}{\sqrt{n}}\right)$. We get:

a) $\bar{X}$ is $N\left(8, \frac{10}{\sqrt{2}}\right) \approx N(8, 7.07107)$, and $P(\bar{X} < 3)$

$$= P\left(\frac{\bar{X}-8}{7.07107} < \frac{3-8}{7.07107}\right) = P(Z < -0.70711)$$
$$= 1/2 - 0.2602 = 0.2398;$$

b) $\bar{X}$ is $N\left(8, \frac{10}{\sqrt{3}}\right) \approx N(8, 5.77350)$, and $P(\bar{X} < 3)$

$$= P\left(\frac{\bar{X}-8}{5.7735} < \frac{3-8}{5.7735}\right) = P(Z < -0.86603)$$
$$= 1/2 - 0.3067 = 0.1933;$$

c) $P(X_i < 0) = P\left(\frac{X_i - 8}{10} < \frac{0-8}{10}\right) = P(Z < -0.8)$

$$= 1/2 - 0.2881 = 0.2119;$$

d) $\bar{X}$ is $N\left(8, \frac{10}{\sqrt{6}}\right) \approx N(8, 4.08248)$, and $P(\bar{X} < 0)$

$$= P\left(\frac{\bar{X}-8}{4.08248} < \frac{0-8}{4.08248}\right) = P(Z < -1.95959)$$
$$= 1/2 - 0.4750 = 0.0250;$$

e) $\bar{X}$ is $N\left(8, \frac{10}{\sqrt{12}}\right) \approx N(8, 2.88675)$, and $P(\bar{X} < 0)$

$$= P\left(\frac{\bar{X}-8}{2.88675} < \frac{0-8}{2.88675}\right) = P(Z < -2.77128)$$

$$= 1/2 - 0.4972 = 0.0028.$$

Because of the averaging out effect, the probability in (b) is lower than in (a); the probabilities in (c), (d) and (e) are decreasing.

What can we say if the X_i's are *not* normally distributed? We can then make use of the so-called *Central Limit Theorem*, which is the topic of the next section.

7.6 The Central Limit Theorem

In Section 6.4 we approximated the binomial distribution by the normal (using de Moivre's theorem). This approximation is a special case of the Central Limit Theorem[1], which is of fundamental and major importance in probability theory.

The Central Limit Theorem

If X_i, $i = 1, \ldots, n$, are random variables with mean μ and variance $\sigma^2 > 0$, then for large n, $\bar{X} = \frac{1}{n}\sum_{i=1}^{n} X_i$ is approximately $N\left(\mu, \frac{\sigma}{\sqrt{n}}\right)$ distributed.

As a rule of thumb, for $n \geqq 30$, the approximation is considered good.

If the distribution of X_i is unimodal and symmetric, the approximation is good even for relatively small n.

Example 7.4

A process for the manufacture of fertilizer produces an average of 20 tons of fertilizer per day, with a variance of 5.76. What is the probability that a five-day period averages less than 18 tons per day?

Solution: In the absence of any information about the distribution of the daily production X_i, we assume that it is nearly normal, so that $\bar{X} = \frac{1}{5}\sum_{i=1}^{5} X_i$,

[1] This theorem has a long history, challenging mathematicians for more than two centuries, until it was finally proved by Chintjin in 1938.

invoking the central limit theorem, may be considered approximately normally distributed. As $E(X_i) = 20$, and $V(X_i) = 5.76$, we get:

$$\bar{X} \text{ is } N\left(20, \sqrt{\frac{5.76}{5}}\right)$$

so that

$$P(\bar{X} < 18) = P\left(\frac{\bar{X} - 20}{\sqrt{1.152}} < \frac{18 - 20}{\sqrt{1.152}}\right) \approx P(Z < -1.86339)$$
$$= 1/2 - 0.4688 = 0.0312$$

which is the probability asked for.

We shall continue our discussion of sampling distributions in the next chapter, on statistical estimation.

References

Chou, Y.: *Statistical Analysis*, 2nd edition. Holt, Rinehart and Winston New York, 1975.

Feller, W.: *An Introduction to Probability Theory and Its Applications*, Vol. 1, 3rd edition. John Wiley & Sons, New York 1968.

Harnett, D. L.: *Statistical Methods*, 3rd edition. Addison-Wesley, Reading, Mass. 1982.

Hawkins, C. A., and J. E. Weber: *Statistical Analysis. Applications to Business and Economics*. Harper & Row, New York 1980.

Kish, L.: *Survey Sampling*. John Wiley & Sons, New York 1965.

Mansfield, E.: *Statistics for Business and Economics*. Norton & Company, New York 1980.

Ross, S. M.: *A First Course in Probability*. Macmillan, New York 1976.

Scheaffer, R. L., W. Mendenhall and L. Ott: *Elementary Survey Sampling*, 2nd edition. Duxbury Press, North Scituate, Mass. 1979.

Wonnacott, T. H., and R. J. Wonnacott: *Introductory Statistics for Business and Economics*, 2nd edition. John Wiley & Sons, New York 1977.

Exercises

7–1 Consider the temperature data of Exercise no. 2 of Chapter 2. Using a random number table, select from this population a simple random sample of size $n = 5$. Specify the random numbers used and the corresponding population elements. From the sample selected, compute the sample mean and the sample standard deviation.

7–2 Same as Exercise no. 1 above, but with $n = 10$. Compare the results with those of Exercise no. 1 and comment.

7–3 Same as Exercise no. 2 above, but with $n = 15$. Compare the results with those of Exercise no. 2 and comment.

7–4 Consider the following population consisting of seventy annual salaries:

$20,600	17,300	19,100	18,100	18,300	20,200	20,400
20,200	19,800	19,100	18,900	21,500	20,600	19,500
17,900	20,700	18,100	19,400	18,500	19,500	19,400
17,500	19,400	17,600	21,400	18,100	20,400	20,900
18,300	17,000	17,100	18,400	18,300	18,300	17,900
20,200	19,400	20,400	20,500	18,700	17,100	20,300
18,300	17,900	18,400	21,400	17,900	17,300	18,100
18,100	16,400	16,600	18,000	19,400	16,500	18,400
19,100	18,400	20,100	19,300	20,300	17,600	18,100
21,400	18,200	20,000	17,300	18,100	21,400	20,400

Using a random number table, select from this population a simple random sample of size n = 10. Specify the random numbers used and the corresponding population elements. From the sample selected, compute the sample mean and the sample standard deviation. Compare these with the results of Example 7.2 in the text, giving the population parameters $\mu = \$18{,}953$ and $\sigma = \$1{,}473$, and comment.

7–5 Same as Exercise no. 4 above, but with n = 15. Compare the results with those of Exercise no. 4 and comment.

7–6 Same as Exercise no. 5 above, but with n = 20. Compare the results with those of Exercise no. 5 and comment.

7–7 Consider the age data of Example 2.3 of Chapter 2. Using a random number table, select from this population a simple random sample of size n = 10. Specify the random numbers used and the corresponding population elements. From the sample selected, compute the sample mean and the sample standard deviation.

7–8 Same as Exercise no. 7 above, but with n = 15. Compare the results with those of Exercise no. 7 and comment.

7–9 Same as Exercise no. 8 above, but with n = 20. Compare the results with those of Exercise no. 8 and comment.

7–10 X is a Poisson-distributed random variable with mean 0.7; Y is a Poisson-distributed random variable with mean 1.2. Assuming that X and Y are independent, determine:

a) $P(X + Y > 3)$
b) $P(X + Y \leqq 6)$
c) $P(1 < X + Y \leqq 5)$
d) $P(2 \leqq X + Y < 7)$.

7–11 A customer enters a post office. Assume that the waiting time X in the queue is Poisson-distributed with mean 5 minutes and the service time Y at the teller is Poisson-distributed with mean 3 minutes. Assume also that X and Y are independent.

a) What is the probability that there is no queue?
b) What is the expected value of the time spent in the post office?
c) Find $P(X + Y \geqq 11)$
d) Find $P(X + Y \leqq 8)$.

7–12 X_1 is a $N(12, 0.7)$ variable; X_2 is a $N(7, 2.1)$ variable. X_1 and X_2 are independent. Calculate:

a) $P(X_1 + X_2 > 19)$
b) $P(X_1 + X_2 \leqq 17.2)$
c) $P(16.5 < X_1 + X_2 \leqq 20.2)$
d) $P(2.1 \leqq X_1 - X_2 < 4.5)$.

7–13 A company operates two retail sale outlets. The weekly sales volume X of the first outlet is $N(13, 1.8)$, measured in thousands of dollars. For the second outlet, the weekly sales volume Y is $N(27, 5.4)$. Assuming that X and Y are independent, find

a) $P(X + Y \leqq 40)$
b) $P(X + Y > 43.5)$
c) $P(35 < X + Y < 45)$.

*7–14 A building contractor buys circular concrete lids from a factory. The diameter X of a lid is $N(110, 0.7)$, measured in centimeters. The lids weigh 1 kg/dm^2. Compute the expected value of the total weight of ten lids, selected at random.

7–15 A random variable X is $\chi^2(1)$ distributed. Compute

a) $P(0.5 \leqq \sqrt{X} \leqq 1.9)$
b) $P(\sqrt{X} \leqq 0.4)$.

7–16 If a random variable X is $N(0, 1)$ distributed, and a random variable Y is $\chi^2(34)$ distributed, and if X and Y are independent, what is

a) $E\left(\frac{X}{\sqrt{Y}}\right)$

b) $V\left(\frac{X}{\sqrt{Y}}\right)$

c) $P\left(2.2 \leqq \frac{X}{\sqrt{Y}} \leqq 2.7\right)$?

7–17 X_1 is a $\chi^2(3)$ distributed random variable, X_2 is a $\chi^2(6)$ distributed random variable, and X_1 and X_2 are independent. Find:

a) $E\left(\frac{X_1}{X_2}\right)$

b) $V\left(\frac{X_1}{X_2}\right)$.

7–18 Y is a $F(1, 40)$ distributed random variable. Compute

a) $E(Y)$
b) $V(Y)$
c) $P(0.2 < \sqrt{Y} \leqq 1.0)$.

7–19 The average age of students attending a university is normally distributed with a mean of 25 and variance of 9.

a) What is the probability that the average age computed from a random sample of 30 students is 24 or less?
b) Repeat part (a) given that there are only 14 students in the sample.

7–20 Refer to Exercise no. 11 of Chapter 6. If a random sample of 25 students is taken what is the probability that the *average* earnings per week is more than $105.20?

7–21 Salaries for recently graduated B. Comm. students are normally distributed with a mean of $22,000 and standard deviation of $500.

a) What is the probability that one recently graduated B. Comm. student earns between $22,250 and $23,000?
b) What is the probability that exactly two students out of a random sample of 10 earn between $22,250 and $23,000?
c) What is the probability that the average salary of 50 randomly selected B. Comm. graduates is over $22,200?

7–22 From a population which is $N(110, 1.5)$ distributed, a random sample of size $n = 10$ is taken. The measurements are: 112.0, 108.5, 112.5, 110.5, 110.0, 111.5, 108.0, 109.5, 110.0, 112.5.

a) Calculate the sample mean $\bar{X}$
b) Determine the standard error $\sigma_{\bar{X}}$ of $\bar{X}$
c) Compute the sample variance s^2
d) Find the sample standard deviation s
e) What is the theoretical distribution of $\bar{X}$?

7–23 A process for the manufacture of fertilizer has produced over the *full period of time it has been in operation,* an average of 10 tons of fertilizer per day, with a variance of 3.23. If the process is observed for a period of eight days, what is the probability that the eight-day average production will be less than 8 tons?

8. Statistical Estimation

After a very brief introduction to estimation in Section 8.1, we define the concept of an estimator in Section 8.2 and the desirable properties of unbiasedness, efficiency and consistency. Section 8.3 is devoted to the relationship between estimation error and sample size, which is illustrated by way of examples.

Confidence intervals are introduced in Section 8.4, treating the case of the mean when the standard deviation is known. In Section 8.5 we provide interval estimates of the mean in the absence of any prior information about the standard deviation. Section 8.6 then considers confidence intervals for the population proportion, with and without correction for finite populations, and in Section 8.7, finally, confidence intervals for the population variance σ^2 are established.

8.1 Introduction

Many statistical investigations involve estimating an unknown parameter of some population. Unless the whole population is observed, the estimation must be based on a sample drawn from the population. Using the data from the sample, a statistic is computed and used as an estimate for the unknown parameter.

Example 8.1

A population is given, for which we know that it is $N(\mu, 1.73)$, but μ is unknown. We want to find μ. How should this be done?

From the previous chapters we see that a good idea might be to calculate the sample mean $\bar{X}$ for a random sample, and then use the value obtained for $\bar{X}$ as a guess of μ. But how confident can we be that we are not much in error?

In the following, we will be able to answer this and similar questions.

8.2 Point Estimation

By an *estimator* we mean an expression for computing a sample statistic, that will be used as an estimate of an unknown population parameter. We want a good estimator to be:

a) *Unbiased*
An unbiased estimator has an expected value equal to the population parameter being estimated.

Example 8.2

$\bar{X}$ is an unbiased estimator of the population mean μ, as $E(\bar{X}) = \mu$, which we showed in Section 7.5.

Example 8.3

s^2 is an unbiased estimator of the population variance σ^2, i.e. $E(s^2) = \sigma^2$.

As s^2 is an important estimator we shall show its unbiasedness in a theorem. For convenience, we work with $(n-1)s^2$ rather than s^2 itself.

Theorem: $E((n-1)s^2) = (n-1)\sigma^2$.

Proof: First we show the identity:

$$(n-1)s^2 = \sum_{i=1}^{n} (X_i - \mu)^2 - n\cdot(\bar{X} - \mu)^2$$

as follows:

$$(n-1)s^2 = \sum_{i=1}^{n} (X_i - \bar{X})^2 = \sum_{i=1}^{n} ((X_i - \mu) - (\bar{X} - \mu))^2$$

$$= \sum_{i=1}^{n} (X_i - \mu)^2 - 2\cdot \sum_{i=1}^{n} (X_i - \mu)\cdot(\bar{X} - \mu) + \sum_{i=1}^{n} (\bar{X} - \mu)^2$$

$$= \sum_{i=1}^{n} (X_i - \mu)^2 - 2(\bar{X} - \mu)\cdot \underbrace{\sum_{i=1}^{n} (X_i - \mu)}_{= n(\bar{X} - \mu)} + n(\bar{X} - \mu)^2$$

$$= \sum_{i=1}^{n} (X_i - \mu)^2 - n(\bar{X} - \mu)^2 .$$

Now we get:

$$E((n-1)s^2) = E\left(\sum_{i=1}^{n}(X_i-\mu)^2\right) - n\cdot E((\bar{X}-\mu)^2)$$

$$= \sum_{i=1}^{n} \underbrace{E((X_i-\mu)^2)}_{= V(X_i) = \sigma^2} - n\cdot V(\bar{X}) = n\sigma^2 - \sigma^2 = (n-1)\sigma^2$$

and we are through with the proof.

Example 8.4

One can prove that $E(s) \neq \sigma$, so that s is *not* an unbiased estimator of σ (the difference $E(s) - \sigma$ is called the *bias* of the estimator σ). Nevertheless, in the absence of a simple unbiased estimator of σ, we shall use s to estimate σ.

Returning to our list of desirable properties of an estimator, we also want it to be:

b) *Efficient*
An efficient estimator has small variance.

Example 8.5

If $\bar{X} = \frac{1}{n}\sum_{i=1}^{n} X_i$, then $\bar{X}$ and X_1 are both unbiased estimators of μ, as $E(\bar{X}) = \mu$, and $E(X_1) = \mu$.
However, $\bar{X}$ is more efficient than X_1, because $V(\bar{X}) = \frac{\sigma^2}{n} < \sigma^2 = V(X_1)$.

c) *Consistent*
If the bias and the variance of an estimator both tend to zero as n becomes very large, then we say that the estimator is *consistent*.

Example 8.6

$E(\bar{X}) = \mu$ and $V(\bar{X}) = \frac{\sigma^2}{n} \to 0, n \to \infty$, so that $\bar{X}$ is a consistent estimator of μ.

Example 8.7

Take an unbalanced coin with $P(\text{head}) = p$, where p is unknown and flip it n times. If X_n is the number of heads obtained, we know that X_n is $\text{Bin}(n, p)$. Then $\frac{1}{n}X_n$ is a consistent estimator of p, because it is *unbiased:*

$$E\left(\frac{1}{n}X_n\right) = \frac{1}{n}E(X_n) = \frac{1}{n}np = p$$

and *efficient:*

$$V\left(\frac{1}{n}X_n\right) = \frac{1}{n^2}V(X_n) = \frac{1}{n^2}np(1-p) = \frac{p(1-p)}{n} \to 0, \quad n \to \infty.$$

Example 8.8

A certain medical treatment was tested on 141 patients and gave success in 113 cases. Give an estimate of the success rate and determine the standard error (standard deviation) of the estimate.

Solution: With a success rate of p (unknown), the number X of successful cases will be Bin(141, p). From Example 8.7 above, we know that X/n is a consistent estimator of p which we will use. The estimate in our particular case is $\frac{X}{n} = \frac{113}{141}$ $= 0.8014$, i.e. 80%.
The standard error $\sigma_{X/n}$ of the estimate is:

$$\sqrt{\frac{p(1-p)}{n}} = \sqrt{\frac{0.8014 \cdot 0.1986}{141}} \approx \sqrt{0.0011287} \approx 0.0336.$$

8.3 Estimation Error and Sampe Size

Example 8.9

The daily electricity consumption of a steel mill is $N(\mu, 6)$ distributed (expressed in MWh), where μ is unknown. Observing the electricity consumption for a number of days, we can use the sample mean $\bar{X}$ as an estimate of μ. If we require a probability of 0.99 that the observed $\bar{X}$ is not more than 3 MWh off from the true μ, how many days are needed for the sample?

Solution: We get:

$$\begin{aligned} 0.99 &= P(|\bar{X}-\mu| \leqq 3) = P(-3 \leqq \bar{X}-\mu \leqq 3) \\ &= P\left(-\frac{3}{\frac{\sigma}{\sqrt{n}}} \leqq \frac{\bar{X}-\mu}{\frac{\sigma}{\sqrt{n}}} \leqq \frac{3}{\frac{\sigma}{\sqrt{n}}}\right) \\ &= 2P\left(0 \leqq \frac{\bar{X}-\mu}{\frac{\sigma}{\sqrt{n}}} \leqq \frac{3}{\frac{\sigma}{\sqrt{n}}}\right) \end{aligned}$$

or

$$0.495 = P\left(0 \leqq Z \leqq \frac{3\sqrt{n}}{\sigma}\right).$$

From a table of the normal distribution we then find:

$$\frac{3\sqrt{n}}{\sigma} = 2.575$$

i.e.

$$\sqrt{n} = \frac{2.575}{3} \cdot \sigma = 5.15$$

so that

$$n = (5.15)^2 = 26.52\,.$$

Consequently, as the sample size must obviously be integer, a sample size of at least $n = 27$ is required.

It is clear from this example that by increasing the sample size we also increase the probability that our estimate is near to the true, but unknown value. The convenience of this increased probability has to be weighed against the cost of a larger sample.

Example 8.10

The opinion of 1,000 people, on the issue of introducing capital punishment, is to be estimated by interviewing a sample of randomly selected persons. From preliminary information, we guess that the proportion p of "yes" – people is 0.3. Determine the sample size n, if we accept a probability of 0.10 that our estimate of p is wrong by 0.05 or more.

Solution: Assume that we get X "yes" from a sample of size n. We know that X is hypergeometric, but can be approximated by $\text{Bin}(n, p)$ and that $\dfrac{X - np}{\sigma_X} = \dfrac{\frac{X}{n} - p}{\frac{1}{n}\sigma_X}$ is approximately $N(0, 1)$, due to the de Moivre theorem (Section 6.4). We get:

$$0.90 = P\left(\left|\frac{X}{n} - p\right| \leqq 0.05\right) = P\left(-0.05 \leqq \frac{X}{n} - p \leqq 0.05\right)$$

$$= P\left(-\frac{0.05}{\frac{1}{n}\sigma_X} \leqq \frac{\frac{X}{n} - p}{\frac{1}{n}\sigma_X} \leqq \frac{0.05}{\frac{1}{n}\sigma_X}\right) = 2 \cdot P\left(0 \leqq \frac{\frac{X}{n} - p}{\frac{1}{n}\sigma_X} \leqq \frac{0.05}{\frac{1}{n}\sigma_X}\right)$$

$$= \text{i.e.} \quad \frac{0.05}{\frac{1}{n}\sigma_X} = 1.645 \quad \text{or} \quad \frac{\sigma_X}{n} = \frac{0.05}{1.645}.$$

a) *Without* finite population correction we get:

$$\sigma_X = \sqrt{np(1-p)}, \quad \text{i.e.} \quad \left(\frac{0.05}{1.645}\right)^2 = \frac{\sigma_X^2}{n^2} = \frac{np(1-p)}{n^2} = \frac{p(1-p)}{n},$$

so that $n = \left(\frac{1.645}{0.05}\right)^2 p(1-p)$. p is unknown and we use the preliminary estimate $p = 0.3$ to get $n = \left(\frac{1.645}{0.05}\right)^2 \cdot 0.3 \cdot 0.7 = (32.9)^2 \cdot 0.21 = 227.3$.

Therefore we conclude that at least 228 people have to be interviewed.

b) *With* finite population correction we get:

$$\sigma_X = \sqrt{np(1-p)} \cdot \sqrt{\frac{N-n}{N-1}} \quad \text{i.e.} \quad \frac{0.05}{1.645} = \frac{\sigma_X}{n}$$

$$= \sqrt{\frac{p(1-p)}{n}} \sqrt{\frac{N-n}{N-1}}, \quad \text{or:} \quad \left(\frac{0.05}{1.645}\right)^2 = \frac{p(1-p)}{N-1} \cdot \frac{N-n}{n}$$

$$= \frac{p(1-p)}{N-1} \cdot \left(\frac{N}{n} - 1\right), \quad \text{so that} \quad \frac{N}{n} - 1 = \frac{N-1}{p(1-p)} \cdot \left(\frac{0.05}{1.645}\right)^2$$

$$\text{or} \quad \frac{N}{n} = 1 + \frac{N-1}{p(1-p)} \cdot \left(\frac{0.05}{1.645}\right)^2 \quad \text{from which, finally;}$$

$$n = \frac{N}{1 + \frac{N-1}{p(1-p)}\left(\frac{0.05}{1.645}\right)^2} = \frac{1{,}000}{1 + \frac{999}{0.3 \cdot 0.7} \cdot \left(\frac{0.05}{1.645}\right)^2}$$

$$= \frac{1{,}000}{1 + \frac{333}{0.07 \cdot 1082.41}} = \frac{1{,}000}{1 + 4.3950} = \frac{1{,}000}{5.395} = 185.3$$

and at least 186 people have to be interviewed.

Remark: What would we do if in Example 8.10 no preliminary information about p were available? We would then not be able to obtain a preliminary estimate of the standard deviation $\sigma_X = \sqrt{np(1-p)}$. One can show that for fixed n and varying p, the standard deviation achieves its maximum for $p = 0.5$. To be on the safe side (obtaining a sample that may be unnecessarily large), we will then use $\sigma_X = \sqrt{n \cdot 0.25}$ for calculating the sample size.

8.4 Interval Estimates of μ when σ is Known

When we give a point estimate of μ, we do not indicate any degree of uncertainty or imprecision of the estimate. This could be done by giving as well the standard error of our estimate. Better still would be to give an *interval* together with an indication of our confidence that the unknown μ belongs to this interval. Such an interval is called a *confidence interval.*

Before we introduce such intervals, we shall introduce the following convenient notation.

Definition: For p such that $0 < p < 1$, the critical point z_p is defined by the relation $P(Z \geqq z_p) = p$ where Z, as usual, is $N(0, 1)$.

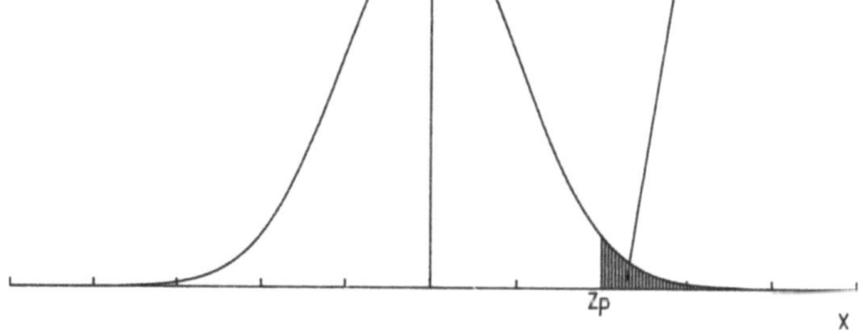

Fig. 8/1: A critical point for the normal distribution.

Example 8.11

From a table of the normal distribution we find:

$$z_{0.05} = 1.64, \quad z_{0.025} = 1.96, \quad z_{0.01} = 2.33, \quad z_{0.005} = 2.57.$$

Example 8.12

It follows that $P(-z_{\alpha/2} \leqq Z \leqq z_{\alpha/2}) = 1 - \alpha$ (see Fig. 8/2).

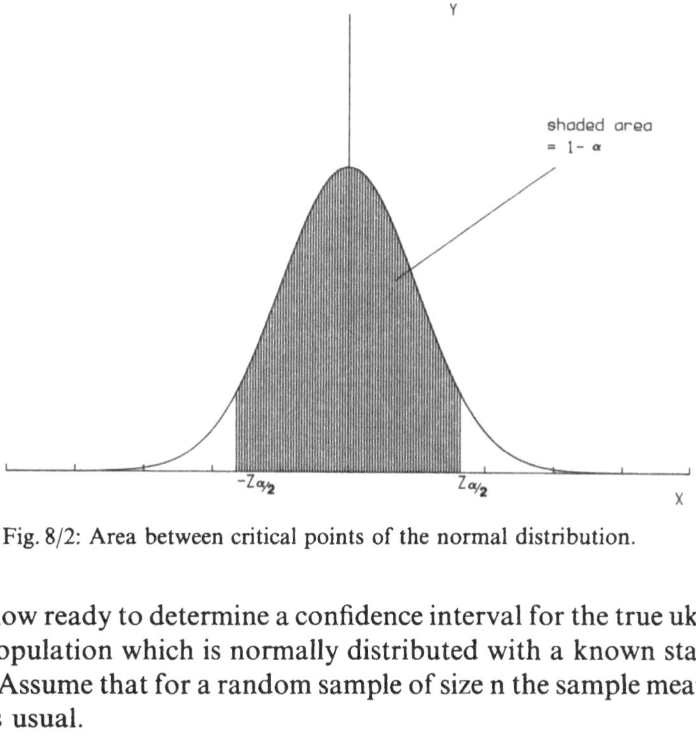

Fig. 8/2: Area between critical points of the normal distribution.

We are now ready to determine a confidence interval for the true uknown mean μ of a population which is normally distributed with a known standard deviation σ. Assume that for a random sample of size n the sample mean is denoted by $\bar{X}$, as usual.

Because $\bar{X}$ is $N\left(\mu, \frac{\sigma}{\sqrt{n}}\right)$ or, equivalently, $\frac{\bar{X} - \mu}{\frac{\sigma}{\sqrt{n}}}$ is $N(0, 1)$, we get:

$$1 - \alpha = P\left(\left|\frac{\bar{X} - \mu}{\frac{\sigma}{\sqrt{n}}}\right| \leqq z_{\alpha/2}\right) = P\left(\left|\bar{X} - \mu\right| \leqq z_{\alpha/2} \cdot \frac{\sigma}{\sqrt{n}}\right)$$

$$= P\left(\bar{X} - z_{\alpha/2} \cdot \frac{\sigma}{\sqrt{n}} \leqq \mu \leqq \bar{X} + z_{\alpha/2} \cdot \frac{\sigma}{\sqrt{n}}\right),$$

and we say that the *interval*

$$\left(\bar{x} - z_{\alpha/2} \cdot \frac{\sigma}{\sqrt{n}},\quad \bar{x} + z_{\alpha/2} \cdot \frac{\sigma}{\sqrt{n}}\right)$$

where $\bar{x}$ is an *observation* of the random variable $\bar{X}$, is a *confidence interval* for μ with *confidence level* $1 - \alpha$.

Warning: Do not confuse this with the following. Similarly to the above, we can obtain

$$1 - \alpha = P\left(|\bar{x} - \mu| \leqq z_{\alpha/2} \cdot \frac{\sigma}{\sqrt{n}}\right)$$

$$= P\left(\mu - z_{\alpha/2} \cdot \frac{\sigma}{\sqrt{n}} \leqq \bar{X} \leqq \mu + z_{\alpha/2} \cdot \frac{\sigma}{\sqrt{n}}\right),$$

so that *for μ known,* we can say that the *random variable* $\bar{X}$ with probability $1 - \alpha$ will belong to the interval $\left(\mu - z_{\alpha/2} \cdot \frac{\sigma}{\sqrt{n}},\ \mu + z_{\alpha/2} \cdot \frac{\sigma}{\sqrt{n}}\right)$.

But we *cannot say* that μ belongs to an interval with any probability, because μ is *not* a random variable, and it either belongs to our confidence interval, or it does not (but we do not know which).

What we *can* say is that the confidence level $1 - \alpha$ will be the proportion of times that μ would belong to our interval, if we repeated the sample and constructed the confidence interval many times. α would then be the proportion of times that the confidence interval obtained did not include μ.

To be specific, assume that a thousand samples, all of size n were taken. If for each sample, a 95% confidence interval for μ was calculated, then we expect that about 950 of these intervals would contain μ, whereas about 50 intervals would not contain μ.

This variation is of course due to the fact that the sample mean $\bar{X}$, due to the randomness in selecting the sample, may be close or not so close to the true (unknown) population mean μ. See the illustrations in Fig. 8/3 and 8/4.

Example 8.13

$\bar{x} = 3.7$, $n = 12$, $\sigma = 1.5$. Construct a confidence interval for μ with confidence level 0.95.

Solution: We have: $0.95 = 1 - \alpha$ i.e. $\alpha = 0.05$, and $z_{\alpha/2} = z_{0.025} = 1.96$.

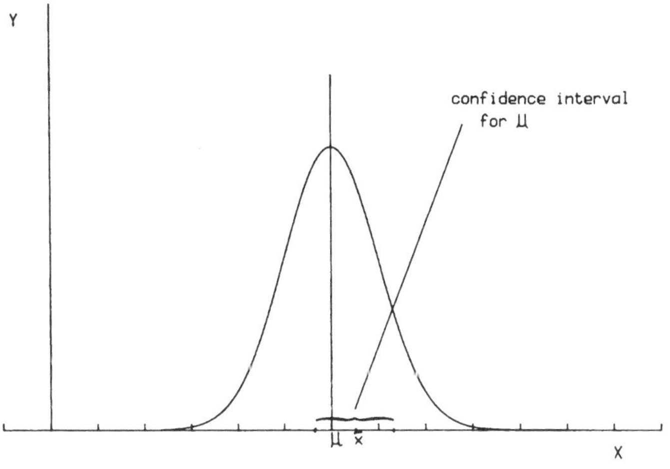

Fig. 8/3: The confidence interval contains μ.

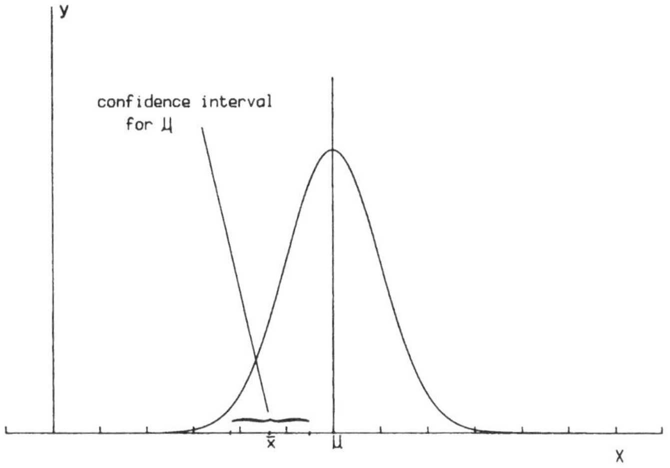

Fig. 8/4: The confidence interval does not contain μ.

Now we get: $\bar{x} + z_{\alpha/2} \cdot \frac{\sigma}{\sqrt{n}} = 3.7 + 1.96 \cdot \frac{1.5}{\sqrt{12}} = 3.7 + 0.85 = 4.55$, and $\bar{x} - z_{\alpha/2} \cdot \frac{\sigma}{\sqrt{n}} = 3.7 - 0.85 = 2.85$, so that $(2.85 \leqq \mu \leqq 4.55) = (2.85, 4.55)$ is a confidence interval for μ with confidence level 0.95.

Example 8.14

As the previous example, but with confidence level 0.99.

Solution: We have: $0.99 = 1 - \alpha$, i.e. $\alpha = 0.01$ and $z_{\alpha/2} = z_{0.005} = 2.57$.

Then $\bar{x} + z_{\alpha/2} \cdot \frac{\sigma}{\sqrt{n}} = 3.7 + 2.57 \cdot \frac{1.5}{\sqrt{12}} = 3.7 + 1.11 = 4.81$, and $\bar{x} - z_{\alpha/2} \cdot \frac{\sigma}{\sqrt{n}}$ $= 3.7 - 1.11 = 2.59$. We conclude that $(2.59, 4.81)$ is a confidence interval for μ with confidence level 0.99.

Remark 1: The confidence interval will obviously be larger, the higher the confidence level $1 - \alpha$.

Remark 2: For finite populations we use $\frac{\sigma}{\sqrt{n}} \cdot \sqrt{\frac{N-n}{N-1}}$ instead of $\frac{\sigma}{\sqrt{n}}$. The reason for this is that the underlying distribution will be hypergeometric so that the finite population correction factor $\sqrt{\frac{N-n}{N-1}}$ is involved (cf. Section 5.4).

Remark 3: Without resorting to normality assumptions or the central limit theorem, one could make use of Chebyshev's inequality (cf. Section 5.2).

8.5 Interval Estimates of μ when σ is Unknown

We have seen that for a sample from a $N(\mu, \sigma)$ population, $\frac{\bar{X} - \mu}{\frac{\sigma}{\sqrt{n}}}$ is $N(0, 1)$.

But what if σ is unknown? We could then use the sample standard deviation s as an estimate of σ. It can be shown that $\frac{\bar{X} - \mu}{\frac{s}{\sqrt{n}}}$ is not normal, but *t-distributed with* $n - 1$ *degrees of freedom* (cf. Section 6.5). Thus we have: $\frac{\bar{X} - \mu}{\frac{s}{\sqrt{n}}}$ is $t(n-1)$. In analogy with the case for the normal distribution we now introduce the following notation.

Definition: For p such that $0 < p < 1$, the critical value $t_p(n)$ is defined by the relation: $P(t \geqq t_p(n)) = p$, where t is $t(n)$.

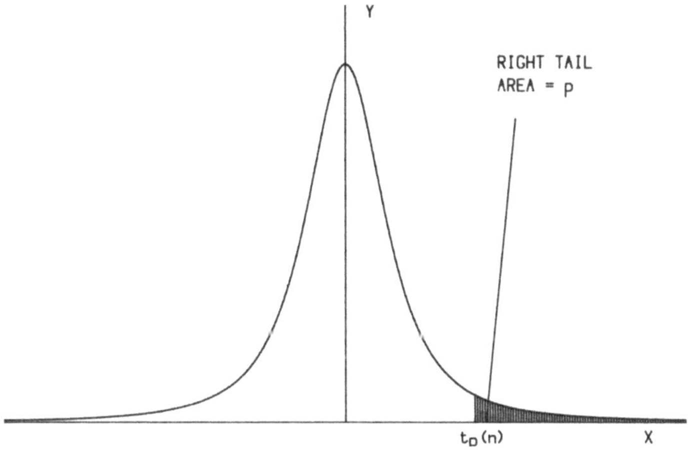

Fig. 8/5: A critical point for the t distribution.

Example 8.15

From a table of critical points for Student's t distribution we find $t_{0.01}(7) = 2.998$, $t_{0.05}(10) = 1.812$, $t_{0.025}(60) = 2.000$, $t_{0.005}(\infty) = 2.576$ (cf. $z_{0.005}$!)

Example 8.16

A sample of size 20 is taken from a $N(\mu, \sigma)$ – distributed population. μ and σ are unknown. $\bar{x} = 10.27$ and $s = 4.16$ were obtained. Construct a 95% confidence interval for μ.

Solution: We proceed as if σ were known, but replace σ by s and use the t-distribution (with $n - 1 = 20 - 1 = 19$ degrees of freedom) instead of the normal distribution. We have:

$1 - \alpha = 0.95$ i.e. $\alpha = 0.05$, and $t_{\alpha/2}(n-1) = t_{0.025}(19)$

$$= 2.093 \quad \text{so that} \quad \bar{x} + t_{\alpha/2}(n-1) \cdot \frac{s}{\sqrt{n}} = 10.27$$

$$+ 2.093 \cdot \frac{4.16}{\sqrt{20}} = 10.27 + 1.95 = 12.22 .$$

Also $\bar{x} - t_{\alpha/2}(n-1) \cdot \frac{s}{\sqrt{n}} = 10.27 - 1.95 = 8.32$, and the 95% confidence interval for μ is $(8.32 \leqq \mu \leqq 12.22) = (8.32, 12.22)$.

For large n (i.e. $n \geqq 30$), the t-distribution is close to the normal, and then we can usually employ the normal approximation, so that $\bar{x} - z_{\alpha/2} \cdot \frac{s}{\sqrt{n}} \leqq \mu \leqq \bar{x} + z_{\alpha/2} \cdot \frac{s}{\sqrt{n}}$ is a confidence interval for μ with confidence level approximately $1 - \alpha$.

For finite populations we shall, of course, use the finite population correction factor (cf. Remark 2 of the previous section).

We shall defer a treatment of interval estimates involving samples from two different populations until the next chapter.

8.6 Interval Estimates of the Population Proportion

We shall only consider the case when the sample size n is large so that the normal approximation can be used. We get, in the same fashion as before:

$$1 - \alpha = P\left(\left|\frac{\frac{X}{n} - p}{\frac{1}{n}\sigma_X}\right| \leqq z_{\alpha/2}\right)$$

from which one can easily obtain:

$$\frac{x}{n} - z_{\alpha/2} \cdot \sqrt{\frac{\frac{x}{n}\left(1 - \frac{x}{n}\right)}{n}} \leqq p \leqq \frac{x}{n} + z_{\alpha/2} \cdot \sqrt{\frac{\frac{x}{n}\left(1 - \frac{x}{n}\right)}{n}}$$

is a confidence interval for the unknown population proportion p, with confidence level $1 - \alpha$. We have used $\frac{x}{n}$ instead of the unknown p to obtain the point estimate for σ_X.

For finite populations the finite population correction factor will be used as well, giving the interval

$$\frac{x}{n} - z_{\alpha/2} \cdot \sqrt{\frac{\frac{x}{n}\left(1 - \frac{x}{n}\right)}{n}} \cdot \sqrt{\frac{N-n}{N-1}} \leqq p \leqq \frac{x}{n} + z_{\alpha/2} \cdot \sqrt{\frac{\frac{x}{n}\left(1 - \frac{x}{n}\right)}{n}} \cdot \sqrt{\frac{N-n}{N-1}}.$$

When the sample size is small, one could either use the binomial distribution (for large populations) or the hypergeometric distribution (for small populations).

Example 8.17

Refer to Example 8.10, on capital punishment. A sample of size $n = 50$ is taken, out of which 17 answer "yes". Determine a 90% confidence interval for the proportion p of "yes"-people in the population.

Solution: *Without* finite population correction we obtain:

$$z_{\alpha/2} \cdot \sqrt{\frac{\frac{x}{n}\left(1 - \frac{x}{n}\right)}{n}} = z_{0.05} \cdot \sqrt{\frac{\frac{17}{50}\left(1 - \frac{17}{50}\right)}{50}}$$

$$= 1.64 \cdot \sqrt{0.004488} \approx 1.64 \cdot 0.06699 \approx 0.110.$$

Therefore, the 90% confidence interval for p is determined by

$$\frac{x}{n} \pm z_{\alpha/2} \cdot \sqrt{\frac{\frac{x}{n}\left(1 - \frac{x}{n}\right)}{n}} = 0.340 \pm 0.110,$$

so that the interval is $(0.230 \leqq p \leqq 0.450)$.

With finite population correction we obtain:

$$z_{\alpha/2} \cdot \sqrt{\frac{\frac{x}{n}\left(1 - \frac{x}{n}\right)}{n}} \cdot \sqrt{\frac{N - n}{N - 1}} = z_{0.05} \cdot \sqrt{\frac{\frac{17}{50}\left(1 - \frac{17}{50}\right)}{50}} \cdot \sqrt{\frac{1000 - 50}{1000 - 1}}$$

$$= 1.64 \cdot \sqrt{0.004488} \cdot \sqrt{\frac{950}{999}} \approx 0.107.$$

The confidence interval is now:

$$(0.340 - 0.107,\ 0.340 + 0.107) = (0.233,\ 0.447).$$

One can also consider the difference between the proportions of two populations, but we shall leave this until the next chapter.

*8.7 Interval Estimates of the Variance

In Sections 8.4 and 8.5 we used samples from a $N(\mu, \sigma)$ population to construct confidence intervals for the mean μ. We shall now consider the variance σ^2. If σ^2 is unknown and we wish to estimate it from a sample, we have seen that the sample variance $s^2 = \frac{1}{n-1}\sum_{i=1}^{n}(X_i - \bar{X})^2$ is a useful estimator of σ^2 as it is unbiased, $E(s^2) = \sigma^2$. We will now see what the sampling distribution of s^2 is.

Theorem: With s^2 being the sample variance $s^2 = \frac{1}{n-1}\sum_{i=1}^{n}(X_i - \bar{X})^2$ of a sample from a $N(\mu, \sigma)$ distributed population, we have:

$$\frac{(n-1)s^2}{\sigma^2} \quad \text{is} \quad \chi^2(n-1).$$

Remark: From the theorem it follows that s^2 is a consistent estimator of σ^2. The unbiasedness has already been shown, and all that would remain to prove is that $V(s^2)$ tends to zero as n tends to infinity. One can show that this is a consequence of the theorem.

As for the normal and t distributions we now introduce the following notation.

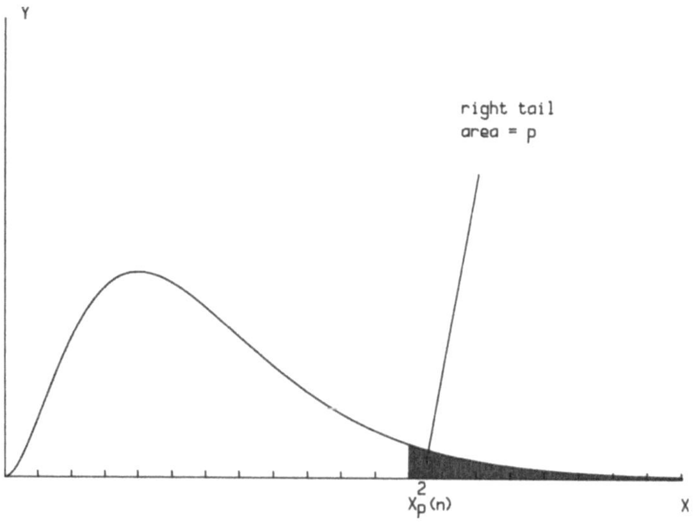

Fig. 8/6: A critical point for the χ^2 distribution.

Definition: For p such that $0 < p < 1$, the critical calue $\chi_p^2(n)$ is defined by the relation:

$$P(\chi^2 \geqq \chi_p^2(n)) = p,$$

where χ^2 is $\chi^2(n)$.

Example 8.18

From a table of critical points of the chi-square distribution we find:

$$\chi_{0.05}^2(4) = 9.49, \quad \chi_{0.01}^2(17) = 33.41,$$
$$\chi_{0.99}^2(8) = 1.65, \quad \chi_{0.90}^2(3) = 0.58$$

Note that because the chi-square distribution is not symmetric, right and left tail areas both have to be tabulated.

Now we can express a confidence interval, with a confidence level of $1 - \alpha$, for the variable $\frac{(n-1)s^2}{\sigma^2}$ as:

$$\chi_{1-\alpha/2}^2(n-1) \leqq \frac{(n-1)s^2}{\sigma^2} \leqq \chi_{\alpha/2}^2(n-1).$$

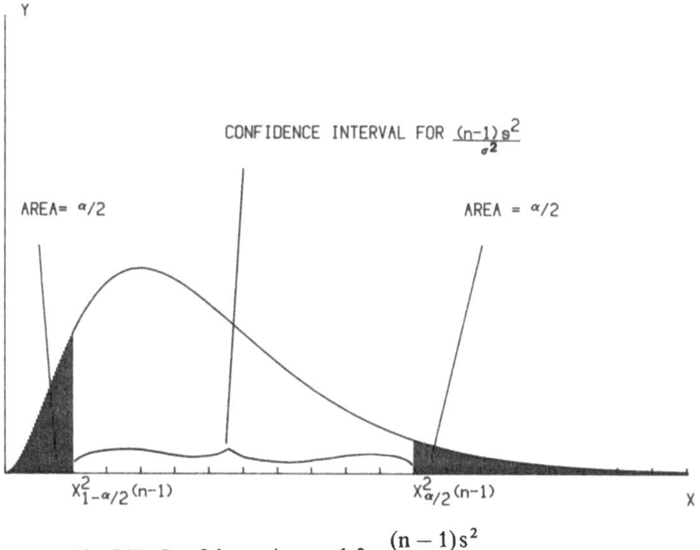

Fig. 8/7: Confidence interval for $\frac{(n-1)s^2}{\sigma^2}$.

It is then easy to see that a confidence interval for σ^2 with confidence level $1-\alpha$ is given by:

$$\frac{(n-1)s^2}{\chi^2_{\alpha/2}(n-1)} \leqq \sigma^2 \leqq \frac{(n-1)s^2}{\chi^2_{1-\alpha/2}(n-1)}.$$

This will be left as an exercise.

Example 8.19

Refer to Example 8.16. Construct a 90% confidence interval for σ^2.

Solution: $1-\alpha = 0.90$ so that $\alpha = 0.10$ and $\alpha/2 = 0.05$. The confidence interval is determined by:

$$\frac{(n-1)s^2}{\chi^2_{\alpha/2}(n-1)} = \frac{19\cdot(4.16)^2}{\chi^2_{0.05}(19)} = \frac{19\cdot(4.16)^2}{30.14} \approx 10.91,$$

and by:

$$\frac{(n-1)s^2}{\chi^2_{1-\alpha/2}(n-1)} = \frac{19\cdot(4.16)^2}{\chi^2_{0.95}(19)} = \frac{19\cdot(4.16)^2}{10.12} \approx 32.49.$$

The interval is therefore $10.91 \leqq \sigma^2 \leqq 32.49$.

Example 8.20

As Example 8.19, but with a 95% confidence level.

Solution: $1-\alpha = 0.95$ so that $\alpha = 0.05$ and $\alpha/2 = 0.025$. We find:

$$\frac{(n-1)s^2}{\chi^2_{\alpha/2}(n-1)} = \frac{19\cdot(4.16)^2}{\chi^2_{0.025}(19)} = \frac{19\cdot(4.16)^2}{32.85} \approx 10.01$$

and

$$\frac{(n-1)s^2}{\chi^2_{1-\alpha/2}(n-1)} = \frac{19\cdot(4.16)^2}{\chi^2_{0.975}(19)} = \frac{19\cdot(4.16)^2}{8.91} \approx 36.90.$$

The interval is therefore (10.01, 36.90).

Remark 1: The point estimate of σ^2 in Examples 8.19 and 8.20 above is of course $s^2 = (4.16)^2 = 17.31$. Because the chi-square distribution is not symmetric, confidence intervals for σ^2 will *not* be symmetric around the point estimate.

Remark 2: If μ is known one can show that $\frac{\sum_{i=1}^{n} (X_i-\mu)^2}{\sigma^2}$ is $\chi^2(n)$, and the confidence interval formulas have to be changed accordingly. We leave out the details of the modifications, which are straightforward.

References

Chou, Y.: *Statistical Analysis,* 2nd edition. Holt, Rinehart and Winston, New York 1975.

Harnett, D. L.: *Statistical Methods,* 3rd edition. Addison-Wesley, Reading, Mass. 1982.

Hawkins, C.A., and J.E. Weber: *Statistical Analysis. Applications to Business and Economics.* Harper & Row, New York 1980.

Lindgren, B.W.: *Statistical Theory,* 3rd edition. Macmillan, New York 1976.

Mansfield, E.: *Statistics for Business and Economics.* Norton & Company, New York 1980.

Mendenhall, W., and J.E. Reinmuth: *Statistics for Management and Economics,* 3rd edition. Duxbury Press, Mass. 1978.

Wonnacott, T.H., and R.J. Wonnacott: *Introductory Statistics for Business and Economics,* 2nd edition. John Wiley & Sons, New York 1977.

Exercises

8–1 The average family income in a small town is a useful variable in deciding whether or not to open a new branch of a store at a shopping center. Past studies indicate that the standard deviation of income is \$2,000.

a) What is the probability that the mean of a random sample of 25 families differs from the true mean by at least 527.2?
b) How large a sample must be taken so that she probability that the sample mean is within \$100 of the true mean is 90%?

8–2 The average tip a waitress receives per night is \$30.00 with a standard deviation of \$7.50.

a) Assume that many random samples of 100 nights are selected and the average tip in each sample computed. Determine an interval within which 90% of all sample means are expected to fall. (Hint: this interval is centered around the population mean.)
b) Assume that very many random samples of 500 nights are selected and the average tip in each sample computed. Determine an interval within which 90% of all sample means are expected to fall.
c) Explain any differences observed between the intervals obtained in parts (a) and (b).

8–3 In any year, the capital-output ratio of the synthetic rubber industry of the contry of Utopia is $N(\mu, 0.12)$. Over a period of 8 years, the average capital-output ratio was 1.84. Determine a 90% confidence interval for the capital-output ratio.

8–4 Solve Exercise no. 3 on the Utopia synthetic rubber industry capital-output ratio, when the standard deviation is unknown, but from the 8-year sample we compute the sample standard deviation $s = 0.12$.

8–5 Fifty shoppers in a department store are randomly selected and asked how much they have spent. It turns out that the average amount spent is \$23.50 (with a standard deviation of \$14.77).

a) Construct a 90% confidence interval for μ (the average spent for all shoppers).
b) What would the 90% confidence interval be if the same data were obtained from a sample of size $n = 20$?

8–6 A random sample of five cans of beer was taken from a production line immediately after filling, and the content of each of the five cans was measured. From experience we know that the distribution of beer content is approximately normal. The following are the sample measurements (in centilitres):

33.0 33.5 33.5 35.0 34.5

Construct a 99% confidence interval for the process mean content per can, μ.

8–7 The statistician at WPZ Consulting Corporation was asked to get an estimate of the sales of TV sets at retail outlets in a city area. From a complete listing of 200 of these outlets he selected 10 outlets at random and found that their sales for the last month was as follows:

Outlets	Sales ($000)
1	10
2	20
3	15
4	40
5	60
6	30
7	25
8	50
9	10
10	25

a) Find the sample mean ($\bar{x}$).
b) Find $\sigma_{\bar{x}}$ (the standard error of the sample mean).
c) Adjust $\sigma_{\bar{x}}$ by the finite population correction factor to account for the fact that the sample was taken without replacement.
d) Find a 95 percent confidence interval for the population mean (i. e. μ) using this adjusted standard deviation.

8–8 25 invoices have been randomly selected from the records of a certain shop. The sample mean is $112.65 and the sample standard deviation is $20.00.

a) Construct a 90 percent confidence interval for the mean value of all incoices.
b) What would the interval be if the sample size were 40 invoices instead of 25?

8–9 A new type of photoflash bulb was tested to estimate the probability, p, that the new bulb would produce the required light output. A sample of 400 bulbs was tested and 360 were observed to function according to specifications.

a) Find a 90% confidence interval estimate for p.
b) How large a sample of bulbs must be tested if we want to estimate the true

fraction which meets the specifications to within 0.01 using a 95% confidence interval? We are certain that the true fraction is approximately 0.9.

c) Same as (b), but with no prior information on the true fraction p.

8–10 A large firm employs a total of 25,000 people in all of its offices and factories. Find a 95% confidence interval estimate for the average years of experience of all employees if a sample of 225 employees reveals an average of 5.2 years with a variance of 144.

8–11 In a 1980 Gallup Poll of 1443 Canadian college students 49% of those interviewed believed that a change in Canada's constitution was likely to occur within the next five years. Find a 95% confidence interval for the population proportion of students believing in the change.

8–12 A cannery prints "Weight 16 oz." on its label. The quality control supervisor selects 9 cans at random and weighs them. He finds the mean to be 15.7 ounces and the standard deviation 0.6 ounces. Find a 90% confidence interval estimate for the mean weight of all "16 oz." cans. Can we say with reasonable certainty that the cannery is cheating its customers?

8–13 Just before an election, a poll showed that 40 out of 400 people sampled would vote for a certain candidate.

a) Determine a 95% confidence interval for the proportion of the population who voted for this candidate.

b) How large should the sample have been in order to estimate the population proportion to within 0.01 (or 1%) with a 95% confidence interval?

8–14 A television advertisement claims that a new model of a mini-car is able to get at least 35 miles per gallon in city traffic. To investigate this claim we test five of the vehicles in city traffic and get the following results:

Car	Miles per gallon (X)	
1	30	
2	32	$\sum X = 160$
3	36	$\sum X^2 = 5192$
4	36	
5	26	

a) Write a 90% confidence interval for the mean of the population from which these cars were taken.

b) Would you accept the 35 m.p.g. claim from the advertisement?

8–15 As general agent for a life insurance company you are interested in the average size of policies sold under a special program for graduating seniors. You take a simple random sample of 100 of this year's sales, and get the following frequency distribution:

Policy size (thousand $)	Number of sales
2.5	20
7.5	40
12.5	25
17.5	10
22.5	5

a) Determine the approximate probability distribution.
b) Estimate the population mean.
c) Estimate the population standard deviation.
d) Make an interval estimate of the population mean, with a 90 percent confidence.
e) Suppose that the population mean is 10. Using the result in (c) above find the probability that if another sample of size $n = 100$ is taken its mean will exceed the population mean by more than 10 percent of its value.

8–16 A grocery chain store adopts a policy of issuing trading stamps on all purchases. Prior sales had averaged $15.50 per customer over the past year, with a standard deviation of $4.80. At the end of a trial period with the new stamps, a random check of 400 customers shows average sales of $16.30.

a) Using a standard deviation of $4.80, write a 95% confidence interval for the new average sales based on the trial period results.
b) Would you be willing to conclude that average sales have changed? (Use the result of part (a).)

8–17 Consider a random sample which consists of the following measurements of compressive strength (in PSI of a certain steal piece):

41,000 44,250 69,400 70,000 80,350.

Construct a 95 percent confidence interval for the average strength of all the steel pieces from which this sample was obtained.

8–18 Consider a time and motion study in which you are interested in estimating the average time that it takes a secretary to execute a certain order form which goes from one department to another. Suppose that an experiment in which a random sample of 40 secretaries were timed in the performance of this task yielded the following results (in seconds):

46.2	61.9	52.5	57.3	51.8	38.0	53.7	56.1	65.4	48.5
51.6	43.0	47.8	60.5	71.1	62.3	56.6	52.5	43.9	52.0
58.1	66.5	33.9	42.7	46.4	53.8	61.2	55.3	48.5	42.9
40.7	52.4	46.6	55.6	58.3	50.4	63.8	35.0	49.5	53.2

Construct a 95 percent confidence interval for the population mean.

8–19 A statistician observes the number of planes landing at a major airport, during 45 randomly selected days. She finds an average of 2,335 planes landing per day with a standard deviation of 391 planes.

a) Construct a 95% confidence interval for μ, the true average number of planes landing per day.
b) Same as (a) above, but with 98% confidence.

8–20 A machine produces a certain kind of rubber tire. 144 tires, randomly selected, yield an average thread depth of 29 mm with a standard deviation of 1.1 mm. Construct a 90% confidence interval for the thread depth.

8–21 Out of 42 professors, randomly selected at a certain university, 32 indicated that they did not oppose course evaluations made by the students. Determine a 99% confidence interval for the true proportion of professors who do not oppose course evaluations.

8–22 Refer to Exercise no. 8.

a) Construct a 90% confidence interval for the variance σ^2.
b) Construct a 95% confidence interval for the variance σ^2.
c) Construct a 98% confidence interval for the variance σ^2.

8–23 Refer to Exercise no. 12. Find a 99% confidence interval for the variance.

8–24 Refer to Exercise no. 14. Find a 90% confidence interval for the variance σ^2.

8–25 Based on Exercise no. 17, find a 95% confidence interval for the variance σ^2.

8–26 Refer to Exercise no. 18.

a) Construct a 90% confidence interval for the variance σ^2.
b) Construct a 98% confidence interval for the variance σ^2.

8–27 Refer to Exercise no. 19. Construct a 99% confidence interval for the variance σ^2.

9. Hypothesis Testing

The theory of confidence intervals will now be carried one step further, to the testing of hypotheses.

In Section 9.1 we introduce the basic problem of testing hypotheses, by way of an example from acceptance sampling. Some basic terminology is also introduced. In Section 9.2 we go into the specific problem of performing hypothesis tests for the unknown mean of a normal distribution, when the variance is known. Both one-sided (left as well as right tail) and two-sided tests are illustrated with examples. The connection with confidence intervals is mentioned.

Section 9.3 extends the results of Section 9.2 to the case when the population variance is not known beforehand, so that it must be estimated using the sample data. In Section 9.4 we show how tests concerning an unknown population proportion can be conducted. Only large samples are considered, but finite as well as infinite populations are covered. Section 9.5 covers two-sample tests of means, for known as well as unknown population variances, and for small as well as large samples. Confidence intervals for the difference between the two population means are also constructed.

In Section 9.6 we look at two-sample tests of proportions, for large samples. In Section 9.7 we use the material covered in Section 8.7 to construct tests concerning the population variance. Two-sided and left-tail tests are treated. In Section 9.8 we then go on to two-sample tests concerning variances, and show how these are done by an F-test.

Section 9.9, finally, shows how the two-sample tests of means, covered in Section 9.5, are modified when a paired difference design can be assumed. It is shown, by way of an example, how this leads to a design with more discriminatory power. Confidence intervals are also constructed, using this design.

9.1 Introduction and Basic Concepts

Example 9.1

A producer of a certain electronic component knows that its life-span, in months, is normally distributed; specifically, it is $N(\mu, 2)$. Due to the particular properties of the production process, μ will be *either* 10 *or* 12 months, but for a given batch of the components it is not known which μ-value applies. A buyer of a batch wants to accept it only if $\mu = 12$, and has decided to test 15 randomly selected elements of the batch (which contains many thousand units). How should the buyer decide whether to accept the batch or not?

This is an example of *acceptance sampling*, and to answer the question we first need to introduce some basic concepts.

Definition: A *hypothesis* H is an assumption about an unknown population parameter θ. A hypothesis of the kind H: $\theta = 4$ is a *simple* hypothesis, whereas a hypothesis of the kind H: $\theta > 3$ or H: $\theta \neq 5$ is a *composite* hypothesis.

Example 9.2

Given a population $N(\mu, \sigma)$ where μ is unknown and σ is known. We are interested in the value of μ and may have the *null hypothesis* H_0:

$$H_0: \ \mu = \mu_0$$

and the *alternative hypothesis* H_1:

$$H_1: \ \mu = \mu_1$$

where $\mu_0 \neq \mu_1$ are given numbers. We assume that exactly one of the hypotheses is true (so that the other must be false) and we want to find out which one (i.e. whether μ equals μ_0 or μ_1). Assume that $\mu_0 < \mu_1$. We select a sample and obtain $\bar{X}$. Clearly a "small" value of the sample mean $\bar{X}$ would lead us to believe

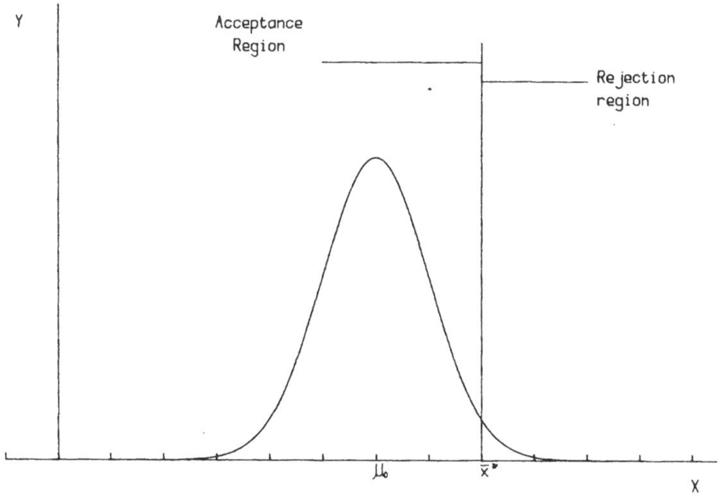

Fig. 9/1: Rejection and acceptance regions.

that H_0 were true, whereas a "large" $\bar{X}$-value would indicate that H_1 might be true. Hence, for some number $\bar{X}^*$, calculated beforehand, we would *reject* H_0 if $X > \bar{X}^*$, but *accept* H_0 if $\bar{X} \leqq \bar{X}^*$. We say that $\bar{X}$ is the *test statistic* and $\bar{X}^*$ the *critical value*.

Thus we have the *decision rule:*

If $X > \bar{X}^*$, reject H_0 (i.e. accept H_1).
If $X \leqq \bar{X}^*$, accept H_0 (i.e. reject H_1).

If H_0 is rejected, we say that the result is *statistically significant.*

Because the rejection region is in the upper (right-hand) tail of the distribution, we say that we use an *upper-tail* (or *right-tail*) *test.*

How should we determine the critical value $\bar{X}^*$?

There is always the risk of making the wrong decision, i.e. rejecting a true H_0, or accepting a false H_0. The first error, rejecting H_0 if it is true, is called a *Type I error;* the other error, accepting H_0 if it is false, is called a *Type II error.* The probabilities of making these errors can of course be calculated, with $\bar{X}^*$ given and the probability distribution of $\bar{X}$ known.

Definition:

$$P(\text{Type I error}) = P(\text{Reject } H_0 | H_0 \text{ true}) = \alpha$$
$$P(\text{Type II error}) = P(\text{Accept } H_0 | H_0 \text{ false}) = \beta$$

α is the *significance level* and $1-\beta$ the *power* of the test (see Figs. 9/2 and 9/3 on the next page).

The significance level α is usually predetermined (e.g. $\alpha = 0.05, 0.01, 0.001$).

How do we find $\bar{X}^*$ if α is given?

Solution: Referring to Example 9.2 we obtain:

$$\alpha = P(\text{Reject } H_0 | H_0 \text{ true}) = P\left(\bar{X} > \bar{X}^* | \bar{X} \quad \text{is} \quad N\left(\mu_0, \frac{\sigma}{\sqrt{n}}\right)\right)$$

$$= P\left(\frac{\bar{X}-\mu_0}{\frac{\sigma}{\sqrt{n}}} > \frac{\bar{X}^*-\mu_0}{\frac{\sigma}{\sqrt{n}}} \,\middle|\, \frac{\bar{X}-\mu_0}{\frac{\sigma}{\sqrt{n}}} \quad \text{is} \quad N(0,1)\right)$$

$$= P\left(Z > \frac{\bar{X}^*-\mu_0}{\frac{\sigma}{\sqrt{n}}}\right).$$

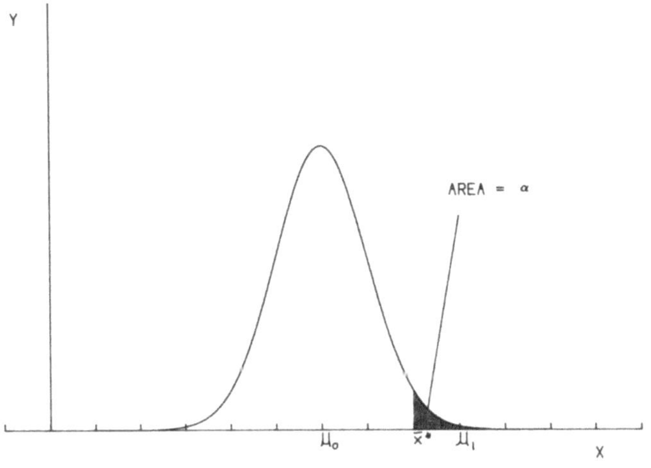

Fig. 9/2: α, the probability of a Type I error.

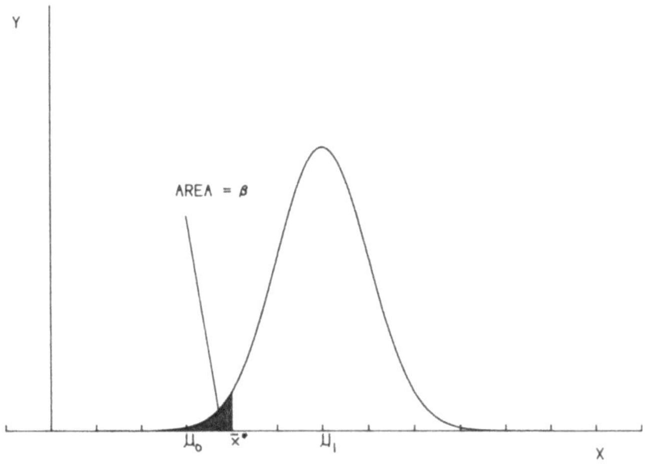

Fig. 9/3: β, the probability of a Type II error.

In other words, $\dfrac{\bar{X}^* - \mu_0}{\dfrac{\sigma}{\sqrt{n}}} = z_\alpha$. Therefore, $\bar{X}^* = \mu_0 + z_\alpha \cdot \dfrac{\sigma}{\sqrt{n}}$. We see that the *lower* the significance level α, the *larger* is the critical value $\bar{X}^*$, and the *larger* is the probability of accepting H_0 (even if it is false). One can show that this implies that β increases. For α and β, reducing one means increasing the other; the only way to reduce both simultaneously is to increase the sample size n.

Thus α, β and $\bar{X}^*$ are connected; when one is given, the other two can be calculated. Specifically, one can easily show that

$$z_\alpha + z_\beta = \frac{\mu_1 - \mu_0}{\frac{\sigma}{\sqrt{n}}}.$$

It is also clear that if H_0 is being rejected for a certain given significance level α_0, it will be rejected as well for all α such that $\alpha \geqq \alpha_0$.

9.2 Testing μ when σ is Known

Example 9.3

For our acceptance sampling problem of Example 9.1 we are testing the null hypothesis:

$$H_0: \ \mu = 12$$

against the alternative hypothesis:

$$H_1: \ \mu = 10.$$

(Note that $\mu_0 = 12 > 10 = \mu_1$, which is the reverse situation of Example 9.2.)

Let $n = 15$, and choose the significance level $\alpha = 0.01$. In other words, the probability of a Type I error (rejecting H_0 if it is true, i.e. erroneously rejecting the batch when it is actually good) is 1%. Let us find the critical value $\bar{X}^*$ and β.

Solution: The decision rule must now obviously be: Accept H_0 if $\bar{X} \geqq \bar{X}^*$ and reject H_0 if $\bar{X} < \bar{X}^*$. Therefore, $\alpha = P(\text{Reject } H_0 | H_0 \text{ true})$ gives:

$$0.01 = P(\bar{X} < \bar{X}^* | \mu = 12) = P\left(\frac{\bar{X} - 12}{\frac{2}{\sqrt{15}}} < \frac{\bar{X}^* - 12}{\frac{2}{\sqrt{15}}} \,\middle|\, \frac{\bar{X} - 12}{\frac{2}{\sqrt{15}}} \text{ is } N(0,1)\right)$$

$$= P\left(Z < \frac{\bar{X}^* - 12}{\frac{2}{\sqrt{15}}}\right).$$

We get:

$$\frac{\bar{X}^* - 12}{\frac{2}{\sqrt{15}}} = -z_{0.01}, \quad \text{i.e.} \quad \bar{X}^* = 12 - z_{0.01} \cdot \frac{2}{\sqrt{15}}$$

$$= 12 - 2.33 \cdot \frac{2}{\sqrt{15}} \approx 10.797.$$

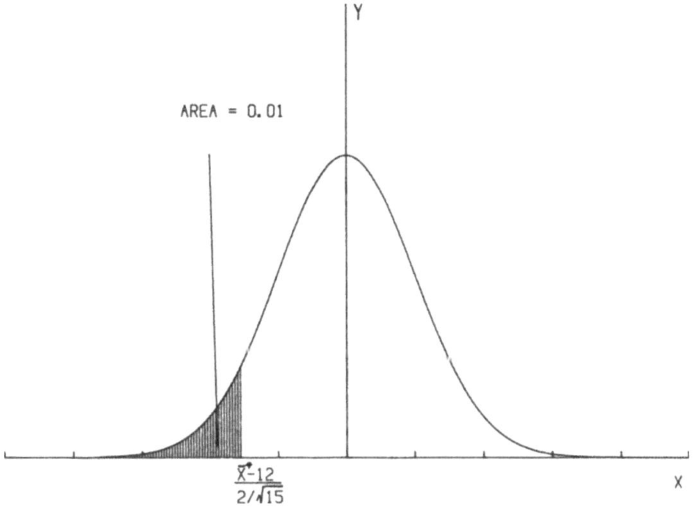

Fig. 9/4: Finding the critical value $\bar{X}^*$ for Example 9.3.

Furthermore,

$$\beta = P(\text{Accept } H_0 | H_0 \text{ false}) = P(\bar{X} \geqq \bar{X}^* | \mu = 10)$$

$$= P\left(\frac{\bar{X}-10}{\frac{2}{\sqrt{15}}} \geqq \frac{\bar{X}^*-10}{\frac{2}{\sqrt{15}}} \,\middle|\, \frac{\bar{X}-10}{\frac{2}{\sqrt{15}}} \text{ is } N(0,1)\right)$$

$$= P\left(Z \geqq \frac{\bar{X}^*-10}{\frac{2}{\sqrt{15}}}\right).$$

But $\bar{X}^* = 10.797$ so that $\dfrac{\bar{X}^*-10}{\frac{2}{\sqrt{15}}} = \dfrac{0.797}{\frac{2}{\sqrt{15}}} \approx 1.543.$

From a table of the normal distribution we now find:

$$\beta = \frac{1}{2} - 0.4382 = 0.0618\,.$$

In this example the producer wants a low α, which is the risk of a good batch being rejected. The consumer wants a low β, being the risk of accepting a bad batch. We say α is *producer's risk* and β is *consumer's risk*.

The test can now be summarized as:

Accept the batch if $\bar{X} \geqq 10.80$, *reject* it otherwise.

We say that this is a *lower-tail* or *left-tail test* (one-sided test).

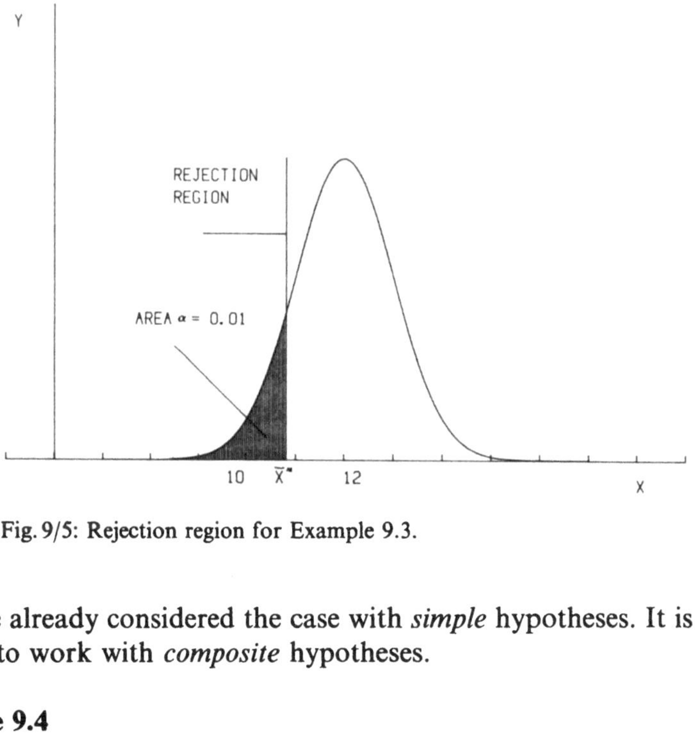

Fig. 9/5: Rejection region for Example 9.3.

We have already considered the case with *simple* hypotheses. It is often more natural to work with *composite* hypotheses.

Example 9.4

In our acceptance sampling case, it may well be that we do not have any prior information about μ, but wish to accept a batch if $\mu \geqq 12$. We would then formulate the hypotheses:

$$H_0: \ \mu \geqq 12$$
$$H_1: \ \mu < 12 .$$

The decision rule for a test of these hypotheses at the 1% level of significance will then be:

$$\text{Accept } H_0 \ \text{ if } \ \bar{X} \geqq \bar{X}^*$$
$$\text{Reject } H_0 \ \text{ if } \ \bar{X} < \bar{X}^* .$$

We get:

$$0.01\,\alpha = P(\text{Reject } H_0 | H_0 \text{ true}) = P(\bar{X} < \bar{X}^* | \mu \geqq 12).$$

We see that because of the composite null hypothesis, there is no single value of μ referred to. Consequently, the distribution of $\bar{X}$ will depend on the choice of hypothesized value of μ, which will also affect the value of α. One way out of this dilemma is to take the *largest* α-value for a true H_0. In our case, this is obtained for $\mu = 12$:

$$\alpha = P(\bar{X} < \bar{X}^* | \mu = 12) = P\left(\frac{\bar{X} - 12}{\frac{\sigma}{\sqrt{n}}} < \frac{\bar{X}^* - 12}{\frac{\sigma}{\sqrt{n}}} \middle| \mu = 12\right)$$

so that: $\dfrac{\bar{X}^* - 12}{\frac{\sigma}{\sqrt{n}}} = -z_\alpha$ and we get the same test as before.

Next, $\beta = P(\text{Accept } H_0 | H_0 \text{ false}) = P(\bar{X} \geqq \bar{X}^* | \mu < 12)$, and because the alternative hypothesis is composite, β will also depend on the actual μ-value. For different μ-values, we can plot the corresponding value of β and thus obtain the so-called *operating characteristic curve:*

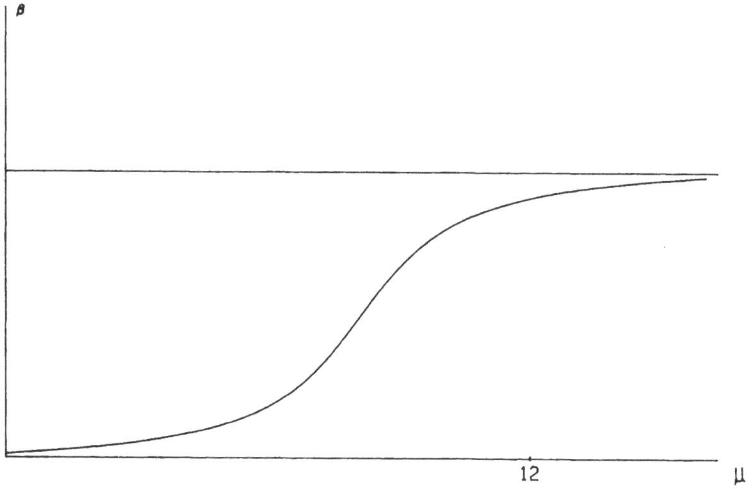

Fig. 9/6: Operating characteristic curve.

The treatment in this book will be restricted to simple null hypotheses, for ease of exposition. For further study, we refer to the books by Chou, by Hawkins and Weber and by Mansfield (see the list of references at the end of this chapter).

We have so far only considered *one-sided* tests. A *two-sided* (*two-tailed*) test would be appropriate, if μ-values on either side of an ideal μ_0 are undesirable.

Example 9.5

A daily train is scheduled to arrive at a certain railway station at 11:00 hours. The actual arrival times are $N(\mu, 0.6)$. We want to test:

$$H_0: \quad \mu = 11$$

against $\quad H_1: \quad \mu \neq 11$

at the 5% level, using a sample of size $n = 9$. The test should obviously be: Reject H_0 if $|\bar{X} - 11| > d^*$, for some appropriately selected d^*. We shall now determine d^*, given the sample size $n = 9$ and the level of significance α:

$$\alpha = P(\text{Reject } H_0 | H_0 \text{ true}) = P\left(|\bar{X} - 11| > d^* \,\middle|\, \bar{X} \text{ is } N\left(11, \frac{\sigma}{\sqrt{n}}\right)\right)$$

$$= P\left(\left|\frac{\bar{X} - 11}{\frac{\sigma}{\sqrt{n}}}\right| > \frac{d^*}{\frac{\sigma}{\sqrt{n}}} \,\middle|\, \frac{\bar{X} - 11}{\frac{\sigma}{\sqrt{n}}} \text{ is } N(0, 1)\right)$$

$$= P\left(|Z| > \frac{d^*}{\frac{\sigma}{\sqrt{n}}}\right)$$

from which one can easily obtain:

$$\frac{d^*}{\frac{\sigma}{\sqrt{n}}} = z_{\alpha/2} \quad \text{or} \quad d^* = z_{\alpha/2} \cdot \frac{\sigma}{\sqrt{n}} = z_{0.025} \cdot \frac{0.6}{\sqrt{9}} = 1.96 \cdot 0.2 = 0.392$$

and the decision rule is:

Accept H_0 if $10.61 \leqq \bar{X} \leqq 11.39$

Reject H_0 if $\bar{X} > 11.39$ or if $\bar{X} < 10.61$.

Remark: A 95% confidence interval for μ is given by $\bar{X} \pm 0.392$. In general, for a two-tailed test, the null hypothesis is accepted for a given α if and only if the hypothesized value of the mean μ belongs to a confidence interval for μ with confidence level $1 - \alpha$.

As the alternative hypothesis H_1 is composite in Example 9.5, β will not be a single number but will depend on the particular hypothesized μ-value. The operating characteristic curve can be graphed, but we shall not do it.

9.3 Testing μ when σ is Unknown

If σ is unknown, we use s as an estimator of σ. The t-distribution now applies, and we modify our expressions accordingly.

Example 9.6

For the one-sided test:

$$H_0:\ \mu = \mu_0$$
$$H_1:\ \mu > \mu_0$$

at level α, we get:

$$\text{Reject} \quad H_0 \text{ if } \bar{X} > \bar{X}^*$$
$$\text{Accept} \quad H_0 \text{ if } \bar{X} < \bar{X}^*$$

where $\bar{X}^* = \mu_0 + t_\alpha(n-1)\cdot\frac{s}{\sqrt{n}}$.

For large n, (i.e. $n \geqq 30$), we use z_α instead of $t_\alpha(n-1)$.

As before, because α represents the upper tail of the distribution, we talk of an *upper-tail test*. Similarly, we also have lower-tail tests and two-sided tests. For two-sided tests, the same relationship as in Section 9.2 holds between acceptance regions and confidence intervals.

Example 9.7

With the set-up of Example 9.6, and with $\mu_0 = 24.3, \bar{X} = 26.5, \alpha = 0.01, n = 18$ and $s = 3.09$, we find:

$$\bar{X}^* = \mu_0 + t_\alpha(n-1)\cdot\frac{s}{\sqrt{n}} = 24.3 + t_{0.01}(17)\cdot\frac{3.09}{\sqrt{18}}$$
$$= 24.3 + 2.567\cdot\frac{3.09}{\sqrt{18}} \approx 26.17\,.$$

We will therefore reject the null hypothesis if $\bar{X} > 26.17$. As $\bar{X} = 26.5$, we will reject H_0 at the 1% level of significance. We will of course also reject H_0 at the 5% level.

9.4 Testing the Proportion

Example 9.8

In Sections 8.3 and 8.6 we considered the problem of estimating the proportion p of voters in favour of capital punishment. Let us now test the hypothesis:

$$H_0:\ p = 0.30$$

against the hypothesis:

$$H_1:\ p = 0.40$$

at 5% level, with a sample size of $n = 85$.

The test should obviously be: Reject H_0 if $\frac{X}{n} > p^*$, where the critical value p^* is to be determined.

$$\alpha = P(\text{Reject } H_0 | H_0 \text{ true}) = P\left(\frac{X}{n} > p^* | p = 0.3\right)$$

$$= P\left(\frac{\frac{X}{n} - 0.3}{\sigma_{\frac{X}{n}}} > \frac{p^* - 0.3}{\sigma_{\frac{X}{n}}} \middle| \frac{\frac{X}{n} - 0.3}{\sigma_{\frac{X}{n}}} \text{ is approximately } N(0, 1)\right)$$

i.e. $z_\alpha \approx \dfrac{p^* - 0.3}{\sigma_{\frac{X}{n}}}$,

and we get:

$$p^* = 0.3 + z_\alpha \sigma_{\frac{X}{n}} = 0.3 + z_\alpha \sqrt{\frac{p(1-p)}{n}}$$

$$= 0.3 + 1.645 \times \sqrt{\frac{0.3 \times 0.7}{85}} \approx 0.382\,.$$

The test is therefore:

Accept H_0 if $\frac{X}{n} \leqq 0.38$

Reject H_0 if $\frac{X}{n} > 0.38$

$$\beta = P(\text{Type II error}) = P(\text{Accept } H_0 | H_0 \text{ false})$$
$$= P\left(\frac{X}{n} \leqq p^* | p = 0.4\right) \approx P\left(Z \leqq \frac{p^* - 0.4}{\sigma_{\frac{X}{n}}}\right)$$

Thus $\frac{p^* - 0.4}{\sigma_{\frac{X}{n}}} = \frac{0.3815 - 0.4}{\sqrt{\frac{0.4 \times 0.6}{85}}} = -\frac{0.0185}{0.0531} = -0.348$ from which we obtain, using a table of the normal distribution:

$$\beta = \frac{1}{2} - 0.1268 = 0.3632,$$

which is quite considerable.

Remark 1: We can easily modify the above using the finite population correction factor $\sqrt{\frac{N-n}{N-1}}$ (remember that $N = 1000$).

Remark 2. We can also see what our test would be if the alternative hypothesis was $H_1: p = 0.20$. The technical details related to Remark 1 and 2 can be done as exercises.

Now let us see how a two-tailed test of the proportion looks:

Example 9.9

Test the hypothesis:

$$H_0: \; p = 0.30$$

against

$$H_1: \; p \neq 0.30.$$

The test should obviously be: Reject H_0 if $\left|\frac{X}{n} - 0.30\right| > d^*$. One can easily show that $d^* = z_{\alpha/2}\sqrt{\frac{p(1-p)}{n}} = 0.097$ for $\alpha = 0.05$ and $n = 85$.

Our two-tail test at 5% level with a sample size of $n = 85$ is therefore:

Reject H_0 if $\frac{X}{n} > 0.397$ or if $\frac{X}{n} < 0.203$

Accept H_0 if $0.203 \leqq \frac{X}{n} \leqq 0.397$.

Remark 1: Again it can be done with finite population correction.

Remark 2: As for two-tailed tests of the mean, we see that $\frac{X}{n} \pm 0.097$ defines a 95% confidence interval for the true proportion.

9.5 Two-Sample Tests of Means

We have so far only considered tests involving one sample. We shall now turn to two-sample tests, and start by considering an illustrative example.

Example 9.10

Assume that the yield (tons/acre) of an oat variety is normally distributed; to be specific it is $N(\mu_1, \sigma_1)$. The yield of another oat variety is $N(\mu_2, \mu_2)$. We want to test:

$$H_0: \ d = \mu_1 - \mu_2 = 0$$

against

$$H_1: \ d = \mu_1 - \mu_2 < 0.$$

Taking samples of sizes n_1 and n_2 respectively, obtaining sample means $\bar{X}_1$ and $\bar{X}_2$, and assuming independence, we know the following:

$$d = \bar{X}_1 - \bar{X}_2 \quad \text{is} \quad N\left(\mu_1 - \mu_2, \sqrt{\frac{\sigma_1^2}{n_1} + \frac{\sigma_2^2}{n_2}}\right).$$

Therefore the test will be:

Accept H_0 if $d \geqq d^*$
Reject H_0 if $d < d^*$

where d^* is yet to be determined.

This is what we now turn to.

As usual, when tests of means are performed, we distinguish between the cases of known and unknown variances.

Case I: σ_1 and σ_2 are *known*

We get:

$$\alpha = P(\text{Type I error}) = P(\text{Reject } H_0 | H_0 \text{ true})$$
$$= P(d < d^* | \mu_1 - \mu_2 = 0) = P\left(\frac{d}{\sigma_d} < \frac{d^*}{\sigma_d} \middle| \frac{d}{\sigma_d} \text{ is } N(0, 1)\right)$$

so that

$$\frac{d^*}{\sigma_d} = -z_\alpha \quad \text{and} \quad d^* = -z_\alpha \sigma_d = -z_\alpha \cdot \sqrt{\frac{\sigma_1^2}{n_1} + \frac{\sigma_2^2}{n_2}}\,.$$

Example 9.11

Assume that we have the following data for our oat yield problem of Example 9.10: $\alpha = 0.01$, $\sigma_1 = 1{,}5$, $\sigma_2 = 2.1$, and the sample sizes are $n_1 = 42$ and $n_2 = 39$. Then we would get:

$$d^* = -z_\alpha \sqrt{\frac{\sigma_1^2}{n_1} + \frac{\sigma_2^2}{n_2}} = -2.326 \sqrt{\frac{(1.5)^2}{42} + \frac{(2.1)^2}{39}} = -0.951\,.$$

Case II: σ_1 and σ_2 are *unknown*

a) For large samples (n_1 and $n_2 \geqq 30$) we can use the normal approximation, and get, using s_1 and s_2 instead of the corresponding unknown σ_1 and σ_2:

$$d^* = -z_\alpha \sqrt{\frac{s_1^2}{n_1} + \frac{s_2^2}{n_2}}\,.$$

b) For small samples (at least one of n_1 and n_2 less than thirty) we have to assume that σ_1 and σ_2 are equal, i.e. $\sigma_1 = \sigma_2 = \sigma$ (unknown). One can then show that:

$$\frac{d - (\mu_1 - \mu_2)}{\sqrt{s_p^2\left(\frac{1}{n_1} + \frac{1}{n_2}\right)}} \quad \text{is} \quad t(n_1 + n_2 - 2)$$

where s_p^2, the so-called *pooled estimate* of σ^2, is defined by:

$$s_p^2 = \frac{(n_1 - 1)s_1^2 + (n_2 - 1)s_2^2}{n_1 + n_2 - 2}\,.$$

Accordingly we have:

$$d^* = -t_\alpha(n_1 + n_2 - 2) \cdot \sqrt{\frac{(n_1 - 1)s_1^2 + (n_2 - 1)s_2^2}{n_1 + n_2 - 2} \cdot \left(\frac{1}{n_1} + \frac{1}{n_2}\right)}\,.$$

Example 9.12

With $\alpha = 0.01$, $s_1 = 1.5$, $s_2 = 2.1$, $n_1 = 42$ and $n_2 = 39$, we get the same result as in Example 9.11 above, i.e. $d^* = -0.951$.

Example 9.13

With $\alpha = 0.01$, $s_1 = 1.7$, $s_2 = 1.8$, $n_1 = 12$, $n_2 = 16$, and assuming $\sigma_1 = \sigma_2 = \sigma$ (unknown) we find:

$$d^* = -t_\alpha(n_1 + n_2 - 2)\cdot\sqrt{\frac{(n_1-1)s_1^2 + (n_2-1)s_2^2}{n_1+n_2-2}\cdot\left(\frac{1}{n_1}+\frac{1}{n_2}\right)}$$

$$= -2.479\cdot\sqrt{\frac{11\cdot(1.7)^2 + 15\cdot(1.8)^2}{12+16-2}\cdot\left(\frac{1}{12}+\frac{1}{16}\right)} = -1.665.$$

We have now treated the different cases for lower-tail tests. For upper-tail tests one can either carry out the necessary modifications of the above procedures, or alternatively, switch the order of μ_1 and μ_2 and thus obtain a lower-tail test.

A two-tailed test of two means would be:

$$H_0:\ \mu_1 - \mu_2 = 0$$
$$H_1:\ \mu_1 - \mu_2 \neq 0.$$

With $d = \bar{X}_1 - \bar{X}_2$ the test is:

Accept H_0 if $|d| \leqq d^*$

Reject H_0 if $|d| > d^*$.

As for the lower-tail test, we distinguish between the cases of known and unknown variances, and in the latter case between large and small samples.

Case I: σ_1 and σ_2 *known*

We get

$$d^* = z_{\alpha/2}\cdot\sqrt{\frac{\sigma_1^2}{n_1}+\frac{\sigma_2^2}{n_2}}.$$

Case II: σ_1 and σ_2 are *unknown*

a) Large n_1, n_2 (both at least thirty):

$$d^* = z_{\alpha/2}\cdot\sqrt{\frac{s_1^2}{n_1}+\frac{s_2^2}{n_2}}.$$

b) Small n_1, n_2 (at least one of them less than thirty), and $\sigma_1 = \sigma_2 = \sigma$:

$$d^* = t_{\alpha/2}(n_1 + n_2 - 2)\cdot\sqrt{\frac{(n_1-1)s_1^2 + (n_2-1)s_2^2}{n_1+n_2-2}\cdot\left(\frac{1}{n_1}+\frac{1}{n_2}\right)}.$$

Example 9.14

Out variety yield as in Example 9.11. Test $\mu_1 = \mu_2$ against $\mu_1 \neq \mu_2$.

For case I we get:

$$d^* = z_{\alpha/2} \cdot \sqrt{\frac{\sigma_1^2}{n_1} + \frac{\sigma_2^2}{n_2}} = 2.576 \cdot \sqrt{\frac{(1.5)^2}{42} + \frac{(2.1)^2}{39}} = 1.052 .$$

For case II (with s_1 instead of σ_1 and s_2 instead of σ_2) we get:

a) Same result as for case I;

b) $$d^* = t_{\alpha/2}(n_1 + n_2 - 2) \cdot \sqrt{\frac{(n_1 - 1)s_1^2 + (n_2 - 1)s_2^2}{n_1 + n_2 - 2} \cdot \left(\frac{1}{n_1} + \frac{1}{n_2}\right)}$$

$$= 2.779 \sqrt{\frac{11(1.7)^2 + 15(1.8)^2}{12 + 16 - 2} \cdot \left(\frac{1}{12} + \frac{1}{16}\right)} = 1.253 .$$

We can also construct confidence intervals for $\mu_1 - \mu_2$, the difference of the two means. As for one-sample tests of means, we then use the formulas for two-sided tests, suitably modified.

Example 9.15

Refer to Example 9.11. A confidence interval for $\mu_1 - \mu_2$ with confidence level $1 - \alpha$ is determined by (Case I):

$$d \pm z_{\alpha/2} \sqrt{\frac{\sigma_1^2}{n_1} + \frac{\sigma_2^2}{n_2}} .$$

With our data we find (cf. Example 9.14):

$$d \pm 1.052$$

for a 99% confidence interval.

Example 9.16

Refer to Example 9.12. A confidence interval for $\mu_1 - \mu_2$ with confidence level $1 - \alpha$ is determined by (Case II a):

$$d \pm z_{\alpha/2} \sqrt{\frac{s_1^2}{n_1} + \frac{s_2^2}{n_2}} .$$

With our data we find (cf. Example 9.14):

$$d \pm 1.052$$

for a 99% confidence interval.

Example 9.17

Refer to Example 9.13. A confidence interval for $\mu_1 - \mu_2$ with confidence level $1-\alpha$ is determined by (Case II b):

$$d \pm t_{\alpha/2}(n_1+n_2-2)\cdot\sqrt{\frac{(n_1-1)s_1^2+(n_2-1)s_2^2}{n_1+n_2-2}\cdot\left(\frac{1}{n_1}+\frac{1}{n_2}\right)}.$$

With our data we find (cf. Example 9.14):

$$d \pm 1.253$$

for a 99% confidence interval.

9.6 Two-Sample Tests of Proportions

In this section we extend the testing of proportions, done in Section 9.4, to include two populations. As a background example we use the capital punishment problem of Sections 8.3 and 8.6 and of Examples 9.8 and 9.9.

Example 9.18

In two cities, the capital punishment supporter proportion is p_1 and p_2, respectively. We want to test:

$$H_0\colon\ p_1 = p_2$$

against

$$H_0\colon\ p_1 \neq p_2\,.$$

The sample sizes are n_1 and n_2 respectively, giving X_1 and X_2 "yes"-answers, respectively, to the question of whether or not capital punishment should be allowed. How should the test be done?

Solution: The test statistic d should obviously be the difference between the sample proportions, i.e. $d = \frac{X_1}{n_1} - \frac{X_2}{n_2}$ and we *accept* H_0 if $|d| \leqq d^*$ and *reject* H_0 if $|d| > d^*$.

To find d^*, we must know the sampling distribution of d. We know that X_1 is $\text{Bin}(n_1, p_1)$ and X_2 is $\text{Bin}(n_2, p_2)$, so that:

$$E\left(\frac{X_1}{n_1}\right) = \frac{1}{n_1}E(X_1) = \frac{1}{n_1}\cdot n_1 p_1 = p_1\,;$$

$$E\left(\frac{X_2}{n_2}\right) = \frac{1}{n_2} E(X_2) = \frac{1}{n_2} \cdot n_2 p_2 = p_2 .$$

Furthermore:

$$V\left(\frac{X_1}{n_1}\right) = \frac{1}{n_1^2} V(X_1) = \frac{1}{n_1^2} \cdot n_1 p_1 (1 - p_1) = \frac{p_1(1 - p_1)}{n_1} = \frac{p_1 q_1}{n_1};$$

$$V\left(\frac{X_2}{n_2}\right) = \frac{1}{n_2^2} V(X_2) = \frac{1}{n_2^2} \cdot n_2 p_2 (1 - p_2) = \frac{p_2(1 - p_2)}{n_2} = \frac{p_2 q_2}{n_2}.$$

Assuming X_1 and X_2 to be statistically independent random variables, we use the normal approximation, and find that $d = \frac{X_1}{n_1} - \frac{X_2}{n_2}$ is approximately distributed as:

$$N\left(p_1 - p_2, \sqrt{\frac{p_1 q_1}{n_1} + \frac{p_2 q_2}{n_2}}\right).$$

Using $\frac{X_1}{n_1} = \hat{p}_1$ to estimate p_1 and $\frac{X_2}{n_2} = \hat{p}_2$ to estimate p_2 we find:

$$\alpha = P(\text{Reject } H_0 | H_0 \text{ true}) = P(|d| > d^* | p_1 = p_2)$$

$$= P\left(\frac{|d|}{\sqrt{\frac{p_1 q_1}{n_1} + \frac{p_2 q_2}{n_2}}} > \frac{d^*}{\sqrt{\frac{p_1 q_1}{n_1} + \frac{p_2 q_2}{n_2}}} \middle| p_1 = p_2\right)$$

$$\approx P\left(|Z| > \frac{d^*}{\sqrt{\frac{\hat{p}_1 \hat{q}_1}{n_1} + \frac{\hat{p}_2 \hat{q}_2}{n_2}}} \middle| Z \text{ is } N(0, 1)\right)$$

from which we obtain the critical value d^*:

$$d^* = z_{\alpha/2} \cdot s_d = z_{\alpha/2} \cdot \sqrt{\frac{\hat{p}_1 \hat{q}_1}{n_1} + \frac{\hat{p}_2 \hat{q}_2}{n_2}} .$$

The modifications for lower-tail and upper-tail tests are obvious.

Example 9.19

Refer to Example 9.18. We have the following data: $\alpha = 0.05$, $X_1 = 26$, $n_1 = 95$, $X_2 = 24$, $n_2 = 78$. Using these we find:

$$d = \frac{X_1}{n_1} - \frac{X_2}{n_2} = \hat{p}_1 - \hat{p}_2 = 0.27368 - 0.30769 = -0.0340$$

$$d^* = z_{\alpha/2}\sqrt{\frac{\hat{p}_1\hat{q}_1}{n_1} + \frac{\hat{p}_2\hat{q}_2}{n_2}}$$
$$= 1.960\sqrt{\frac{0.27368 \cdot 0.72632}{95} + \frac{0.30769 \cdot 0.69231}{78}} = 0.136.$$

We have $|d| \leqq d^*$, because $|-0.0340| = 0.0340 \leqq 0.136$. Therefore, we *cannot* reject the null hypothesis at the 5% level of significance. Neither can we reject H_0 for any other $\alpha \leqq 0.05$.

Remark: Confidence intervals for the difference between two population proportions could be constructed by suitably modifying our two-sided tests above. We leave this as an exercise for the reader.

*9.7 Testing the Variance

In Section 8.7 we considered interval estimates of variances. Our results were based on the fact that $\frac{(n-1)s^2}{\sigma^2}$ is $\chi^2(n-1)$ distributed if the underlying population has a $N(\mu, \sigma)$ distribution. This fact will now be used to construct hypothesis tests for the variance.

Example 9.20

For a $N(\mu, \sigma)$ population where μ and σ are both unknown, we wish to test the hypothesis:

$$H_0: \ \sigma^2 = \sigma_0^2$$

against

$$H_0: \ \sigma^2 \neq \sigma_0^2$$

where σ_0^2 is a given number. How should this be done?

Solution: Using the sample variance s^2 as an estimator of σ^2, the test should obviously accept H_0 if and only if

$$\chi^2_{1-\alpha/2}(n-1) \leq \frac{(n-1)s^2}{\sigma_0^2} \leqq \chi^2_{\alpha/2}(n-1).$$

In other words

$$\textit{Reject}\ H_0 \text{ if } s^2 > \frac{\sigma_0^2}{n-1}\chi^2_{\alpha/2}(n-1)$$

or if

$$s^2 < \frac{\sigma_0^2}{n-1}\chi^2_{1-\alpha/2}(n-1)$$

$$\textit{Accept}\ H_0 \text{ if } \frac{\sigma_0^2}{n-1}\chi^2_{1-\alpha/2}(n-1) \leqq s^2 \leqq \frac{\sigma_0^2}{n-1}\chi^2_{\alpha/2}(n-1).$$

Example 9.21

Using the data of Example 8.16 ($n = 20, \bar{x} = 10.27$ and $s = 4.16$), we perform a two-sided test of the hypothesis that $\sigma^2 = 34.3$, at the 10% level.

Solution: $\alpha = 0.10$ so that $\alpha/2 = 0.05$, and

$$\frac{\sigma_0^2}{n-1}\chi^2_{1-\alpha/2}(n-1) = \frac{34.3}{19}\cdot 10.12 \approx 18.27$$

$$\frac{\sigma_0^2}{n-1}\chi^2_{\alpha/2}(n-1) = \frac{34.3}{19}\cdot 30.14 \approx 54.41\,.$$

As we have $s^2 = (4.16)^2 = 17.31$, our test statistic is in the left tail rejection region, so that H_0 is rejected.

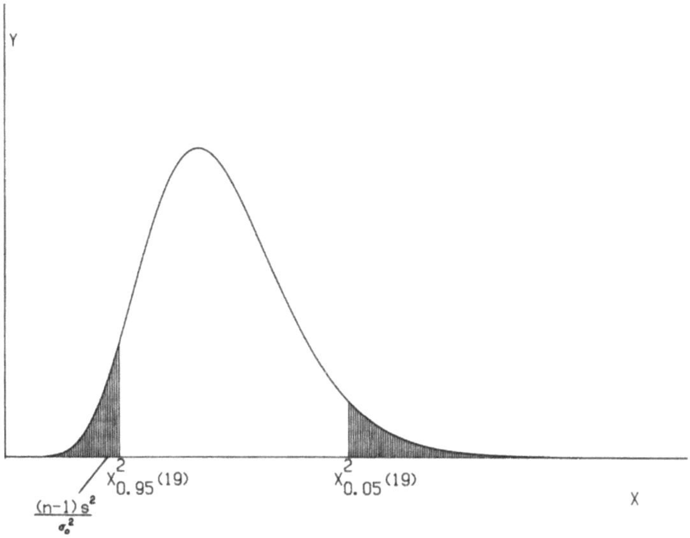

Fig. 9/7: Rejection region for the chi-square distribution of Example 9.21.

Example 9.22

As Example 9.21, but with $\alpha = 0.05$.

Solution: With $\alpha/2 = 0.025$ we find

$$\frac{\sigma_0^2}{n-1}\chi^2_{1-\alpha/2}(n-1) = \frac{34.3}{19}\cdot 8.91 \approx 16.08$$

$$\frac{\sigma_0^2}{n-1}\chi^2_{\alpha/2}(n-1) = \frac{34.3}{19}\cdot 32.85 \approx 59.30\,.$$

As $s^2 = 17.31$, our test statistic falls into neither of the rejection regions, so that the null hypothesis *cannot* be rejected at the 5% level.

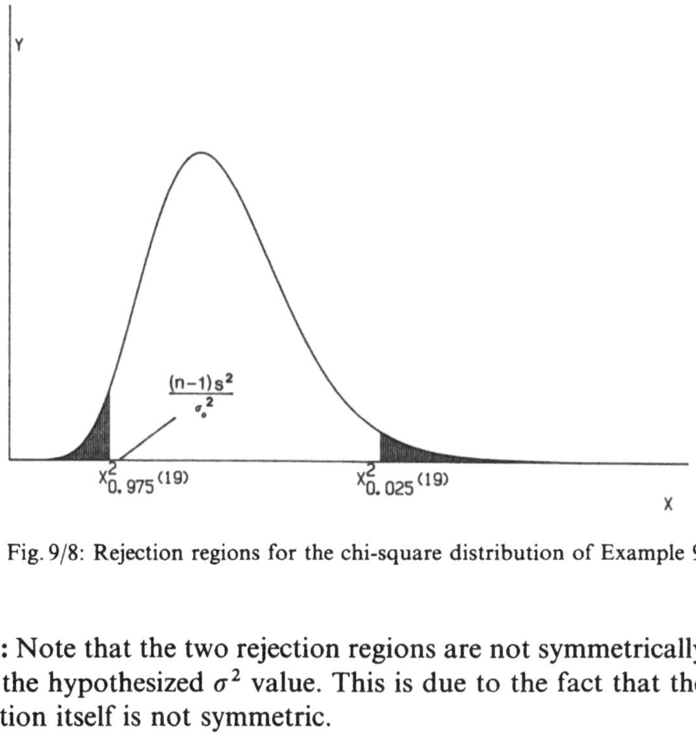

Fig. 9/8: Rejection regions for the chi-square distribution of Example 9.22.

Remark: Note that the two rejection regions are not symmetrically positioned around the hypothesized σ^2 value. This is due to the fact that the chi-square distribution itself is not symmetric.

Example 9.23

Using the data of Example 9.21, perform a lower-tail test of the hypothesis:

$$H_0:\ \sigma^2 = \sigma_0^2$$

where $\sigma_0^2 = 22.5$. Use a significance level of 1%.

Solution: The alternative hypothesis is now:

$$H_1:\ \sigma^2 < \sigma_0^2$$

so that the test is:

$$\textit{Reject}\quad H_0 \text{ if } s^2 < \frac{\sigma_0^2}{n-1}\chi^2_{1-\alpha}(n-1)$$

$$\textit{Accept}\quad H_0 \text{ if } s^2 \geqq \frac{\sigma_0^2}{n-1}\chi^2_{1-\alpha}(n-1).$$

We obtain:

$$\frac{\sigma_1^2}{n-1}\chi^2_{1-\alpha}(n-1) = \frac{22.5}{19}\cdot\chi^2_{0.99}(19) = \frac{22.5}{19}\cdot 7.63 \approx 9.04.$$

With $s^2 = (4.16)^2 = 17.31$ we have

$$s^2 \geqq \frac{\sigma_0^2}{n-1}\chi^2_{1-\alpha}(n-1)$$

so that we *cannot* reject H_0 at the 1% level.

Upper-tail tests are very similar to lower-tail tests, and we leave it to the reader to carry out the necessary modifications.

*9.8 Two-Sample Tests of Variances

We shall now extend the testing of variances from the previous section to include two populations.

Example 9.24

A company is selling a certain commodity through two retail outlets. The weekly sales at the two outlets are independent and $N(\mu_1, \sigma_1)$ and $N(\mu_2, \sigma_2)$ distributed, respectively. For inventory management purposes, one is interested to know if the two variances σ_1^2 and σ_2^2 are equal or not. Thus we test:

$$H_0:\ \frac{\sigma_1^2}{\sigma_2^2} = 1$$

against

$$H_1:\ \frac{\sigma_1^2}{\sigma_2^2} \neq 1.$$

How can we do this?

Solution: Taking sample sizes of n_1 and n_2, respectively, we know that $\frac{(n_1-1)s_1^2}{\sigma_1^2}$ is $\chi^2(n_1-1)$ distributed and that $\frac{(n_2-1)s_1^2}{\sigma_2^2}$ is $\chi^2(n_2-1)$ distributed (cf. Section 8.7). From a theorem in Section 7.4, on the ratio of independent chi-square variables, we then get:

$$\frac{\dfrac{(n_1-1)s_1^2}{\sigma_1^2}\Big/(n_1-1)}{\dfrac{(n_2-1)s^2}{\sigma_2^2}\Big/(n_2-1)} \quad \text{is} \quad F(n_1-1,\, n_2-1).$$

If H_0 is true, i.e. $\sigma_1^2 = \sigma_2^2$, then the composite variable reduces to $\frac{s_1^2}{s_2^2}$, which will be our test statistic F:

$$F = \frac{s_1^2}{s_2^2}.$$

Although the test is two-tailed, we shall arrange so that the rejection region is in the upper tail only, by simply always putting the larger of the two sample variances in the *numerator*. At level α, the test is therefore:

Reject H_0 if $F > F_{\alpha/2}(n_1-1, n_2-1)$
Accept H_0 if $F \leqq F_{\alpha/2}(n_1-1, n_2-1)$.

Example 9.25

With $n_1 = 11$, $n_2 = 8$, $s_1^2 = 2.43$ and $s_2^2 = 0.412$ we compute:

$$F = \frac{s_1^2}{s_2^2} = \frac{2.43}{0.412} \approx 5.90.$$

From an F-table we find $F_{0.05}(10, 7) = 3.64$, so that H_0 is *rejected* at 10% level of significance, and we conclude that the two variances are not equal.

We also see that $F_{0.01}(10, 7) = 6.62$, so that we *cannot* reject H_0 at the 2% level.

Example 9.26

Assume that $n_1 = 11$, $n_2 = 8$, $s_1^2 = 2.44$ and $s_2^2 = 4.91$. Arranging so that the larger sample variance is in the numerator, we find $F = \frac{4.91}{2.44} \approx 2.01$.

With $F_{0.05}(7, 10) = 3.14$ we therefore cannot reject H_0 at the 10% level. $F_{0.01}(7, 10) = 5.20$, so that we cannot reject H_0 at 2% level either.

Example 9.27

In Section 9.5, when two-sample tests of means were considered we had to assume equal variance for the two populations in the small sample case. We now see that the F test developed in this section can be used to test if the assumption of equal variances is justified.

Remark: We have only looked at two-tailed tests in this section. One-tail tests can also be considered. (See the books by Chou, by Hawkins and Weber or by Ott in the list of references at the end of this chapter).

*9.9 Paired Two-Sample Tests of Means

Example 9.28

A Swedish car company is suffering from worker absenteeism. A new health insurance plan is proposed to remedy the situation, and is tried during a month on an experimental basis at eight of the company's various divisions. The average number of monthly worker absence hours is recorded for each of the eight divisions, with the old and with the new plan. The result is summarized in Fig. 9/9.

From these data, can we conclude that the new plan reduces absenteeism?

	Monthly absence hours, per worker		
Division	Old Plan	New Plan	Difference
1	7.69	6.99	0.70
2	6.64	6.51	0.13
3	6.26	6.28	−0.02
4	8.34	7.17	1.17
5	5.56	5.34	0.22
6	7.03	6.84	0.19
7	6.77	6.81	−0.04
8	7.08	6.94	0.14
TOTAL	55.37	52.88	2.49

Fig. 9/9: Worker absenteeism with the old and the new plans

Solution: We assume that the absenteeism is $N(\mu_1, \sigma_1)$ distributed with the old plan and $N(\mu_2, \sigma_2)$ with the new. We want to test:

$$H_0: \mu_1 - \mu_2 = 0$$

against

$$H_1: \ \mu_1 - \mu_2 > 0.$$

This is a two-sample test of means, which we covered in Section 9.5. Therefore we can proceed according to familiar lines.

As the samples are small, we have to assume that $\sigma_1 = \sigma_2 = \sigma$. Then we know that with $d = \bar{X}_1 - \bar{X}_2$, the variable:

$$\frac{d - (\mu_1 - \mu_2)}{\sqrt{s_p^2\left(\frac{1}{n_1} + \frac{1}{n_2}\right)}}$$

is $t(n_1 + n_2 - 2)$ distributed, where $s_p^2 = \frac{(n_1 - 1)s_1^2 + (n_2 - 1)s_2^2}{n_1 + n_2 - 2}$ is the pooled sample variance.

For our data we obtain:

$$\sum X_{1i} = 55.37, \quad \sum X_{1i}^2 = 388.2627,$$
$$\sum X_{2i} = 52.88, \quad \sum X_{2i}^2 = 351.9284 \quad (n_1 = n_2 = 8).$$

Next, we remember the shortcut expression for the sample variance (cf. Section 3.2):

$$s_1^2 = \frac{1}{n_1 - 1}\left(\sum X_{1i}^2 - \frac{(\sum X_{1i})^2}{n_1}\right),$$

from which we obtain:

$$(n_1 - 1)s_1^2 = \sum X_{1i}^2 - \frac{(\sum X_{1i})^2}{n_1} = 388.2627 - \frac{(55.37)^2}{8} \approx 5.03309.$$

Similarly,

$$(n_2 - 1)s_2^2 = 351.9284 - \frac{(52.88)^2}{8} \approx 2.3916,$$

so that:

$$s_p^2 = \frac{(n_1 - 1)s_1^2 + (n_2 - 1)s_2^2}{n_1 + n_2 - 2} \approx \frac{5.03309 + 2.3916}{8 + 8 - 2} \approx 0.5303.$$

Our test, at level α, is:

Accept H_0 if $d \leqq d^*$
Reject H_0 if $d > d^*$.

where $d^* = t_\alpha(n_1 + n_2 - 2) \cdot \sqrt{s_p^2 \left(\frac{1}{n_1} + \frac{1}{n_2}\right)}$.

For $\alpha = 0.05$ we find:

$$d^* \approx t_{0.05}(14) \cdot \sqrt{0.5303 \left(\frac{1}{8} + \frac{1}{8}\right)} \approx 1.761 \cdot 0.3641 \approx 0.64 .$$

Our test statistic d is given by:

$$d = \bar{X}_1 - \bar{X}_2 = \frac{\sum X_{1i}}{n_1} - \frac{\sum X_{2i}}{n_2} = \frac{55.37}{8} - \frac{52.88}{8} \approx 0.31 ,$$

so that we *cannot* reject H_0. Not even at the 10% level can we reject H_0, as we would then have $d^* \approx t_{0.10}(14) \cdot 0.364 \approx 1.345 \cdot 0.3641 \approx 0.49$. In other words, using our test we have insufficient evidence to infer that the new plan reduces worker absenteeism.

On the other hand, if for each division we consider the difference in absenteeism under the old and the new plans, $X_{1i} - X_{2i} = d_i$, we find that this is $\frac{2.49}{8} = 0.31125$, on the average. This suggests that the new plan is better than the old. The reason why our t-test above (without pairing the observations in the samples) could not detect this difference is that the variation *within* each of the two samples is sizeable ($s_p^2 = 0.5303$, so that $s_p \approx 0.73$) compared to the difference *between* the two sample means (0.31).

Therefore we take another approach (*paired samples*):

Assuming that $X_{1i} - X_{2i}$ are independent, $i = 1, \ldots, n$, then $\bar{d} = \frac{1}{n} \sum_{i=1}^{n} (X_{1i} - X_{2i})$ is approximately $N\left(\mu_1 - \mu_2, \frac{\sigma}{\sqrt{n}}\right)$ distributed, where σ^2 is estimated by $s_d^2 = \frac{1}{n-1} \sum_{i=1}^{n} (d_i - \bar{d})^2$.

Our test for paired samples is then:

Accept H_0 if $\bar{d} \leq \bar{d}^*$
Reject H_0 if $\bar{d} > d^*$

where d^* is given by:

$$\bar{d}^* = t_\alpha(n-1) \cdot \frac{s_d}{\sqrt{n}} .$$

For the data in our example, we find:

$$\sum d_i = 2.49, \quad \sum d_i^2 = 1.9819,$$

so that:

$$s_d^2 = \frac{1}{n-1}\left(\sum d_i^2 - \frac{(\sum d_i)^2}{n}\right) = \frac{1}{7}\left(1.9819 - \frac{(2.49)^2}{8}\right) \approx 0.1724,$$

from which we get:

$$\bar{d}^* \approx t_{0.05}(7) \cdot \frac{\sqrt{0.1724}}{\sqrt{8}} \approx 1.895 \cdot 0.1468 \approx 0.28\,.$$

With $\bar{d} = 0.31$ and $\bar{d}^* = 0.28$, we find that $\bar{d} > \bar{d}^*$, so that H_0 is *rejected* at the 5% level.

For $\alpha = 0.025$ we get

$$\bar{d}^* \approx t_{0.025}(7) \cdot 0.1468 = 2.365 \cdot 0.1468 \approx 0.35$$

so that we *cannot* reject H_0 at the 2.5% level of significance.

Remark: The above example shows us that the same set of data can lead us to different conclusions, depending on the test design adopted. With the assumption of a paired design, we managed to construct a test with more discriminatory power. This was not possible without the paired design assumption.

Lowel-tail and two-tailed tests using the paired difference design are straightforward, and we shall instead turn to confidence intervals.

Example 9.29

Using the same data as in our absenteeism example, compute:

a) a 95% confidence interval
b) a 99% confidence interval
c) a 90% confidence interval

for the difference in absence hours.

Solution: The confidence interval is

$$\left(\bar{d} - t_{\alpha/2}(n-1) \cdot \frac{s_d}{\sqrt{n}}, \quad \bar{d} + t_{\alpha/2}(n-1) \cdot \frac{s_d}{\sqrt{n}}\right),$$

making use of the paired design assumption. Now we get:

a) $\alpha = 0.05$ so that:

$$t_{\alpha/2}(n-1)\cdot\frac{s_d}{\sqrt{n}} \approx t_{0.025}(7)\cdot 0.1468 \approx 0.35\,.$$

The interval is:

$$(0.31 - 0.35,\ 0.31 + 0.35) = (-0.04,\ 0.66).$$

b) $\alpha = 0.01$ so that:

$$t_{\alpha/2}(n-1)\cdot\frac{s_d}{\sqrt{n}} \approx t_{0.005}(7)\cdot 0.1468 \approx 3.499\cdot 0.1468 \approx 0.51$$

and the interval is:

$$(0.31 - 0.51,\ 0.31 + 0.51) = (-0.20,\ 0.82)\,.$$

c) $\alpha = 0.10$ so that:

$$t_{\alpha/2}(n-1)\cdot\frac{s_d}{\bar{n}} \approx t_{0.05}(7)\cdot 0.1468 \approx 0.28$$

and the interval is:

$$(0.31 - 0.28,\ 0.31 + 0.28) = (0.03,\ 0.59)\,.$$

References

Chou, Y.: *Statistical Analysis,* 2nd edition. Holt, Rinehart and Winston, New York 1975.

Hamburg, M.: *Statistical Analysis for Decision Making,* 2nd edition. Harcourt, Brace, Jovanovich, New York 1977.

Harnett, D. L.: *Statistical Methods,* 3rd edition. Addison-Wesley, Reading, Mass. 1982.

Hawkins, C. A., and J. E. Weber: *Statistical Analysis. Applications to Business and Economics*. Harper & Row, New York 1980.

Lapin, L. L.: *Statistics for Modern Business Decisions,* 3rd edition. Harcourt, Brace, Jovanovich, New York 1982.

Mansfield, E.: *Statistics for Business and Economics,* Norton & Company, New York 1980.

Ott, L.: *An Introduction to Statistical Methods and Data Analysis,* Duxbury Press, North Scituate, Mass. 1977.

Wonnacott, T. H. and R. J. Wonnacott: *Introductory Statistics for Business and Economics,* 2nd edition. John Wiley & Sons, New York 1977.

Exercises

9–1 From a population which is normally distributed with unknown mean and standard deviation 0.72 a sample of size 17 is taken. Using a significance level of 5%:

a) construct a lower-tail test of the hypothesis that $\mu = 2.56$.

b) construct a two-sided test of the hypothesis that $\mu = 2.49$.
c) construct an upper-tail test of the hypothesis that $\mu = 2.52$.

9–2 A sample of size $n = 12$ is taken from a $N(\mu, 32.5)$ distributed population.

a) If the sample mean $\bar{X}$ is 88.3, what can we conclude using a two-sided test of the hypothesis $\mu = 85.0$ at 5% level of significance?
b) With $\bar{X} = 75.9$ and $\alpha = 0.02$, use a lower-tail test of the hypothesis $\mu = 72.6$.
c) With $\bar{X} = 83.0$ perform an upper-tail test of the hypothesis $\mu = 83.0$ using a significance level of 1%.

9–3 A company buying a certain type of industrial diesel engine believes that its output is $N(\mu, 1.5)$ kW. Measuring the output from 39 engines gave a sample mean output of 31.2 kW.

a) Perform a test of the hypothesis $\mu = 30.0$ against the alternative hypothesis $\mu = 32.0$. Use $\alpha = 0.05$.
b) Calculate the probability of a Type II error.
c) What would the sample size have to be, at least, in order for β not to exceed 10%?

9–4 A shipment of oranges comes from either Sicily or Lebanon; it is unknown which. The weight, in grams, of each orange is $N(95, 8)$ for Sicilian and $N(104, 8)$ for Lebanese oranges.

a) Formulate a decision rule for testing the hypothesis: "The oranges come from Sicily" at 1% level, with a sample size of 15 oranges.
b) What is the probability of a Type II error?
c) From the sample, $\bar{X} = 100.2$ was obtained. What is the conclusion?

9–5 Consider a random sample which consists of the following measurements of compressive strength (in PSI) of a certain item

41, 44, 69, 70, 80.

At a 5% level of significance test the appropriate hypothesis that the above sample comes from a population with a mean of 65 PSI.

9–6 Test the hypothesis that the average length of local telephone calls made in a certain community is 4 minutes, if a random sample of 100 such calls had a mean of 3.4 minutes and a standard deviation of 2.8 minutes. Use a level of significance of $\alpha = 0.05$.

9–7 The Golf Ball Manufacturing Company wishes to produce golf balls that are no less than 1.7 inches in diameter. A sample of 64 balls is randomly selected ($\bar{X} = 1.68$ inches; $s = 0.12$ inches). With a critical probability of 1%, do the golf balls meet the company's standards?

9–8 A random sample of electronic pagers used by on-site foremen of a large construction company showed an average life of 1.26 years, with a standard deviation of 0.41 years. Under ordinary conditions, these pagers are known to have an average life of 1.39 years. $\alpha = 0.05$. Test the null hypothesis that the pagers lasted 1.39 years.

9–9 In a sample of 25 light bulbs, it is found that the mean service life is 1,580 hours, and that the sample variance is 14,400 hours. Test the hypothesis that the mean life is 1,600 hours against the alternative that it is not with α specified at 0.01.

9–10 A manufacturer of wire claims that the mean breaking strength of a competitor's 30 pound wire is really less than 30 pounds. A sample of 50 pieces of the competitor's 30-pound wire has been drawn and each tested. The following results were obtained:

$\bar{x} = 28$ pounds $s = .9$ pounds.

Does the evidence support the manufacturer's claim at the .05 level of significance that the mean breaking strength of the competitor's wire is less than 30 pounds?

9–11 A union claims that its workers take an average of 13 minutes for coffee. The management of a company wishes to challenge this claim, maintaining that coffee breaks are longer. A sample of 400 coffee breaks shows an average time of 14 minutes with a standard deviation of 10 minutes. Should the management challenge the union, if it is willing to take a 5% chance of incurring a strike by rejecting a truthful claim?

9–12 At a corporation, merit increases are awarded by the division directors, at an average of $200. The personnel manager suspects that a certain division director is too generous in awarding merit increases, and takes a random sample of 17 employees from this division. She finds a mean increase of $215.75 with a standard deviation of $19.81. If the increases are independent and normally distributed, is there enough evidence to support the personnel manager's suspicion? Test this at $\alpha = 0.05$.

9–13 A manufacturer of batteries wishes to be reasonably sure that less than 5% of its batteries are defective. 300 batteries are selected at random from a large lot and tested individually. 10 are found to be defective. By using $\alpha = .01$ decide whether the manufacturer has sufficient evidence to conclude that the percentage of defectives in the entire lot is less than 5%.

9–14 In Boston in 1968, Dr. Benjamin Spock was tried for conspiracy to violate the Selective Service Act. About 29% of the people eligible for jury duty were women, but of the 700 people the judge had selected in his previous few trials, only 15% were women. How would you rate the judge's fairness?

9–15 The government is interested in selecting one of two fuel suppliers for missile fuel. The two suppliers are identical in all respects. Therefore, to choose between the two, the government decided to sample 100 gallons of fuel from each supplier to determine the average time a gallon of each brand of fuel lasted. It was found that Supplier A's fuel lasted 960 minutes, with a standard deviation of 92 minutes, while Supplier B's fuel lasted 900 minutes with a standard deviation of 90 minutes.

a) Calculate a 90% confidence interval for the difference between the mean times of the two suppliers.
b) Is there a significant difference between the two suppliers? Assume that we wish to reject a true null hypothesis no more than 5% of the time.
c) Which supplier do you think the government should use?

9–16 Two machines produce identical bolts. The lengths on the bolts produced by the two machines are believed to be normally distributed and to have the same variance. It is now suspected that the average length of bolts produced by machine one is longer than those produced by the other. Two independent samples are taken and the relevant sample data are shown below. Perform an appropriate test.

$n_1 = 80$	$n_2 = 100$	$\alpha = 0.01$
$\bar{X}_1 = 2.6$	$\bar{X}_2 = 2.5$	
$s_1^2 = .55$	$s_2^2 = .046$.	

9–17 Of 50 male professors, randomly selected, the average annual salary (rounded to the nearest thousand) was $28,000, with a standard deviation of $2,000. The average annual salary of 30 female professors was $22,000 with a standard deviation of $1,000. Calculate a 90% confidence interval estimate for the difference in the population average of salaries of all male and female professors.

9–18 A manufacturer claims that the nylon cord his company produces is stronger than cotton cord. We are given the following information:

	Nylon Cord	Cotton Cord
Sample size	$n_1 = 10$	$n_2 = 8$
Average breaking strength	$\bar{X}_1 = 105$	$\bar{X}_2 = 101$
Variance	$s_1^2 = 74$	$s_2^2 = 70$

Can we conclude that nylon cord is indeed stronger than the cotton one at $\alpha = 1\%$?

9–19 A legislator is concerned about the difference between the salaries paid to male and female employees who do the same work. Assuming that executive salaries for both males and females have a nearly normal distribution with roughly the same standard deviation, he collected random samples from each group:

Salaries	n	$\bar{X}$	s^2
Male	10	48.2	10.20
Female	12	45.6	8.02

(thousands of dollars)

Find the appropriate 95% confidence interval and interpret its meaning for the legislator.

9–20 A nutritionist wishes to compare the effectiveness of two weight reducing diets. The following data are obtained from two independent samples:

	Diet 1	Diet 2
Sample size	$n_1 = 15$	$n_2 = 10$
Average weight loss	$\bar{X}_1 = 9$	$\bar{X}_2 = 11$
Sample variance	$s_1^2 = 20$	$s_2^2 = 30$

a) Find a 90% confidence interval for the difference between Diets 1 and 2.
b) At $\alpha = 10\%$ is there sufficient evidence that Diet 1 produces a smaller weight loss than Diet 2?
c) In view of (a) and (b), what are your conclusions?

9–21 A consumer research organization is interested in estimating the difference between the mean life (usable mileage) of two brands of 40,000 mile steelbelted radial tires. For this purpose, the organization collected information pertaining to the two brands and the results are recorded below:

	n	$\bar{X}$	s
Brand I	10	38.2	6.3
Brand II	12	35.6	7.4
		(thousands of miles)	

Find the 98% confidence interval estimate for the difference between the population parameters μ_1 and μ_2.

9–22 A bio-rythm fanatic claims that his advice on when to take days off will reduce the number of accidents or close calls while on the job. A sample of eight bus drivers were asked to accept the fanatic's advice, which would not change their total hours on the job. The number of accidents or close calls was then recorded. Later, the comparable figures for the preceding period were looked up in the files:

Employee No.	Accidents or Close Calls During Preceding Year	Accidents or Close Calls During Bio-Rythm Year
1	3	1
2	3	3
3	3	2
4	2	1
5	1	2
6	3	1
7	2	1
8	4	3

a) Calculate the 90% confidence interval estimate for the difference between the population means.
b) Do the results convince you, one way or the other? Explain why or why not.

9–23 Participative management is a managerial practice that encourages employees to participate in the decision-making process of an organization, whereas autocratic management does not. Two companies, one of which practices participative management and the other autocratic management are compared in terms of employees' attitudes toward their respective employers. An attitude survey was conducted and the following results were obtained: 65 of the 100 employees selected from Company A, which practices participative management were satisfied with their employer, whereas 45 of the 100 employees selected from Company B, which practices autocratic management were satisfied with their employer.

a) Is there sufficient evidence to conclude at a significance level of 5% that the employees are equally satisfied, against the alternative hypothesis that they are not?
b) Find a 95% confidence interval for the difference between the two population proportions.
c) What conclusions can be made in view of (a) and (b)?

9–24 From a normally distributed population, a sample of size $n = 25$ is taken. With a sample variance $s^2 = 44.4$ perform

a) a lower-tail test of H_0: $\sigma^2 = 46.0$ at the 1% level;
b) a lower-tail test of H_0: $\sigma^2 = 41.9$ at the 5% level;
c) an upper tail test of H_0: $\sigma^2 = 45.0$ at the 5% level.

9–25 A certain statistical study involves testing the difference between the means of two populations. A random sample from one of the populations has 17 observations and a variance of 23.7. A random sample from the other population has 24 observations and a variance of 6.9. As both samples are small, we have to assume equal population variances for the test described in Section 9.5. At the 2% level of significance, is this assumption justified?

9–26 To evaluate the impact of unionization in a depressed industry, two industrial relations students compared wages in a unionized factory with those in an identical non-unionized factory. A random selection of workers was polled. On the basis of the following results, the students concluded that unionized wages were significantly higher.

	Union Factory	Non-Union Factory
	\$4.10	\$3.50
	3.80	3.10
	2.00	1.40
	3.40	2.80
	3.20	2.60
	2.40	1.80
	2.80	2.30
Means	3.10	2.50
Variances	$.56\bar{3}$	$.53\bar{3}$

a) Can this statement be made correctly at a significance level of $\alpha = .05$ if a paired difference design is used?
b) What would the conclusion be if a paired difference design is not justifiable?

9–27 Eight persons are selected at random and tested to see how long it takes to associate a particular product with an advertising layout. They are exposed to two different layouts and tested after each. Time to recognition is measured in seconds. The results were as follows:

Person	Recognition Time Layout 1	Recognition Time Layout 2
1	3	4
2	1	2
3	1	3
4	2	1
5	1	2
6	2	3
7	3	3
8	1	3

a) Construct a 90% confidence interval estimate for the difference in recognition times.
b) Give an interpretation of the results indicated by the confidence interval. Do you think the difference is substantial? Explain why or why not.

9–28 Prof. Pushover and Prof. Stickler teach two sections of the same management course, and students in their sections do exactly the same term project. Reacting to complaints that Prof. Pushover marks more generously than Prof. Stickler, the two professors have decided to compare the grades they award for term projects. A sample of 8 projects is selected and evaluated by both of them. The following results occur:

Project Author	Pushover's Grade	Stickler's Grade
H. Adams	78	71
G. Boyle	67	61
F. Choquette	75	69
E. Deer	65	57
D. Ewert	81	74
C. Flynn	63	58
B. Glenn	77	73
A. Hephurn	70	65
Mean	72	66
Standard Deviation	6.65	6.74

a) Is there sufficient evidence to be 95% confident that Prof. Pushover is more generous than Prof. Stickler?
b) Construct a 90% confidence interval for the difference in grades.
c) Is there sufficient evidence that the marks for the two sets of grades have different variances?

9–29 An MBA student sends questionnaires to a random sample of 200 companies. Only 48 of these companies respond. The student requires at least 100 responses to have a valid data base for his project, so he sends out questionnaires to an additional 150 randomly selected companies. This time, however, he encloses self-addressed envelopes for responses. Fifty-four companies respond to this second batch of questionnaires. Can he conclude with 95% confidence that the self-addressed envelopes have significantly helped his response rate?

9–30 A government office has access to ten typists. Half of these have new typewriters, the others do not. All of the typists are given similar reports to type. The resulting typing times are given below:

Old Machines	New Machines
90 min.	75 min.
86 min.	71 min.
93 min.	79 min.
91 min.	77 min.
85 min.	73 min.

a) Is there sufficient evidence to be 95% confident that the new machines produce more quickly?
b) Is there sufficient evidence to refute (with 95% confidence) the assumption of equal variance which we need in order to pool variance?

10. Chi-Square Tests and Nonparametric Techniques

In Section 6.6 we introduced the chi-square distribution and in Section 7.4 we presented some results relating it to the normal, t and F distributions. Then we used it for constructing interval estimates of the variance, in Section 8.7. We also employed it for hypothesis testing of the variance, in Sections 9.8 and 9.9. In this chapter we shall show a few other applications of the chi-square distribution, testing for independence of two or more separate random variables in Section 10.1, for the equality of several proportions in Section 10.2, and for goodness of fit in Section 10.3.

The testing for independence which we shall be dealing with in Section 10.1 does not involve any distribution parameter μ, σ etc. We say that it is a *nonparametric* test. Also, as it does not involve any assumption about the underlying distribution (normal, t, etc.) we say that it is a *distribution free* test. We shall present nonparametric tests of central tendency in Section 10.4, of randomness in Section 10.5, and of correlation in Section 10.6.

Although strictly speaking nonparametric and distribution free tests are not the same, the term "nonparametric methods" usually refers to both types of tests. There are many nonparametric tests available; most of the (parametric) tests discussed in Chapter 9 have a nonparametric counterpart. As a nonparametric test generally is easier to perform and requires less computational effort than its parametric analogue, we may ask why we use parametric tests at all. The answer is that a nonparametric test is usually less powerful (efficient) than its parametric counterpart. A nonparametric test is therefore preferred when computational and/or procedural simplicity is important. Besides, nonparametric tests have also been developed for qualitative data (i.e. when observations are only given on an ordinal or nominal scale).

On the other hand, some tests that assume, say, normality about the underlying distribution may still perform quite well, even if the assumption is violated. Such a test is said to be *robust* against violation of this assumption. The analysis of variance test, which we shall deal with in Chapter 11, is an example of a robust parametric test.

10.1 Testing for Independence

Example 10.1

The eye colour and hair colour of 100 randomly selected people are recorded. The number of persons belonging to each category, i. e. the actual frequencies, are shown in Fig. 10/1.

eyes \ hair	fair	dark	
blue	36	21	57
brown	16	27	43
	52	48	100

Fig. 10/1: Actual frequency table for Example 10.1.

Such a table, in which the number of observations are entered according to two different classifications, is called a *contingency table*.

Judging from these figures, would we say that the eye colour and the hair colour of a person are statistically dependent or not?

Solution: If the two attributes were independent, we would expect to find about $\frac{52}{100} \times \frac{43}{100} \times 100 = 22.36$ fair-haired, brown-eyed people in our sample. In other words, 22.36 is the *expected* frequency, assuming independence. Computing all the expected frequencies we obtain the following *expected frequency table:*

eyes \ hair	fair	dark	
blue	29.64	27.36	57.00
brown	22.36	20.64	43.00
	52.00	48.00	100.00

Fig. 10/2: Expected frequency table for Example 10.1.

The discrepancies between the actual frequencies, f_a (*a* for *a*ctual), and the expected frequencies, f_e (*e* for *e*xpected), are used to form a test statistic:

$$\chi^2 = \sum \frac{(f_a - f_e)^2}{f_e}.$$

If the value of this expression is large, there must be at least one considerable discrepancy between an actual and expected frequency (the division by f_e is only to "scale" the different expressions in the sum to make them comparable). This is an indication that there *is* some dependence between the two classifications. We can now be more precise.

One can show that if the following null hypothesis is true:

H_0: The classifications are independent,

then the above sum has a chi-square distribution (approximately), with the number of degrees of freedom determined by:

$$(\text{No. of rows} - 1) \times (\text{No. of columns} - 1).$$

In our case we obtain:

$$(2-1) \times (2-1) = 1 \text{ degree of freedom.}$$

The test statistic becomes:

$$\chi^2 = \sum \frac{(f_a - f_e)^2}{f_e} = \frac{(36 - 29.64)^2}{29.64} + \frac{21 - 27.36)^2}{27.36}$$
$$+ \frac{(16 - 22.36)^2}{22.36} + \frac{(27 - 20.64)^2}{20.64} \approx 1.3647 + 1.4784$$
$$+ 1.8090 + 1.9598 \approx 6.61.$$

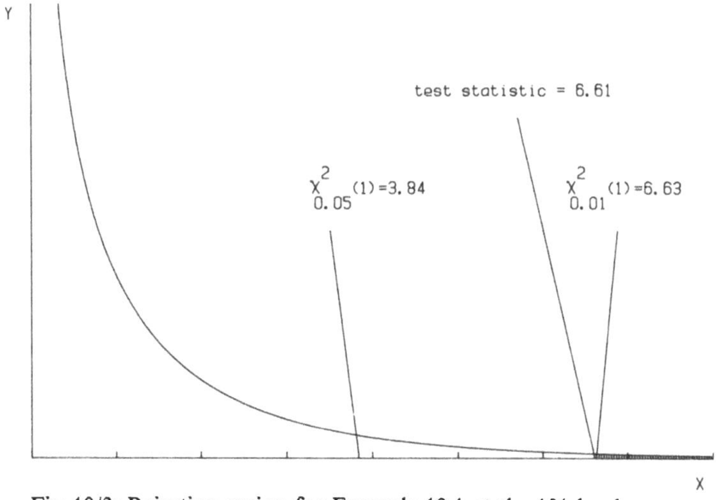

Fig. 10/3: Rejection region for Example 10.1 at the 1% level.

Clearly, this must be an upper-tail test, so that we reject the null hypothesis if the test statistic falls in the right tail of the distribution.

From a chi-square table we find $\chi^2_{0.05}(1) = 3.84$, $\chi^2_{0.01}(1) = 6.63$. As the value of our test statistic, 6.61, exceeds the value of $\chi^2_{0.05}(1)$, we conclude that the null hypothesis (about independence) can be *rejected* at the 5% level. On the other hand, $6.61 < 6.63 = \chi^2_{0.01}(1)$, and we *cannot* reject the null hypothesis at the 1% level.

Remark: In our test above the expected frequencies need not be integer as the actual frequencies do. An attempt to correct for the error which this introduces is done by continuity correction (similar to what we did in Section 6.4 when the binomial distribution was approximated by the normal). Using this correction (also referred to as *Yates correction*) the test statistic is:

$$\chi^2 = \sum \frac{(|f_a - f_e| - 0.5)^2}{f_e} .$$

The correction is particularly beneficial when the number of degrees of freedom is low. We shall not go into any details.

10.2 Testing for Equality of Several Proportions

Example 10.2

(Capital punishment supporters). Three cities, A, B and C are considered, and a sample of 300 people yields the contingency table in Fig. 10/4.

answer \ city	A	B	C	
"yes"	12	15	6	33
"no"	88	105	74	267
	100	120	80	300

Fig. 10/4: Actual frequencies for Example 10.2

Let us now test the hypothesis:

$$H_0: \; p_A = p_B = p_C$$

where p_A is the proportion of "yes"-answers in city A, etc.

How could this be done?

Solution: If H_0 is true, then in our sample there should be e.g. about $\frac{33}{300} \times 100$ "yes" in A and about $\frac{267}{300} \times 80$ "no" in C. These are the expected frequencies which are computed in the table below.

answer \ city	A	B	C	
"yes"	11.0	13.2	8.8	33.0
"no"	89.0	106.8	71.2	267.0
	100.0	120.0	80.0	300.0

Fig. 10/5: Expected frequencies for Example 10.2.

The discrepancy between the *expected* frequencies, f_e and the corresponding *actual* frequencies, f_a is used to form a test statistic

$$\chi^2 = \sum \frac{(f_a - f_e)^2}{f_e}.$$

As in the previous section we can perform a χ^2-test by measuring the discrepancy between actual and expected frequencies:

$$\chi^2 = \sum \frac{(f_a - f_e)^2}{f_e} = \frac{(12 - 11.0)^2}{11.0} + \frac{(15 - 13.2)^2}{13.2} + \frac{(6 - 8.8)^2}{8.8} + \frac{(88 - 89.0)^2}{89.0} + \frac{(105 - 106.8)^2}{106.8} + \frac{(74 - 71.2)^2}{71.2} \approx 1.38.$$

The number of degrees of freedom is:

(No. of rows -1) $\times$ (No. of columns -1) $= (2 - 1) \times (3 - 1) = 2$.

A test at the level α should obviously be:

Reject H_0 if $\chi^2 > \chi^2_\alpha(2)$.

We find $\chi^2_{0.05}(2) = 5.99$ so that we *cannot* reject H_0 at the 5% level. In fact, $\chi^2_{0.10}(2) = 4.61$ and we therefore can not reject H_0 even at the 10% level.

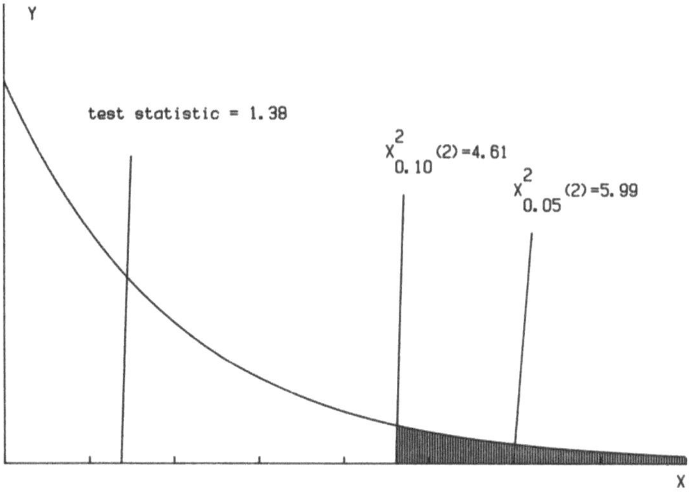

Fig. 10/6: Rejection region for Example 10.2 at the 10% level.

Example 10.3

With H_0: $p_A = p_B = p_C = 1/4$
we should get the following expected frequencies

answer \ city	A	B	C	
"yes"	25.0	30.0	20.0	75.0
"no"	75.0	90.0	60.0	225.0
	100.0	120.0	80.0	330.0

Fig. 10/7: Expected frequencies for Example 10.3

and

$$\chi^2 = \frac{(12-25.0)^2}{25.0} + \frac{(15-30.0)^2}{30.0} + \frac{(6-20.0)^2}{20.0} + \frac{(88-75.0)^2}{75.0} + \frac{(105-90.0)^2}{90.0} + \frac{(74-60.0)^2}{60.0} = 32.08.$$

With $\chi^2_{0.005}(2) = 10.60$ we see that we can reject our null hypothesis at the 0.5% level.

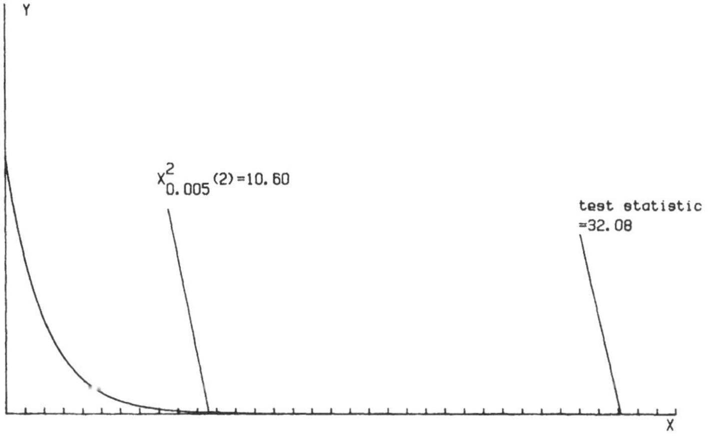

Fig. 10/8: Rejection region for Example 10.3 at the 0.5% level.

Remark 1: Example 10.2 can be interpreted as testing for independence between capital punishment opinion and city homestead of a person. Conversely, Example 10.1 can be interpreted as testing for equality of the proportions of blue eyed persons among dark and fair-haired people.

Remark 2: For the chi-square tests of this and the previous section the expected frequencies should always be at least 5 (otherwise the chi-square approximation of the test statistic might be poor). If this is not the case, the problem can be modified by aggregating columns and/or rows so that the criterion is satisfied. We leave out the details here (but see Example 10.5).

Remark 3: In a slightly different situation we consider proportions within one sample resulting from just one classification scheme. We illustrate this by an example.

Example 10.4

Suppose that a newspaper maintains that the political party situation in Canada is:

Liberal: 44%, Progressive Conservative 34%,
National Democratic Party: 20%, Other: 2%.

A random sample of 1829 voters gave the following:

Liberal: 878 (48%), P.C.: 512 (28%),
NDP: 421 (23%), Other: 18 (1%).

Can we conclude that the newspaper is wrong?

Solution: We have:

$$H_0:\quad p_1 = 0.44,\ p_2 = 0.34,\ p_3 = 0.20,\ p_4 = 0.02\,.$$

With n_i, $i = 1, 2, 3, 4$ being the actual frequencies (f_a) ($\sum n_i = n = 1829$), the expected frequencies (f_e) are $E(n_i) = np_i = 1829\,p_i$. Computing these, we obtain the table in Fig. 10/9 below.

Party	i	Actual frequency, n_i	Expected frequency, $E(n_i)$
Liberal	1	878	804.76
PC	2	512	621.86
NDP	3	421	365.80
Other	4	18	36.58
Total:		1829	1829.00

Fig. 10/9: Actual and expected frequencies for Example 10.3.

Now,

$$\chi^2 = \frac{(878-804.76)^2}{804.76} + \frac{(512-621.86)^2}{621.86} + \frac{(421-365.80)^2}{365.80} + \frac{(18-36.58)^2}{36.58} \approx 43.84\,.$$

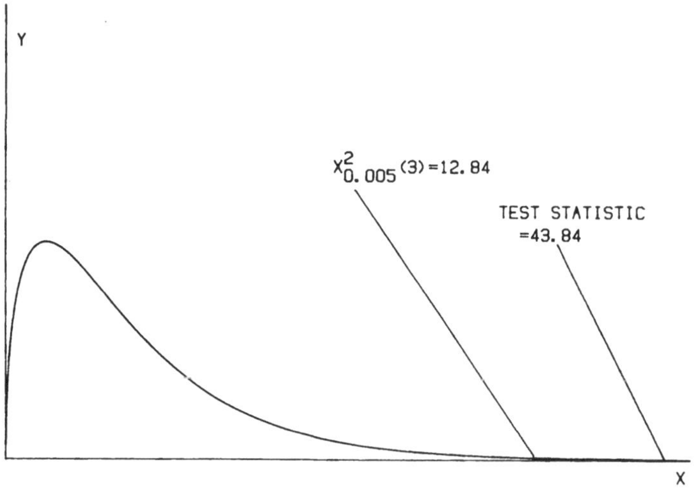

Fig. 10/10: Rejection region for Example 10.4 at the 0.5% level.

One can show that χ^2 is $\chi^2(3)$ if H_0 is true, and we *reject* H_0 if $\chi^2 > \chi^2_\alpha(3)$.

$\chi^2_{0.005}(3) = 12.84$ so that we can *reject* at the 1/2% level the hypothesis that the newspaper is correct.

In general, for r political parties, the test statistic would be $\chi^2(r-1)$ distributed, if the null hypothesis were true.

Remark 4: In our last example we were implicitly dealing with the *multinomial* distribution (a generalization of the binomial): If there are k possible outcomes of an experiment, with probabilities $p_1, p_2, \ldots, p_k$ $\left(\text{i.e. } \sum_{j=1}^{k} p_j = 1\right)$ and if $X_1, X_2, \ldots, X_k$ denote the number of times out of n $\left(\text{i.e. } \sum_{i=1}^{k} X_i = n\right)$ that each respective outcome occurs, then

$$P(X_1 = n_1, X_2 = n_2, \ldots, X_k = n_k) = \frac{n!}{n_1!\, n_2! \ldots, n_k!} \cdot p_1^{n_1} \cdot p_2^{n_2} \ldots p_k^{n_k}.$$

10.3 Testing for Goodness of Fit

Another application of the chi-square test is to assess whether a set of obtained observations conforms to a given theoretical distribution.

Example 10.5

In a large factory, the number of accidents each day have been recorded over a period covering 130 working days, as follows:

No. of accidents in a day	No. of days
0	69
1	42
2	15
3	4
$\geqq 4$	0
Total:	130

Fig. 10/11: Data for Example 10.5.

Perform a chi-square test to see if the number of accidents per day is Poisson-distributed with mean 0.9.

Solution: Given that the null hypothesis is true, we can compute the expected frequencies and compare them with the actual frequencies, in the usual way. The expected frequencies are of course obtained as follows: P(x), the probability of x accidents in a day, is found from a Poisson table (or calculated from $e^{-0.9} \cdot \frac{(0.9)^x}{x!}$). Then this probability is multiplied by 130, the total number of days: 130P(x). We organize the results in a table:

x, No. of accidents in a day	P(x), probability of x accidents in a day	130P(x), expected No. of days with x accidents in a day
0	0.4066	52.9
1	0.3659	47.6
2	0.1647	21.4
3	0.0494	6.4
≧ 4	0.0134	1.7
	1.0000	130.0

Fig. 10/12: Computing expected frequencies for Example 10.5.

The actual and expected frequencies can now be summarized as follows:

No. of accidents	Actual frequency, f_a		Expected frequency, f_e	
0	69		52.9	
1	42		47.6	
2	15		21.4	
3	4	4	6.4	8.1
≧ 4	0		1.7	
Total:	130		130.0	

Fig. 10/13: Actual and expected frequencies for Example 10.5.

Remembering that all expected frequencies must be at least 5, the last two groups have been combined into a new group with an expected frequency of 8.1. We have now four groups, so that the test statistic

$$\chi^2 = \sum \frac{(f_a - f_e)^2}{f_e}$$

will be approximately chi-square distributed with three degrees of freedom, provided that the following null hypothesis H_0 is true:

H_0: the sample comes from a $P(0.9)$ distribution.

The number of degrees of freedom is:

$$(\text{no. of groups } -1) = 4 - 1 = 3\,.$$

Numerically, we find

$$\chi^2 = \sum \frac{(f_a - f_e)^2}{f_e} = \frac{(69 - 52.9)^2}{52.9} + \frac{(42 - 47.6)^2}{47.6} + \frac{(15 - 21.4)^2}{21.4} + \frac{(4 - 8.1)^2}{8.1} \approx 9.55\,.$$

With $\chi^2_{0.05}(3) = 7.81$, $\chi^2_{0.01}(3) = 11.34$ we find that the null hypothesis can be rejected at the 5% level but not at the 1% level.

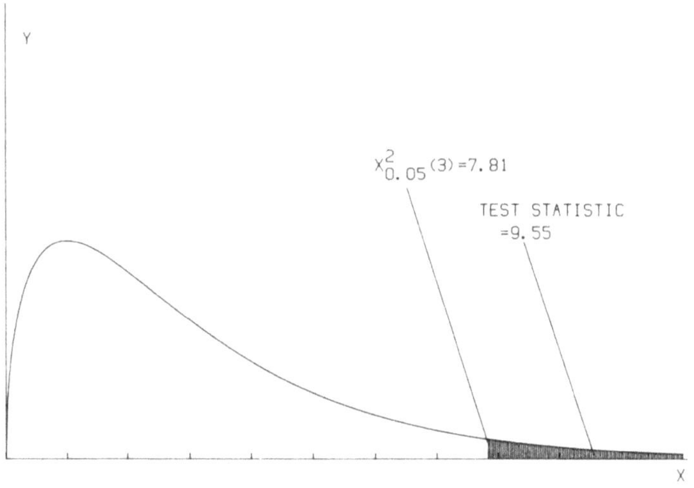

Fig. 10/14: Rejection region for Example 10.5 at the 5% level.

Example 10.6

In Example 10.5 we concluded, at the 5% level, that the sample does *not* come from a $P(0.9)$ distribution. But maybe it comes from a Poisson distribution with a parameter other than $\lambda = 0.9$? We could repeat the test with various values of the parameter λ. Another approach is to *estimate* λ from the available data. The null hypothesis is then:

H_0: the sample comes from a Poisson distribution.

Assuming that this null hypothesis is true, we can than estimate λ as the average number of accidents per day. The total number of accidents is:

$$0 \times 69 + 1 \times 42 + 2 \times 15 + 3 \times 4 + 4 \times 0 = 84$$

and as the total number of days is 130 we find the following estimate of λ:

$$\frac{84}{130} \approx 0.646 .$$

The probabilities $P(x)$ would therefore be:

$$e^{-\lambda} \cdot \frac{\lambda^x}{x!} \approx e^{-0.646} \cdot \frac{(0.646)^x}{x!} \approx 0.5241 \cdot \frac{(0.646)^x}{x!}$$

and the expected frequencies $130P(x)$:

x	P(x)	130P(x)	
0	0.5239	68.1	
1	0.3384	44.0	
2	0.1093	14.2	
3	0.0236	3.1	} 17.8
≧4	0.0038	0.5	
Total:	0.9990	129.9	

Fig. 10/15: Expected frequencies for Example 10.6.

Three groups have now to be combined to ensure that all expected frequencies are at least 5. We obtain the test statistic χ^2:

$$\chi^2 = \sum \frac{(f_a - f_e)^2}{f_e} = \frac{(69 - 68.1)^2}{68.1} + \frac{(42 - 44.0)^2}{44.0} + \frac{(19 - 17.8)^2}{17.8} \approx 0.18 .$$

This value of the test statistic is quite low (in favour of H_0) and should be compared with the value 9.55 which we obtained in Example 10.5 using the *same data*. The reason for this difference is that we have now used the data to estimate λ and have consequently been able to produce a better fit. This is reflected in the number of degrees of freedom, which now is obtained as follows:

(no. of groups – no. of estimated parameters -1)
$= 3 - 1 - 1 = 1$.

As $\chi^2_{0.10}(1) = 2.71$ we can now *not* reject the null hypothesis even at the 10% level. In fact, the low test statistic value of 0.18 strongly indicates that the null hypothesis is correct. Summarizing, the data seems to indicate that the sample comes froms a Poisson distribution with a mean of about 0.646.

Other distributions

In a similar way, we can perform chi-square goodness of fit tests for the binomial distribution, the uniform distribution, the normal distribution etc., but we leave out the details here. Let us just remark that when continuous distributions are being tested for goodness of fit, it is preferable to work with *cumulative* actual and expected frequencies. This reduces the impact of round-off errors; the problem with expected frequencies smaller than 5 is also alleviated.

10.4 Nonparametric Tests of Central Tendency

The Sign Test

Example 10.7

(Small sample.) The marketing department of a company producing long-life electric light bulbs claims that the bulbs last 1500 hours. The burning life of eleven bulbs was measured, resulting in the following data:

1220, 1360, 1740, 1450, 1630, 2360, 1290, 1320, 860, 1400, 1270.

Is the marketing department's claim justifiable?

Solution: We shall apply the sign test to the following null hypothesis:

H_0: Median bulb life is 1500 hours,

against the alternative hypothesis that the median bulb life is less than 1500 hours. We argue as follows. If the median life is 1500 hours, then the probability that a bulb selected at random will last for less than 1500 hours is 0.5. Further, the probability that it will last for at least 1500 hours is also 0.5. Therefore the number x of bulbs with a life of less than 1500 hours will have a binomial distribution Bin (11, 0.5) (remember that we have a total of eleven bulbs in our sample):

$$P(x) = \binom{11}{x} \cdot (0.5)^x \cdot (1 - 0.5)^{11-x} = \binom{11}{x} \cdot (0.5)^{11}.$$

In our case, $x = 8$, and from a table, or computing directly, we find the probability 0.1133 that x is 8 or more. Consequently, the null hypothesis cannot be rejected, not even at the 10% level, even though data suggest that the median is less than 1500. On the other hand, $P(x \geqq 9) = 0.0327$, so that if nine observations had been less than 1500, we would have rejected the null hypothesis at the 5% level.

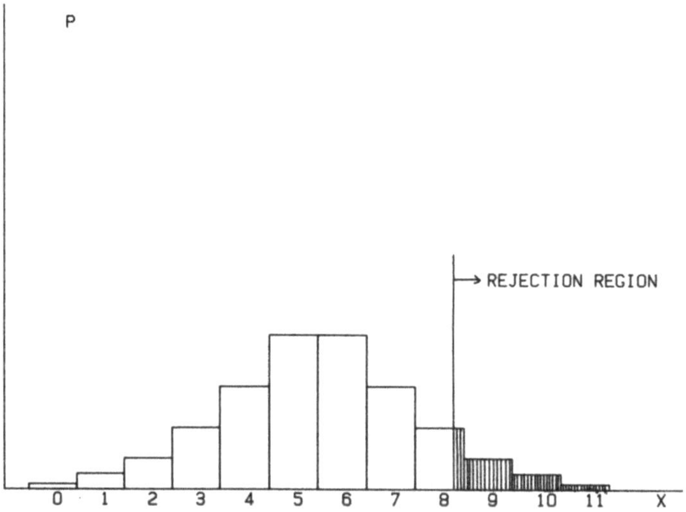

Fig. 10/15: Rejection region for Example 10.7 at the 5% level.

Example 10.8

(Large sample) If in Example 10.7 the sample size had been 90 instead of 11, with 53 observations of less than 1500 hours, what would the conclusion be?

Solution: We can now use the normal approximation of the binomial distribution. x is Bin (n, p) with $n = 90$, $p = 0.5$. Therefore

$$E(x) = np = 90 \cdot 0.5 = 45; \; V(x) = np(1 - p) = 90 \cdot 0.5 \cdot 0.5 = 22.5.$$

Now we get (without continuity correction, for simplicity's sake):

$$P(x \geqq 53) = P\left(\frac{x - 45}{\sqrt{22.5}} \geqq \frac{53 - 45}{\sqrt{22.5}}\right)$$
$$\approx P(Z \geqq 1.6865) \approx 0.0458.$$

Thus, with a z-score of 1.6865 we get a right-tail area of 0.0458.

That is, the null hypothesis (median bulb life is 1500 hours) can be rejected at the 5% level (but only just).

Example 10.9

(Paired samples) From each of eight positions in a company we select randomly one male and one female employee of equivalent standing (regarding age, seniority, rank etc.). The salaries are as follows:

Female	Male	Sign of difference (Male-Female)
$18,000	$20,000	+
14,000	15,000	+
24,000	22,000	−
16,000	17,000	+
29,000	32,000	+
15,000	15,000	0
17,000	18,000	+
21,000	20,000	−

We want to test if female salaries are lower than male. How should this be done?

Solution: The null hypothesis is:

H_0: Female and male salaries have the same median.

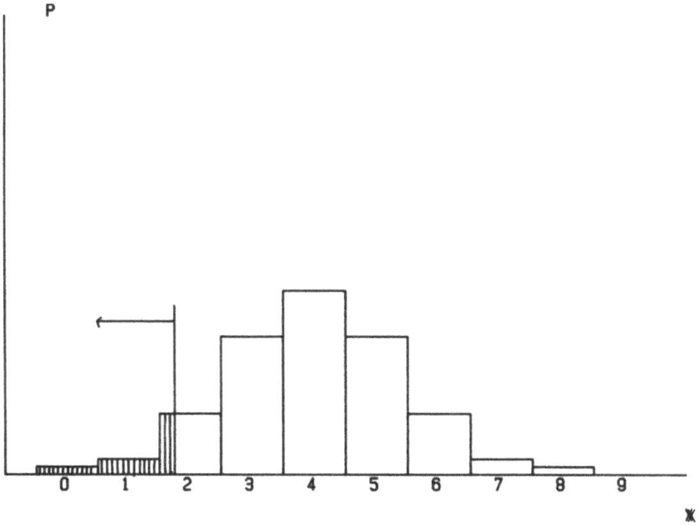

Fig. 10/16: Rejection region for Example 10.9 at the 5% level.

In analogy with our discussion of the light bulb examples, we realize that the number x of cases with a higher female salary than the corresponding male one (a minus sign) should be Bin (8, 0.5) distributed. In our example, $x = 2$ and we find $P(x \leqq 2) = 0.1445$. In order for us to reject the null hypothesis at the 5% level, we must obtain a P-value of less than 0.05. As this is not the case, we *cannot* reject the null hypothesis at the 5% (in fact, not even at the 10%) level.

Remark 1: In Example 10.7 and 10.8 we performed upper-tail tests; in Example 10.9 we had a lower-tail test.

Wilcoxon's Rank Sum Test

We shall now test the hypothesis that two different populations have the same distribution. We are not interested in knowing what the distributions actually are, only if they are identical or not.

Example 10.10

(Independent samples) Four female and six male employees of a firm are randomly selected and their salaries recorded. The result is as follows:

Sample A (Female)	Sample B (Male)
$18,000	$20,000
14,000	22,000
24,000	15,000
19,000	21,000
	32,000
	25,000

We want to test if male and female salaries have the same distribution or not. How could this be done?

Solution: We shall use the Wilcoxon rank sum test (equivalent to the so-called Mann-Whitney U-test) of the null hypothesis.

H_0: the two distributions are identical

against

H_1: the two distributions are *not* identical.

The first step in the test is to rank all observations, jointly, according to size, giving each a rank number. We obtain

Observation ($1000's)	14	15	18	19	20	21	22	24	25	32
Sample	A	B	A	A	B	B	B	A	B	B
Rank	1	2	3	4	5	6	7	8	9	10

Fig. 10/17: Ranking data for Example 10.10.

The next step is to add the rank numbers for each sample to obtain the *rank sum* T_A (and T_B):

$$T_A = 1 + 3 + 4 + 8 = 16$$
$$(T_B = 2 + 5 + 6 + 7 + 9 + 10 = 39).$$

Remark 2: With $n_A \leqq n_B$ being the sample sizes we have:

$$T_A + T_B = \frac{(n_A + n_B)(n_A + n_B + 1)}{2}$$

and one can show that for $n_A \geqq 10$,

$$\frac{T_A - \frac{1}{2} n_A (n_A + n_B + 1)}{\sqrt{\frac{1}{12} n_A n_B (n_A + n_B + 1)}} \quad \text{is}$$

approximately $N(0, 1)$, so that a normal test can be used.

Now we consider the rank sum for the *smaller* of the two samples (T_A) and *reject* H_0 if $T_A \leqq T_L$ or $T_A \geqq T_U$ where T_L (L for lower) and T_U (U for upper) are tabulated.

For our example, $n_A = 4, n_B = 6$ which gives us $T_L = 12$, $T_U = 32$ for a two-tailed, 5% level test. Thus $T_L < T_A < T_U$ and we *cannot* reject the null hypothesis about equal salaries. For $\alpha = 0.10$, one finds the same conclusion.

Remark 3: If both sample sizes are at least 10, the normal approximation can be used.

Remark 4: With H_1: "female salaries are lower than male", we would reject H_0 if $T_A \leqq T_L$ but not if $T_A \geqq T_U$; i.e., the test would be a lower-tail test, and we would reject the null hypothesis at $\alpha = 2.5\%$.

Remark 5: If ties occur *within* a sample, they may be broken arbitrarily. In case a tie (or a sequence of equal observations) straddles the two samples, the average of the two (or more) ranks involved are assigned to each observation, as in Fig. 10/18 below.

Observation...	141	143	143	143	149	152	...
Sample ...	A	B	B	A	A	B	...
Rank ...	7	9	9	9	11	12	...

Fig. 10/18: Averaging ranks in case of ties.

Remark 6: The Wilcoxon rank sum test can also be used for data given on an *ordinal* scale as only ranking is needed.

Remark 7: In case the two samples are equal size, $n_A = n_B$, whichever of T_A and T_B can be used. It is easy to see that the same conclusion will always be arrived at, using either T_A or Z_B in this case.

The Wilcoxon Signed-Rank Test

This test can be used to test the difference of the medians of two *symmetric* distributions (paired samples). This has already been done with the sign test without the assumption of symmetry (Example 10.9).

Example 10.11

(Paired samples) Consider the data of Example 10.9. Computing the difference for each pair, the absolute difference and the *rank* of the absolute difference we obtain the following table:

Female	Male	Difference ($1000's) male-female	Absolute difference	Rank of absolute difference
$18,000	$20,000	2	2	~~5~~ 5.5
14,000	15,000	1	1	~~1~~ 1.5
24,000	22,000	−2	2	~~6~~ 5.5
16,000	17,000	1	1	~~2~~ 2.5
29,000	32,000	3	3	7
15,000	15,000	0	0	–
17,000	18,000	1	1	~~3~~ 2.5
21,000	20,000	−1	1	~~4~~ 2.5

As before, we want to test if female salaries are lower than male.

Solution: First we compute a column of differences, then the absolute values of these, and finally a rank column of the absolute differences (zero differences are not ranked). For ties, average values are given, as in our example. Finally the rank sums T_+ and T_- of the ranks corresponding to a positive or negative difference are calculated. For our example, we get:

$$T_+ = 5.5 + 2.5 + 2.5 + 7 + 2.5 = 20$$
$$T_- = 8$$

and the test statistic $T = \min(T_+, T_-) = \min(20, 8) = 8$.

With a sample size of $n = 8$, but 7 rankings we put $n = 7$ and with a lower-tail test, we see from a table that we *cannot* reject the null hypothesis at the 5% level (as this would have required $T \leqq 4$). This conclusion is the same as the one we reached in Example 10.9.

Remark 8: One can show that for $n \geqq 10$,

$$\frac{T - \frac{1}{4}n(n+1)}{\sqrt{\frac{1}{24}n(n+1)(2n+1)}}$$

is approximately $N(0, 1)$, so that a normal test can be used.

Remark 9: The deletion of the observations relating to zero differences may appear a strange practice. It would take us too far to look deeper into this issue; let us only say that it is commonly done.

10.5 A Nonparametric Test of Randomness

One of the most crucial assumptions for a statistical investigation is that the sample taken is truly random. In this section we shall describe the *runs test* which is used to test the hypothesis of randomness of observations.

Example 10.12

It has been suggested that strikes in the British automobile industry are a random phenomenon. To investigate this, a major plant in the industry was observed for a number of consecutive weeks; if there was a strike sometime during a week it received the label "S" (for "strike"), otherwise "N" (for "no strike"). The following data were obtained:

Age	Test score	I	T
23	17.6	8	0
24	12.6	3	4
25	14.0	5	1
26	7.9	0	5
27	11.2	1	3
28	9.9	0	3
29	15.5	2	0
32	13.3	1	0
34	12.9	0	0
Total:		20	16

Fig. 10/20: Data and computations for Example 10.13.

Remark: The Kendall test is also suitable for purely ordinal (rank) data. The Kendall coefficient of rank correlation (always between -1 and $+1$, inclusive) is for n observations defined as:

$$r = \frac{S}{\frac{n}{2}(n-1)}.$$

We obtain $r = \dfrac{S}{\frac{n}{2}(n-1)} = \dfrac{-4}{\frac{9}{2}(9-1)} = 1/9 \approx -0.11.$

References

Chou, Y.: *Statistical Analysis,* 2nd edition. Holt, Rinehart and Winston, New York 1975.

Gibbons, J. D.: *Nonparametric Methods for Quantitative Analysis.* Holt, Rinehart and Winston, New York 1976.

Hamburg, M.: *Statistical Analysis for Decision Making,* 2nd edition. Harcourt, Brace, Jovanovich, New York 1977.

Hawkins, C. A., and J. E. Weber: *Statistical Analysis. Applications to Business and Economics.* Harper & Row, New York 1980.

Lapin, L. L.: *Statistics for Modern Business Decisions,* 3rd edition. Harcourt, Brace, Javanovich, New York 1982.

Mansfield, E.: *Statistics for Business and Economics,* Norton & Company, New York 1980.

Ott, L.: *An Introduction to Statistical Methods and Data Analysis,* Duxbury Press, North Scituate, Mass. 1977.

Wonnacott, T. H., and R. J. Wonnacott: *Introductory Statistics for Business and Economics,* 2nd edition. John Wiley & Sons, New York 1977.

Exercises

10–1 A market research firm desires to determine whether the inclusion of a dollar bill in a questionnaire would increase the number of responses. Three hundred questionnaires, half with dollar bills, half without, are sent to 300 persons selected at random; the following results are obtained:

	Responded	No Response	Total
Dollar bill included	97	53	150
Dollar bill not included	80	70	150
Total	177	123	300

Is there a significant evidence at 5% to indicate that the inclusion of a dollar bill is related to the number of responses to the questionnaire?

10–2 The management of a firm wants to know how its employees feel about working conditions, particularly whether there are differences in sentiment between various departments. A study based on random samples of the employees of four departments yielded the results shown in the following table:

	Dept. A	Dept. B	Dept. C	Dept. D
Working conditions are very good	65	112	85	80
Working conditions are average	27	67	60	44
Working conditions are poor	8	21	15	16

Test the hypothesis that the distribution of the proportions of employees who think that working conditions are very good, average, and poor is the same for all four departments. Use a level of significance of 0.05.

10–3 In late 1957 a bureau of Business Research polled a sample of 500 men engaged in different fields of business in a certain state, to determine whether there were any differences in attitude towards the prospects for over-all business activity in the coming year. The results of this poll were as follows:

	Bankers	Manufacturers	Merchants	Farmers
Increased activity	40	55	80	75
Decreased activity	15	30	40	50
No appreciable change	20	25	30	40

Test the null hypothesis that the distribution of the true proportions corresponding to the three categories is the same for all four kinds of businessmen. Use a level of significance of 0.05.

10–4 The Vice-President of Finance for a large firm wants to determine whether there is a difference between the two internal auditors (Smith and Jones) with regard to the types of errors they are able to detect in the customer billing statements. A random sample of 100 faulty billings was selected and classified according to type of mistake and the auditor detecting the mistake. The results are given below:

Smith (type of error detected)	Jones (type of error detected)
9 addition errors	6 addition errors
13 prices wrong	8 prices wrong
21 wrong items	24 wrong items
9 combination and other	10 combination and other

Is there a relationship between auditor and type of error detected at a significance level of 10%?

10–5 A firm selling four products wishes to determine whether sales are distributed similarly among four general classes of customers. A random sample of 1000 sales records provides the following information:

	Product			
Customer group	1	2	3	4
Professionals	85	23	56	36
Businessmen	153	44	128	75
Factory Workers	128	26	101	45
Farmers	34	7	15	44

At $\alpha = 5\%$ test the null hypothesis that both methods of classification are independent.

10–6 Suppose that 100 United States senators were polled in an effort to ascertain their attitude toward capital punishment. The senators are classified according to their party affiliation and opinion on the issue. The results of the poll are tabulated as follows:

	Attidude Toward Capital Punishment		
Party Affiliation	Favour	Opposed	No opinion
Democrats	22	33	5
Republicans	18	17	5

Test the null hypothesis that the senator's opinion on capital punishment is independent of party affiliation at $\alpha = .01$.

10–7 To put a one-year warranty into effect, the buyers of a small appliance are asked to mail a postcard on which several questions relating to the purchase are asked.

From a large number of these postcards, a random sample of 100 is selected for analysis. The following frequencies, based on the sample of postcards, describe the purchasers according to place of purchase and source of product knowledge.

	Place of Purchase			
Source of Knowledge	Department Store	Discount Store	Appliance Store	Total
Friend	10	5	5	20
Newspaper	15	30	5	50
Magazine	5	5	20	30
Total	30	40	30	100

a) Using a 5 percent level of significance, test the null hypothesis that there is no relationship between place of purchase and source of knowledge.
b) Would the conclusion in (a) above be different if the one percent level were used?
c) Suppose that the management of the company had assumed before it obtained the sample results above that 40 percent of the purchases are influenced by friends, 40 percent by newspaper advertisements, and 20 percent by magazine advertisements. At the 1 percent level of significance test this hypothesis.

10–8 A company's marketing research staff members desire to test how they can influence the percentage of questionnaires returned. Believing that the creation of an impression of personal attention may be important, they send out 1,000 questionnaires: 500 are obviously mimeographed, 300 are offset – printed to look typewritten, 200 are actually original typed copies. Of these, 120 mimeographed questionnaires are returned, 100 offset questionnaries are returned and 80 typed questionnaires are returned. By using the 1% level of significance what can one conclude?

10–9 We want to decide whether a cubic die is perfectly balanced. For this purpose the die is rolled 300 times with the following results:

Face	1	2	3	4	5	6
Frequency	35	40	32	60	68	65

Test to see if the die is perfectly balanced, with $\alpha = .01$.

10–10 A famous application of the chi-square goodness of fit test is the von Bortkiewicz[1] study of the number of soldiers in the Prussian army being kicked to death by horses. He obtained the following data for ten army divisions during twenty years:

[1] Ladislaus von Bortkiewicz, Polish mathematician and statistician, 1868–1931.

Deaths per year and division	No. of cases
0	109
1	65
2	22
3	3
4	1
5	0
$\geqq 6$	0

a) Test if the number of deaths per year in a division follows a Poisson distribution with $\lambda = 0.9$. Use $\alpha = 0.05$.
b) Test if the number of deaths per year in a division follows a Poisson distribution. Use $\alpha = 5\%$. (Hint: Use the fact that 122 deaths are recorded).

10–11 A real estate company wishes to determine whether a difference exists between prices of residential homes in two areas: Westmount and Beaconsfield. Six houses from Westmount and nine from Beaconsfield were randomly selected and the selling prices (in thousands of dollars) are recorded in the table below:

Westmount	Beaconsfield
110	87
127	210
96	90
215	115
182	124
153	171
	99
	102
	136

Use the appropriate nonparametric statistic to decide whether there is a difference in the probability distribution of house prices in the two urban communities. (Use $\alpha = .05$)

10–12 Suppose a physician uses the Wilcoxon rank-sum test on a sample of eight patients treated with penicillin and on a group of ten patients to whom sulfa was administered, and that he obtains the following results for the number of days required to cure a virulent strain of a certain disease:

(A) Penicillin 15, 9, 12, 22, 14, 9, 10, 15
(B) Sulfa 7, 8, 10, 6, 7, 7, 4, 13, 11, 5

a) Rank the sample data and calculate T_A and T_B.
b) The doctor's null hypothesis is that the treatments are equally effective. For-

mulate his decision rule, assuming that in the future he will use the treatment he finds most effective but that otherwise he will test further. (Use $\alpha = .05$).

c) What action should the doctor take?

10–13 Rown Realty Company wishes to determine whether a difference exists between prices of cottages in two areas: Bear Island and Deer Mountain. Five cottages from the Bear Island area and seven from the Deer Mountain area were randomly selected and the prices (in thousands of dollars) are recorded in the table below:

Bear Island	Deer Mountain
23	37
25	22
21	34
40	32
20	47
	26
	19

Use the appropriate nonparametric statistic to see whether there is a difference in the probability distribution of cottage prices in the two resort areas. (Use $\alpha = .05$).

10–14 Suppose two methods, A and B, are used to teach English to two different groups, I and II, of randomly selected adult immigrants. After a period of time, a standard examination is administerd. The test scores are below:

Group I Test Score (by A)	Group II Test Score (by B)
93	85
93	76
92	84
99	72
98	73
87	68
85	

Test, at alpha = 5%, to see whether Method A yields higher scores. (Assume no particular distribution for scores.)

10–15 An experiment is designed to compare the effectiveness of two methods, I and II, of teaching reading. The subjects are 12 sets of identical twins. One child is randomly selected from each set of twins and assigned to class I; the other is assigned to class II. The two classes are taught with the two methods respectively. The test scores in a standard reading comprehension examination are below:

Twin Pair	1	2	3	4	5	6	7	8	9	10	11	12
Class I Test Score	70	95	80	73	61	96	66	75	90	77	89	90
Class II Test Score	75	92	71	63	64	84	51	78	84	59	78	74

Test to see if the two probability distributions are different. ($\alpha = 1\%$).

10–16 A pharmaceutical research statistician suspects that a chemical treatment for a certain illness changes the body temperature. 12 patients with the illness are selected at random. Their body temperatures are recorded before and after having-received the treatment. The results, given in degrees Celsius, are as follows:

Patient	Before	After
1	37.1	37.2
2	36.9	36.4
3	37.0	36.7
4	37.3	38.5
5	37.7	39.1
6	36.8	37.4
7	36.9	37.8
8	37.4	37.7
9	36.8	37.5
10	37.1	36.9
11	36.7	36.7
12	37.2	37.5

Test the null hypothesis that the two population distributions are identical using $\alpha = 10\%$.

10–17 For determining the effectiveness of an industrial safety program, data on accidents were collected. The average monthly losses of man-hours due to accidents in 10 plants "before" and "after" the program was instituted are shown in the following table:

Plant	Before	After
1	28	19
2	37	38
3	8	7
4	65	53
5	43	31
6	14	19
7	15	13
8	6	4
9	28	26
10	115	100

At $\alpha = 10\%$ test the null hypothesis that the distribution of "before" and "after" is the same versus the alternative hypothesis that the distributions are different.

10–18 Many large supermarket chains produce their own goods for sale under a house label. They advertise that, although the house brands are of the same quality as the national brands, they can be sold at lower prices because of lower production costs. A comparison of the daily sales (number of units sold) of eleven products at a certain supermarket produced the following data:

	National Brand	House Brand
Catsup	303	237
Corn (canned)	504	428
Bread	205	127
Margarine	157	136
Dog food	205	49
Peaches (canned)	273	302
Cola	394	147
Green beans	93	248
Ice cream	188	188
Cheese	126	147
Beer	303	29

It is desired to compare the sales of the national brand and house brand products.

a) What type of experimental design is represented here?
b) Perform a test of the hypothesis that the probability distributions of the sales of national and house brands are identical. The research hypothesis of interest is that the sales of national brands tend to exceed those of house brands. Use $\alpha = .01$.

10–19 An investor is considering a particular stock on the stock market. The following is the daily closing price of the stock for a certain sequence of trading days (one row per week):

$16.80	16.25	15.70	17.00	14.95
17.20	16.80	16.65	16.30	16.10
16.65	16.70	16.90	16.50	15.95
16.30	16.25	16.50	16.40	16.05
16.50	16.60	16.75	16.55	16.10

Is the stock price random over time?

10–20 Suppose that the investor of the previous problem considers another stock over the same time period, with the following closing price:

\$27.65	27.20	27.55	27.40	27.25
27.50	27.65	27.80	27.50	26.90
26.85	26.50	25.90	25.50	25.00
26.10	26.35	27.05	26.85	26.35
26.85	27.20	27.50	27.90	27.10

Are the prices of the two stocks correlated?

11. Analysis of Variance and Experimental Design

In Chapter 9 we tested hypotheses about the equality of means from two different populations, using t-tests. We shall now extend the problem and consider several populations. A notable fact is that we perform tests about *means* by considering *variances*. The technique is called *analysis of variance* (ANOVA) and was originally developed for application in agriculture.

In Section 11.1 we introduce a problem that will serve as a basis for the presentation and discussion of the ANOVA technique. We also familiarize the reader with the notational apparatus to be used and establish the fundamental ANOVA identity. Section 11.2 is devoted to one-way (one-factor) ANOVA. We use the ANOVA table in its most common format, and illustrate the computations by solving a numerical example.

In Section 11.3 we discuss the crucial, yet often badly neglected issue of experimental design. This leads us in a natural way over to two-way (two-factor) analysis of variance, which is covered in Section 11.4. Finally, in Section 11.5 we give a very brief treatment of randomized block and Latin square designs.

11.1 Introduction

Example 11.1

Consider the weekly output from four different machines. For each machine, a sample is taken:

Machine \ Sample (week)	j = 1	2	3	4	5	6	$\bar{X}_i$
i = 1	670	840	780	610	900	–	760
2	600	800	690	650	–	–	685
3	800	810	730	690	750	720	750
4	970	840	930	790	920	–	890
							$\bar{\bar{X}} = 774.5$

How do we test the hypothesis, that the four machines have equal average weekly output? The alternative hypothesis is that the four machine means are *not* all equal, i.e. at least two means differ.

Analysis

In general, with a sample size of n_i for row $i = 1, \ldots, k$ (rows are often called *treatments* in ANOVA) we get the average $\bar{X}_i$ for row i:

$$\bar{X}_i = \frac{1}{n_i} \sum_{j=1}^{n} X_{ij}.$$

Remark: The n_i:s can, but do not have to be the same. The overall average $\bar{\bar{X}}$ is $\left(\sum_{i=1}^{k} n_i = N\right)$:

$$\bar{\bar{X}} = \frac{1}{N} \sum_{i,j} X_{ij} = \frac{1}{N} \sum_{i=1}^{k} n_i \bar{X}_i.$$

In our example, $k = 4, n_1 = n_4 = 5, n_2 = 4$ and $n_3 = 6$ so that $\bar{\bar{X}} = \frac{1}{20} \sum_{i,j} X_{ij}$ $= \frac{1}{20} \sum_i n_i \bar{X}_i = \frac{1}{20} (5\bar{X}_1 + 4\bar{X}_2 + 6\bar{X}_3 + 5\bar{X}_4)$.

We assume that all X_{ij} are $N(\mu_i, \sigma)$ and independent. Note that the variance is the same for all treatments.

We want to test

$$H_0: \ \mu_1 = \mu_2 = \ldots = \mu_k$$

against $H_1: \ \mu_l \neq \mu_m$, for some l and m.

Paradoxically, this test about *means* can be done by looking at *variations* in the data. One can easily show the following identity.

$$\underbrace{\sum_{i,j} (X_{ij} - \bar{\bar{X}})^2} = \underbrace{\sum_{i=1}^{k} n_i (\bar{X}_i - \bar{\bar{X}})^2} + \underbrace{\sum_{i,j} (X_{ij} - \bar{X}_i)^2}$$

total variation, total sum of squares, SS (Total)	between groups variation, between groups sum of squares, treatment sum of squares, explained variation, SS (Between groups), SS (Treatment)	within groups variation, within groups sum of squares, unexplained variation, error sum of squares, SS (Within groups), SS (Error)

Exercise: Prove the identity.

11.2 One-Way Analysis of Variance

Now we divide each of the sums of squares on the right hand side by the appropriate degrees of freedom to obtain the mean square; then we take the following ratio:

$$F = \frac{\dfrac{SS\ (\text{Between})}{k-1}}{\dfrac{SS\ (\text{Within})}{N-k}}.$$

If the machines (treatments, groups) are equivalent, as much variation should occur within groups as between; hence the above ratio should not be excessive. A *large* ratio, indicating much variation between groups compared to within, suggests that the machines are *not* equivalent. In fact, one can show that the ratio F is F distributed, or more specifically $F(k-1, N-k)$, provided that H_0 is true. Therefore, we *reject* H_0 at the α level of significance if $F > F_\alpha(k-1, N-k)$.

Summarizing, we obtain the ANOVA table as in Fig. 11/1.

Source of variation	Sum of Squares (SS)	Degrees of freedom	F
Between groups; treatments; explained	$\sum_{i=1}^{k} n_i(\bar{X}_i - \bar{X})^2$ = SS (Between)	$k-1$	$\dfrac{\dfrac{SS\ (\text{Between})}{k-1}}{\dfrac{SS\ (\text{Within})}{N-k}}$
Within groups; error; unexplained	$\sum_{i=1}^{k} \sum_{j=1}^{n_i} (X_{ij} - \bar{X}_i)^2$ = SS (Within)	$N-k$	
TOTAL:	$\sum_{i=1}^{k} \sum_{j=1}^{n_i} (X_{ij} - \bar{X})^2$ = SS (Total)	$N-1$	

Fig. 11/1: Analysis of variance (ANOVA) table.

Calculation-wise, one can show that with $T = \sum_{i,j} X_{ij}$ (total sum of all observations) and $T_i = \sum_{j=1}^{n_i} X_{ij}$ (sum of all observations in sample i), so that $T = \sum_{i=1}^{k} T_i$, we have:

$$\text{SS (Between)} = \sum_{i=1}^{k} \frac{T_i^2}{n_i} - \frac{T^2}{N} \; T_i^2$$

$$\text{SS (Within)} \;\; = \sum_{i,j} X_{ij}^2 - \sum_{i=1}^{k} n_i$$

Adding both these expressions, terms cancel out and we get:

$$\text{SS (Total)} = \sum_{i,j} X_{ij}^2 - \frac{T^2}{N}.$$

Warning: These calculations often involve the difference between two large, about equally sized numbers, so numerical precision is important.

Returning to our example, we get:

$$T = T_1 + T_2 + T_3 + T_4 = 3800 + 2740 + 4500 + 4450 = 15490$$

and $N = 20$, so that:

$$\text{SS (Between)} = \sum \frac{T_i^2}{n_i} - \frac{T^2}{N} = 12100400 - 11997005 = 103395$$

$$\text{SS (Within)} \;\; = \sum X_{ij}^2 - \sum \frac{T_i^2}{n_i} = 12211500 - 12100400 = 111100$$

and

$$F = \frac{\dfrac{\text{SS (Between)}}{k-1}}{\dfrac{\text{SS (Within)}}{N-k}} = \frac{\dfrac{103395}{4-1}}{\dfrac{111100}{20-4}} = \frac{34465}{6943.75} = 4.963\,.$$

The ANOVA table for this problem would therefore be as follows:

Source of variation	SS	d.f.	F
Between groups	103395	3	4.963
Within groups	111100	16	
Total	214495		

In an F-table we find $F_{0.05}(3, 16) = 3.24$. The ANOVA test is an upper-tail test, i. e. the rejection region is in the right tail of the F distribution. We have $F = 4.963 > 3{,}24 = F_{0.05}(3, 16)$, so that H_0 is *rejected* at the 5% level; i. e. we conclude that the machines are *different*.

We also find that $F_{0.01}(3, 16) = 5.29$ so that H_0 can *not* be rejected at the 1% level.

Remark: We have only considered one variable (source of between-groups variation) or *factor*. If different operators were using the machines in our example, this would be a second factor which we might like to find the effect of. This would lead us to *two-factor* ANOVA.

One can show that the denominator in the F ratio, i.e. the expression

$$\frac{\sum_{i,j} (X_{ij} - \bar{X}_i)^2}{N - k}$$

which we also denote $\frac{SS\,(\text{Within})}{N-k}$ or $\frac{SS\,(\text{Error})}{N-k}$ is an estimate of σ^2, the common variance. This estimate is pooled from all the groups and is a generalization of the pooled variance from two samples, which we considered in Section 9.5 on two-sample tests. Therefore we denote $\frac{SS\,(\text{Within})}{N-k}$ by s^2 and can use it to construct a confidence interval of the mean μ_i, with confidence level $1 - \alpha$:

$$\bar{X}_i \pm t_{\alpha/2}(N-k) \cdot \frac{s}{\sqrt{n_i}}$$

for $i = 1, \ldots, k$.

Also, we obtain a confidence interval for the difference between the two means μ_l and μ_m:

$$\bar{X}_l - \bar{X}_m \pm t_{\alpha/2}(N-k) \cdot s \cdot \sqrt{\frac{1}{n_l} + \frac{1}{n_m}}\,.$$

From the data in Example 11.1 we find:

$$s^2 = \frac{SS\,(\text{Within})}{N-k} = \frac{111\,100}{20-4} = 6943.75$$

and

$$s = \sqrt{s^2} = \sqrt{6943.75} = 83.329\,.$$

Example 11.2

From Example 11.1 we can compute a 95% confidence interval for μ_4:

$$\bar{X}_4 \pm t_{0.025}(N-k) \cdot \frac{s}{\sqrt{n_4}} = 890 \pm \underbrace{t_{0.025}(20-4)}_{2.120} \cdot \frac{83.329}{\sqrt{5}} = 890 \pm 79.00.$$

The confidence interval is therefore $811 \leqq \mu_4 \leqq 969$.

Example 11.3

From Example 11.1 we determine a 90% confidence interval for $\mu_2 - \mu_3$:

$$(\bar{X}_2 - \bar{X}_3) \pm t_{0.05}(N-k) \cdot s \cdot \sqrt{\frac{1}{n_2} + \frac{1}{n_3}}$$

$$= (685 - 750) \pm \underbrace{t_{0.05}(16)}_{1.746} \cdot 83.329 \cdot \sqrt{\frac{1}{4} + \frac{1}{6}} = -65 \pm 93.9.$$

The confidence interval is $(-158.9, 28.9)$.

*11.3 Experimental Design

The analysis of variance uses data on one or more variables. The measurements (observations) of these variables are often obtained in an experimental situation. This applies typically to data from marketing, management and production studies. Data can also arise from nonexperimental situations; this is particularly true for financial and economic data.

We describe research conducted on already available (i.e. nonexperimental) data as *ex post facto* research ("after the fact" research). This is in contrast to *experimental* research, in which at least some of the data are generated experimentally as part of the research project. In an experimental research design, the investigator is manipulating one or more variables that are under his control, and measures the effects of this manipulation on the dependent variable(s). To describe the research design, we have to specify how the subjects (experimental units) are assigned to *experimental groups,* for different "treatments" (manipulation of a variable being considered). A group that is given no treatment is called a *control group*. For example, let us assume that the manager of a company is considering a new labour productivity increasing incentive for a factory. How should he ascertain the value of this incentive? An obvious procedure would be to take a sample of subjects (factory workers) and treat some of them, the experimental group, with the incentive. The others, the control group, are not subjected to the incentive. Afterwards we try to distinguish any difference between the two groups. It is important, however, that any discrepancy in performance is really due to the incentive and not to any other, extraneous factor. If extraneous factors have significantly influenced the results, the whole experiment will be questionable and the research results useless.

Let us start by describing some inadequate research designs. Having analyzed these, we will be in a better position to appreciate the proper research designs which we will then turn to.

Inadequate Research Designs

First we introduce some convenient notations. Let X denote an independent variable that is manipulated by the researcher. If we have several such variables we denote them by $X_1, X_2, X_3, \ldots$. By $\sim X$ (or $\sim X_1$, $\sim X_2$, $\sim X_3, \ldots$) we indicate that the variable is *not* manipulated, even though the researcher has the power to do so. By $\textcircled{X}$ (or $\textcircled{X_1}, \textcircled{X_2}, \textcircled{X_3}, \ldots$) we indicate that the researcher does *not* have the power to manipulate the variable; it is not under his/her control. The dependent variable is denoted by Y. Specifically, Y_b is the dependent variable *before* manipulation of $X(X_1, X_2, X_3, \ldots)$ and Y_a is the dependent variable *after* manipulation of $X(X_1, X_2, X_3, \ldots)$.

In Fig. 11/2 we show the so-called *One-Shot Case Study* or *One Group* design.

$$X \qquad Y_a$$

Fig. 11/2: One Group Design

In this design, the independent variable X is manipulated, after which the dependent variable Y_a is measured. For example, recalling the productivity incentive situation, the incentive would be introduced, and the resulting productivity measured afterwards.

It is immediately obvious why this design is blatantly inadequate: What are we comparing Y_a against? Is it better or worse than before? We have obviously no chance of knowing, unless Y is measured before the experiment as well.

Let us just mention that this design has an ex post facto counterpart:

$$\textcircled{X} \qquad Y_a$$

This is perhaps less ridiculous than the experimental version, because we are at least dealing with variables that are not under our control.

A natural improvement is the *One Group Before-After* design shown in Fig. 11/3.

Y_b X Y_a

Fig. 11/3: One Group Before-After Design

Now we have measured the dependent variable before (*pretest*) the manipulation, Y_b, as well as after (*posttest*), Y_a. Suppose that our incentive program was tested in this way, and that a significant increase $Y_b - Y_a$ occurred. Does this prove the effectiveness of the program? The answer is "no"; the productivity may have risen because of other factors (maybe it is going up all the time).

Also, the workers involved in the experiment may have learnt during the "before" measurement how to achieve a high rating and used this for the "after" measurement; this effect is called *sensitization.*

The sensitization effect is not present in the *Two Groups Simulated Before-After* design.

	X	Y_a
Y_b		

Fig. 11/4: Two Groups Simulated Before-After Design.

The horizontal line in Fig. 11/4 indicates that two groups are involved; one which is manipulated and measured afterwards and another which is only measured beforehand. Although the sensitization effect is now eliminated, the changing environment (other factors) issue is still not resolved.

An attempt to deal with the extraneous factor issue is made in the *Experimental and Control Groups* design:

X	Y_a	Experimental
$\sim$X	Y_a	Control

Fig. 11/5: Experimental and Control Groups Design.

This design suffers in one essential aspect. Although a control group is used to compare with the experimental group, it could still happen that extraneous factors distort the result. We must therefore deliberately make sure that the experimental and control groups are equal in this respect, either by *randomiz-*

ation (randomly assigning subjects to the experimental or the control group) or by *matching* the subjects of the two groups against each other.

We have now become familiarized with the main pitfalls of poor research design and shall describe some acceptable designs.

Adequate Research Designs

We begin by the most basic of all good research designs. It is illustrated in Fig. 11/6.

Randomization	X	Y_a	Experimental
	$\sim X$	Y_a	Control

Fig. 11/6: Experimental and Control Groups Design with Randomized Assignment

This is the same design as in Fig. 11/5 except that the assignment of subjects to the experimental or the control group is done randomly. Given a "sufficient" sample size, this will cause the extraneous factor effect to cancel out. It may also be prudent to use the *blind* experiment technique: the subjects do not know if they belong to the experimental or the control group (this is of course only possible for certain types of experiments). One may even consider a *double blind* experiment, in which not even the researcher knows, at the time of the experiment, which group a particular subject beongs to. Some book keeping is of course necessary so that one can afterwards find out which group the subjects belonged to.

An extension of the design shown in Fig. 11/6 is obtained if we consider two different variables jointly. For example, let us reconsider our productivity incentive program and add fringe benefits as another variable. Formally, our variable would be $X = (X_1, X_2)$ where X_1 stands for incentives and X_2 for benefits. A possible design would then be:

Randomization	$\sim X_1, \sim X_2$	Y_a	Control
	$X_1, \sim X_2$	Y_a	Experimental 1
	$\sim X_1, X_2$	Y_a	Experimental 2
	X_1, X_2	Y_a	Experimental 3

Fig. 11/7: Experimental and Control Groups with Two Independent Variables.

In this design, the Control and Experimental 1 groups act as a control and experimental group when only X_1 is manipulated; similarly Control and Experimental 2 are used if we wish to investigate the effect of manipulating X_2 only. However, we can also use Experimental 2 as the *control* group (and Experimental 3 as the experimental group) for analyzing the effects of X_1, given that X_2 is manipulated. A similar argument holds for using Experimental 1 and 3 for analyzing X_2, given that X_1 is manipulated. By drawing the Fig. 11/7 diagram as follows:

	$\sim X_2$	X_2
$\sim X_1$	Control	Experimental 2
X_1	Experimental 1	Experimental 3

Fig. 11/8: 2 × 2 Factorial Design.

we see that a one-way analysis of variance approach is suitable. We also say that we have a *2 × 2 factorial design*. If each of the factors can be set at various levels we could then obtain $m \times n$ factorial designs; with three factors we would have an $m \times n \times p$ factorial design (suitable for two-way ANOVA), etc.

If we add the pretest feature to the design in Fig. 11/6 we obtain the following, which is the classical research design for the social and behavioural sciences:

Randomization	Y_b	X	Y_a	Experimental
	Y_b	$\sim X$	Y_a	Control

Fig. 11/9: Experimental and Control Groups Design and Randomized Assignment and Pretest.

This design can be extended to obtain even stronger designs; for instance, if we particularly wish to control the sensitization effect we could use the following design:

	Y_b	X	Y_a	Experimental
Randomization	Y_b	$\sim X$	Y_a	Control 1
		X	Y_a	Control 2

Fig. 11/10: A Three Group Strong Design.

or even:

	Y_b	X	Y_a	Experimental
	Y_b	~X	Y_a	Control 1
Randomization		X	Y_a	Control 2
		~X	Y_a	Control 3

Fig. 11/11: A Four Group Strong Design.

These two designs offer excellent abilities to reduce or eliminate the effect of extraneous factors; therefore we say that they are *strong* designs.

We now end the discussion of research designs, having covered the basic principles and warned against some of the main pitfalls in research methodology. We saw that factorial designs provided a logical set-up for an analysis of variance approach. Having already covered one-way ANOVA in Sections 11.1 and 11.2 let us now turn to two-way ANOVA.

*11.4 Two-Way Analysis of Variance

In one-way ANOVA we only considered one source of variation, i.e. one factor or variable. Now we extend this approach to include two factors.

Example 11.4

Consider Example 11.1. Let us change the situation by assuming that there are three machine operators, each of whom operates a machine. The data below apply, now with different headings (indicating a completely different research design):

	Operator			
Machine	j = 1	2	3	$\bar{X}_{i.}$
i = 1	850	790	620	753.3
2	830	720	680	743.3
3	830	750	710	763.3
4	830	920	780	843.3
$\bar{X}_{.j}$	835	795	697.5	$\bar{\bar{X}} = 775.8$

Two sources of variation, under control of the investigator, are now present. The first is due to the difference in machines, as before; the second is due to the difference in operators, which was not considered before. We introduce the following general notation (with r rows and q columns):

$$\bar{X}_{i\cdot} = \frac{1}{q}\sum_{j=1}^{q} X_{ij} \qquad \text{(row average),} \qquad i = 1, \ldots, r$$

$$\bar{X}_{\cdot j} = \frac{1}{r}\sum_{i=1}^{r} X_{ij} \qquad \text{(column average),} \qquad j = 1, \ldots, q$$

where r denotes the number of rows and q the number of columns (so that $N = rq$). All rows have the same number of elements. Also:

$\mu_{i\cdot}$ = true (unknown) row mean, $i = 1, \ldots, r$
$\mu_{\cdot j}$ = true (unknown) column mean, $j = 1, \ldots, q$.

Two hypotheses can now be tested, one about equal row means (which is what we have done before), and one about equal column means.

One can easily show the identity:

$$\underbrace{\sum_{i,j}(X_{ij}-\bar{\bar{X}})^2}_{\substack{\text{total variation,}\\ \text{total sum of}\\ \text{squares,}\\ \text{SS (Total)}}} = \underbrace{\sum_{i=1}^{r} q(\bar{X}_{i\cdot}-\bar{\bar{X}})^2}_{\substack{\text{between rows}\\ \text{variation,}\\ \text{between rows}\\ \text{sum of squares,}\\ \text{SS (Rows)}}} + \underbrace{\sum_{j=1}^{q} r(\bar{X}_{\cdot j}-\bar{\bar{X}})^2}_{\substack{\text{between columns}\\ \text{variation,}\\ \text{between columns}\\ \text{sum of squares,}\\ \text{SS (Columns)}}}$$

$$+ \underbrace{\sum_{i,j}(X_{ij}-\bar{X}_{i\cdot}-\bar{X}_{\cdot j}+\bar{\bar{X}})^2}_{\substack{\text{unexplained variation,}\\ \text{error sum of squares,}\\ \text{SS (Error)}}}$$

Exercise: Prove the identity.

Remark: It is also quite common to talk about variation between *blocks* and *treatments* instead of between rows and columns. We shall talk of SS(Rows) and SS(Columns) to avoid confusion.

The two-way analysis of variance table will then look as follows:

Source of variation	Sum of squares (SS)	Degrees of freedom	F
Between rows	$\sum_{i=1}^{r} q(\bar{X}_{i\cdot} - \bar{X})^2 = SS(Rows)$	$r-1$	$\dfrac{\frac{SS(Rows)}{r-1}}{\frac{SS(Error)}{(r-1)(q-1)}}$
Between columns	$\sum_{j=1}^{q} r(\bar{X}_{\cdot j} - \bar{X})^2 = SS(Columns)$	$q-1$	$\dfrac{\frac{SS(Columns)}{(r-1)(q-1)}}{\frac{SS(Error)}{(r-1)(q-1)}}$
Error	$\sum_{i,j}(X_{ij} - \bar{X}_{i\cdot} - \bar{X}_{\cdot j} + \bar{X})^2 = SS(Error)$	$(r-1)(q-1)$	
Total	$\sum_{i,j}(X_{ij} - \bar{X})^2 = SS(Total)$	$rq-1$	

Fig. 11/12: Two-way analysis of variance (ANOVA) table.

If the null hypothesis about equal row means is true (against the alternative that they are not all equal), then one can show that the F-ratio:

$$\frac{\frac{SS(Rows)}{r-1}}{\frac{SS(Error)}{(r-1)(q-1)}} \quad \text{is} \quad F((r-1), (r-1)(q-1)) \quad \text{distributed.}$$

Similarly, one can show that if the null hypothesis about equal column means is true (against the alternative that they are not all equal), then the F-ratio:

$$\frac{\frac{SS(Columns)}{q-1}}{\frac{SS(Error)}{(r-1)(q-1)}} \quad \text{is} \quad F((q-1), (r-1)(q-1)) \quad \text{distributed.}$$

Calculation-wise, one can show that with T being the total sum of all observations, as before, and with

$$T_{i\cdot} = q\bar{X}_{i\cdot} = \sum_{j=1}^{q} X_{ij} \quad \text{(row sum)}, \quad i = 1, \ldots, r$$

$$T_{\cdot j} = r\bar{X}_{\cdot j} = \sum_{i=1}^{r} X_{ij} \quad \text{(column sum)}, \quad j = 1, \ldots, q$$

so that $T = \sum_{i=1}^{r} T_{i\cdot} = \sum_{j=1}^{q} T_{\cdot j}$, we have:

$$\begin{aligned} SS(\text{Rows}) &= \sum_{i=1}^{r} \frac{T_{i\cdot}^2}{q} - \frac{T^2}{N} \\ SS(\text{Columns}) &= \sum_{j=1}^{q} \frac{T_{\cdot j}^2}{r} - \frac{T^2}{N} \\ SS(\text{Error}) &= \sum_{i,j} X_{ij}^2 - \sum_{i=1}^{r} \frac{T_{i\cdot}^2}{q} - \sum_{j=1}^{q} \frac{T_{\cdot j}^2}{r} + \frac{T^2}{N}. \end{aligned}$$

These expressions are generally used for the ANOVA table; as before, we should take care not to lose any numerical precision when they are computed, as they often involve the difference of large numbers of about the same size.

Returning to our example, we get $r = 4$, $q = 3$, $N = rq = 12$ and:

$$T = T_{1\cdot} + T_{2\cdot} + T_{3\cdot} + T_{4\cdot} = 2260 + 2230 + 2290 + 2530 = 9310$$

and

$$T = T_{\cdot 1} + T_{\cdot 2} + T_{\cdot 3} = 3340 + 3180 + 2790 = 9310.$$

Also, $\sum_{i,j} X_{ij}^2 = 7\,299\,900$.

Thus we obtain:

$$SS(\text{Rows}) = \frac{1}{q} \sum_{i=1}^{r} T_{i\cdot}^2 - \frac{T^2}{N} = \frac{1}{3}(2260^2 + 2230^2 + 2290^2 + 2530^2) - \frac{9310^2}{12}$$

$$= \frac{1}{3} \cdot 21\,725\,500 - \frac{86\,676\,100}{12} \approx 7\,241\,833.3 - 7\,223\,008.3 = 18\,825$$

$$SS(\text{Columns}) = \frac{1}{r} \sum_{j=1} T_{\cdot j}^2 - \frac{T^2}{N} = \frac{1}{4}(3340^2 + 3180^2 + 2790^2) - \frac{9310^2}{12}$$

$$= \frac{1}{4} \cdot 29\,052\,100 - \frac{86\,676\,100}{12} \approx 7\,263\,025 - 7\,223\,008.3 = 40\,016.7$$

$$SS(\text{Error}) = \sum_{i,j} X_{ij}^2 - \sum_{i=1}^{r} \frac{T_{i\cdot}^2}{q} - \sum_{j=1}^{q} \frac{T_{\cdot j}^2}{r} + \frac{T^2}{N}$$

$$\approx 7\,299\,900 - 7\,241\,833.3 - 7\,263\,025 + 7\,223\,008.3 = 18\,050.$$

Let us now test the null hypothesis H_0: The machines have equal output

i.e. H_0: $\mu_{1\cdot} = \mu_{2\cdot} = \mu_{3\cdot} = \mu_{4\cdot}$

against the alternative hypothesis that not all of the four machines have the same output.

The appropriate F-ratio is:

$$\frac{\dfrac{SS(\text{Rows})}{r-1}}{\dfrac{SS(\text{Error})}{(r-1)(q-1)}} = \frac{\dfrac{18825}{4-1}}{\dfrac{18050}{(4-1)(3-1)}} = \frac{\dfrac{18825}{3}}{\dfrac{18050}{6}} \approx 2.086 .$$

From an F-table we find $F_{0.05}(3,6) = 4.76$.

We therefore *cannot* reject the null hypothesis about equal machine output.

Let us then test the null hypothesis H_0: The operators are equally efficient

i.e. H_0: $\mu_{\cdot 1} = \mu_{\cdot 2} = \mu_{\cdot 3}$

against the alternative hypothesis that not all of the three operators are equally efficient.

The appropriate F-ratio is:

$$\frac{\dfrac{SS(\text{Columns})}{q-1}}{\dfrac{SS(\text{Error})}{(r-1)(q-1)}} = \frac{\dfrac{40016.7}{3-1}}{\dfrac{18050}{(4-1)(3-1)}} = \frac{\dfrac{40016.7}{2}}{\dfrac{18050}{6}} \approx 6.651 .$$

From an F-table we find $F_{0.05}(2,6) = 5.14$ and $F_{0.01}(2,6) = 10.92$.

Therefore, we can *reject* the null hypothesis about equally efficient operators at the 5% level of confidence, but *not* at the 1% level.

*11.5 Randomized Block and Latin Square Designs

Consider the machine output problem of Example 11.1. Assume that a close investigation of the actual conditions surrounding the experiment reveals that a new raw material for the machines is to be used from week no. 4 onwards. What effect will this have on our experiment? The obvious answer is that this extraneous factor might confound the results, as it enters in a systematic way. A method to remove this undesired effect would be to use a *randomized block design*. In our example this means that instead of using the old raw material for the first three weeks and then switching to the new, the weeks would be selected at random for use with the new raw material.

For instance, the new raw material might be used in weeks 2, 3 and 5, and the old in weeks 1, 4 and 6.

Consider now the machine output problem of Example 11.4, and assume that a four-machine, four-operator test is being performed, yielding 16 observations. Suppose now that we also wish to obtain some indication of the effect on the output of each of four possible raw materials, A, B, C and D. Using a $4 \times 4 \times 4$ factorial design might seem appropriate, for a total of 64 measurements. However, the following design would require only 16 measurements.

Machine \ Operator	j = 1	2	3	4
i = 1	B	A	D	C
2	C	B	A	D
3	D	C	B	A
4	A	D	C	B

Fig. 11/13: A Latin Square Design.

In Fig. 11/13 each raw material occurs exactly once in each row and exactly once in each column. Such a design is called a *Latin Square* design. These designs are appropriate when there are three factors present, all having the same number of levels. Latin squares of different sizes can easily be constructed, or found in tables. Examples are:

B	A	C
A	C	B
C	B	A

3×3 Latin square

D	A	B	C
A	B	C	D
B	C	D	A
C	D	A	B

4×4 Latin square

A	E	D	C	B
B	A	E	D	C
C	B	A	E	D
D	C	B	A	E
E	D	C	B	A

5×5 Latin Square

Fig. 11/14: Latin squares.

References

Chou, Y.: *Statistical Analysis,* 2nd edition. Holt, Rinehart and Winston, New York 1975.

Hamburg, M.: *Statistical Analysis for Decision Making,* 2nd edition. Harcourt, Brace, Jovanovich, New York 1977.

Hawkins, C.A., and J.E. Weber: *Statistical Analysis. Applications to Business and Economics,* Harper & Row, New York 1980.

Kerlinger, F.N.: *Foundations of Behavioral Research,* 2nd edition. Holt, Rinehart and Winston, New York 1973.

Kleinbaum, D.G., and L.L. Kupper: *Applied Regression Analysis and other Multivariable Methods,* Duxbury Press, North Scituate, Mass. 1978.

Lapin, L.L.: *Statistics for Modern Business Decisions,* 3rd edition. Harcourt, Brace, Jovanovich, New York 1982.

Mansfield, E.: *Statistics for Business and Economics,* Norton & Company, New York 1980.

Ott, L.: *An Introduction to Statistical Methods and Data Analysis,* Duxbury Press, North Scituate, Mass. 1977.

Wonnacott, T.H., and R.J. Wonnacott: *Introductory Statistics for Business and Economics,* 2nd edition. John Wiley & Sons, New York 1977.

Exercises

11–1 A marketing research institute studied the effect of four different colours on product recognition time. The study involved twenty people randomly assigned to four groups with five people in each. Each colour was then exposed to each person. The recognition time (in seconds) was measured. The following data were obtained:

$\bar{x}_1 = 0.69$, $\bar{x}_2 = 0{,}98$, $\bar{x}_3 = 1.19$, $\bar{x}_4 = 0.72$

SS(Total) = 2.06 and SS(Error) = 0.82

a) What are the null and alternative hypotheses in this study?
b) Construct the analysis of variance table;
c) Test the null hypothesis using a level of significance of 0.05.

11–2 A university commerce student is considering three possible careers in the furniture industry: finance, sales and personnel management. Since he is interested in rapid advancement, he has surveyed the advancement of top executives in each of these areas. Shown below are the ages at which current executive level rank was reached.

Finance	Retail Sales	Personnel
46	38	45
48	43	44
52	39	47
43	45	46·
47	36	46

At the 5% level of significance, can this student conclude that the three areas offer him the same opportunity?

$$\sum_{i=1}^{n} x_i = 665 \qquad \sum_{i=1}^{n} x_i^2 = 29719.$$

11–3 In the table below are shown the amounts obtained (in kg/hr) of a certain chemical product, when a production process was operating at three different temperature levels. The replicates are data values from random sampling.

Temperature level	Replicate 1	2	3	4
30 °C	17.2	16.5	16.9	18.1
35 °C	20.6	22.4	21.0	20.7
40 °C	19.1	19.3	19.9	19.5

Does the temperature at which the process is operated have any effect on the rate of production of this chemical? Test, using $\alpha = 0.05$.

11–4 A marketing research study examined the comparative effect of six different promotional techniques and obtained the results shown in the table below. State the conclusions that one can derive from the analysis of variance table. Use a 5% level of significance.

Source	d.f.	ss
Promotional technique	5	26.37
Error	9	15.82
Total	14	42.19

11–5 A soft drink company carried out a pilot study regarding customer preferences for the colour of a new drink. Three different colours were considered: orange, yellow, green. Fifteen test areas with similar sales potential were selected, and each colour was assigned randomly to five of the areas for test marketing.

The following table shows the amounts (in litres) sold.

Orange	Yellow	Green
31.4	27.7	29.9
28.2	25.2	30.3
30.6	28.6	31.8
27.5	24.7	31.7
28.9	27.1	32.4

Suppose it is desired to control the α risk at .05. Are the mean sales the same for the different colours?

11–6 The much feared Marquis DeSade decided to test the effectiveness of three different methods of lecturing his sadistics course. 18 students were randomly selected to be taught by the three different methods. The course results are recorded below.

Method A	Method B	Method C
88	89	76
92	92	89
76	81	95
85	76	84
81	92	96
79	78	86

a) Test at $\alpha = 5\%$ to see whether the differences among the three sample means are significant.
b) Construct a 90% confidence interval for the average performance using method A.

11–7 During the past four years, four different textbooks have been used in a certain statistics course and the final examination results for the students are recorded in the following table:

	Textbook 1	2	3	4
	60	80	97	67
	80	81	84	84
	69	73	93	78
	65	69	79	61
		75	92	
		72		
Total	274	450	445	380

$$\sum_i \sum_j X_{ij}^2 = 122115.$$

At $\alpha = 5\%$ can we conclude that students' scores are significantly affected by textbooks? (Show H_0, H_1, the ANOVA table and your conclusion).

11–8 To test whether the average lives of two makes of a battery are different at a significance level of .05, a random sample of students who used either make of battery was asked to keep a record of the time that elapsed before their battery died. The observed battery lives are recorded below (in hours):

Always-ready Brand:	10.9	12.4	9.5	16.6	14.4	8.2
Daracill Brand:	13.7	11.4	8.5	6.5	7.9	

a) Use a two-sample t-test to determine if there is a significant difference in average battery lives.
b) Use analysis of variance to conduct the same test.
c) Square the t_α and the t statistic from part (a) and compare these with the F_α and F statistic of Part (b). What assumption did we make in both approaches?

11–9 a) Fill in the analysis of variance table below.
b) How many treatments are there in this problem?
c) State reasonable null and alternative hypotheses. If you were willing to commit Type I errors only 1% of the time, what critical value of F would you use?
d) What is your conclusion?

Source of Variation	Sum of Squares	Degrees of Freedom	F Ratio
Treatments	78.400		8.124
Error	38.600	12	
Total			

11–10 Consider Exercise no. 3. Assume that each replicate was performed at a different pressure. Conduct a two-way analysis of variance test to determine whether

a) the pressure, or
b) the temperature

has a significant effect. Use $\alpha = 0.05$.

11–11 Consider Exercise no. 5. Assume that each locality (observation) is associated with a different average income level. Conduct a two-way analysis to determine whether

a) the colour, or
b) the income

has a significant effect. Use $\alpha = 0.01$ and 0.05.

11–12 Consider Exercise no. 6. Assume that each row of the data refers to students with a different number of other courses already taken. Perform a two-way analysis of variance to see if the number of courses taken, and/or the teaching technique has a significant effect on student performance.

12. Simple Linear Regression

We have now come to one of the most fruitful subjects within statistics, namely regression. Regression analysis describes how variables are related. To be specific, the value of one variable (for the purpose of the analysis called the *dependent* variable) is predicted or explained by the value(s) of the so-called *independent* variable(s).

The background of the term "regression" is very interesting. It originates from a study by Galton who compared the heights of men and their sons and grandsons. He found that tall men usually had tall sons and grandsons, but that the relationship between father and son was (statistically) stronger than between father and grandson. The height of grandsons tended to be closer to the population average than the height of sons, which itself in turn tended to be closer to the average than the father's height. In other words, deviations from the average height tend to *regress* back to the average in subsequent generations. Galton used this fact to predict the height of children and this method became known as regression analysis. Today, the term serves as a name for a much larger area within statistics.

In Section 12.1 we introduce the basic problem, and some basic terminology is explained. Our treatment is built around an example relating annual incomes and expenditures for families in Japan. Section 12.2 is devoted to the method of least squares and will serve as a foundation for the rest of this and the subsequent chapter. Section 12.3 deals with the estimators $\hat{\alpha}$ and $\hat{\beta}$, and Section 12.4 with correlation analysis and ANOVA. In Section 12.5 we show how to estimate the expected value of the dependent variable for a given value of the independent variable, and in Section 12.6 we predict the dependent variable for a given value of the independent variable.

In Section 12.7 we show how to solve simple linear regression problems by computer, and analyze the computer output resulting from the introductory Japanese income problem.

As in many other places elsewhere in this book, an equal sign (=) is often used when it really should be an approximately equal sign (≈). This is done for presentation purposes.

12.1 Introduction

Example 12.1

Consider the following sample data from April, 1960, concerning urban families in Japan:

Income (yen per month)	Average Income (x)	Average Expenditure (y)
10,000–14,999	12,500	14,100
15,000–19,999	17,700	18,500
20,000–24,999	22,300	22,600
25,000–29,999	27,300	25,800
30,000–34,999	32,200	31,000
35,000–39,999	37,300	34,600
40,000–44,999	42,300	39,800
45,000–49,999	47,200	42,000
50,000–59,999	54,300	49,600
60,000–69,999	64,300	57,000

Fig. 12/1: Data for the Japanese income problem.

Does this set of data suggest a relation between the average income x and average expenditure y? If there is a relationship, what mathematical form does it take? And how do we determine such a relationship, if it exists?

To investigate this problem more closely, we first plot x and y in a *scatter diagram:*

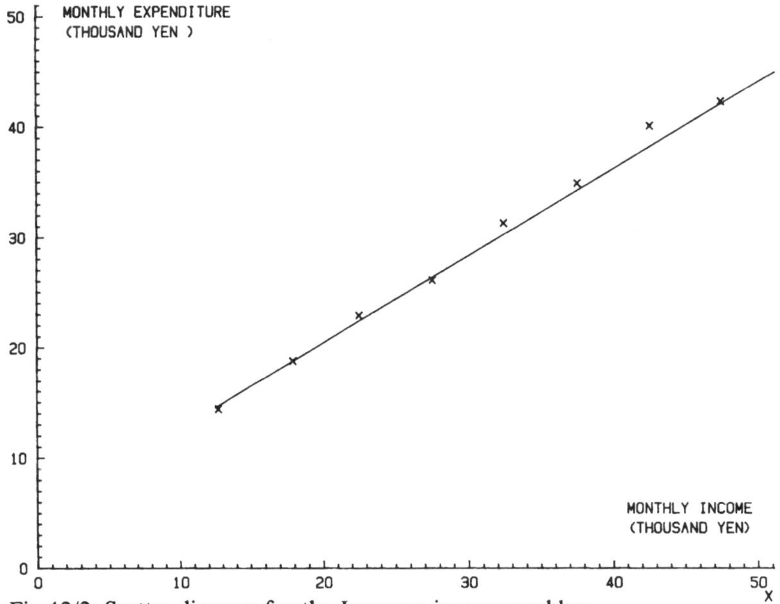

Fig. 12/2: Scatter diagram for the Japanese income problem.

From the diagram it is obvious that there is a relation between x and y (as we indeed expected). Is the relation *linear*, i.e. do coefficients α and β exist so that $y = \alpha + \beta x$? In *linear regression analysis* we describe the relation between x and y in linear form and try to find the best possible line, i.e. a line which in some sense gives the best possible fit to the observed data.

Remark 1: It is of course extremely unlikely for all points to be exactly on a straight line and we shall therefore *specify* the *model*

$$y = \alpha + \beta x + \varepsilon$$

where the *error term* ε is a random variable with zero mean and variance σ^2.

We can then write $E(Y|x)$ (the conditional expectation of Y, given x; also denoted by $\mu_{Y|x}$) as $E(Y|x) = \alpha + \beta x$.

Remark 2: If the relation is not linear, we might still be able to use linear regression by a suitable transformation of the data. As an example, let us consider the famous Cobb-Douglas production function $Y = \gamma K^{\alpha} L^{\beta}$ where Y is output, K capital and L labour and α, β and γ are constants. It is transformed by taking logarithms:

$$\log Y = \log \gamma + \alpha \log K + \beta \log L,$$

and the linear model can still be used if we work with logarithms of the data on Y, K and L.

Remark 3: It may be, as we just saw, that three or more variables are related to each other. We could then specify a *multiple linear regression* model

$$y = \alpha + \beta_1 x_1 + \beta_2 x_2 + \ldots + \beta_k x_k + \varepsilon,$$

where $y, x_1, \ldots, x_k$ are variables and $\alpha, \beta_1, \ldots, \beta_k$ are constants. y is called the *dependent* variable and $x_1, \ldots, x_k$ the *independent* variables.

Which of the variables is to be labelled as dependent will usually be clear from case to case. Otherwise it is a matter of judgement, convention or taste. When there is only one independent variable, we talk of *simple* linear regression. We shall in this chapter limit ourselves to this case, and leave a discussion of multiple linear regression to the next chapter.

Remark 4: *Warning:* Even if we could conclude that there is a relation $y = \alpha + \beta x$ between x and y, this does not mean that there has to be a direct *causal* relation between x and y. There may be a third variable z hidden, which directly affects x and y in the same direction. For example, let:

x = total daily volume of ice-cream sold in the Montreal region.
y = total daily volume of soft drink sold in the Montreal region.

Then x and y are probably not directly causally related to each other, but rather both dependent on z = daily highest afternoon temperature in the Montreal region.

Remark 5: It may be that our linear regression analysis will tell us that our data do not firmly support the linear relation $y = \alpha + \beta x$. Still x and y could be related, but the relation may be *nonlinear* ($y = \alpha + \frac{\beta}{x}$ or $y = \alpha \cdot e^{-\beta x}$ or $y = \alpha\sqrt{\beta - x^2}$, etc.).

Remark 6: It may be that our data for y and x give a good fit to a straight line, say for $15 \leqq x \leqq 35$:

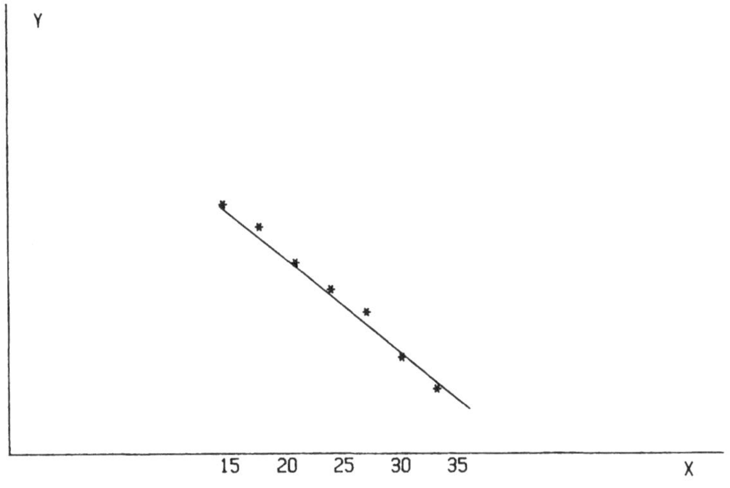

Fig. 12/3: Good fit to a straight line for $15 \leqq x \leqq 35$.

Having found a regression line $y = \alpha + \beta x$, we can then, for given x, use the line to *predict* y. But this can of course only be done for $15 \leqq x \leqq 35$ and for circumstances similar to those for which the data were obtained. The true hidden relation may significantly deviate from our regression line outside the interval $15 \leqq x \leqq 35$:

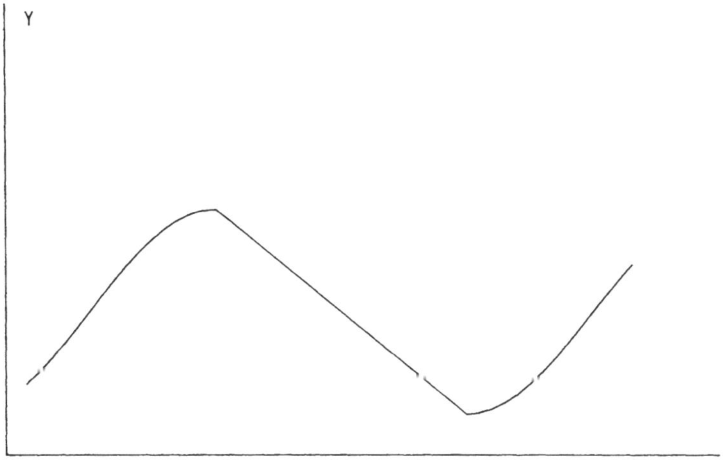

Fig. 12/4: Poor fit to a straight line outside $15 \leqq x \leqq 35$.

12.2 The Method of Least Squares

Consider the following problem. Given n pairs of observations of the variables x and y: (x_i, y_i), $i = 1, \ldots, n$. How can we find a "best" regression line $y = \hat{\alpha} + \hat{\beta}x$? More specifically, how do we find $\hat{\alpha}$, $\hat{\beta}$ such that $\sum_{i=1}^{n} (y_i - \hat{y}_i)^2$ is minimal, where $\hat{y}_i$ is the "fitted" y_i – value, i.e. $\hat{y}_i = \hat{\alpha} + \hat{\beta}x_i$? We refer to $\sum_i (y_i - \hat{y}_i)^2$ as the *sum of squared errors*, SSE, because $y_i - \hat{y}_i$ is the *error* we make if the observed value y_i is replaced by the fitted value $\hat{y}_i$. This error can be interpreted as the vertical distance from the point (x_i, y_i) to the fitted line $y = \hat{\alpha} + \hat{\beta}x$.

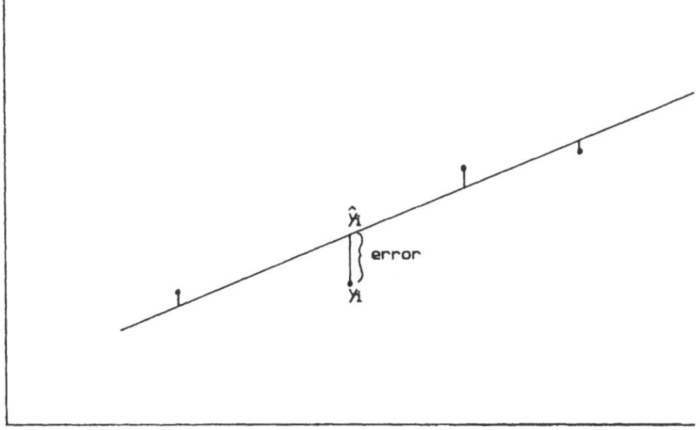

Fig. 12/5: Observed points and fitted line.

We have:

$$SSE = \sum_{i=1}^{n} (y_i - \hat{y}_i)^2 = \sum_{i=1}^{n} (y_i - \hat{\alpha} - \hat{\beta}x_i)^2 .$$

In this expression, let us temporarily replace $\hat{\alpha}$ by α and $\hat{\beta}$ by β. x_i and y_i are given values, so we can now regard SSE as a function of the two *variables* α and β.

We want to find α and β such that SSE is minimized; the solution $\alpha = \hat{\alpha}$ and $\beta = \hat{\beta}$ is called the *least squares estimate* of α and β. Differentiating SSE with respect to α and β and putting the two derivatives equal to zero: $\frac{\partial}{\partial\alpha}(SSE) = \frac{\partial}{\partial\beta}(SSE) = 0$ gives us, after some calculations (which we shall leave out here[2]):

$$\hat{\beta} = \frac{\sum(x_i - \bar{x})(y_i - \bar{y})}{\sum(x_i - \bar{x})^2} = \frac{n\sum x_i y_i - (\sum x_i)(\sum y_i)}{n\sum x_i^2 - (\sum x_i)^2}$$

$$\hat{\alpha} = \bar{y} - \hat{\beta}\bar{x} = \frac{1}{n}(\sum y_i - \hat{\beta}\sum x_i)$$

where $\bar{x} = \frac{1}{n}\sum_1^n x_i$ and $\bar{y} = \frac{1}{n}\sum_1^n y_i$.

Example 12.2

From our Japanese data we obtain the following table (fill it in *columnwise* and not row-wise). For convenience, figures are given in thousands of yen:

i	x_i	y_i	$x_i y_i$	x_i^2	y_i^2
1	12.5	14.1	176.25	156.25	198.81
2	17.7	18.5	327.45	313.29	342.25
3	22.3	22.6	503.98	497.29	510.76
4	27.3	25.8	704.34	745.29	665.64
5	32.2	31.0	998.20	1036.84	961.00
6	37.3	34.6	1290.58	1391.29	1197.16
7	42.3	39.8	1683.54	1789.29	1584.04
8	47.2	42.0	1982.40	2227.84	1764.00
9	54.3	49.6	2693.28	2948.49	2460.16
10	64.3	57.0	3665.10	4134.49	3249.00
Total	357.4	335.0	14025.12	15240.36	12932.82

Fig. 12/6: Table for computing $\hat{\alpha}$ and $\hat{\beta}$ for the Japanese data.

[2] The reader who is familiar with differential calculus of two variables is encouraged to do the calculations. As an intermediate step one obtains the so-called *normal equations:*

$$n\hat{\alpha} + \hat{\beta}\sum X_i = \sum y_i$$
$$\hat{\alpha}\sum x_i + \hat{\beta}\sum x_i^2 = \sum x_i y_i .$$

We get:

$$\hat{\beta} = \frac{n\sum x_i y_i - (\sum x_i)(\sum y_i)}{n\sum x_i^2 - (\sum x_i)^2} = \frac{10 \cdot 14025.12 - 357.4 \cdot 335.0}{10 \cdot 15240.36 - (357.4)^2}$$

$$= \frac{20522.2}{24668.84} = 0.8319$$

$$\hat{\alpha} = \bar{y} - \hat{\beta}\bar{x} = \frac{1}{n}(\sum y_i - \hat{\beta}\sum x_i) = \frac{1}{10}(335 - 0.8319 \cdot 357.4) = 3.768.$$

Remark: It is convenient to work with the notation

$$S_{xx} = \sum (x_i - \bar{x})^2$$
$$S_{yy} = \sum (y_i - \bar{y})^2$$
$$S_{xy} = \sum (x_i - \bar{x})(y_i - \bar{y}).$$

Using this notation one can easily show:

$$\hat{\beta} = \frac{S_{xy}}{S_{xx}}$$

$$SSE = \sum (y_i - \hat{y}_i)^2 = S_{yy} - \frac{(S_{xy})^2}{S_{xx}}$$

$$s_x^2 = \frac{1}{n-1} S_{xx} \quad \text{(the sample variance of x)}$$

$$s_{xy} = \frac{1}{n-1} S_{xy} \quad \text{(the sample } \textit{covariance} \text{ of x and y)}$$

etc.

12.3 The Estimators $\hat{\alpha}$ and $\hat{\beta}$

We state the assumptions of the linear model: The random variables Y_i are statistically independent with mean $\alpha + \beta x_i$, variance $= \sigma^2$. Alternatively, we could say that Y_i satisfies the relationship

$$Y_i = \alpha + \beta x_i + \varepsilon_i,$$

with ε_i being independent variables for different i:s, having zero mean and standard deviation σ.

Now that we have estimated the true but unknown regression line $y = \alpha + \beta x$, we are of course interested to know something about the estimators $\hat{\alpha}$ and $\hat{\beta}$.

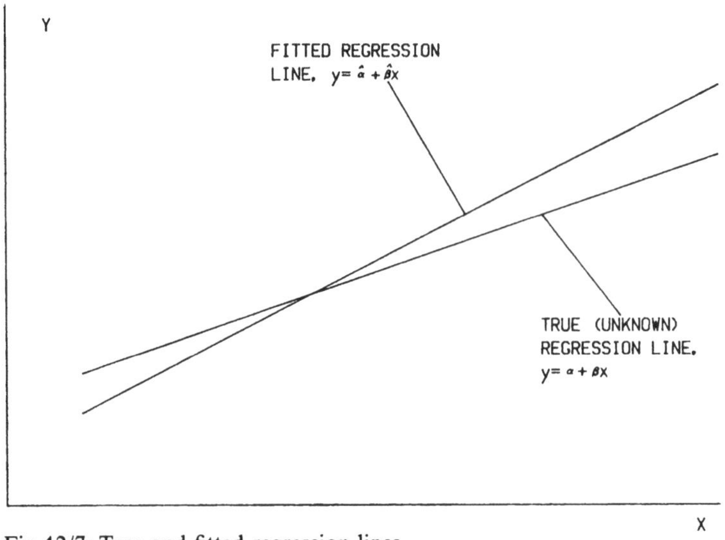

Fig. 12/7: True and fitted regression lines.

It is not very difficult to show the following:

Theorem:

$$E(\hat{\alpha}) = \alpha,\ V(\hat{\alpha}) = \sigma^2 \sqrt{\frac{1}{n} + \frac{\bar{x}^2}{\sum (x_i - \bar{x})^2}} = \sigma^2 \sqrt{\frac{1}{n} + \frac{\bar{x}^2}{S_{xx}}}$$

$$E(\hat{\beta}) = \beta,\ V(\hat{\beta}) = \frac{\sigma^2}{\sum (x_i - \bar{x})^2} = \frac{\sigma^2}{S_{xx}}.$$

It is left to the reader to prove the theorem as an exercise.

$\hat{\alpha}$ and $\hat{\beta}$ are described as *linear estimators,* because they are linear expressions of the observed values y_i (note that we consider x_i as predetermined). From the theorem above we see that they are unbiased. Regarding their variance, one has the following famous result, which we give without proof:

The Gauss-Markov Theorem[3]

Of all linear unbiased estimators, $\hat{\alpha}$ and $\hat{\beta}$ have minimum variance.

Let us now concentrate on $\hat{\beta}$. In order to carry out tests and construct confidence intervals regarding $\hat{\beta}$ we have to know its distribution. Assuming that ε_i is

[3] Karl Friedrich Gauss, German mathematician, 1777–1855.
Andrey Andreyevitch Markov, Russian mathematician, 1856–1922.

$N(0, \sigma)$, one can show that

$$\frac{\hat{\beta}-\beta}{\sqrt{s^2 \cdot \frac{1}{\sum(x_i-\bar{x})^2}}} = \frac{\hat{\beta}-\beta}{\frac{s}{\sqrt{S_{xx}}}} = \frac{\hat{\beta}-\beta}{s} \cdot \sqrt{S_{xx}}$$

is t-distributed with $n-2$ degrees of freedom and where $s^2 = \frac{1}{n-2}\sum(y_i - \hat{y}_i)^2$, called the *residual variance*, is an unbiased estimator of σ^2. We also say that s is the *standard error of the estimate.* One can show that

$$s^2 = \frac{1}{n-2}\left(S_{yy} - \frac{(S_{xy})^2}{S_{xx}}\right) = \frac{\sum y_i^2 - \hat{\alpha}\sum y_i - \hat{\beta}\sum x_i y_i}{n-2}.$$

For our example, we get:

$$s^2 = \frac{12932.82 - 3.768 \cdot 335 - 0.8319 \cdot 14025.12}{8} = \frac{3.043}{8} = 0.3804,$$

so that:

$$s = 0.617.$$

Knowing the probability distribution for $\hat{\beta}$, we can now proceed to test hypotheses and construct confidence intervals for β.

Example 12.3

Perform a two-sided test of the hypothesis H_0: $\beta = 0$ using our Japanese data. In this example we test if x contributes any information about y. $\beta = 0$ would indicate that x is of no value for predicting y, using the linear model.

Solution: Our test statistic is

$$t = \frac{\hat{\beta}-\beta}{s} \cdot \sqrt{\sum(x_i-\bar{x})^2} = \frac{0.8319-0}{0.617}\underbrace{\sqrt{15240.36 - \frac{(357.4)^2}{10}}}_{\sqrt{2466.884} = 49.6677} = 67.0$$

and with $t_{0.005}(8) = 3.355$ we *reject* H_0 at the 1% level; our test statistic is so large so that we can be very confident that H_0 is false. This means that there *is* a linear relationship between x and y.

Example 12.4

Find a 98% confidence interval for β.

Solution: We know (cf. Section 9.3) that the interval is determined by:

$$\hat{\beta} \pm t_{0.01}(n-2) \cdot \frac{s}{\sqrt{\sum x_i^2 - \frac{1}{n}(\sum x_i)^2}} = 0.8319 \pm 2.896 \cdot \frac{0.617}{49.6677}$$

$= 0.8319 \pm 0.0360$, so that the interval is $(0.7959, 0.8679)$.

One can also construct confidence intervals for α and perform tests like H_0: $\alpha = 0$ (the regression line passes through the origin), etc. We shall leave this out.

12.4 Correlation Analysis and ANOVA for Regression

A measure of the strength of the linear relationship (or the *linear correlation*) between x and y is given by the *correlation coefficient* r (also referred to as the *Pearson product moment coefficient of correlation*):

Definition: The *correlation coefficient* r is given by:

$$r = \frac{\sum_{i=1}^{n} (x_i - \bar{x})(y_i - \bar{y})}{\sqrt{\sum_{i=1}^{n} (x_i - \bar{x})^2 \cdot \sum_{i=1}^{n} (y_i - \bar{y})^2}} = \frac{S_{xy}}{\sqrt{S_{xx} S_{yy}}}.$$

It is generally easier to calculate r from the equivalent expression:

$$r = \frac{n\sum x_i y_i - (\sum x_i)(\sum y_i)}{\sqrt{\{n\sum x_i^2 - (\sum x_i)^2\}\{n\sum y_i^2 - (\sum y_i)^2\}}}.$$

Example 12.5

From our Japanese income data we obtain:

$$r = \frac{10 \cdot 14025.12 - 357.4 \cdot 335.0}{\sqrt{\{10 \cdot 15240.36 - (357.4)^2\} \cdot \{10 \cdot 12932.82 - (335)^2\}}}$$

$$= \frac{20522.2}{\sqrt{24668.84 \cdot 17103.2}} = 0.99910.$$

One can show that $-1 \leq r \leq 1$ always holds; our r-value above is therefore quite high, indicating a very strong linear relationship.

Since the numerator in the expression for r is the same as that of $\hat{\beta}$, and the denominators are positive in both cases, $r > 0$ will indicate a positive slope of the regression line, $r < 0$ a negative slope. $r = 0$ implies no linear correlation between x and y. r near to 0 indicates a weak linear relationship; r near to $+1$ or -1 a strong one:

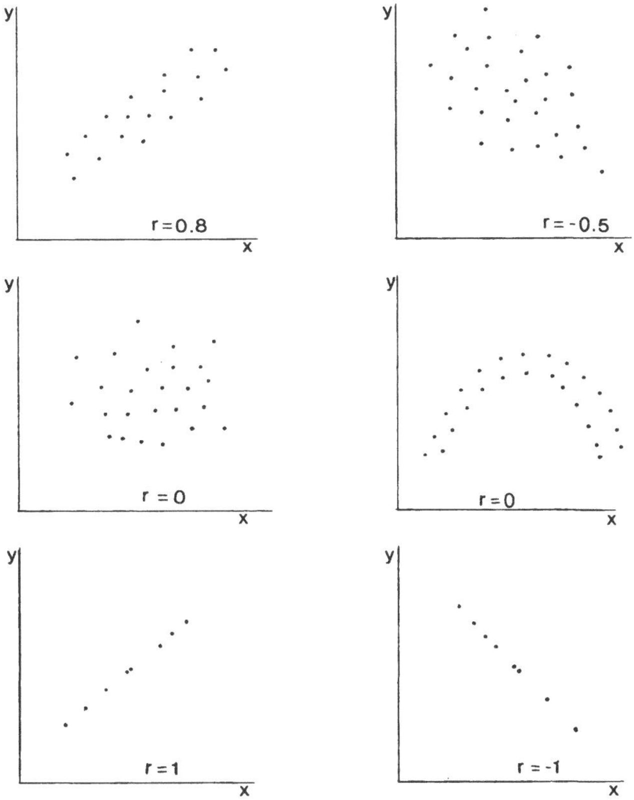

Fig. 12/8: The correlation coefficient for various scatter diagrams.

One can show that:

$$r = \frac{\sum(y_i - \bar{y})^2 - \sum(y_i - \hat{y}_i)^2}{\sum(y_i - \bar{y})^2} = 1 - \frac{\sum(y_i - \hat{y}_i)^2}{\sum(y_i - \bar{y})^2}$$

and from this we see that $0 \leqq r^2 \leqq 1$. r^2 is called the *coefficient of determination* and has an interesting interpretation. We can write:

$y_i - \bar{y}$	$=$	$(\hat{y}_i - \bar{y})$	$+$	$(y_i - \hat{y}_i)$
total deviation		explained deviation		unexplained deviation

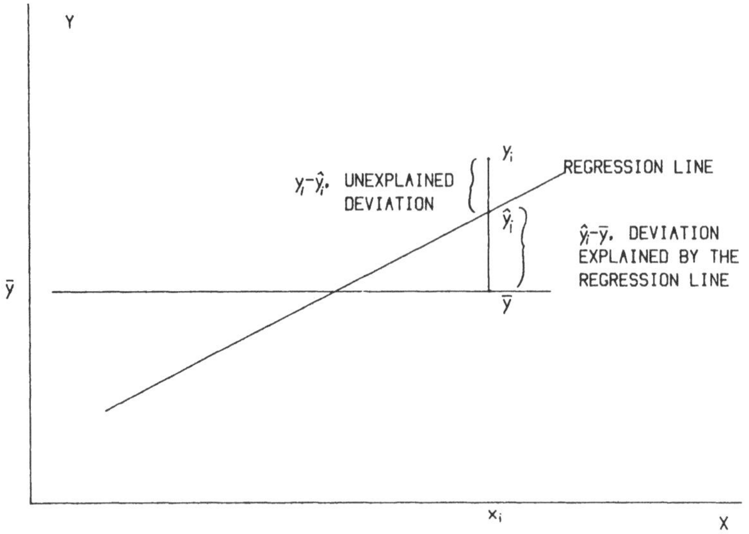

Fig. 12/9: Explained, unexplained and total deviation.

Squaring both sides and summing, one can show:

$$\underbrace{\Sigma(y_i-\bar{y})^2}_{\text{total variation}} = \underbrace{\Sigma(\hat{y}_i-\bar{y})^2}_{\text{explained variation}} + \underbrace{\Sigma(y_i-\hat{y}_i)^2}_{\text{unexplained variation}}$$

The explained variation is accounted for by our linear regression line, but the unexplained variation is the remaining variation around the regression line. The less the latter is, the closer the fit to the straight line. We see that: $r^2 = 1 - \frac{\text{unexplained variation}}{\text{total variation}} = \frac{\text{explained variation}}{\text{total variation}}$, so that r^2 near to 1 indicates a very good fit and r^2 near to 0 a poor one.

Example 12.6

From our Japanese income data, we find $r^2 = (0.9991)^2 = 0.9982$ which is very good indeed. In practice, r^2-values over 0.95 are considered good.

Analysis of Variance for Regression

Returning to our expression for the variation in y we shall now regard it as an ANOVA identity:

$$\underbrace{\sum_i (y_i - \bar{y})^2}_{\substack{\text{total variation,}\\ S_{yy},\\ \text{SS (Total)}}} = \underbrace{\sum_i (\hat{y}_i - \bar{y})^2}_{\substack{\text{variation explained}\\ \text{by regression,}\\ \text{SS (Regression)}}} + \underbrace{\sum_i (y_i - \hat{y}_i)^2}_{\substack{\text{unexplained variation,}\\ \text{sum of squared}\\ \text{errors, SSE,}\\ \text{SS (Error)}}}$$

As for ordinary ANOVA one can then establish the table:

Source of Variation	Sum of Squares (SS)	d.f.	F
Regression	$\sum_i (\hat{y}_i - \bar{y})^2$ $= \text{SS (Regression)}$	1	$F = \dfrac{\text{SS(Regr.)}}{\dfrac{\text{SS(Error)}}{n-2}}$
Unexplained, residual variation	$\sum_i (y_i - \hat{y}_i)^2$ $= \text{SS (Error)}$	$n-2$	
Total	$\sum_i (y_i - \hat{y})^2 = \text{SS(Total)}$	$n-1$	

Fig. 12/10: ANOVA table for simple linear regression.

As for ordinary ANOVA one can show that F is $F(1, n-2)$ if $\beta = 0$. This means that an F-test can be used to test the null hypothesis:

H_0: $\beta = 0$

against H_0: $\beta \neq 0$.

If $\beta = 0$ we have $Y = \alpha + \varepsilon$ so that the true regression line would be $y = \bar{y}$ (assuming, for simplicity, that α is correctly estimated: $\alpha = \hat{\alpha} = \bar{y}$); see Fig. 12/11 on the next page.

Remark 1: Note that $\dfrac{\text{SS(Error)}}{n-2} = s^2$, so that $F = \dfrac{\text{SS(Regression)}}{s^2}$.

Also, as $\text{SS(Total)} = S_{yy}$ and $\text{SS(Error)} = \text{SSE} = S_{yy} - \dfrac{(S_{xy})^2}{S_{xx}}$ we have:

$$\text{SS(Regression)} = \text{SS(Total)} - \text{SS(Error)}$$
$$= S_{yy} - \left(S_{yy} - \frac{(S_{xy})^2}{S_{xx}}\right) = \frac{(S_{xy})^2}{S_{xx}} = \hat{\beta} \cdot S_{xy}.$$

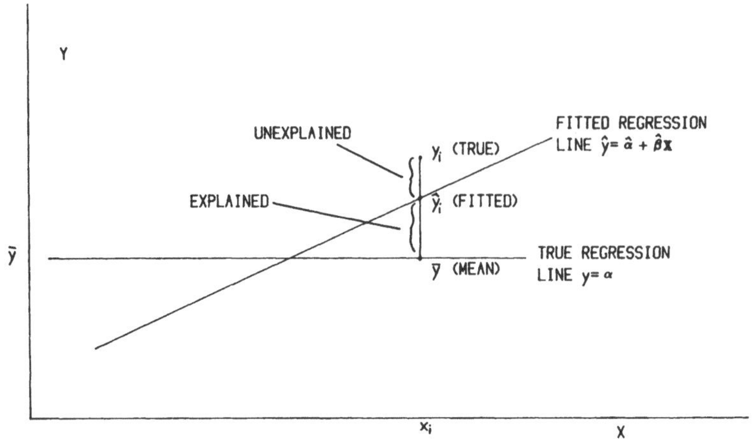

Fig. 12/11: Horizontal true regression line.

Example 12.7

From our Japanese example we find:

$\mathrm{SS(Regression)} = \hat{\beta}\cdot S_{xy} = 0.8319\cdot 2052.22 = 1707.24$ and $s^2 = 0.3804$ so that

$$F = \frac{\mathrm{SS(Regression)}}{s^2} = \frac{\hat{\beta}\cdot S_{xy}}{s^2} = \frac{1707.24}{0.3804} = 4488.0\,.$$

From an F-table we find $F_{0.01}(1,8) = 11.26$ so that H_0 is *rejected* at the 1% level.

Remark 2: The F-test is equivalent to a t-test for $\beta = 0$. We remember that $(t(n))^2 = F(1, n)$ (see the end of Section 7.4). In fact, our t-statistic was 67.0, and $(67.0)^2 = 4488.0$, which was our F-statistic. Also,

$$(t_{0.005}(8))^2 = (3.355)^2 = 11.26 = F_{0.01}(1,8)\,.$$

In general[4], $(t_\alpha(n))^2 = F_{2\alpha}(1, n)$.

[4] Proof: $1 - \alpha - 0.5 = P(0 \leqq t \leqq t_\alpha(n)) = \frac{1}{2}P(t^2 \leqq t_\alpha^2(n))$.
Therefore, $1 - 2\alpha = P(t^2 \leqq t_\alpha^2(n)) = P(F \leqq t_\alpha^2(n))$.
But $1 - 2\alpha = P(F \leqq F_{2\alpha}(1, n))$. Consequently, $(t_\alpha(n))^2 = F_{2\alpha}(1, n)$.

Remark 3: As we have seen that the t and F tests for the significance of β are equivalent, one may ask why we bother with both, when one of them will do. The answer is that for *simple* linear regression they are equivalent, but not for *multiple* linear regression. In the latter case, we shall need both tests, as we shall see in the next chapter.

12.5 Estimating the Expected Value of Y for a Given x

We talk of the *conditional* distribution of Y when we think of x as given. The mean $\mu_{Y|x}$ of this distribution, once x is known, is given by the *true* regression line, $\mu_{Y|x} = \alpha + \beta x$. One can prove the following:

Theorem: $\hat{\alpha} + \hat{\beta}x$ is $N\left(\alpha + \beta x, \sigma\sqrt{\frac{1}{n} + \frac{(x-\bar{x})^2}{\sum(x_i - \bar{x})^2}}\right)$.

In other words, $\hat{\alpha} + \hat{\beta}x$ is an unbiased estimator of $\mu_{Y|x}$. The notation Y | x ("Y, given x") is equivalent to $Y = \alpha + \beta x + \varepsilon$. Based on the above theorem, a test of the hypothesis: H_0: $E(Y|x^*) = y^*$, where x^* and y^* are given values would use the test statistic $t = \dfrac{\hat{y} - y^*}{s\sqrt{\frac{1}{n} + \frac{(x^* - \bar{x})^2}{\sum(x_i - \bar{x})^2}}}$, the sampling distribution of which is $t(n-2)$, provided that the null hypothesis is true.

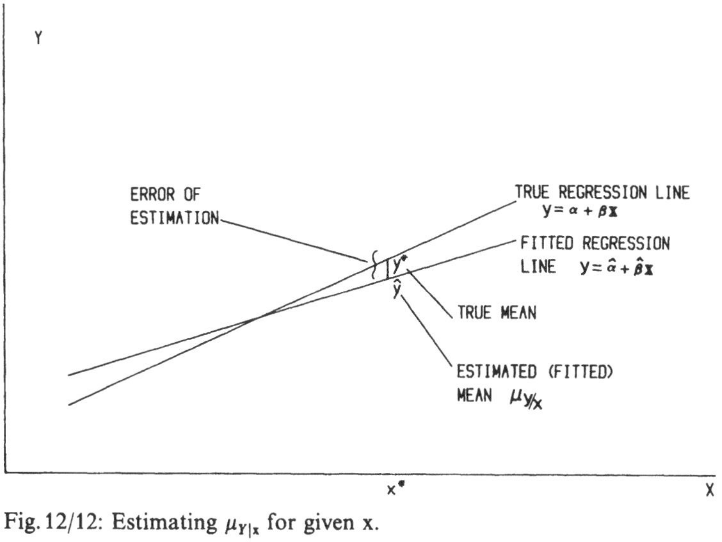

Fig. 12/12: Estimating $\mu_{Y|x}$ for given x.

Example 12.8

Perform a two-sided test of H_0: $E(Y|x = 41.5) = 37.2$ using our Japanese data.

Solution: Our test statistic t is:

$$t = \frac{\hat{y} - y^*}{s\sqrt{\frac{1}{n} + \frac{(x^* - \bar{x})^2}{\sum(x_i - \bar{x})^2}}} = \frac{\overbrace{\hat{\alpha} + \hat{\beta}\cdot 41.5}^{\hat{y}} - 37.2}{0.617\sqrt{\frac{1}{10} + \frac{(41.5 - 35.74)^2}{2466.884}}}$$

$$= \frac{3.768 + 0.8319\cdot 41.5 - 37.2}{0.617\cdot 0.336822} = 5.25$$

and with $t_{0.005}(8) = 3.355$, we *reject* H_0 at the 1% level.

Example 12.9

Does $y^* = 23.4$ belong to a 95% confidence interval for $E(Y|x = 23.5)$?

Solution: The confidence interval is defined by:

$$\hat{\alpha} + \hat{\beta}\cdot 23.5 \pm t_{0.025}(8)\cdot s\cdot\sqrt{\frac{1}{n} + \frac{(23.5 - 35.74)^2}{\sum(x_i - \bar{x})^2}}$$

$= 23.332 \pm 2.306\cdot 0.617\cdot 0.4009 = 23.33 \pm 0.57$; so that the interval is $[22.76, 23.90]$, and $y^* = 23.4$ belongs indeed to this interval.

12.6 Predicting Y for a Given x

In trying to predict Y, when x is given, there are two errors involved: first, the possible error we have committed in not finding the exact true regression line; second, the random error ε of Y, given x and the true regression line $\alpha + \beta x$. The error in predicting a *single* value of Y will therefore, in general, exceed the error in estimating the *expected* value of Y.

One can show that the variance of the prediction error $Y - \hat{y}$ is $\sigma^2\left(1 + \frac{1}{n} + \frac{(x^* - \bar{x})^2}{\sum(x_i - \bar{x})^2}\right)$, and that the $t(n-2)$ distribution applies.

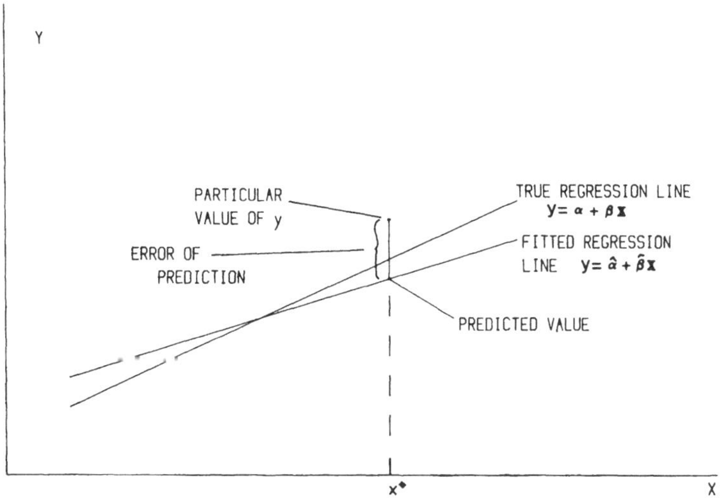

Fig. 12/13: Predicting Y for a given x.

Example 12.10

Construct a 99% confidence interval for $Y|x = 48.6$.

Solution: The interval is defined by:

$$\hat{y} \pm t_{0.005}(8) \cdot s \sqrt{1 + \frac{1}{n} + \frac{(48.6 - 35.74)^2}{\sum(x_i - \bar{x})^2}}$$

$$= \hat{\alpha} + \hat{\beta} \cdot 48.6 \pm 3.355 \cdot 0.617 \cdot \sqrt{1 + \frac{1}{10} + 0.0670} = 44.198 \pm 2.236$$

so that the interval is (41.96, 46.43).

Hypothesis testing is straightforward, and we do not go into the details.

Remark 1: We have been talking of s^2 as an estimator of σ^2. We could have written $s^2_{Y|x}$ or $s^2_{y \cdot x}$ to indicate that this is the variance of Y, *given x*. If we looked at the *overall* (sample) variance of Y, $\frac{\sum(y_i - \bar{y})^2}{n-1}$, we could denote this by s^2_y. We see that we get:

$$r^2 = 1 - \frac{s^2_{y \cdot x}}{s^2_y} \cdot \frac{n-2}{n-1}$$

which for large n is very near to: $1 - \frac{s^2_{y \cdot x}}{s^2_y}$.

Remark 2: As a check on the calculations for finding $\hat{\alpha}$ and $\hat{\beta}$, one can use the following (which can be proved to be always true):

$$\bar{y} = \hat{\alpha} + \hat{\beta}\bar{x}$$
$$\sum(y_i - \hat{y}_i) = 0 .$$

Exercise: Show that these two relationships hold!

12.7 Solving Regression Problems by Computer

There are many computer packages available today for solving various statistical problems. Although the packages differ in some respects, familiarity with one package usually enables one to run another package without much difficulty. It is as with automobiles: if you know how to drive one car, you know how to drive them all.

We shall use the SPSS system, which is available on many CDC computers. SPSS (*S*tatistical *P*ackage for the *S*ocial *S*ciences) is a system of computer programs for various types of statistical analysis. We shall only consider the REGRESSION program and assume that it is run using keypunched cards.

A card deck for solving the Japanese regression problem looks as follows (read from the bottom to the top):

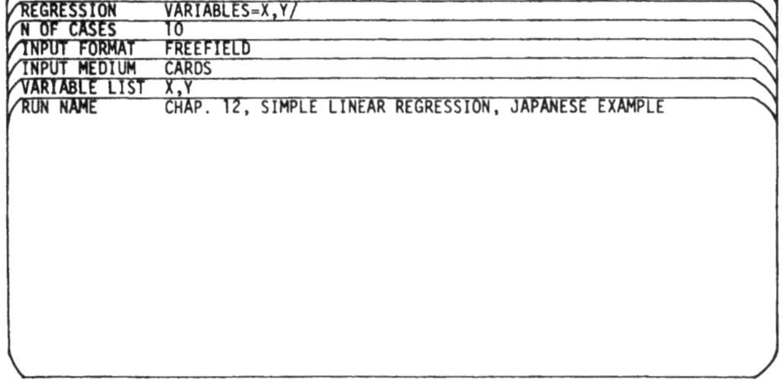

Fig. 12/15: SPSS input deck.

The SPSS input control cards for our Japanese regression problem are almost self-explanatory. Here are just a few comments.

- All SPSS control cards have two portions:
  a *control field* (columns 1 to 15)
  a *specification field* (columns 16 to 80).
- The control field always begins in column 1, and never exceeds 15 characters.
- A *variable name* is a string of at most eight alphanumeric (letter or digit) characters, starting with a letter and with no blanks (e.g. X, X1 or INCOME).
- The order in the VARIABLE LIST must be the same as in the READ INPUT DATA.
- On the REGRESSION card, the variables to be used are listed.
- Directly following REGRESSION= is the name of the *dependent* variable, followed by WITH (within blanks) and a list of the *independent* variables. (2) is needed but has a meaning only for step-wise regression (which we shall not go into); RESID=0 enables us to plot the residuals.
- OPTIONS and STATISTICS. We do not go into these.
- READ INPUT DATA. Indicates the beginning of the data cards.
- All variable observations for a case occur on one card, i.e. there is one card for each case. Numbers should be separated by spaces and/or commas. On a card, the numbers should refer to variables in the same order as indicated on the VARIABLE LIST card, but need not start in column 1 or be restricted to any other specific columns.

There are many other options and control possibilities, but we shall not go into them.

If the card deck for the Japanese regression problem is submitted for an SPSS run, part of the resulting output will look as follows:

From Fig. 12/16 and 12/17 on the next page we can see that almost all aspects of linear regression that we have covered so far are dealt with: the coefficients with t-tests of significance, correlation and ANOVA, predictions etc.

An interesting aspect is the computer cost for obtaining all this information. The problem took less than 0.3 seconds to solve on a CDC Cyber computer. If we assume that an hour's computation time is worth $600 (a reasonable figure), we can conclude that it costs less than 5 cents to obtain all this information! This low figure should emphasize how cheap the use of a modern high speed digital

```
CHAP. 12, SIMPLE LINEAR REGRESSION, JAPANESE EXAMPLE                83/03/03,   18.12.58.      Page 2

FILE   NONAME   (CREATION DATE = 83/03/03.)
* * * * * * * * * * * * * * * * * * * * * * * * M U L T I P L E    R E G R E S S I O N * * * * * * * * * * * * * *

DEPENDENT VARIABLE..  Y

MEAN RESPONSE    33500.00000     STD. DEV.   13785.33843

FINAL STEP.

MULTIPLE R                 .99910     ANALYSIS OF VARIANCE      DF         SUM OF SQUARES           MEAN SQUARE
R SQUARE                   .99821     REGRESSION                1.      1707257790.96218      1707257790.06218
ADJUSTED R SQUARE          .99799     RESIDUAL                  8.         3062209.03781           382776.12973
STD DEVIATION           618.68904     COEFF OF VARIABILITY      1.8 PCT

----------------------- VARIABLES IN THE EQUATION -------------------

VARIABLE            B          STD ERROR B        _____T_____      __BETA___
                                                  SIGNIFICANCE     ELASTICITY

X             .83190778     .12456558E-01       66.784723         .9991044
                                                     .000           .88753
(CONSTANT)    3767.6158     486.29037           7.7476669
                                                     .000

ALL VARIABLES ARE IN THE EQUATION.


COEFFICIENTS AND CONFIDENCE INTERVALS.

VARIABLE            B          STD ERROR B             T             95.0 PCT CONFIDENCE INTERVAL

X             .83190778     .12456558E-01       66.784723         .80318294    ,  .86063263
CONSTANT      3767.6158     486.29037           7.7476669         2646.2294    ,  4889.0023
```

Fig. 12/16: Part of SPSS output.

```
SIMPLE LINEAR REGRESSION, JAPANESE EXAMPLE                            81/03/03.      18.12.58.      PAGE 3

FILE   NONAME · (CREATION DATE = 83/03/03.)
* * * * * * * * * * * * * * * * * * * * * * * * M U L T I P L E    R E G R E S S I O N * * * * * * * * *

OBSERVATION    Y VALUE          Y ESTIMATE          RESIDUAL              -2SD                    0.0

    1.         14100.00          14166.46           -66.46312                                   · I
    2.         18500.00          18492.38           7.616410                                      I·
    3.         22600.00          22319.16           280.8406                                      I
    4.         25800.00          26478.70           -678.6983                       ·             I
    5.         31000.00          30555.05           444.9536                                      I
    6.         34600.00          34797.78           -197.7761                              ·      I
    7.         39800.00          38957.32           842.6849                                      I
    8.         42000.00          43033.86           -1033.663                  ·                  I
    9.         49600.00          48940.21           659.7915                                      I
   10.         57000.00          57259.29           -259.2863                             ·       I

NOTE - (*)  INDICATES ESTIMATE CALCULATED WITH MEANS SUBSTITUTED
       R  INDICATES POINT OUT OF RANGE OF PLOT

NUMBER OF CASES PLOTTED        10.
NUMBER OF 2 S.D. OUTLIERS       0 OR       0 PERCENT OF THE TOTAL
```

Fig. 12/17: Part of SPSS output.

computer is for statistical purposes. Most microcomputers, like the Apple, the IBM Personal Computer, the Hewlett-Packard HP-85 etc., also have special software (programs) developed for regression and other types of statistical analysis.

References

Chou, Y.: *Statistical Analysis,* 2nd edition. Holt, Rinehart and Winston, New York 1975.

Hamburg, M.: *Statistical Analysis for Decision Making,* 2nd edition. Harcourt, Brace, Jovanovich, New York 1977.

Harnett, D. L.: *Statistical Methods,* 3rd edition. Addison-Wesley, Reading, Mass. 1982.

Hawkins, C.A., and J.E. Weber: *Statistical Analysis. Applications to Business and Economics.* Harper & Row, New York 1980.

Klecka, W., N. H. Nie and C. Hadlai Hull: *SPSS Primer.* McGraw-Hill, New York 1975.

Kleinbaum, D.G., and L.L. Kupper: *Applied Regression Analysis and Other Multivariable Methods,* Duxbury Press, North Scituate, Mass. 1978.

Mansfield, E.: *Statistics for Business and Economics,* Norton & Company, New York 1980.

Nie, N.H., C. Hadlai Hull, J.G. Jenkins, K. Steinbrenner and D.H. Bent: *Statistical Package for the Social Sciences,* 2nd edition. McGraw-Hill, New York 1975.

Ott, L.,: *An Introduction to Statistical Methods and Data Analysis,* Duxbury Press, North Scituate, Mass. 1977.

Wonnacott, T.H., and R.J. Wonnacott: *Introductory Statistics for Business and Economics,* 2nd edition. John Wiley & Sons, New York 1977.

Exercises

12–1 An analysis is conducted to determine the relationship between the performance rating score received by nine civil engineers and the length of their tenure. Suppose that the following data is obtained:

Performance Rating	1	2	3	4	5	6	7	8	9
Length of Tenure	1	3	1	3	2	4	4	4	5

a) Find the regression line using tenure as the independent variable.
b) Based on the fitted regression line, what would the performance rating be if the length of tenure were two years?

12–2 The table below presents data for a random sample of $n = 8$ students with regard to the hours of study during a three-week period and the grade earned at an examination at the end of this time period for a course in business statistics.

Sampled Student	Hours of Study	Examination Grade
1	20	64
2	16	61
3	34	84
4	23	70
5	27	88
6	32	92
7	18	72
8	22	77

a) Determine the regression equation for estimating the examination grade given the number of hours of study, and enter the regression line on a scatter diagram. Carry the calculations to one place beyond the decimal point.

b) Use the regression equation to estimate the examination grade for a student who devotes 30 hours to study of the course material.

c) Construct a 90 percent approximate prediction interval for estimating the examination grade for a student who devotes 30 hours to study, based on using the standard error of estimate.

12–3 Refer to Exercise no. 1 above.

a) Does the data provide sufficient evidence, at a 5% level of significance, that performance rating tends to increase as the length of tenure increases?

b) Find the correlation between the variables.

c) What is the coefficient of determination for this data? What does it explain?

12–4 Among other appropriate courses, a secretarial school offers a six-week course in typing. The director of the school is interested in predicting the typing speed of a course participant who has just completed the course, as judged by the typing speed of the participant at the end of the first week of the course. The director selects a random sample of ten beginning participants. At the end of the first week and at the end of the sixth week they are timed in typing a standard short business letter. The results are given in the following table:

	Typing Time in Minutes	
Participant	At the end of week 1	At the end of week 6
A	9.0	4.6
B	10.8	5.4
C	11.8	5.5
D	13.0	7.8
E	12.8	6.4
F	12.0	7.4
G	12.6	6.2
H	11.8	5.4
I	8.0	3.4
J	11.6	6.2

a) Plot the data in the form of a scatter diagram, being sure to identify the scales properly. On the basis of the diagram, is a linear estimating equation appropriate here?

b) Estimate the parameters in the linear equation from which typing time at the end of the course can be estimated from typing time at the end of the first week of the course. Interpret the parameter estimates specifically in terms of this problem.

c) Construct a 90 percent confidence interval for β, the slope of the regression line.

d) On the basis of the evidence in the sample, could one use the results of the analysis to predict the time to type a standard business letter at the end of the course from a similar time after the first week of the course? Why or why not?
e) Compute the coefficient of correlation.

12–5 A data processing company performs adjustments of magnetic tape drives as part of its service contracts. A statistician is studying the relation between the number of minutes required for a customer service call to adjust tape drives and the number of tape drives adjusted. She has collected the following random sample data:

Number of Tape Drives Adjusted	Number of Minutes Required on Call
7	327
6	272
2	100
5	228
4	197
6	279
3	148
1	66
5	238
3	142
8	377
5	239

a) Draw a scatter diagram for this data.
b) Would the assumption of a linear relationship appear to be reasonable? Why or why not?
c) Obtain the estimated regression equation using the number of tape drives as the independent variable.
d) Compute the coefficient of correlation.
e) Construct a 95% confidence interval for the mean time required for service calls involving 4 tape drives.
f) Construct a 95% confidence interval for β, the slope of the regression line.
g) Test whether or not $\beta = 0$ at a significance level of 05.

12–6 Given the following data for the U.S. Federal Reserve Bank discount rate and bank debits, 1962–1968:

Debits ($trillion)	x	3.43	3.75	4.52	5.13	5.94	6.35	7.99
Discount rate (%)	y	3.00	3.38	3.88	4.38	4.50	4.25	5.25

a) Assuming the regression of y on x to be linear, find the least-squares line for the data.
b) Estimate σ^2 (in other words, calculate s^2).
c) Determine a 95% confidence interval for β, the coefficient for x.
d) Calculate r and r^2 for the above data. What is the conclusion?

12–7 To determine the price for a new product, a company conducted a number of pilot studies in ten market areas with virtually identical sales potential. The product was test marketed in each of the areas, with varying price. The following data were recorded:

Area	Unit Price	Sales volume (in thousands of units)
	X	Y
1	$ 8.00	17
2	8.50	16
3	9.00	14
4	9.50	12
5	10.00	10
6	10.50	8
7	11.00	9
8	11.50	7
9	12.00	7
10	12.50	5

a) Determine the least-squares linear regression line using price as the independent variable.
b) Calculate the coefficient of determination. What does it explain?
c) Obtain a 95% confidence interval for the expected sales volume if the price of the product is $9.45.
d) Test if $\beta = 0$, using a significance level of 0.05.
e) How does a price reduction of $1.20 affect the expected sales volume?

12–8 Because the wage bill is a major component of total cost, we might expect a direct relationship between the wage rate in the trinket industry and the price of trinkets. The wage and trinket selling prices of 12 randomly chosen trinket firms are presented below:

Company no.	Average Wage	Trinket Price
1	$5.90	$3.45
2	6.00	3.50
3	7.30	3.80
4	5.00	3.25
5	7.40	3.85
6	4.50	3.10
7	5.10	3.30
8	5.50	3.40
9	6.40	3.60
10	6.50	3.65
11	7.00	3.75
12	5.40	3.35

a) Find the equation of the least squares line that relates average wages to prices.
b) What would you expect the trinket price to be for a firm with an average wage of \$4.50, based on the regression performed in part (a)?
c) How do you explain the discrepancy between the price you expect in question (b) and the price you actually see for Company 6?

12–9 A car dealer is concerned about the effect of advertising on radio. He wants to know if it is affecting sales – for better or worse. The data of his regression analysis is summarized below, where X = advertising budget for each of 12 weeks, and Y = number of cars sold during each of these weeks.

$\sum X = 780$ $\sum Y = 276$ $\sum XY = 20740$
$\sum X^2 = 5420$ $\sum Y^2 = 9228$

a) Construct a 95% confidence interval for the advertising coefficient in this regression.
b) Test the hypothesis that advertising is responsible for increasing car sales to above what they otherwise would be.

12–10 The Eltrym Scotch Company wishes to know whether or not disposable family income is a reliable indicator for predicting company sales. Some relevant data were collected and are shown below.

Year	Disposable Income (\$ Billions)	Company Sales (\$ Millions)
1959	337	404
1960	350	412
1961	364	425
1962	385	429
1963	405	436
1964	438	440
1965	473	447
1966	512	458
1967	546	569
1968	591	477

A least squares regression analysis was performed with the following results:

$$\hat{S} = 265.55425 + 0.41842\ I$$

where: $\hat{S}$ = estimate of sales in \$ millions.
I = Disposable Income in \$ billions.

$SSE = 7795.461$
$SS_{yy} = 19884.100$
$s_{\hat{\beta}} = 0.11879$

a) What is the exact meaning of the slope coefficient?
b) Calculate a 95% confidence interval for the average company sales for all years when disposable income is \$600,000,000,000.

c) If, in one year, disposable income were \$550,000,000,000, what would you estimate company sales to be? Use a 90% confidence level.

12–11 Consider Exercise no. 8, on the trinket industry.

a) Use SPSS (or any other computer package) to calculate the equation of the least squares line that relates average wages to prices.
b) Test to see if the slope is significant at $\alpha = 5\%$.
c) Find r and r^2. Comment.

12–12 A least squares linear regression and correlation analysis was conducted on data obtained from a random sample of 102 salesmen of a large company with the following results:

$Y = -10 + X$, where $X =$ age in years of the salesmen (from 30tp 50); $Y =$ annual commission in thousands of dollars; $n = 102$; and $s = 3$ (expressed in thousands of dollars).

The coefficient of determination was found to be .64.

a) The sales manager objected to the results of the equation, because the value, $\alpha = -10$, did not seem reasonable to him. Explain briefly how you would reply to the sales manager.
b) Interpret the regression coefficient, $b = 1$, specifically in terms of this problem.
c) Test the null hypothesis H_0: there is no correlation in the population ($\varrho = 0$); that is, for all 30 to 50 year old salesmen of this company, is there any correlation between age and annual commissions? Use a 99% confidence level.

(To compute an observed t-value for correlation, use: $t = \frac{r\sqrt{n-2}}{\sqrt{1-r^2}}$)

d) Would a 40 year old salesman who received \$18,000 in annual sales commission be considered a "poor performer" or just an average salesman? Why?
e) What would the minimum annual sales commission be expected to be for the top 60% of all 40 year old salesmen?

12–13 It is claimed that the variance in commercial credit institutions' rates of interest reflects the different standards the institutions use in screening applications. The lower the rate, the higher the standards and thus the less likely the account is to default in payment. The data in the table represents the interest rates charged by eight randomly selected credit institutions and their default rates.

Interest Rates (percent)	Number of Defaults (per 1000 loans)
7.0	39
6.5	38
5.5	18
6.0	36
8.0	36
8.5	45
6.0	39
6.5	36

a) What is the dependent variable?
b) Estimate the linear regression equation.
c) Explain the meaning of $\hat{\alpha}$ and $\hat{\beta}$.
d) Calculate s^2 and comment.
e) Is the independent variable significant in predicting the dependent variable? ($\alpha = 5\%$)
f) Calculate the correlation coefficient and the coefficient of determination and comment on the result.

13. Multiple Linear Regression

The previous chapter was devoted to simple linear regression. We showed how one variable, called the independent variable, could be related to another, the dependent variable. A natural extension is to study how the behaviour of one variable can be linearly related to several other variables. Such an analysis is called *multiple linear regression analysis,* which we shall deal with in this chapter.

Section 13.1 introduces the reader to the need for multiple regression by considering an example in which aggregate Canadian investment is regressed on lagged gross national expenditures. It is argued that the interest rate should be included in the regression as well. In Section 13.2 we describe the least squares approach to multiple linear regression and apply it to our example. Section 13.3 covers the concept and the use of dummy variables, and touches on the difficulties posed by multicollinearity and serial correlation. In Section 13.4 we perform hypothesis tests and construct confidence intervals for multiple regression. Section 13.5 briefly treats how quadratic and higher order terms may be introduced into the regression equation, how partial F-tests are conducted and introduces the concepts of stepwise regression and heteroscedasticity. Section 13.6 ends the chapter by discussing some issues in the building of linear regression models.

13.1 Introduction

Example 13.1

Consider the annual data of some variables for the Canadian economy, as displayed in Fig. 13/1 on the next page.

CON: Consumer Expenditure (millions of 1961 $),
INV: Non-Inventory Investment Expenditure (millions of 1961 $),
RLAG: Yield on Long-Term Government Bonds, lagged one year (%),
YLAG: Gross National Expenditure, lagged one year (millions of 1961 $).

Using these data, we wish to fit the following simple linear regression model:

$$\text{INV} = \beta_0 + \beta_1 \text{YLAG} + \varepsilon .$$

Year	YLAG	CON	INV	RLAG
1963	42349	28408	7282	5.11333
1964	44531	30121	8523	5.08750
1965	47519	31950	9499	5.18333
1966	50685	33619	10542	5.20833
1967	54207	35221	10417	5.69000
1968	56016	36966	10415	5.93667
1969	59292	38672	11105	6.74583
1970	62448	39571	11159	7.58417
1971	64014	41674	11920	7.91250
1972	67585	44533	12666	6.94750
1973	71515	48083	14150	7.23167

Fig. 13/1: Canadian economic data (Source: Bank of Canada).

The SPSS input might look like:

```
RUN NAME        CHAP. 13, SIMPLE LINEAR REGRESSION, INV ON YLAG
VARIABLE LIST   DATE, YLAG, CON, INV, RLAG
INPUT MEDIUM    CARDS
INPUT FORMAT    FREEFIELD
N OF CASES      11
REGRESSION      VARIABLES = YLAG, INV/
                REGRESSION= INV WITH YLAG(2) RESID=0/
OPTIONS         6,7,21
STATISTICS      4,9
READ INPUT DATA
```

Fig. 13/2: Part of SPSS input for Example 13.1

The results from SPSS (see Figure 13/3 below), are:

$$\begin{aligned} \text{INV} &= -38.32 + 0.1904\ \text{YLAG} \\ &\qquad (0.037) \qquad (10.6) \end{aligned}$$

$R^2 = 0.926$

S.D. (Standard deviation) = 1889

F-statistic = 113

S.E. (Standard error) = 541.0

In other words, $\hat{\beta}_0 = -38.32$, $\hat{\beta}_1 = 0.1904$, indicating that if YLAG increases by \$1, INV will increase by \$0.1904. The numbers in brackets below the coefficients indicate the corresponding t-statistic for testing the hypothesis that this particular coefficient is zero. For instance, for β_1 we have:

$$\frac{\hat{\beta}_1}{\frac{s}{\sqrt{S_{xx}}}} = \frac{\hat{\beta}_1}{s_{\hat{\beta}_1}} = \frac{0.1904}{0.01792} = 10.6,$$

```
SIMPLE LINEAR REGRESSION, INVESTMENT ON INCOME                                84/03/05
FILE   NONAME   (CREATION DATE =  84/03/05.)
* * * * * * * * * * * * * * * * * * * * * * * * *  M U L T I P L E   R E G R E S S I O N  * * * * * * * * * * * * * * *

DEPENDENT VARIABLE..      INV
MEAN RESPONSE     10698.00000      STD. DEV.      1888.95341
FINAL STEP.

MULTIPLE R              .96238       ANALYSIS OF VARIANCE   DF       SUM OF SQUARES        F         SIGNIFICANCE
R SQUARE                .92617       REGRESSION             1.       33047191.61774    112.90644          .000
ADJUSTED R SQUARE       .91797       RESIDUAL               9.        2634258.38226
STD DEVIATION        541.01329       COEFF OF VARIABILITY   5.1 PCT

-------------------- VARIABLES IN THE EQUATION ---------------------
VARIABLE            B              STD ERROR B         T             BETA
                                                   SIGNIFICANCE   ELASTICITY

YLAG           .19043356        .17921904E-01     10.625744        .9623788
                                                       .000        1.00358
(CONSTANT)    -38.315196        1023.4886       -.37435880E-01
                                                       .971

ALL VARIABLES ARE IN THE EQUATION.


COEFFICIENTS AND CONFIDENCE INTERVALS.
VARIABLE          B            STD ERROR B           T                 95.0 PCT CONFIDENCE
YLAG          .19043356      .17921904E-01     10.625744             .14989142    ,  .2
CONSTANT     -38.315196      1023.4886        -.37435880E-01        -2353.6061    ,  22
```

Fig. 13/3: Part of SPSS output for Example 13.1.

where $s_{\hat{\beta}_1}$ is the *standard error* of $\hat{\beta}_1$. With a t-statistic of 10.6, β_1 is highly significant (in fact, $\alpha = 0.000$ according to the SPSS output).

S.D. = 1899 refers to the sample standard deviation of Y:

$$\sqrt{\frac{1}{n-1}\Sigma(y_i-\bar{y})^2} = \sqrt{\frac{1}{n-1}S_{yy}} = s_y = 1888.9534\,.$$

The F statistic refers to ANOVA for regression, and we have:

$$F = 112.90644 = (10.625744)^2 = (t)^2\,,$$

as we indeed expected (cf. Remark 2 of Section 12.4).

S.E. = 541.0 refers to s, the standard error of the estimate,

$$\sqrt{\frac{1}{n-2}\Sigma(y_i-\hat{y}_i)^2} = \sqrt{\frac{1}{n-2}SSE} = \sqrt{\frac{1}{9}\cdot 2\,634\,258.38226} = 541.01328\,.$$

Although the fit of the regression equation

$$INV = \beta_0 + \beta_1 YLAG + \varepsilon$$

is not bad in view of the above analysis and statistics, we suspect that the investment variable could be even better explained. For instance, economic theory as well as common sense tells us that the interest rate will influence the investments. Therefore, we would wish to include *both* YLAG and RLAG as independent variables on the right-hand side. But how should this be done? We shall address this issue in the next section.

13.2 Least-Squares Estimation

In practice, it may occur that we get a low r^2-value in a simple linear regression model, because there is a third variable which affects our results. Instead of assuming

$$Y = \alpha + \beta x + \varepsilon,$$

we could then specify the model:

$$Y = \beta_0 + \beta_1 x_1 + \beta_2 x_2 + \varepsilon$$

and use *multiple* linear regression, i.e. compute values of the coefficients β_0, β_1 and β_2.

In general, for k independent (right-hand side) variables, the problem of computing the regression coefficients can be formulated as follows:

How do we find $\beta_0, \beta_1, \ldots, \beta_k$ so that $\sum_i (y_i - \hat{y}_i)^2$ is minimal, where:

$$\hat{y}_i = \beta_0 + \beta_1 x_{i1} + \beta_2 x_{i2} + \ldots, + \beta_k x_{ik}, \quad i = 1, \ldots, n$$

and x_{ij} is observation no. i of variable no. j?

Solution: In analogy with the simple linear regression case, the least-squares estimates $\hat{\beta}_0, \hat{\beta}_1, \ldots, \hat{\beta}_k$ are obtained using differential calculus. The formulas for computing the $\hat{\beta}_j$ can be given in an elegant form only by using matrix algebra:

$$\text{With } y = \begin{pmatrix} y_1 \\ y_2 \\ \vdots \\ y_n \end{pmatrix}, \qquad X = \begin{pmatrix} 1 & x_{11} & x_{12} & \ldots & x_{1k} \\ 1 & x_{21} & x_{22} & \ldots & x_{2k} \\ \vdots & \vdots & \vdots & \vdots & \vdots \\ 1 & x_{n1} & x_{n2} & \ldots & x_{nk} \end{pmatrix},$$

$$\beta = \begin{pmatrix} \beta_0 \\ \beta_1 \\ \vdots \\ \beta_k \end{pmatrix} \quad \text{and} \quad \varepsilon = \begin{pmatrix} \varepsilon_1 \\ \varepsilon_2 \\ \vdots \\ \varepsilon_n \end{pmatrix},$$

we find that the model equations can be written $y = X\beta + \varepsilon$. One can show that the solution is given by: $\hat{\beta} = (X^T X)^{-1} X^T y$, (where -1 stands for matrix inverse and T for matrix transpose).

The calculations are complicated and are today always done on the computer.

Remark 1: The column of 1 : s in the X-matrix is inserted for technical reasons, to deal with the intercept term, β_0.

Remark 2: For simple linear regression, graphical representation is possible in two dimensions, and we have used this fact to illustrate various aspects (correlation, error, fitted vs true line etc.). For multiple linear regression with two independent variables, graphical representation is possible in the three-dimensional space. Instead of a regression *line* we must now talk of a regression *plane:*

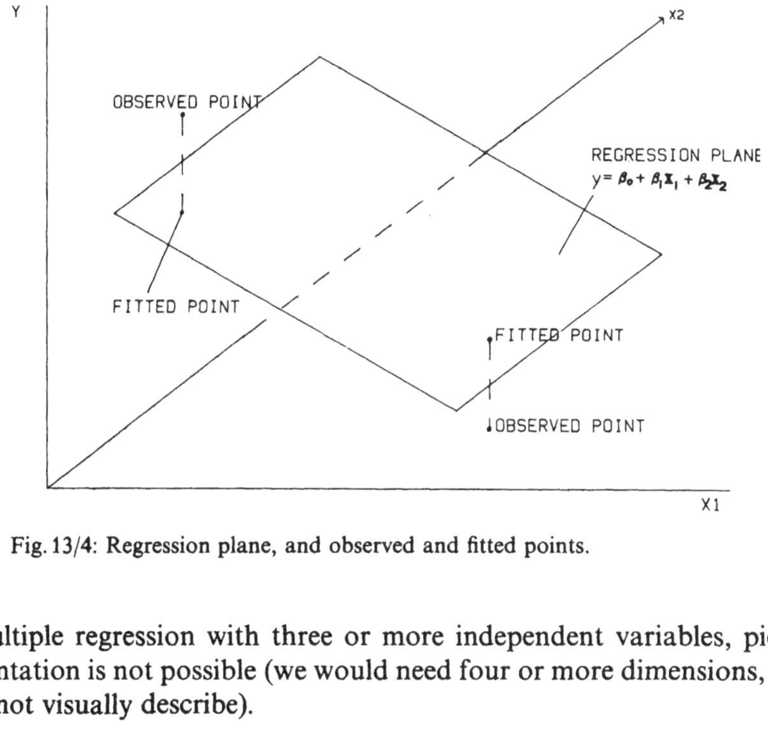

Fig. 13/4: Regression plane, and observed and fitted points.

For multiple regression with three or more independent variables, pictorial representation is not possible (we would need four or more dimensions, which we cannot visually describe).

Example 13.2

Consider Example 13.1. Let us specify the multiple linear regression model

$$\text{INV} = \beta_0 + \beta_1 \text{YLAG} + \beta_2 \text{RLAG} + \varepsilon$$

and compute the least squares coefficient estimates.

Solution: The SPSS input might now look like:

```
RUN NAME          CHAP. 13, MULTIPLE LINEAR REGRESSION, INV ON YLAG AND RLAG
VARIABLE LIST     DATE, YLAG, CON, INV, RLAG
INPUT MEDIUM      CARDS
INPUT FORMAT      FREEFIELD
N OF CASES        11
REGRESSION        VARIABLES=YLAG, INV, RLAG/
                  REGRESSIONS=INV WITH YLAG, RLAG(2) RESID=0/
OPTIONS           6,7,21
STATISTICS        4,9
READ INPUT DATA
```

Fig. 13/5: Part of SPSS input for Example 13.2.

and part of the resulting SPSS is shown in Fig. 13/6 below.

```
CHAP. 13, MULTIPLE LINEAR REGRESSION, INV ON YLAG AND RLAG              84/03/04.      12.04.05.             PAGE 2

FILE   NONAME   (CREATION DATE = 84/03/04.)
* * * * * * * * * * * * * * * * * * * * * * * * * M U L T I P L E   R E G R E S S I O N * * * * * * * * * * * * * *

DEPENDENT VARIABLE..   INV

MEAN RESPONSE    10698.00000      STD. DEV.    1888.95341

FINAL STEP.

MULTIPLE R            .97975      ANALYSIS OF VARIANCE     DF       SUM OF SQUARES          MEAN SQUARE
R SQUARE              .95991      REGRESSION               2.       34251073.19430       17125536.59715
ADJUSTED R SQUARE     .94989      RESIDUAL                 8.        1430376.80570         178797.10071
STD DEVIATION      422.84406      COEFF OF VARIABILITY     4.0 PCT

--------------------- VARIABLES IN THE EQUATION ----------------------

VARIABLE            B              STD ERROR B         T            BETA
                                                  SIGNIFICANCE   ELASTICITY

YLAG             .26200700       .30935799E-01    8.4693786      1.3240837
                                                       .000        1.38077
R LAG          -714.04985        275.18001       -2.5948464      -.4056725
                                                       .032        -.41650
(CONSTANT)      382.22305        816.18836        .46830250
                                                       .652

ALL VARIABLES ARE IN THE EQUATION.

COEFFICIENTS AND CONFIDENCE INTERVALS.

VARIABLE          B             STD ERROR B          T              95.0 PCT CONFIDENCE INTERVAL

YLAG           .26200700       .30935799E-01    8.4693786         .19066899    ,    .33334500
RLAG        -714.04985         275.18001       -2.5948464       -1348.6154     ,  -79.484257
CONSTANT     382.22305         816.18836        .46830250       -1499.9087     ,   2264.3548
```

Fig. 13/6: Part of SPSS output from Example 13.2.

From Fig. 13/6 we conclude that the fitted regression equation is:

$$\begin{aligned}
\text{INV} &= \underset{(0.462)}{382.22} + \underset{(8.47)}{0.2620}\,\text{YLAG} - \underset{(2.59)}{714.05}\,\text{RLAG} \\
\text{R}^2 &= 0.960 \\
\text{S.D.} &= 1889 \\
\text{F-statistic} &= 95.8 \\
\text{S.E.} &= 422.8.
\end{aligned}$$

In other words, $\hat{\beta}_0 = 382.22$, $\hat{\beta}_1 = 0.2620$ and $\hat{\beta}_2 = -714.05$. This implies that if YLAG increases by \$1, all other things being equal, INV will increase by

$ 0.2620. If RLAG increases by 1 percentage point, all other things being equal, INV will decrease by $ 714.05 million.

To be able to analyze the other information given, we must first see how hypothesis tests are carried out. We shall deal with that in Section 13.4.

13.3 Dummy Variables, Multicollinearity and Serial Correlation

Dummy Variables

Example 13.3

For a random sample of employees of a certain company we record the sex, the number of years of schooling and the annual salary. Suppose that we get the following:

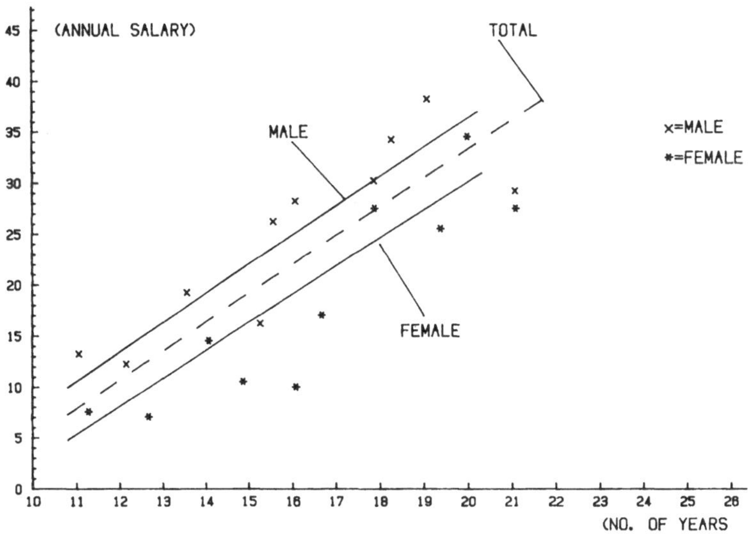

Fig. 13/7: Scatter diagram for Example 13.3.

How can we fit a linear regression model to this data?

Solution: We see that if we consider the male and female observations separately, we obtain two different regression lines. If we consider the male and female data together but disregard sex, we get a line between the male and the female lines, but with a poor fit.

We can include information on schooling as well as on sex by introducing a $0-1$ *dummy variable* x_2 to express the qualitative information about male or female:

$$x_2 = \begin{cases} 1 & \text{if male} \\ 0 & \text{if female} \end{cases}.$$

We would then fit

$$y = \beta_0 + \beta_1 x_1 + \beta_2 x_2 + \varepsilon .$$

From this we could conclude, for instance, that male salaries are $\tilde{\beta}_2$ higher than female, all other things being equal:

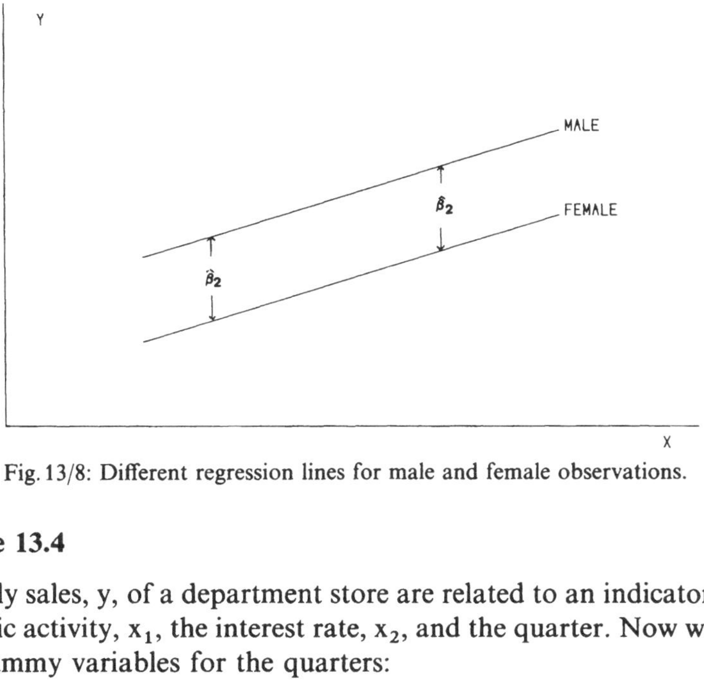

Fig. 13/8: Different regression lines for male and female observations.

Example 13.4

Quarterly sales, y, of a department store are related to an indicator of general economic activity, x_1, the interest rate, x_2, and the quarter. Now we introduce *three* dummy variables for the quarters:

$$x_3 = \begin{cases} 1 & \text{in quarter 1} \\ 0 & \text{otherwise} \end{cases}$$

$$x_4 = \begin{cases} 1 & \text{in quarter 2} \\ 0 & \text{otherwise} \end{cases}$$

$$x_5 = \begin{cases} 1 & \text{in quarter 3} \\ 0 & \text{otherwise} \end{cases}$$

We specify:

$$y = \beta_0 + \beta_1 x_1 + \beta_2 x_2 + \beta_3 x_3 + \beta_4 x_4 + \beta_5 x_5 + \varepsilon .$$

As fourth-quarter sales are always highest, we expect $\hat{\beta}_3$, $\hat{\beta}_4$ and $\hat{\beta}_5$ to be negative (Why?).

In general, if a qualitative variable has k levels, then $k - 1$ dummy variables are needed.

Remark: One can show that multiple regression on only qualitative variables is equivalent to ANOVA. We shall not go into the details.

Multicollinearity

Example 13.5

The following data are given for company sales in different geographical territories of a country.

Territory	y Sales	x_1 Population	x_2 Advertizing Outlay
1	34	5.0	5.0
2	29	4.2	4.5
3	43	8.5	10.0
4	21	1.4	2.5
5	35	3.6	5.0
6	27	1.3	3.0

Fig. 13/9: Data for Example 13.5.

Fitting $y = \beta_0 + \beta_1 x_1 + \beta_2 x_2 + \varepsilon$
we find:

$$R^2 = 0.8672$$
$$F = 9.795 \qquad (F_{0.05}(2,3) = 9.55).$$

From this we see that

$$H_0 : \beta_1 = \beta_2 = 0$$

can be *rejected* at the 5% level.

However, for the β_1 and β_2 coefficients we obtain the following t-statistics:

$$\frac{\hat{\beta}_1}{s_{\hat{\beta}_1}} = \frac{0.41428}{2.323} = 0.178 \qquad (t_{0.025}(3) = 3.182)$$

$$\frac{\hat{\beta}_2}{s_{\hat{\beta}_2}} = \frac{2.2476}{2.323} = 0.968 \qquad (t_{0.025}(3) = 3.182)$$

so that *neither* of the coefficients are significant at the 5% level.

The reason for this apparent contradiction is that x_1 and x_2 are highly correlated, so that x_2 does not provide much more information about y than x_1 does. The regression does therefore not "know" which of the two variables to give the credit for explaining y.

This phenomenon is called *collinearity* or more generally *multicollinearity* if three or more independent variables are linearly related. Let us consider an example.

Suppose, for quarterly data, that one tries with *four* quarterly dummy variables, e.g.

$$x_i = \begin{cases} 1 & \text{for quarter i} \\ 0 & \text{otherwise} \end{cases}$$

with $i = 1, 2, 3, 4$.

One would then find that the regression breaks down. The reason is multicollinearity; we see that $x_1 + x_2 + x_3 + x_4 = 1$ so that the quarterly dummies are completely dependent (because knowing the value of any three of them means knowing the value of the fourth).

Serial correlation

The error terms ε_i (the residuals) may be correlated, particularly when time-series data are used. This violates our assumptions for the linear model. One can test for serial correlation (also called autocorrelation) using the so-called *Durbin-Watson statistic.* Various techniques are available to eliminate the effects of serial correlation. We shall not go into these.

13.4 Hypothesis Tests for Multiple Regression

As for the simple linear regression model we assume that the random variables Y_i are statistically independent with variance σ^2. One can then show that the residual variance s^2 given by:

$$s^2 = \frac{1}{n-(k+1)} \sum (y_i - \hat{y}_i)^2 = \frac{1}{n-(k+1)} \cdot \text{SSE}$$

is an unbiased estimator of σ^2. k stands for the number of independent variables, as usual.

Example 13.6

For our investment function of Example 13.2,

$$\text{INV} = \beta_0 + \beta_1 \text{YLAG} + \beta_2 \text{RLAG} + \varepsilon$$

we found:

$$\text{SSE} = 1\,430\,376.8$$

so that

$$s^2 = \frac{1}{n-(k+1)} \text{SSE} = \frac{1}{11-(2+1)} 1\,430\,376.8 = 178\,797.1,$$

$$\text{i.e.} \quad s = 422.84406,$$

which is what the computer output (Fig. 13/6) stated. We note that this standard error is considerably smaller than 541.0 which was obtained when only YLAG was used as an independent variable (Example 13/1 and Fig. 13/3).

Now we come to the β_j coefficients. We remember that for the simple linear regression case we had:

$$\frac{\hat{\beta} - \beta}{s} \cdot \sqrt{S_{xx}} \quad \text{is } t(n-2) \text{ distributed, where } s_{\hat{\beta}} = \frac{s}{\sqrt{S_{xx}}}.$$

In the general case, using analogous assumptions, similar results hold, except that S_{xx} is replaced by another number (related to $(X^T X)^{-1}$) and the degrees of freedom are $n-(k+1)$. SPSS provides us with $s_{\hat{\beta}_j}$.

Example 13.7

Find a 95% confidence interval for β_1.

From the SPSS output of Figure 13/6 we find:

$$\hat{\beta}_1 = 0.2620$$
$$s_{\hat{\beta}_1} = 0.0309\,.$$

Therefore, the interval is determined by:

$$\hat{\beta}_1 \pm t_{0.025}(n-(k+1)) \cdot s_{\hat{\beta}_1} = 0.2620 \pm t_{0.025}(8) \cdot 0.0309 = 0.2620 \pm 0.0713$$

so that the interval is:

$$0.1907 \leqq \beta_1 \leqq 0.3333 .$$

This interval is directly provided by the SPSS output.

Example 13.8

Perform a two-sided test of the hypothesis:

$$H_0 : \beta_2 = 0 .$$

Solution: From the SPSS output of Fig. 13/6 we find:

$$\hat{\beta}_2 = -714.05$$
$$s_{\hat{\beta}_2} = 275.18 .$$

Our test statistic is:

$$t = \frac{\hat{\beta}_2 - 0}{s_{\hat{\beta}_2}} = \frac{-714.05}{275.18} = -2.595$$

(which is provided by the SPSS output).

With $t_{0.025}(8) = 2.306$ we can therefore *reject* H_0 at the 5% level, but with $t_{0.010}(8) = 2.896$ we *cannot* reject H_0 at the 2% level. From the SPSS output we see that the significance of $\hat{\beta}_2$ is 3.2%.

Remark 1: Sometimes the F-statistic instead of the t-statistic is given for a β_j. Remember that then $(t_{\alpha/2}(n-(k+1)))^2 = F_\alpha(1, n-(k+1))$ (cf. Remark 2 of Section 12.4).

We shall now see how we can test for β_1 and β_2 *simultaneously:*

$$H_0 : \beta_1 = \beta_2 = 0$$
$$H_1 : \text{Either } \beta_1 \neq 0 \text{ or } \beta_2 \neq 0 \text{ or both.}$$

We do this by an F-test using ANOVA for regression. In analogy with the case for simple linear regression one can show that:

$$\frac{\dfrac{SS(\text{Regression})}{k}}{\dfrac{SS(\text{Error})}{n-(k+1)}} \quad \text{is} \quad F(k, n-(k+1)) \text{ distributed } \textit{if } H_0 \textit{ is true.}$$

Here we have, as before:

$$SS(\text{Total}) = SS(\text{Regression}) + SS(\text{Error})$$
$$\Sigma(y_i - \bar{y})^2 = \Sigma(\hat{y}_i - \bar{y})^2 + \Sigma(y_i - \hat{y}_i)^2 .$$

Example 13.9

In our case, we find from the SPSS output of Figure 13/6:

$$\begin{aligned} &SS(\text{Regression}) && = 34\,251\,073.2 \\ &SS(\text{Error}) && = 1\,430\,376.8 \\ &k = 2,\ n-(k+1) && = 11-(2+1) = 8 \end{aligned}$$

Therefore,

$$F = \frac{\dfrac{SS(\text{Regression})}{k}}{\dfrac{SS(\text{Error})}{n-(k+1)}} = \frac{\dfrac{34\,251\,073.2}{2}}{\dfrac{1\,430\,376.8}{8}} = 95.78$$

and with $F_{0.01}(2,8) = 8.65$ we can *reject* H_0 at the 1% level. Actually, the SPSS output provides the F-statistic 95.78 and also gives the significance of less than 0.1%.

Remark 2: We define the *(multiple) coefficient of determination* R^2 (R is called the *multiple correlation coefficient*) by:

$$R^2 = 1 - \frac{\sum(y_i - \hat{y}_i)^2}{\sum(y_i - \bar{y})^2} = 1 - \frac{SS(\text{Error})}{SS(\text{Total})}.$$

It is easy to see that our F-statistic can also be expressed as

$$F = \frac{\dfrac{R^2}{k}}{\dfrac{(1-R^2)}{n-(k+1)}}.$$

Example 13.10

We find:

$$\begin{aligned} R^2 = 1 - \frac{SS(\text{Error})}{SS(\text{Total})} &= \frac{SS(\text{Regression})}{SS(\text{Regression}) + SS(\text{Error})} \\ &= \frac{34\,251\,073.2}{34\,251\,073.2 + 1\,430\,376.8} = 0.95991\,. \end{aligned}$$

SPSS provides R^2 directly.

While R^2 provides a measure of the fit of the regression equation, the F-statistic tells us if the regression equation is significantly "better" than just $\hat{y} = \bar{y}$ (i.e. a horizontal regression plane).

We can have a high R^2 but low F as indicated in Fig. 13/10:

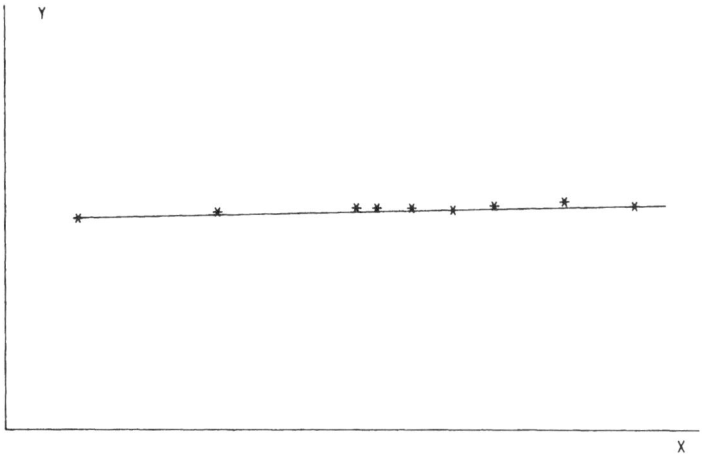

Fig. 13/10: High R^2, low F.

or a low R^2 but high F:

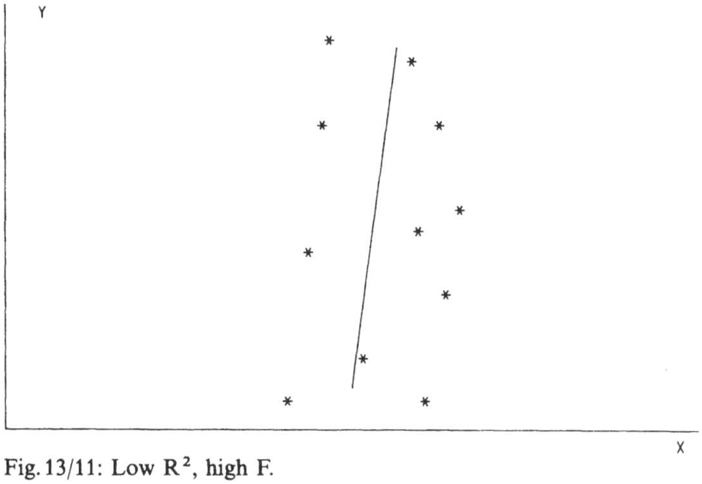

Fig. 13/11: Low R^2, high F.

or R^2 and F both low, or R^2 and F both high.

Exercise: Draw diagrams like in Fig. 13/10 and 13/11 for the last two cases!

We can also use our multiple linear regression equation for estimation and prediction.

Example 13.11

What is the estimated mean investment INV if YLAG = 61 000 and RLAG = 6.9?

Solution: Inserting into our regression equation INV = 382.22 + 0.2620 YLAG − 714.05 RLAG we find:

$$\text{INV} = 382.22 + 0.2620 \cdot 61\,000 - 714.05 \cdot 6.9 = 11437\,.$$

This is also the predicted value of INV, given the YLAG and RLAG values.

One can construct confidence intervals and test hypotheses regarding the expected and predicted values of the dependent variable, given prescribed levels of the independent variables. We shall not go into this.

13.5 Other Aspects of Linear Regression

Quadratic and higher order terms

It may sometimes be desirable to include higher order terms in a regression.

Example 13.12

The linear model $y = \beta_0 + \beta_1 x_1 + \beta_2 x_2 + \varepsilon$ may be augmented to:

$$Y = \beta_0 + \beta_1 x_1 + \beta_2 x_2 + \beta_3 x_1 x_2 + \beta_4 x_1^2 + \beta_5 x_2^2\,,$$

including now also the *interaction* term $x_1 x_2$ and the *quadratic* terms x_1^2 and x_2^2. Cubic terms (e.g. x_2^3) and even higher order terms ($x_1 x_2^4$, x_1^6 etc.) may be included as well as other terms (e^{x_2} etc.). Multicollinearity may easily arise, though.

Partial F-tests

Example 13.13

With the model

$$Y = \beta_0 + \beta_1 x_1 + \beta_2 x_2 + \ldots + \beta_8 x_8 + \varepsilon$$

we may wish to test:

$$H_0 : \beta_1 = \beta_4 = \beta_7 = 0$$

against

$$H_1 : \text{not } H_0 .$$

This is done by ANOVA for regression as follows:

a) Run the partial model (x_1, x_4, x_7 removed):

$$y = \beta_0 + \beta_2 x_2 + \beta_3 x_3 + \beta_5 x_5 + \beta_6 x_6 + \beta_8 x_8 + \varepsilon$$

and obtain $SSE_{partial}$.

b) Run the complete model (with all variables) and obtain $SSE_{complete}$ and s^2.

c) Compute $F = \dfrac{(SSE_{partial} - SSE_{complete})/3}{s^2}$ (three β: s tested) which should be $F(3, n - (8 + 1))$ distributed if H_0 is true.

Stepwise regression

Instead of deciding a priori which independent variables should be used, one may use *stepwise regression* when variables are brought into the model stepwise, one by one. This could be done in an order prescribed by the model builder, or left to be decided on by the computer, based on t-statistics. SPSS can do this, but we leave out the details.

Heteroscedasticity

It may be that the variance σ^2 of the error term ε is not constant, but grows with growing independent variables. This is called *heteroscedasticity*, and special tricks are required to deal with this case. We shall leave them out.

*13.6 Model Building

We shall now draw on the material developed in this and the previous chapter to show how linear regression models may be constructed. As usual we use an example to illustrate our treatment.

Example 13.14

From our annual Canadian economic data of Example 13.1 we might build the model (time subscripts are inserted for clarity):

$$\begin{aligned}
&\text{CON}_t = 1390.43 + 0.6346\,\text{YLAG}_t && R^2 = 0.926\\
&\qquad\quad (1.00) \qquad (26.1) && F = 681\\
& && \text{S.D.} = 6097\\
& && \text{S.E.} = 733.8
\end{aligned}$$

$$\begin{aligned}
&\text{INV}_t = 382.22 + 0.2620\,\text{YLAG}_t - 714.05\,\text{RLAG}_t && R^2 = 0.960\\
&\qquad\quad (0.468) \quad (8.47) \qquad\qquad (2.59) && F = 95.8\\
& && \text{S.D.} = 95.8\\
& && \text{S.E.} = 422.8
\end{aligned}$$

$$\begin{aligned}
&Y_t = \text{CON}_t + \text{INV}_t + \text{GOV}_t && \text{(identity)}\\
&\text{YLAG}_t = Y_{t-1} && \text{(definition)}.
\end{aligned}$$

Here GOV is government expenditure (millions of 1961 \$, data not given).

The first two of these equations have been estimated from our data using multiple linear regression; the third is an "identity", i.e. an equation which according to economic theory must always hold true and the fourth is a definition. The four equations together form what we call a *simultaneous equation model*. As we can see, the variables CON, INV, Y and YLAG can be solved for from the equations; accordingly these variables are referred to as *endogenous*. RLAG and GOV, on the other hand, cannot be obtained from within the model and are therefore called *exogenous*. A rule of thumb is that a model has as many endogenous variables as it has equations; it may have any number of exogenous variables. Solving for the endogenous variables, given the values of the exogenous variables, is called *simulation*.

Estimating simultaneous equation models using the least-squares technique separately for each equation may produce *biased* coefficients, and more sophisticated methods like *two-stage least squares* or *maximum likelihood estimation* have to be used. They are beyond the scope of this book.

With a model like this one can *simulate* the actual historical development to test the model's "tracking" properties. If these are found satisfactory, the model could be used for *forecasting* (simulating into the future) or *policy analysis* (experimenting with different economic policies for the past or the future).

We end this section by another example, of a single-equation model.

Example 13.15

When the government borrows from the public to pay for an underbalanced budget, it competes with private enterprise for investment funds. The cost of borrowing is therefore pushed up, causing investment to be cut back. But this decrease in investment spending is not immediate, as firms will have to buy the equipment already ordered. Cut-backs will however affect new orders, so that the investment will decrease after some delay.

DATE	IME	YD	YDDIF	RL	RL2	RL4	RL6	TREND
1961 Q1	565.00	6219.79	8.18	5.17	4.90	5.43	5.27	1.00
1961 Q2	661.00	6473.01	181.54	5.11	5.23	5.17	5.35	2.00
1961 Q3	553.00	7486.99	−218.83	4.98	5.17	4.90	5.43	3.00
1961 Q4	539.00	6725.73	232.22	4.92	5.11	5.23	5.17	4.00
1962 Q1	569.00	6668.41	448.63	4.92	4.98	5.17	4.90	5.00
1962 Q2	703.00	6970.09	497.08	5.03	4.92	5.11	5.23	6.00
1962 Q3	602.00	8257.58	770.59	5.41	4.92	4.98	5.17	7.00
1962 Q4	605.00	7050.68	324.95	5.10	5.03	4.92	5.11	8.00
1963 Q1	608.00	6825.49	157.08	5.08	5.41	4.92	4.98	9.00
1963 Q2	756.00	7258.62	288.53	4.97	5.10	5.03	4.92	10.00
1963 Q3	653.00	8733.71	476.14	5.17	5.08	5.41	4.92	11.00
1963 Q4	670.00	7373.43	322.75	5.13	4.97	5.10	5.03	12.00
1964 Q1	731.00	7388.13	562.64	5.20	5.17	5.08	5.41	13.00
1964 Q2	899.00	7379.27	120.65	5.22	5.13	4.97	5.10	14.00
1964 Q3	726.00	8767.14	33.43	5.22	5.20	5.17	5.08	15.00
1964 Q4	815.00	7703.24	329.81	5.10	5.22	5.13	4.97	16.00
1965 Q1	795.00	7794.41	406.28	5.02	5.22	5.20	5.17	17.00
1965 Q2	1009.00	7764.97	385.70	5.11	5.10	5.22	5.13	18.00
1965 Q3	900.00	9384.67	617.52	5.32	5.02	5.22	5.20	19.00
1965 Q4	1014.00	8257.10	553.86	5.39	5.11	5.10	5.22	20.00
1966 Q1	1031.00	8215.80	421.39	5.53	5.32	5.02	5.22	21.00
1966 Q2	1242.00	8266.99	502.02	5.62	5.39	5.11	5.10	22.00
1966 Q3	1028.00	9946.50	561.83	5.81	5.53	5.32	5.02	23.00
1966 Q4	1132.00	8557.28	300.18	5.79	5.62	5.39	5.11	24.00
1967 Q1	1151.00	8532.98	317.18	5.57	5.81	5.53	5.32	25.00
1967 Q2	1348.00	8749.72	482.73	5.72	5.79	5.62	5.39	26.00
1967 Q3	1013.00	10104.43	157.94	6.02	5.57	5.81	5.53	27.00
1967 Q4	1006.00	8990.69	433.41	6.44	5.72	5.79	5.62	28.00

Fig. 13/12: Data for Example 13.15.

The government wants to know how the investment in machinery and equipment depends on some other economic variables and what delays are involved.

Fig. 13/12 contains data on the dependent variable and several other variables. Construct a model that explains the dependent variable by regression with some of the other variables. Use at least 20 observations for the regression, and at least three independent variables.

Variables

IME: Business investment in machinery and equipment (millions of 1961 $)
YD: Disposable personal income in Canada (millions of 1961 $)
YDDIFF: Annual change of disposable personal income (millions of 1961 $)

RL: Average Yield on Government of Canada Bonds with lives of 10 years and over (%)
RL2: RL of two quarters ago (%)
RL4: RL of four quarters ago (%)
RL6: RL of six quarters ago (%)
TREND: Trend variable
Qi: Qi = 1 in quarter i, 0 otherwise.

Solution: When properly constructing a model, we should explain why the independent variables that we have chosen can be expected to provide significant information about the dependent variable. We should also have some prior expectations about the sign and significance of most estimated coefficients. The discussion of the model constructed should also include an account of the meaning of all statistics relating to the model. A comparison of the actual findings and the prior expectations should also be made. Due to space limitations, we will only show the end product. After some preliminary thinking and experimenting we arrive at the following model:

$$\text{IME} = \beta_0 + \beta_1 \text{YD} + \beta_2 \text{RL4} + \beta_3 \text{Q1} + \beta_4 \text{Q2} + \beta_5 \text{Q3}\,.$$

Part of the SPSS output which results when this regression is run is displayed in Fig. 13/13.

MEAN RESPONSE 833.00000 STD. DEV. 230.33792

FINAL STEP.

			DF	SUM OF SQUARES	MEAN SQUARE	F	SIGNIFICANCE
MULTIPLE R	.95146	ANALYSIS OF VARIANCE	DF	SUM OF SQUARES	MEAN SQUARE	F	SIGNIFICANCE
R SQUARE	.90528	REGRESSION	5.	1296807.61317	259361.52263	42.05065	.000
ADJUSTED R SQUARE	.88375	RESIDUAL	22.	135692.38683	6167.83576		
STD DEVIATION	78.53557	COEFF OF VARIABILITY	9.4 PCT				

-------------------- VARIABLES IN THE EQUATION ------------------

VARIABLE	B	STD ERROR B	T / SIGNIFICANCE	BETA / ELASTICITY
YD	.26817397	.23708215E-01	11.311437	1.1829645
			.000	2.55074
Q2	185.54472	42.272891	4.3892129	.3552065
			.000	.05569
Q1	66.121723	42.844163	1.5433076	.1265833
			.137	.01984
RL4	-45.786004	78.326110	-.58455609	-.0486162
			.565	-.28670
Q3	-350.09386	49.479991	-7.0754632	-.6702191
			.000	-.10507
(CONSTANT)	-1028.3398	334.09240	-3.0780100	
			.006	

Fig. 13/13: Partial SPSS output for the model
$\text{IME} = \beta_0 + \beta_1 \text{YD} + \beta_2 \text{RL4} + \beta_3 \text{Q1} + \beta_4 \text{Q2} + \beta_5 \text{Q3}$.

It turns out that this model is quite acceptable; the regression has good F and R^2 values. The YD coefficient is positive, and the RL4 coefficient negative, as we might expect. The signs of dummy variable coefficients also appear reasonable. The t statistics of the individual coefficients are not so good, however; in particular the RL4 is poor. On balance, though, we must consider this model a good compromise between all the different requirements of a model, with regards to statistics and theoratically sound structure.

Remark: To caution the reader against any undue optimism regarding the faith in the data concerning its ability to reject an unsound specification, let us play the devil's advocate and try the specification:

$$\text{IME} = \beta_0 + \beta_1 \text{YD} + \beta_2 \text{RL2} + \beta_3 \text{Q2}.$$

Part of the SPSS output from fitting this model is shown in Figure 13/14 below.

```
MEAN RESPONSE      833.00000        STD. DEV.        230.33792

FINAL STEP.

MULTIPLE R             .87213    ANALYSIS OF VARIANCE   DF         SUM OF SQUARES    MEAN SQUARE      F      SIGNIFICANCE
R SQUARE               .76061    REGRESSION              3.          1089572.61718   363190.87239   25.41815         .000
ADJUSTED R SQUARE      .73069    RESIDUAL               24.           342927.38282    14288.64095
STD DEVIATION       119.53510    COEFF OF VARIABILITY   14.3 PCT

-------------------- VARIABLES IN THE EQUATION -----------------

VARIABLE          B          STD ERROR B          T            BETA
                                             SIGNIFICANCE   ELASTICITY

YD              .10250332   .28156718E-01   3.6404569      .4521609
                                              .001          .97496
Q2           202.65334     53.928821        3.7577929      .3879592
                                              .001          .06082
RL2          420.78157    104.52643         4.0255996      .4883362
                                              .000         2.64729
(CONSTANT)  -2235.0036    459.68529        -4.8620298
                                              .000
```

Fig. 13/14: Partial SPSS output for the model
$\text{IME} = \beta_0 + \beta_1 \text{YD} + \beta_2 \text{RL2} + \beta_3 \text{Q2}$.

This time, although the R^2 and F statistics are not as good as before, they are still quite acceptable. Looking at the individual coefficients, we see that they all have significant t statistics. But what about their signs? The YD coefficient is positive, as we expect it to be, but the RL2 coefficient is *negative,* contrary to economic theory and common sense. Add to this the fact that the RL2 coefficient is significant as well, and we realize that we should not always put too much faith in our models. The reason why the second model produced such good statistics may be due to some peculiarity in the data, or perhaps pure coincidence. Proper caution and skepticism should therefore always be exercised whenever a model is used. In the words of Henri Theil, "It requires maturity to realize that models are to be used but not to be believed."[2]

[2] H. Theil: "Principles of Econometrics", John Wiley & Sons, New York 1971, p. vi.

References

Chou, Y.: *Statistical Analysis,* 2nd edition. Holt, Rinehart and Winston, New York 1975.

Hamburg, M.: *Statistical Analysis for Decision Making,* 2nd edition. Harcourt, Brace, Jovanovich, New York 1977.

Harnett, D.L.: *Statistical Methods,* 3rd edition. Addison-Wesley, Reading, Mass. 1982.

Hawkins, C.A., and J.E. Weber: *Statistical Analysis. Applications to Business and Economics,* Harper & Row, New York 1980.

Klecka, W., N.H. Nie and C. Hadlai Hull: *SPSS Primer*. McGraw-Hill, New York 1975.

Kleinbaum, D.G., and L.L. Kupper: *Applied Regression Analysis and Other Multivariable Methods,* Duxbury Press, North Scituate, Mass. 1978.

Mansfield, E.: *Statistics for Business and Economics,* Norton & Company, New York 1980.

Nie, N.H., C. Hadlai Hull, J.G. Jenkins, K. Steinbrenner and D.H. Bent: *Statistical Package for the Social Sciences,* 2nd edition, McGraw-Hill, New York 1975.

Ott, L.: *An Introduction to Statistical Methods and Data Analysis,* Duxbury Press, North Scituate, Mass. 1977.

Wonnacott, T.H. and R.J. Wonnacott: *Introductory Statistics for Business and Economics,* 2nd edition. John Wiley & Sons, New York 1977.

Exercises

13–1 A firm wishes to determine the relationship between its sales and two independent variables: advertising expenditures and base prices, both in hundreds of dollars. Ten cities are selected and the data for a given month is shown below:

City	Sales $ Y	Advertising Expenditures $ X (000)	Base Price $ Z (00)
1	22	25	60
2	30	26	44
3	24	28	54
4	27	30	48
5	30	32	64
6	30	34	70
7	32	35	60
8	35	36	60
9	34	38	72
10	36	38	68

On the next page is a partial SPSS output for the above data.

a) What is the regression equation for the above data?
b) Find a 95% confidence interval for β_1.
c) Interpret $\hat{\beta}_2$.
d) Test $H_0 : \beta_1 = \beta_2 = 0$ using $\alpha = 5\%$.
e) What is the predicted value of Y if $X = 34{,}000$ and $Z = 5600$?

```
DEPENDENT VARIABLE..   Y          SALES

MEAN RESPONSE        30.00000    STD. DEV.       4.59468

FINAL STEP

MULTIPLE R           .90919     ANALYSIS OF VARIANCE    DF        SUM OF SQUARES     MEAN SQUARE    F  SIGNIFICANCE
R SQUARE             .82663     REGRESSION              2.          157.06040         78.53020    16.68847    .002
ADJUSTED R SQUARE    .77710     RESIDUAL                7.           32.93960          4.70566
STD DEVIATION       2.16925     COEFF OF VARIABILITY    7.2 PCT

-------------------- VARIABLES IN THE EQUATION ---------------------

VARIABLE           B          STD ERROR B       F             BETA
                                             ------------  ----------
                                             SIGNIFICANCE  ELASTICITY

X               1.0979894     .21749838      25.484978     1.1421757
                                                  .001       1.17851
Z               -.18924080    .11012557       2.7986218    -.8784974
                                                  .138       -.37850
(CONSTANT)      5.9998614     5.2204323       1.3102930
                                                  .288

ALL VARIABLES ARE IN THE EQUATION
```

Partial computer output for Exercise no. 1.

13–2 The Eihtak Ltée company has divided Canada into about 200 sales territories: In each territory it has an exclusive distributor selling to and otherwise servicing the retail outlets. The marketing analyst assumed that the sales in each territory would be influenced by the population of the territory, the amount of promotion effort which the company expends, and the efficiency of the local distributor. She decided to investigate this relationship by the use of multiple regression analysis. Seven of the sales territories were selected at random for analysis. The data resulting from the analysis are displayed in the table below.

Territory	Y Sales (Thousands of units per year)	X_1 Population (Millions of persons)	X_2 Advertising (Radio spots per day)	X_3 Distributor Efficiency Index (*)
027	6	0.7	12	3
063	5	0.4	10	2
093	10	1.2	20	1
100	12	2.0	14	2
142	5	0.8	5	4
155	15	3.0	7	3
171	12	1.5	22	1

(*) Each distributor was rated 1, 2, 3, 4 with 1 being the highest rating for excellence throughout and 4 representing minimum efficiency as indicated by these criteria.

The marketing analyst then used a multiple regression computer program, of which some output appears on the next page.

```
DEPENDENT VARIABLE..   Y          SALES

MEAN RESPONSE        9.28571     STD. DIV.       3.98868

FINAL STEP

MULTIPLE R            .99915     ANALYSIS OF VARIANCE     DF       SUM OF SQUARES  MEAN SQUARES     F       SIGNIFICANCE
R SQUARE              .99831     REGRESSION               3.            95.26733      31.75578   590.885231       .000
ADJUSTED R SQUARE     .99662     RESIDUAL                 3.              .16124        .05375
STD DEVIATION         .20181     COEFF OF VARIABILITY     2.5 PCT

--------------------- VARIABLES IN THE EQUATION ---------------------

VARIABLE            B            STD ERROR B          T            BETA
                                                 SIGNIFICANCE   ELASTICITY

X1            4.1851954        .10658341          1541.8859     .9400316
                                                       .000       .61812
X3           -.43154540        .21287146          4.1101544    -.1204093
                                                       .136      -.10623
X2            .14897915        .17890786E-01      15.875338     .2366828
                                                       .028       .20628
(CONSTANT)   2.6170041         .98086466          7.1185352
                                                       .076
ALL VARIABLES ARE IN THE EQUATION.
```

Partial computer output for Exercise no. 2.

a) Write the estimated multiple regression equation for the linear model.
b) Estimate expected sales when $X_1 = 1.4$, $X_2 = 11$, $X_3 = 3$.
c) By what percentage is the variability of sales reduced when the population, the advertising and the distributor efficiency are considered in the regression model?
d) Test whether or not a relation between sales and the three factors does indeed exist. (use $\alpha = .05$).
e) By how much would sales change if the population were half a million persons less? What is the underlying assumption?

13–3 A property developer wished to estimate the selling price of house lots in a North Vancouver city district. She recorded for each of 20 recently sold house lots:

y = selling price of the lot (in thousands of dollars)
x_1 = area of the lot (in hundreds of square meters)
x_2 = average elevation of the lot (in meters above the sea level)
x_3 = slope of the lot (difference, in meters between the largest and smallest elevation of the lot)

She then used a regression-analysis computer program, obtaining the following output:

MULTIPLE R	.8854
R SQUARE	.7838
STD. ERROR OF EST.	.6075

ANALYSIS OF VARIANCE

	DF	SUM OF SQUARES	MEAN SQUARE	F-RATIO
REGRESSION	3	21.409	7.136	19.345
RESIDUAL	16	5.903	.369	

ANALYSIS OF INDIVIDUAL VARIABLES

VARIABLE	COEFFICIENT	STD ERROR	F-VALUE
(CONSTANT)	−2.491		
AREA	.099	.058	2.935
ELEVATION	.029	.006	23.327
SLOPE	.086	.031	7.841

a) What is the multiple linear regression equation relating selling price to the area, elevation and slope of a house lot?
b) What percentage of the variation in selling price is explained by the three independent variables?
c) Test the hypothesis that the regression equation is not a useful predictor of y (at $\alpha = .05$).
d) Which variable shows the strongest explanatory relationship to selling price in the presence of the other variables? Explain.
e) Which shows the weakest? Explain.

13–4 The president of a large railway company has attempted to study the effect of two types of promotional expenditures on the use of commuter train services.

The use of the commuter services is measured in dollars at the end of each month. Twenty-four consecutive months were selected and analyzed. The two types of promotional expenditures were reduced monthly rates (x_1, in thousands of dollars) and higher frequency of trains (x_2, in thousands of dollars). The sales (y) were measured in tens of thousands of dollars. Different monthly expenditures were employed and the results analyzed.

A partial computer print-out for the least-squares multiple regression is shown below.

Source	DF	Sum of Squares	Mean Square	F-Value	PR>F	R-Square
Model	2	114.678	57.339	47.703	.0001	.9304
Error	21	25.241	1.202			
Total	23	139.919				

Parameter	Estimate	T for H_0 Parameter = 0	PR > |T|	Std. Error of Estimate
Intercept	2.13438	3.50	.0001	.61036
x_1	3.02925	25.18	.0001	.12028
x_2	0.70575	5.87	.0001	.12028

a) State the least-squares prediction equation for this model from the above results.
b) Assume that the expenditures for the two promotional types are:

$x_1 = \$3,000$
$x_2 = \$5,000$.

What would this model estimate the resulting sales to be?

c) Test the effectiveness of each expenditure individually with respect to the above results. Secondly, test the whole model through the use of the analysis of variance F test.

d) Discuss the R-square value in the above print-out in some detail.

13–5 Feminists have alleged that the Colossal Corporation performs salary discrimination against its female employees. To evaluate this claim, information is taken from a random sample of employees. The following is aportion of the SPSS print-out of the regression of Y against X_1, X_2 and X_3, where

Y = Annual Income　　X_1 = Years of Experience
X_2 = Years of Education　　X_3 = 1 if female, 0 if male.

Analysis of Variance	DF	Sum of Squares	Mean Square	F
Regression	3	73 335 840.63210	24 445 280.21070	936.60076
Residual	46	1 200 622.04048	26 100.47914	

Variables in the Equation

Variable	B	Std. Error B	F / Significance
X_1	731.81370	76.870030	90.633126 0
X_2	1207.5334	548.78300	4.8416901 .014
X_3	−865.37041	494.50012	3.0624657 .040
(Constant)	9103.2734	141.52093	4137.6506 0

a) On how many observations is this regression based?

b) Test if this regression is significant, using $\alpha = 0.01$.

c) Compute s, the standard error of the estimate.

d) Test the hypothesis that female employees have lower annual salaries than male employees when education and experience are taken into account.

13–6 In the table on the next page are shown the year-end closing prices of a certain common stock (Y) during ten years from 1972 to 1981, and these three independent variables: X_1, the prime interest rate; X_2, the price-earnings ratio; and X_3, quarterly dividend in cents:

Year	Stock Price (Y)	Prime Interest Rate (X_1)	Price-Earnings Ratio (X_2)	Quarterly Dividend (X_3)
1972	40.	.06	10	.25
1973	35.	.07	11	.50
1974	30.	.08	20	.20
1975	20.	.09	12	.15
1976	10.	.10	8	.10
1977	15.	.08	7	.10
1978	20.	.06	9	.15
1979	30.	.06	13	.40
1980	40.	.07	15	.45
1981	20.	.09	5	.20

The following table shows part of the SPSS output for the above table and model:

$$Y = \beta_0 + \beta_1 X_1 + \beta_2 X_2 + \beta_3 X_3 + \varepsilon.$$

```
DEPENDENT VARIABLE..    Y

MEAN RESPONSE       26.00000        STD. DEV.        10.48809

FINAL STEP.

MULTIPLE R              .88412  ANALYSIS OF VARIANCE      DF      SUM OF SQUARES   MEAN SQUARE       F      SIGNIFICANCE
R SQUARE                .78167  REGRESSION               3.          773.85281      257.95094    7.16042       .02
ADJUSTED R SQUARE       .67250  RESIDUAL                 6.          216.14719       36.02453
STD DEVIATION          6.00204  COEFF OF VARIABILITY  23.1 PCT

------------------ VARIABLES IN THE EQUATION ------------------        ------- VARIABLES NOT IN EQUATION -----------
VARIABLE           B         STD ERROR B        T            BETA        VARIABLE   PARTIAL   TOLERANCE        F
                                           SIGNIFICANCE  ELASTICITY                                    SIGNIFICANCE

  X1         -249.53036     164.96625     -1.5126146     -.3401846
                                                .181      -.72940

  X2          .66012497     .49842602      1.3244192      .2719338
                                                .234       .27928

  X3          36.504790     16.748408      2.1795975      .5123297
                                                .072       .35101

(Constant)    28.576735     15.910676      1.7960730
                                                .123

ALL VARIABLES ARE IN THE EQUATION.

COEFFICIENTS AND CONFIDENCE INTERVALS.

VARIABLE           B         STD ERROR B        T          95.0 PCT CONFIDENCE INTERVAL

  X1         -249.53036     164.96625     -1.5126146     -653.18605   ,   154.12534
  X2          .66012497     .49842602      1.3244192     -.55947299   ,   1.8797229
  X3          36.504790     16.748408      2.1795975     -4.4768682   ,   77.486440
CONSTANT      28.576735     15.910676      1.7960730     -10.355076   ,   67.508546
```

a) What is the estimated regression model for the above data?
b) What percentage of the variation in the year-end closing price is explained by the variables prime interest rate, price-earnings ratio and quarterly dividend?
c) Find a 95% confidence interval for β_2.
d) What interpretation can we give to β_1?
e) Test the hypothesis that the three parameters β_1, β_2 and β_3 are simultaneously different from zero at an α-level of 10%.

f) If X_1 and X_3 are fixed but X_2 is allowed to increase by 5 units, what happens to the stock price?

13–7 A marketing experiment was designed by a statistician to study the effects of two types of promotional expenditures on sales (Y) of a line of food products sold in supermarkets. Sixteen localities were selected for the test. They were similar in market potential and were representative of the target market for this line of products. Various combinations of media advertising expenditures (X) and point-of-sale expenditures (Z) were specified for the study, and the localities were assigned at random to one of these X, Z combinations.

The statistician then used a certain regression analysis computer program, obtaining the output below.

```
ORDINARY LEAST SQUARES

DEPENDENT VARIABLE     Y

RIGHT-HAND            ESTIMATED           STANDARD            T-
 VARIABLE             COEFFICIENT          ERROR           STATISTIC

    C                   2.13437           .610361             3.497
    X                   3.02925           .120281            25.185
    Z                   .705750           .120281             5.867

LOG OF LIKELIHOOD FUNCTION =                    -12.7821
R-SQUARED =                                       .9809
DURBIN-WATSON STATISTIC (ADJ. FOR 0. GAPS) =     1.9635
SUM OF SQUARED RESIDUALS =                      3.76157
STANDARD ERROR OF THE REGRESSION =               .537914
SUM OF RESIDUALS =                              .682121E-11
NUMBER OF OBSERVATIONS =                         16.000
MEAN OF DEPENDENT VARIABLE =                    15.2069
F-STATISTIC ( 2., 13.) =                        334.349

ESTIMATE OF VARIANCE-COVARIANCE MATRIX OF ESTIMATED COEFFICIENTS

                      C                   X                   Z

            + + + + + + + + + + + + + + + + + + + + + + + + + + + + + + +

C           +     .372540          -.506365E-01         -.506365E-01
X           +   -.506365E-01        .144676E-01         -.100414E-17
Z           +   -.506365E-01       -.100414E-17          .144676E-01
                      1                   2                   3
```

a) Write the estimated multiple regression equation for the linear model.
b) By what percentage is the variability of locality sales reduced when the media and point-of-sale promotional expenditures are considered in the regression model?
c) Test whether or not a relation between sales and the two types of promotional expenditures does indeed exist. (Use $\alpha = .05$).
d) Estimate β_1 and β_2, each with a 95 percent confidence interval.
e) Estimate expected sales when $X = 5.4$ and $Z = 2.3$.

13–8 A commerce student wishes to estimate stock prices for the Pirstorp Company, based on data relating to the period 1960 to 1979. He collects data for the following variables:

X_1 = time (a trend variable)
X_2 = Y (market unit price of stock)
X_3 = earnings per share
X_4 = Financial Review Stock Price Index

The student wishes to examine two models:

Model I $\quad Y = \beta_0 + \beta_3 X_3 + \varepsilon$

Model II $\quad Y = \beta_0 + \beta_3 X_3 + \beta_4 X_4 + \varepsilon.$

Using a certain multiple linear regression computer program, he obtains partial printouts for Models I and II as follows:

Model I

```
REGRESSION COEFFICIENT                      .60985

STD. ERROR OF REG. COEF.                    .182

COMPUTED T-VALUE                           3.356

                ANALYSIS OF VARIANCE FOR THE REGRESSION
SOURCE OF VARIATION              D.F.  SUM OF SQ.  MEAN SQ.  F VALUE
ATTRIBUTABLE TO REGRESSION         1     55.419     55.419    11.260
DEVIATION FROM REGRESSION (SSE)   18     88.594      4.922
TOTAL                             19    144.013
```

Model II

```
VARIABLE    REG.COEF.   STD. ERROR COEF.    COMPUTED T    BETA COEF.

   3         .28279        .12171            2.32359       .28766
   4        1.61899        .27776            5.82867       .72159

                ANALYSIS OF VARIANCE FOR THE REGRESSION

SOURCE OF VARIATION              D.F.  SUM OF SQ.  MEAN SQ.  F VALUE
ATTRIBUTABLE TO REGRESSION         2    114.466     57.233    32.930
DEVIATION FROM REGRESSION (SSE)   17     29.547      1.738
TOTAL                             19    144.013
```

The data used for the variables X_1, X_2, X_3 and X_4 are given below:

X_1 Trend Variable	X_2 Market Unit Price	X_3 Earnings Per share	X_4 Financial Review Stock Price Index
1.000	1.000	1.000	1.000
2.000	1.286	1.921	.982
3.000	1.124	3.095	1.029
4.000	1.200	2.410	1.057
5.000	1.124	4.286	1.085
6.000	1.638	5.794	1.314
7.000	2.048	4.841	1.485
8.000	1.876	3.604	1.600
9.000	1.838	5.983	1.577

X_1 Trend Variable	X_2 Market Unit Price	X_3 Earnings Per share	X_4 Financial Review Stock Price Index
10.000	2.704	5.126	2.000
11.000	4.857	10.222	2.571
12.000	5.857	9.539	2.771
13.000	5.810	11.634	2.628
14.000	7.048	8.142	2.914
15.000	9.333	6.746	3.657
16.000	8.190	8.190	3.542
17.000	7.905	4.841	3.971
18.000	5.552	4.063	3.600
19.000	4.762	5.238	4.200
20.000	5.429	6.206	4.685

a) From the information given above determine:
   i) β_0 (i.e. the intercept for Models I and II);
   ii) R^2 and R for both models.
   iii) Standard error of the regression estimate for both models.
b) Test the significance of the regression coefficients in Model I and Model II.
c) Which one of the two models above gives the best explanation of stock prices? Give reasons for the answer by comparing and contrasting the two models. Use the R^2, the standard deviations of the regression coefficients and the t-values of the analysis.

13–9 A farmer wishes to know how fertilization and rainfall affect the yield of one of his crops. He uses the following random observation as a basis for estimating a multiple linear regression model:

Crop Yield (Tons/Hectar)	35	74	85	62	59	61	80	65	67	66	23	44
Fertilizer (kg/Hectar)	235	518	591	581	358	465	500	457	408	555	180	281
Rainfall (cm)	37	45	50	28	57	35	60	43	74	32	63	58

a) Use a multiple linear regression computer package to estimate this model.
b) Find a 95% confidence interval for the coefficient relating to rainfall.
c) Test if the regression is significant at a level of 5%.
d) What would the expected yield be if 315 kg/ha of fertilizer was used and rainfall turned out to be 52 cm?

14. Time Series and Forecasting

A *time series* is a sequence of numbers relating to a variable which changes over time. Examples of time series are: the total annual value of Volkswagen motor vehicles sold in Canada, for 1960 to 1980; the daily closing price of gold at the London Exchange, for the year 1982; the lowest overnight temperature recorded in the city of Chicago, for each month during the period from March 1973 to November 1979; the number of children born in Sweden weekly, during this century.

Whereas a time series pertains to measurements of *one* variable at *several* points in time, *cross section* data pertain to *several* variables at the *same* point in time. Most statistical data in business and economics are of either the time series or the cross section type. In the previous chapters, most of the data we have been working with have been cross section data; the attention will now be focussed on analysing time series data.

In Section 14.1 our goal is to develop methods for appropriately smoothing a given time series, to facilitate a better understanding of its movements. The moving average as well as the exponential smoothing methods are covered. Then in Section 14.2 the classical multiplicative time series model is explained, and its various components discussed. Section 14.3 shows how the trend and seasonal components can be isolated; the trend is obtained by linear regression, and the seasonal factor by the ratio-to-moving average method.

Modern time series analysis, which is a fast growing speciality, is very briefly sketched in Section 14.4. Finally, in Section 14.5 we put the time series tools that we have developed to use by constructing forecasts.

14.1 Smoothing Methods

Example 14.1

Consider the data in Example 13.15 of YD, disposable personal income in Canada. We repeat the data here, for convenience:

DATE	YD
1961 Q1	6219.79
1961 Q2	6473.01
1961 Q3	7486.99
1961 Q4	6725.73
1962 Q1	6668.41
1962 Q2	6970.09
1962 Q3	8257.58
1962 Q4	7050.68
1963 Q1	6825.49
1963 Q2	7258.62
1963 Q3	8733.71
1963 Q4	7373.43
1964 Q1	7388.13
1964 Q2	7379.27
1964 Q3	8767.14
1964 Q4	7703.24
1965 Q1	7794.41
1965 Q2	7764.97
1965 Q3	9384.67
1965 Q4	8257.10
1966 Q1	8215.80
1966 Q2	8266.99
1966 Q3	9946.50
1966 Q4	8557.28
1967 Q1	8532.98
1967 Q2	8749.72
1967 Q3	10104.43
1967 Q4	8990.69

Fig. 14/1: Disposable personal income in Canada, YD (millions of 1961 $).

If we plot the data of Fig. 14/1 in a diagram we get Fig. 14/2 on the next page, where consecutive observations have been joined by lines. The pracitce of joining adjacent observation points in this way is quite common in time series analysis and facilitates a visual comprehension of the series.

It is only when we have plotted the time series that we see the clear pattern in this time series; a relatively steady rise over time, broken by sharp peaks for the third quarter of each year. We realize the truth in the expression: "A picture paints a thousand words".

In order to obtain a deeper understanding of the behaviour of a time series, we may want to *smooth* the series. That is, we would like to generate from the series

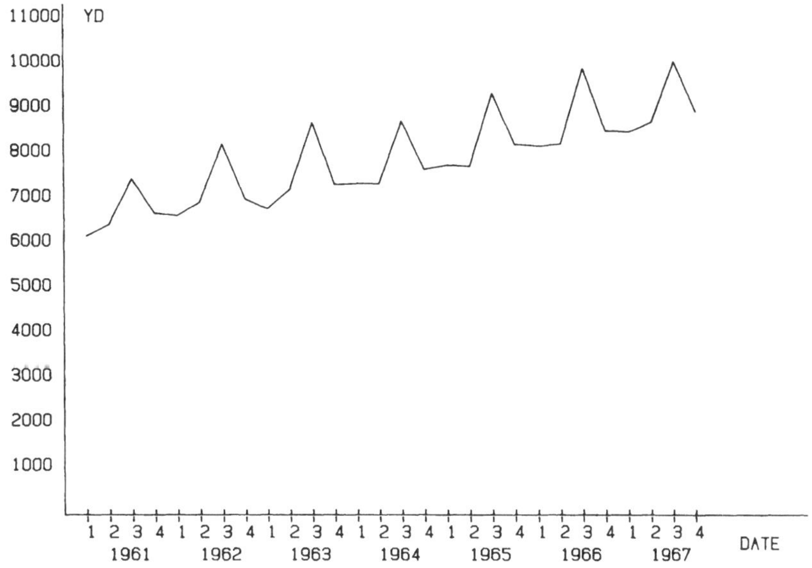

Fig. 14/2: Disposable personal income in Canada, YD (millions of 1961 $).

a smooth curve which displays the long-term movements of the series. In our example, we would wish to even out the jerkiness caused by the third quarter peaks.

We shall discuss two smoothing methods, taking *moving averages* and performing *exponential smoothing*. We start with the first.

Definition: An *m-point moving average* of a time series is obtained by taking the average of m adjacent observations and plotting it at the midpoint of the m observations.

Example 14.2

For our disposable personal income series, YD of Example 14.1, we can compute a three-point moving average series $\overline{YD_t}$, as follows:

t	YD_t	$\overline{YD_t}$
1961 Q1	6219.79	–
1961 Q2	6473.01	6726.60
1961 Q3	7486.99	6895.24
1961 Q4	6725.73	6960.37
1962 Q1	6668.41	6788.07
1962 Q2	6970.09	7298.69
1962 Q3	8257.58	7426.11
1962 Q4	7050.68	7377.91
1963 Q1	6825.49	
⋮	⋮	⋮

Fig. 14/3: Three-quarter moving averages for the time series of Example 14.1.

We notice that by taking three-point moving averages, we obtain a smoothed series which has two observations less than the original series (one less at the start and one less at the end). For a two-point moving average, we would lose one observation, for a five-point moving average four observations are lost, etc.

If we examine the moving averages $\overline{YD_t}$ of Example 14.2 we find that most but not all of the smoothed values will include a contribution from a third quarter. For instance, the first smoothed value (pertaining to 1961 Q2) which is 6726.60, includes a contribution from the third quarter of 1961:

$$\frac{6219.79 + 6473.01 + 7486.99}{3} = 6726.60\,.$$

However, the smoothed value pertaining to 1962 Q1 does *not* include a contribution from the third quarter of 1961 or 1962:

$$\frac{6725.73 + 6668.41 + 6970.09}{3} = 6788.07\,.$$

We realize that a suitable smoothing of our time series would be by four-point moving averages, since the sharp peaks occur with a periodicity of four. However, taking a four-point moving average over the four quarters of 1964, and plotting the result at the midpoint of the four observations would put us between the second and third quarter time points of 1964. In general, when an even-point moving average time series is formed, we take averages of adjacent moving averages, so that the resulting time series can be compared to the original one. We then say that we use *centered* moving averages.

Example 14.3

Consider the following data for United States quarterly exports (goods and services) EX_t in billions of U.S. dollars:

quarter \ Year	1965	1966	1967	1968	1969
I	8.6	10.3	11.3	11.8	11.8
II	10.4	11.0	11.8	13.0	14.7
III	9.5	10.4	11.0	12.6	13.9
IV	10.7	11.7	12.2	13.2	15.3

Constructing a four-quarter moving average time series from this data we obtain the table in Fig. 14/4 below. Note that the table is filled in *column-wise*.

Date	EX_t	Four-point moving average $\overline{EX}_t$	Centered four-point moving average $\overline{\overline{EX}}_t$
1965 Q1	8.6		
Q2	10.4		
		9.8	
Q3	9.5		10.012
		10.225	
Q4	10.7		10.3
		10.375	
1966 Q1	10.3		10.488
		10.6	
Q2	11.0		10.725
		10.85	
Q3	10.4		10.975
		11.1	
Q4	11.7		11.2
		11.3	
1967 Q1	11.3		11.375
		11.45	
Q2	11.8		11.512
		11.575	
Q3	11.0		11.638
		11.7	
Q4	12.2		11.85
		12.0	
1968 Q1	11.8		12.2
		12.4	
Q2	13.0		12.525
		12.65	
Q3	12.6		12.65
		12.65	
Q4	13.2		12.862
		13.075	
1969 Q1	11.8		13.238
		13.4	
Q2	14.7		13.662
		13.925	
Q3	13.9		
Q4	15.3		

Fig. 14/4: Four-point and centered four-point moving averages.

Plotting the original versus the centered four-point moving average smoothed series of this example we obtain the following diagram:

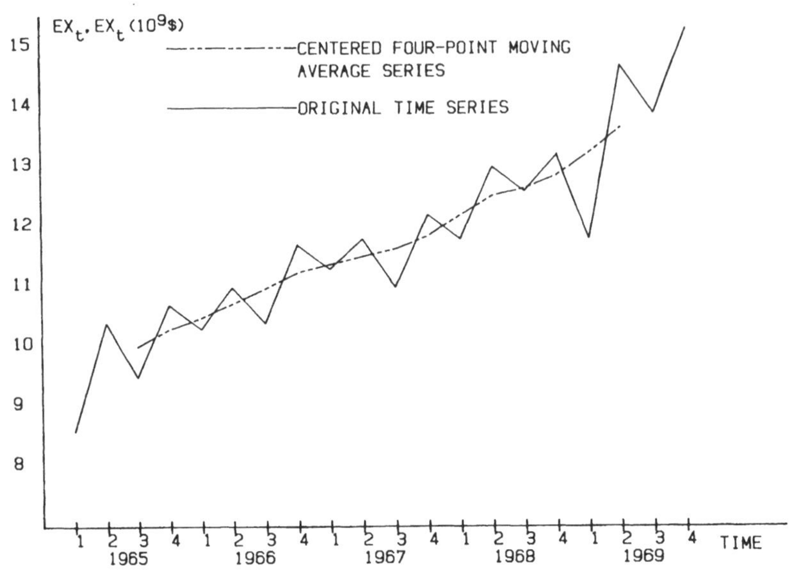

Fig. 14/5: Original and smoothed series from Example 14.3.

Looking at the plots in Fig. 14/5 we are again reminded of how useful the pictorial representation is. (We can hardly overemphasize the importance of the visual aspect in time series analysis. The first step in any time series analysis should always be to obtain a time plot of the series to be investigated.) From the smoothed series in Fig. 14/5 we can clearly see that a steady upward moving trend is present. This information can be used to try to explain the movements of the time series by considering it as a sum or a product of various components, of which the trend would be one. This decomposition approach will be taken in the next section.

A drawback of the moving average method for smoothing a time series is that we lose observation points. This is a disadvantage if for instance we want to forecast the time series beyond the period for which we have observations.

In Example 14.3 the last observed value was for the fourth quarter of 1969, and if we wanted to make a prediction of the next (i.e. the 1970 Q1) value, based on smoothed values, we find that we have no later smoothed data than 1969 Q2. A smoothing method which does not suffer from this weakness is the *exponential smoothing* method which computes a smoothed value for each original observation. It is a very simple smoothing technique with minimal calculation and data-storing requirements. It works as follows.

Consider any time series X_t, $t = 1, 2, 3, \ldots$ The exponentially smoothed series Y_t, $t = 1, 2, 3, \ldots$ is obtained by first assigning the value X_1 to Y_1 and then successively:

$$Y_2 = \alpha X_2 + (1 - \alpha) Y_1$$
$$Y_3 = \alpha X_3 + (1 - \alpha) Y_2$$
$$\vdots$$

or in general, for $t > 1$:

$$Y_t = \alpha X_t + (1 - \alpha) Y_{t-1}$$

α is a given (predetermined) constant, $0 \leqq \alpha < 1$, which we refer to as the *smoothing constant.* We see that the exponentially smoothed series is very simple to compute; the smoothed value Y_t is simply the arithmetic weighted average of the original time series value X_t and the previous smoothed value Y_{t-1}.

Example 14.4

Using a smoothing constant $\alpha = 0.6$ we obtain the following result using the United States export data EX_t from Example 14.3, for the years 1968 and 1969:

Date	EX_t	Y_t
1968 Q1	11.8	11.8
Q2	13.0	12.52
Q3	12.6	12.568
Q4	13.2	12.947
1969 Q1	11.8	12.259
Q2	14.7	13.724
Q3	13.9	13.830
Q4	15.3	14.712

Fig. 14/6: Original and smoothed series from Example 14.4.

Then we plot the original and smoothed values from Example 14.4 and obtain Fig. 14/7 below:

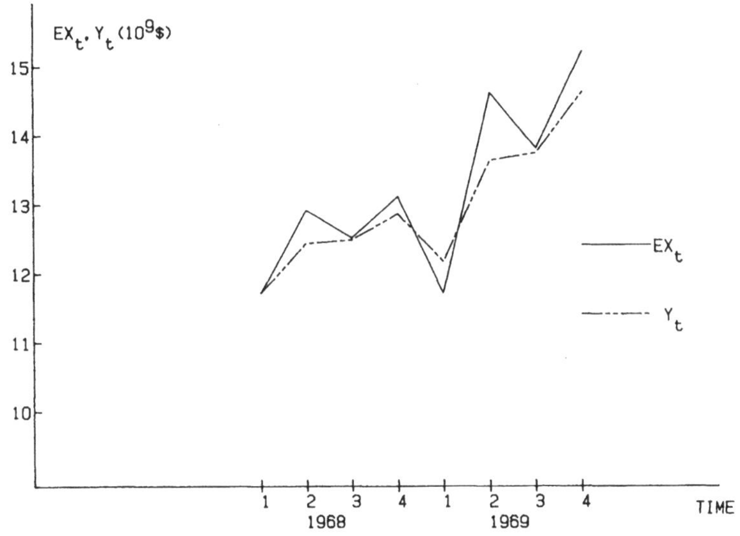

Fig. 14/7: Original and smoothed series from Example 14.4.

It is clear from the exponential smoothing formula that large values of the smoothing constant α (i.e. α near 1) will produce a series Y_t which is near to the original one; little smoothing has been done. Conversely, small values of α (i.e. near 0) will produce a very smooth series. The choice of a suitable value of α is usually up to the statistician; if a very smooth series is desired (or if the original series moves very erratically), $\alpha = 0.1$ or 0.2 may be satisfactory. If little smoothing is desired (or if the original series does not fluctuate much), $\alpha = 0.9$ or 0.8 could be used. The reader is urged to try $\alpha = 0.1$ and $\alpha = 0.9$ on the data in Example 14.4 and compare the outcomes in view of the above discussion.

Let us now look closer at the smoothing equation. By using it successively for periods back into the past we find the following:

$$Y_t = \alpha X_t + (1-\alpha)\underbrace{Y_{t-1}}$$
$$\underbrace{Y_{t-1}} = \alpha X_{t-1} + (1-\alpha)\underbrace{Y_{t-2}}$$
$$Y_{t-2} = \alpha X_{t-2} + (1-\alpha)Y_{t-3}$$
$$\vdots$$

By making all substitutions we get:

$$\begin{aligned} Y_t &= \alpha X_t + (1-\alpha)\{\alpha X_{t-1} + (1-\alpha)Y_{t-2}\} \\ &\alpha X_t + (1-\alpha)\alpha X_{t-1} + (1-\alpha)^2 Y_{t-2} \\ &\alpha X_t + (1-\alpha)\alpha X_{t-1} + (1-\alpha)^2\{\alpha X_{t-2} + (1-\alpha)Y_{t-3}\} \\ &\alpha X_t + (1-\alpha)\alpha X_{t-1} + (1-\alpha)^2\alpha X_{t-2} + (1-\alpha)^3 Y_{t-3} \end{aligned}$$

We see that all preceding X_t : s are reflected in the current smoothed value Y_t, and that the weights of these are α, $(1-\alpha)\alpha$, $(1-\alpha)^2\alpha, \ldots$ which decrease exponentially (hence the name exponential smoothing). Thus, the further back in time we go, the less weight is assigned to X_t. The rate of this decrease is obviously dependent on α; with an α near to one, the decrease is very rapid.

14.2 The Classical Time Series Model

We shall now explain the traditional model for analyzing a time series by decomposing it into separate components. The basic assumption is that any time series Y_t can be considered to consist of four components:

$$Y_t = T_t \cdot C_t \cdot S_t \cdot R_t$$

where T_t is the *long-term* (or *secular*) *trend*,
C_t is the *cyclical* effect,
S_t is the *seasonal* effect, and
R_t is the *residual* (*random*) effect.

The above equation is referred to as the *multiplicative* model where the four components T, C, S and R are multiplied to give the Y-value. The *additive* model specifies Y as the sum of the four components; however, we shall only consider the multiplicative model.

Long-term trends often appear in time series data, such as population growth, data for oil consumption, air pollution, crime rate, etc.

Cyclical effects are present when the time series exhibits a wave-like pattern. Examples of this are the trade (business) cycle of GNP data and the total shipping tonnage ordered in the world annually. Cyclical effects are not as easily predictable as seasonal effects to which we shall now come.

Seasonal effects are upward and downward movements, regularly occurring, usually on an annual basis. Examples are sales volumes of many commodities like house heating oil, camping equipment, motor cars, snow-blowers, lawn-mowers, etc. Seasonal effects are predictable and occur at more or less given times of the year.

Residual (or random) effects account for everything not explained by trend, cyclical or seasonal variation. They can be caused by weather, political events, unpredicted technological developments or consumer attitude changes.

Every time series contains random variation. In addition, it may include one, two or all three of the other components. In the next section we shall study some of the separately.

14.3 Isolating and Analyzing Various Components of the Multiplicative Model

Analysis of Trend

The trend component of a time series expresses its long-term movement over time. Trend curves can be of essentially three different types; either increasing, decreasing or a mixture of both. Some commonly used trend curves of the increasing type are the *exponential* (expressing, for instance, world population growth):

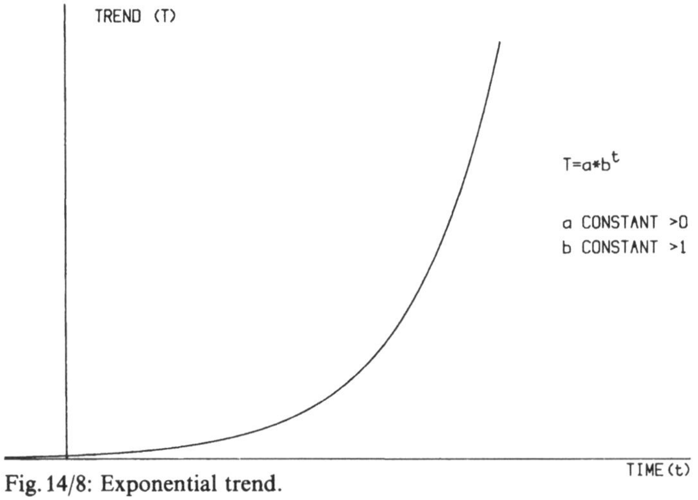

Fig. 14/8: Exponential trend.

and the *linear* (say, hydroelectric power generation in Sweden):

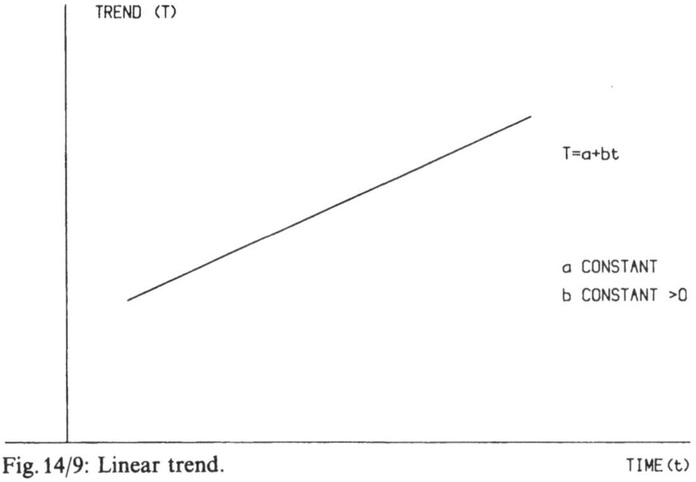

Fig. 14/9: Linear trend.

Other common trend curves are the *logistic* and the *Gompertz* trend curves, but we shall not discuss them.

Decreasing trend curves can again be exponential (for instance known unexploited world reserves of silver):

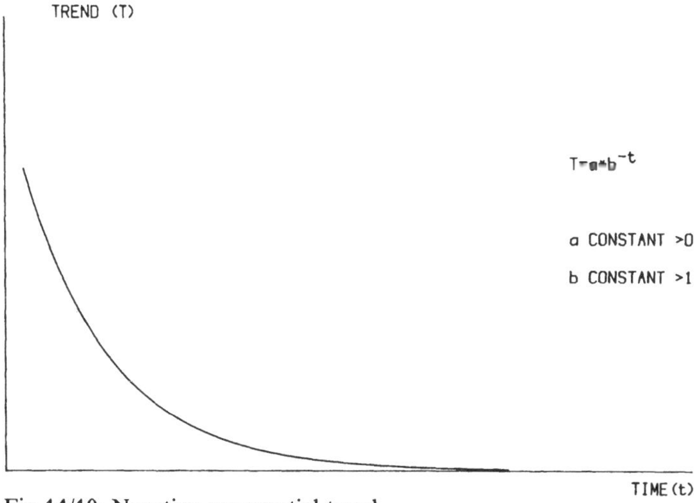

Fig. 14/10: Negative exponential trend.

and linear (for instance depletion of inventory stocks with no replenishment and constant average demand rate):

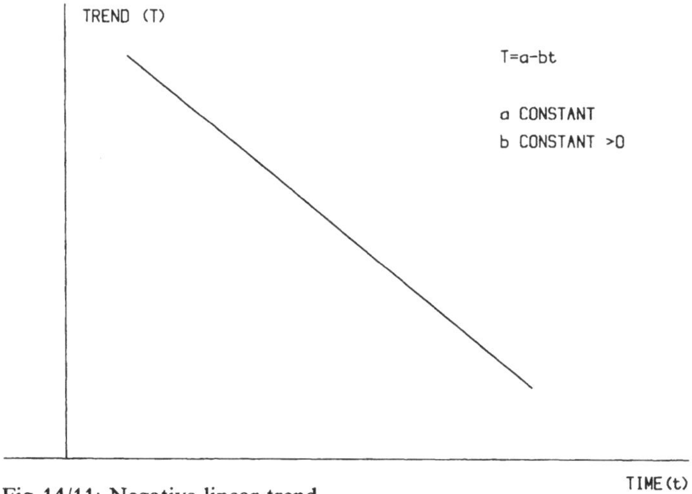

Fig. 14/11: Negative linear trend.

Regarding mixed trends, we might consider parabolic trend (say, bicycle sales or product life cycle):

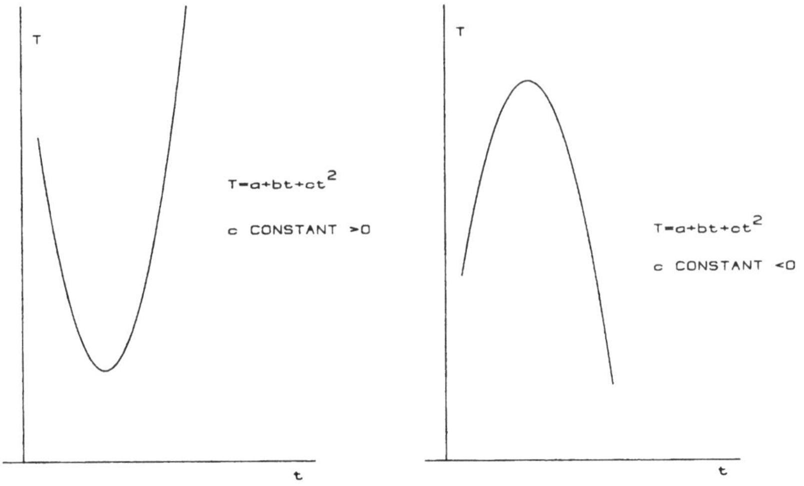

Fig. 14/12: Parabolic trends.

Suppose that a plot of the time series being investigated indicates that a linear trend might be applicable. We could then use linear regression to determine a linear trend line. However, we must be well aware that the theoretical assumptions for using linear regression (uncorrelated residuals, etc.) may well be violated. In spite of this, it is common procedure in time series analysis to use regression analysis anyway.

Example 14.5

Consider the following quarterly data on the number of unemployed people in Canada:

Date	Unemployed (thousands)	Date	Unemployed (thousands)
1976 Q1	776	1978 Q1	1001
Q2	707	Q2	933
Q3	709	Q3	880
Q4	705	Q4	829
1977 Q1	910	1979 Q1	969
Q2	839	Q2	859
Q3	827	Q3	761
Q4	825	Q4	746

Fig. 14/13: Unemployment figures for Canada.

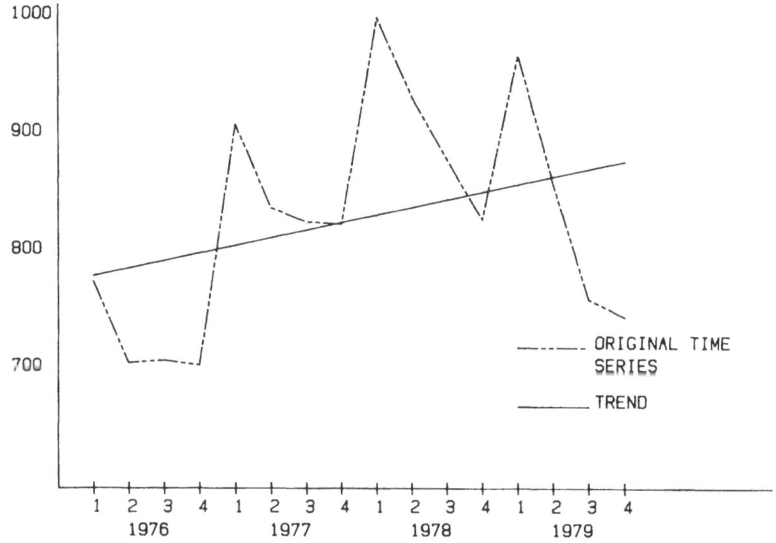

Fig. 14/14: Time series plot and trend line for Example 14.5.

Using simple linear regression, as in Chapter 12, we fit the linear model

$$Y = \beta_0 + \beta_1 t + \varepsilon$$

to this data and compute the least-squares regression line. We put $t = 1$ for 1976 Q1, $t = 2$ for 1976 Q2 etc., so that $t = 16$ for 1979 Q4. The regression line then becomes (the reader is urged to do the computations):

$$Y = 774.6 + 6.485t.$$

This trend line is also drawn in the diagram in Figure 14.14 above. As we see, the fit is not very good. This is reflected by the r^2-value of the regression, which is 0.11; a rather low figure. It is clear that a further analysis of the time series is required.

Seasonal Effect: The Ratio-to-Moving Average Method

We shall now show how the seasonal component (index) of a time series can be computed. We shall use the so-called *ratio-to-moving average* method, which uses moving averages to calculate seasonal indices, S_t. When these are obtained, the original time series can be *deseasonalized*, i. e. the seasonal effect S_t removed. The idea underlying the ratio-to-moving average method is the following:

By forming a suitable moving average smoothed series $\bar{Y}_t$, we can assume that the seasonal component S_t and the random component R_t have been removed.

In other words, we would have:

$$\bar{Y}_t = T_t \cdot C_t .$$

Forming the ratio between the original series Y_t and the smoothed series $\bar{Y}_t$ we would then get:

$$\frac{Y_t}{\bar{Y}_t} = \frac{T_t \cdot C_t \cdot S_t \cdot R_t}{T_t \cdot C_t} = S_t \cdot R_t .$$

By averaging this ratio we then eliminate the random effect R_t; what remains is S_t.

The method is best illustrated by way of a numerical example.

Example 14.6

We shall apply the ratio-to-moving average method to our Canadian unemployment time series of Example 14.5. Because of the seasonality of the time series, a four-quarter centered moving average appears appropriate. The table in Fig. 14/15 below shows how the ratios $Y_t/\bar{Y}_t$ are calculated. The table is filled in columnwise:

Date	Original time series Y_t	Four-quarter moving average, $\bar{Y}_t$	Centered $\bar{Y}_t$, i.e. $\bar{\bar{Y}}_t$	Ratio $Y_t/\bar{\bar{Y}}_t$
1976 Q1	776			
Q2	707			
		724.25		
Q3	709		741.00	0.9568
		757.75		
Q4	705		774.25	0.9106
		790.75		
1977 Q1	910		805.50	1.1297
		820.25		
Q2	839		835.25	1.0045
		850.75		
Q3	827		861.625	0.9598
		873.00		
Q4	825		884.75	0.9325
		896.50		
1978 Q1	1001		903.125	1.1084
		909.75		
Q2	933		910.25	1.0250
		910.75		
Q3	880		906.75	0.9705
		902.75		
Q4	829		893.50	0.9278
		884.25		
1979 Q1	969		869.375	1.1146
		854.50		
Q2	859		844.125	1.0176
		833.75		
Q3	761			
Q4	746			

Fig. 14/15: Finding $S_t \cdot R_t$ for Example 14.6.

For each of the four quarters, we then average the $S_t \cdot R_t$-values obtained in the last column, in order to establish the seasonal factor S_t. We get:

Year \ Quarter	Q1	Q2	Q3	Q4
1976	–	–	0.9568	0.9106
1977	1.1297	1.0045	0.9598	0.9325
1978	1.1084	1.0250	0.9705	0.9278
1979	1.1146	1.0176	–	–
Average	1.1176	1.0157	0.9624	0.9236

Fig. 14/16: Finding the seasonal factors S_t for Example 14.6.

The seasonal factors (components) have now been found; for instance, for the second quarter it is 1.0157.

Remark: The above ratio-to-moving average method for computing the seasonal factors can be further refined. The careful reader may have noticed that the average[1] of the seasonal factors obtained by the above procedure is 1.0048. This number should obviously be 1, and so we may want to scale the four seasonal factors accordingly. We shall not go into this.

Deseasonalized data are useful for many purposes. They can be used for a further analysis to isolate the cyclical component C_t. It is also common practice to express figures for unemployment, price level, imports and exports etc. in deseasonalized form. The seasonal index is an important tool for short-term forecasting.

Example 14.7

The deseasonalized series, i. e. $T_t \cdot C_t \cdot R_t$, resulting from our Examples 14.5 and 14.6 is calculated in the table in Fig. 14/17 on the next page. As usual, the results are conveniently filled in columnwise.

Plotting the original time series of Example 14.5 together with the trend and the deseasonalized series we obtain Fig. 14/18 on the next page.

We shall return to the use of the seasonal factors in the section on forecasting.

[1] As a matter of fact, not the arithmetic but the *geometric* mean should be taken, if we wanted to be completely correct.

Date	Original time series Y_t	Seasonal factor S_t	Deseasonalized series $T_t \cdot C_t \cdot R_t$
1976 Q1	776	1.1176	694
Q2	707	1.0157	696
Q3	709	0.9623	737
Q4	705	0.9236	763
1977 Q1	910	1.1176	814
Q2	839	1.0157	826
Q3	827	0.9623	859
Q4	825	0.9236	893
1978 Q1	1001	1.1176	896
Q2	933	1.0157	919
Q3	880	0.9623	914
Q4	829	0.9236	898
1979 Q1	969	1.1176	867
Q2	859	1.0157	846
Q3	761	0.9623	791
Q4	746	0.9236	808

Fig. 14/17: Deseasonlized data for Example 14.5.

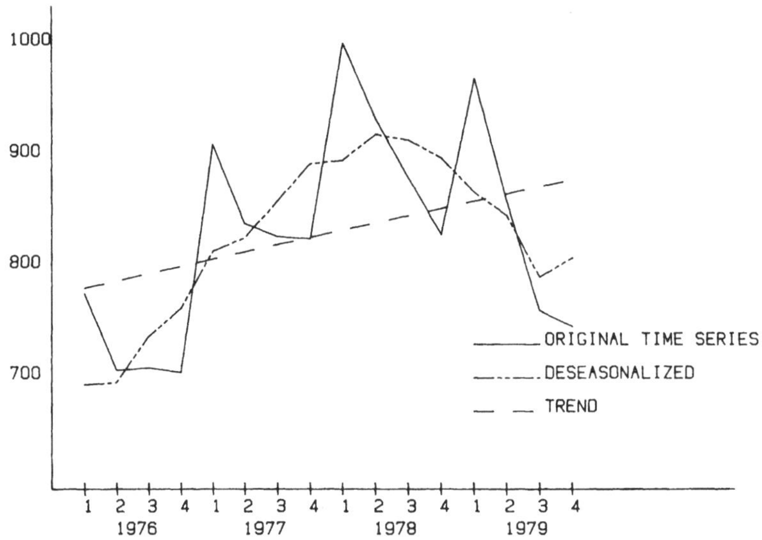

Fig. 14/18: Original, trend and deseasonlized data for Example 14.5.

The ratio-to-moving average method for isolating the seasonal variation component of a time series is closely related to the multiplicative model. If an additive model is adopted, we can use a dummy variable approach in a multiple linear regression context (e.g. Sections 13.3 and 13.6 of the previous chapter). For Example 14.5 we might then specify the model:

$$Y_t = \beta_0 + \beta_1 t + \beta_2 Q1 + \beta_3 Q2 + \beta_4 Q3 + \varepsilon_t$$

and then determine the coefficients β_0, β_1, β_2, β_3 and β_4 by the least-squares method. (The reader is referred to the previous chapter for details.) By looking at the deseasonlized series plot in Fig. 14/8 we get the impression that a negative parabolic trend might be even better:

$$Y_t = \beta_0 + \beta_1 t + \beta_2 t^2 + \beta_3 Q1 + \beta_4 Q2 + \beta_5 Q3 + \varepsilon_t$$

where β_2 would be negative.

*14.4 Modern Time Series Analysis

The random component R_t of a time series may often exhibit *serial correlation.* We may assume that it can be expressed as

$$R_t = \phi R_{t-1} + \varepsilon_t$$

where the error terms ε_t are independent with zero mean. The coefficient ϕ may be estimated and the resulting expression used for R_t to provide an improved time series model.

In general, a time series X_t may be expressed by a number of its past values in a so-called *autoregressive* model:

$$X_t = \delta + \phi_1 X_{t-1} + \phi_2 X_{t-2} + \ldots + \phi_p X_{t-p} + \varepsilon_t$$

which is said to be of type AR(p). Looking back at our exponential smoothing of Section 14.1, we see that we were using a special type of an AR(1) model.

Rather than using an autoregressive model, we may specify the time series X_t as:

$$X_t = \mu + \varepsilon_t + \theta_1 \varepsilon_{t-1}$$

where the error terms ε_t and ε_{t-1} are independent N(0, 1) variables. This is a moving-average model and can be generalized to:

$$X_t = \mu + \varepsilon_t + \theta_1 \varepsilon_{t-1} + \theta_2 \varepsilon_{t-2} + \ldots + \theta_q \varepsilon_{t-p}.$$

We say that this is a moving-average model of order q; it is of type MA(q). Combining the autoregressive and moving-average models we get a mixed autoregressive-moving-average model of order (p, q); we say that it is of type ARMA(p, q).

Estimating the coefficients of an ARMA model and using it to study a time series is referred to as the *Box-Jenkins' method* after the two statisticians who pioneered it.[2] Box-Jenkins models have attracted much attention lately by practitioners as well as researchers of time series analysis. We shall not go further into the Box-Jenkins methodology and refer to the books by Bowerman and O'Connell, by Granger and by Thomopoulos. (See the list of references at the end of this chapter.)

14.5 Forecasting

An important aspect of time series analysis is to attempt to forecast the development of a time series beyond the period for which we have observations. This is of course a very tricky issue, since we can never be sure of what the future will contain. Forecasts are necessary, though, for planning and other purposes, and we have to do the best we can.

We shall show how the classical time series model can be used for forecasting. Other forecasting methods, which we will not cover, include the use of econometric models (such as we developed in Section 13.6) and Box-Jenkins models.

Example 14.8

Consider the Canadian unemployment data of Example 14.5. We shall prepare a forecast for the unemployment for each quarter of 1980.

Solution: The simplest conceivable forecast is always to take the latest observation available and use it as a guess for future values. In our case, the latest observation is 746 (for 1979 Q4); we may use it as a forecast for 1980 Q1, Q2, Q3 and Q4. This is obviously very naive. A slightly more realistic method would involve the exponential smoothing technique, but we skip this and move on to the classical time series model. Using the trend line from Example 14.5 we have:

$$T_t = 774.6 + 6.485t$$

where 1980 Q1 corresponds to $t = 17$, 1980 Q2 to $t = 18$ etc. We also employ the seasonal factors S_t obtained in Example 14.6. The forecast values are $T_t \cdot S_t$, which are computed in the table in Figure 14/19 below:

[2] Their book: G.E.P. Box and G.M. Jenkins: *Time Series Analysis. Forecasting and Control*, revised edition, Holden-Day, San Francisco, 1976, is written at a much higher level than this text, and is therefore not included in the list of references.

Date	T_t	S_t	Forecast $T_t \cdot S_t$	Actually realized value
1980 Q1	884.85	1.1176	988.9	955
Q2	891.33	1.0157	905.3	909
Q3	897.82	0.9623	864.0	817
Q4	904.30	0.9236	835.2	785

Fig. 14/19: Forecast and actual values for Example 14.8.

The forecast values are not bad, in light of the actually observed figures, which are entered in the table in Fig. 14/19, although they were not used for making the forecast. As discussed earlier, though, a negative parabolic trend would probably have given an even better forecast.

References

Bowerman, B. L., and R. T. O'Connell: *Time Series and Forecasting: An Applied Approach*. Duxbury Press, North Scituate, Mass. 1979.

Chou, Y.: *Statistical Analysis*, 2nd edition. Holt, Rinehart and Winston, New York 1975.

Granger, C. W. J.: *Forecasting in Business and Economics*. Academic Press, New York 1980.

Hamburg, M.: *Statistical Analysis for Decision Making*, 2nd edition, Harcourt, Brace, Jovanovich, New York 1977.

Harnett, D. L.: *Statistical Methods*, 3rd edition. Addison-Wesley, Reading, Mass. 1982.

Lapin, L. L.: *Statistics for Modern Business Decisions*, 3rd edition. Harcourt, Brace, Jovanovich, New York 1982.

Makridakis, S., and S. C. Wheelwright: *Forecasting Methods and Applications*. John Wiley and Sons, New York 1978.

Mansfield, E.: *Statistics for Business and Economics*. Norton & Company, New York 1980.

Nelson, C. R.: *Applied Time Series Analysis for Managerial Forecasting*, Holden-Day, San Francisco 1973.

Neter, J., W. Wasserman and G. S. Whitmore: *Applied Statistics*, 2nd edition. Allyn & Bacon, Boston, Mass. 1982.

Summers, G. W., W. S. Peters and C. P. Armstrong: *Basic Statistics in Business and Economics*, 3rd edition. Wadsworth, Belmont, California 1981.

Thomopoulos, N. T.: *Applied Forecasting Methods*. Prentice-Hall, Englewood Cliffs, New Jersey 1980.

Wonnacott, T. H., and R. J. Wonnacott: *Introductory Statistics for Business and Economics*, 2nd edition. John Wiley & Sons, New York 1977.

Exercises

14–1 Using the data in Example 14.1 in the text, from 1965, first quarter, to 1967, last quarter, compute a five-point moving average series. Plot the original and the smoothed data.

14–2 Using the same data as in Exercise no. 1 above, compute a centered four-point moving average series. Plot the original and the smoothed data.

The following data represent the quarterly revenue, in thousands of dollars, of a certain restaurant.

Year	Quarter	Revenue
1970	I	12.0
	II	15.6
	III	21.9
	IV	16.7
1980	I	13.3
	II	18.1
	III	24.0
	IV	17.4
1981	I	15.3
	II	18.4
	III	25.4
	IV	20.4

a) Plot the time series.
b) Construct a centered 4-point moving average series.
c) Plot the smoothed series together with the original one.

14–4 Using the same data as in Exercise no. 1 above, compute an exponentially smoothed series, for an α-value of 0.7. Plot the original and the smoothed data.

14–5 Using the same data as in Exercise no. 1 above, compute an exponentially smoothed series, for an α-value of 0.4. Plot the original and the smoothed data.

14–6 Using the Canadian unemployment data of Example 14.5 in the text, compute an exponentially smoothed series for an α-value of 0.9. Plot the original and the smoothed data.

14–7 Using the same data as in Exercise no. 1 above, determine the least-squares linear trend line.

14–8 Consider the United States export data of Example 14.3 in the text.

a) Find the least-squares linear trend line.
b) Using the ratio-to-moving average method, compute the seasonal factors.
c) Produce a forecast for 1970 based on the trend and seasonal components.

14–9 A French car manufacturer has released the following data about the number of cars exported to Canada in the past 3 years.

	1980	1981	1982
Quarter 1	8,000	9,000	11,000
Quarter 2	12,000	15,000	18,000
Quarter 3	11,000	14,000	16,000
Quarter 4	9,000	11,000	16,000

a) Compute centered four-point moving average values for this time series.
b) Compute the seasonal index for each quarter.
c) Assume that 1980 Q1 is quarter 1 for the time series and that the trend line is given by $T_t = 8{,}227 + 657t$ (where t is the time measured in quarters for the time series.) What is the trend projection for the number of cars to be exported to Canada for each quarter in 1983?

14–10 Consider the restaurant revenue data of Exercise no. 3 above.

a) Determine the least-squares trend line.
b) Compute the seasonal index for each quarter by the ratio-to-moving average method.
c) Construct a forecast for the subsequent six quarters.

14–11 Add to the Canadian unemployment figures of Example 14.5 in the text the following data:

Date	Unemployment (Thousands)
1980 Q1	955
Q2	909
Q3	817
Q4	785
1981 Q1	952
Q2	865
Q3	839
Q4	935

a) Determine the least squares trend line.
b) Compute the seasonal index for each quarter by the ratio-tomoving average method.
c) Construct a forecast for the subsequent six quarters.

15. Index Numbers

Example 15.1

According to Statistics Canada, the average hourly earnings for workers in the Canadian manufacturing industry were as follows during the first nine months of 1979:

Month (1979)	Jan.	Feb.	Mar.	Apr.	May	June	July	Aug.	Sept.
Earnings ($/hour)	7.15	7.18	7.24	7.32	7.38	7.41	7.45	7.47	7.57

Does this mean that the average worker in September 1979 was

$$\frac{7.57}{7.15} \cdot 100 - 100 = 5.87\% \text{ better off than in January 1979?}$$

The answer is that he was not, because the purchasing power of the dollar he received in September 1979 due to inflation was less than that of the January 1979 dollar.

How can we then adjust for this decrease in the purchasing power of the dollar, so that comparisons can be made at different points in time? An *index number* will accomplish this by compensating for the change in purchasing power of the dollar. The specific index number we use in this example is the so-called *consumer price index* (CPI), which is of a weighted aggregate price index type.

In Section 15.1 we shall deal with simple as well as aggregate price and quantity index numbers, and in Section 15.2 different weighting methods for aggregate index numbers are discussed.

From a mathematical viewpoint, the material in this chapter is at a much lower level than in the preceding chapters; it is put at the end of the book simply because it naturally follows after the time series chapter.

15.1 Price and Quantity Indices

Example 15.2

The following figures show the total production of beer in Canada, for the first eight months of 1979:

Month	Jan.	Feb.	Mar.	Apr.	May	June	July	Aug.
Beer Production (million gallons)	31.2	28.4	38.7	39.2	45.7	50.9	48.5	50.2

To express the change over time in the beer production, we may express the beer production in any month as a percentage of, say, the March production. We have then formed a simple quantity index with March 1979 as the *base month:*

Month Jan. (1979)	Feb.	Mar.	Apr.	May	June	July	Aug.	
Beer production index (March 1979 = 100)	80.6	73.4	100.0	101.3	118.1	131.5	125.3	129.7

Fig. 15/1: Monthly Canadian beer production indices, March 1979 = 100.

If instead we choose May 1979 as the base month we would obtain:

Month (1979)	Jan.	Feb.	Mar.	Apr.	May	June	July	Aug.
Beer production index (May 1979 = 100)	68.3	62.1	84.7	85.8	100.0	111.4	106.1	109.8

Fig. 15/2: Monthly Canadian beer production indices, May 1979 = 100.

The selection of base period is made to suit the purpose for which the index numbers will be used. It is generally preferable to choose the base such that the indices are not too far from 100; this will facilitate an appreciation and comparison of the figures.

Simple price indices involve comparisons of prices instead of quantities.

Example 15.3

The following table shows the price of milk (in dollars per gallon) in a certain major city in the United States, from 1965 to 1970:

Year	1965	1966	1967	1968	1969	1970
Milk price ($/gallon)	1.08	1.12	1.16	1.19	1.22	1.24

Computing a milk price index with 1969 as the base year, we obtain:

Year	1965	1966	1967	1968	1969	1970
Milk price index (1969 = 100)	88.5	91.8	95.1	97.5	100.0	101.6

Fig. 15/3: Milk price indices, 1969 = 100.

Simple price indices can be used to compare the price development of the same commodity in different states or countries, or over different periods. They can also be used to compare the price developments of different commodities.

15.2 Different Weighting Methods

Regarding the issue of the purchasing power of the dollar, a simple price index for a certain commodity will obviously not be enough. Neither will a straightforward averaging of the price indices for various commodities into a simple aggregate price index do because the outlays for certain basic commodities, like dairy products, will be much heavier than the outlays for footwear. A general price index should therefore *weight* the prices of all commodities considered in relation to their importance in a normal household budget. Such an index is called a *weighted aggregate price index*.

The weights can be included in the price index in different ways. The *Laspeyres price index* I_n is calculated by the formula:

$$I_n = \frac{\sum p_n q_0}{\sum p_0 q_0} \times 100$$

where p are commodity prices and q the quantities in which the commodities are bought. The subscript 0 indicates the base period (year) and n the period (year) for which the index is calculated. The sums are taken over the various commodities that are included in the index. This set of commodities is often referred to as the index "market basket". The quantities are usually supposed to be the amounts of the various commodities that an average family would buy in a year. The value of the market basket would then be $\sum p_0 q_0$ in the base year; the same market basket would cost $\sum p_n q_0$ in the current year.

Example 15.4

Consider the following data for the price of three common family market basket commodities:

Commodity Price	1965	1970	1975	1980
Milk (¢/qt.)	26.7	33.2	37.1	41.5
Flour (¢/lb.)	12.3	14.1	20.3	24.2
Potatoes (¢/lb.)	11.1	27.3	20.5	26.8

Assume further that the average family annual purchases of these commodities are as follows, for the years 1965 and 1975.

Commodity quantity	1965	1975
Milk (qt.)	360	350
Flour (lb.)	80	90
Potatoes (lb.)	160	175

A simple 1970 aggregate price index, with 1965 as the base year, would then be:

$$\frac{33.2 + 14.1 + 27.3}{26.7 + 12.3 + 11.1} \times 100 = 148.9\,.$$

This index does not give enough emphasis to the purchase of milk, as it completely neglects the quantities purchased. If we compute the 1970 Laspeyres index we see that quantities are as well taken into account:

$$\frac{33.2 \cdot 360 + 14.1 \cdot 80 + 27.3 \cdot 160}{26.7 \cdot 360 + 12.3 \cdot 80 + 11.1 \cdot 160} \times 100 = 141.0\,.$$

If we compute the Laspeyres price index for each of the four years, using 1965 as the base year, we obtain the following table:

Year	1965	1970	1975	1980
Laspeyre price index (1965 = 100)	100.0	141.0	147.6	171.1

Fig. 15/4: The Laspeyre price index for Example 15.4.

Instead of letting the index weights be given by the base year quantities as in the Laspeyres index, we may use the current year quantities. Then we get the *Paasche index:*

$$I_n = \frac{\sum p_n q_n}{\sum p_0 q_n} \times 100\,.$$

(The same notation is used as in the definition of the Laspeyres index.)

Computing the Paasche price index for 1975, using 1965 as the base year, we find:

$$\frac{37.1 \cdot 350 + 20.3 \cdot 90 + 20.5 \cdot 175}{26.7 \cdot 350 + 12.3 \cdot 90 + 11.1 \cdot 175} \times 100 = 148.4\,.$$

If we compare the Paasche and Laspeyres price indices for 1975, 148.4 and 147.6 respectively, we see that they are not much different. If the quantities of the market basket items change significantly, the discrepancy between the two indices can become quite sizeable. Whereas the Laspeyres index focusses on the consumer habits in the base year, the Paasche index concentrates on the consumer habits of the current year. An index which is a compromise between the two is the "Fisher ideal price index", calculated as:

$$\sqrt{(\text{Laspeyres index}) \times (\text{Paasche index})}\,.$$

Our Fisher ideal price index for 1975, using 1965 as the base year, would therefore be:

$$\sqrt{148.4 \times 147.6} = 148.0\,.$$

The Consumer Price Index

The most important of all price indices used in economics and industry is the consumer price index. The Canadian CPI (consumer price index) uses many different commodities and the market basket represents the purchases by clerical worker and wage earner families. Thus the CPI is a cost of living indicator. It is calculated using a modification of the Laspeyres index, and currently uses 1971 as the base year.

Example 15.5

Including the CPI numbers in our Example 15.1 we obtain the following table:

Month (1979)	Jan.	Feb.	Mar.	Apr.	May	June	July	Aug.	Sep.
Earnings ($/hour)	7.15	7.18	7.24	7.32	7.38	7.41	7.45	7.47	7.57
CPI (1971 = 100)	182.7	184.4	186.6	187.9	189.7	190.6	192.1	192.8	194.5
Earnings (1971 $/hour)	3.91	3.89	3.88	3.90	3.89	3.89	3.88	3.87	3.89
Earnings index (in fixed prices) (Jan = 100)	100.0	99.5	99.1	99.5	99.4	99.3	99.1	99.0	99.5

Fig. 15/5: Real hourly earnings. (The figures in the two bottom rows have been calculated to five decimal places and then rounded off)

In the bottom row of the table in Figure 15/5 above we display *real earnings* in percent of Jan. 1979 earnings (1971 $/hr); this is a *real wage* index. We talk of real values when they have been deflated by a price index.

Let us close by remarking that the choice of base year or month for an index series is free; it is also immediately clear how we can transform[1] an index series from one base year (month) to another:

Month	Jan.	Feb.	Mar.	Apr.	May	June	July	Aug.	Sept.
CPI (Mar. 1979 = 100)	97.9	98.8	100.0	100.7	101.7	102.1	102.9	103.3	104.2

Fig. 15/16: Transformed consumer price indices.

References

Chou, Y.: *Statistical Analysis*, 2nd edition. Holt, Rinehart and Winston, New York 1975.

Hamburg, M.: *Statistical Analysis for Decision Making*, 2nd edition. Harcourt, Brace, Jovanovich, New York 1977.

[1] This is only approximately true for weighted aggregate indices, because of changing weights.

Harnett, D. L.: *Statistical Methods,* 3rd edition. Addison-Wesley, Reading Mass. 1982.
Hawkins, C. A., and J. E. Weber: *Statistical Analysis. Applications to Business and Economics.* Harper & Row, New York 1980.
Lapin, L. L.: *Statistics for Modern Business Decisions,* 3rd edition, Harcourt, Brace, Jovanovich, New York 1982.
Mansfield, E.: *Statistics for Business and Economics,* Norton & Company, New York 1980.
Neter, J., W. Wasserman and G. A. Whitmore: *Applied Statistics,* 2nd edition. Allyn and Bacon, Boston, Mass. 1982.
Ott, L.: *An Introduction to Statistical Methods and Data Analysis,* Duxbury Press, North Scitutate, Mass. 1977.
Summers, G. W., W. S. Peters and C. P. Armstrong: *Basic Statistics in Business and Economics,* 3rd edition. Wadsworth, Belmont, California 1981.
Wonnacott, T. H., and R. J. Wonnacott: *Introductory Statistics for Business and Economics,* 2nd edition. John Wiley & Sons, New York 1977.

Exercises

15–1 Using the data in Example 15.1 in the text, compute a simple earnings index series, using June 1979 as the base month.

15–2 Calculate a simple index for the following stock price using 1975 as the base year.

Year	1975	1976	1977	1978	1979	1980	1981	1982
Stock Price ($)	9.5	10.9	11.2	14.0	13.5	14.5	15.1	16.2

15–3 Using the data in Example 15.4 in the text, compute a simple aggregate price index series, using 1975 as the base year.

15–4 Using the data in Example 15.4 in the text, compute:

a) A Laspeyres price index series, using 1975 as the base year.
b) The Paasche price index for 1965, using 1975 as the base year.

15–5 Consider the following price and quantity data:

	Price ($/unit)		Quantity (units)	
	1976	1977	1976	1977
Electricity	2.38	2.51	75	78
Gas	14.60	15.10	9.6	10.2
Water	.33	.34	303	305
Telephone	2.80	2.95	65	66

Calculate the Laspeyres and the Paasche price indices for 1977, using 1976 as the base year.

15–6 The costs (in cents per pound) of six common meat products are given below for five years:

Year	Ground Beef	Round Steak	Rib Roast	Ham	Frying Chicken	Pork Chops
1975	52	97	110	108	55	120
1976	58	98	115	115	59	105
1977	62	102	120	110	65	115
1978	67	110	130	107	72	122
1979	70	115	139	99	79	135

Using 1976 as the base year, compute the following indices:

a) The simple price index for each type of meat for 1978.
b) The simple aggregate index of meat prices for 1978.
c) The Laspeyres meat price index for 1978. In 1976 the average family bought 125 lb. of ground been, 65 lb. of round steak, 50 lb. of rib roast, 60 lb. of ham, 105 lb. of frying chicken and 75 lb. of pork chops.
d) The Paasche meat index for 1978. In 1978 the average family bought 140 lb. of ground beef, 60 lb. of round steak, 55 lb. of rib roast, 70 lb. of ham, 115 lb. of frying chicken and 60 lb. of pork chops.
e) Fisher's ideal index for the meat prices in 1978.

Tables

Table No. 1: Random Numbers (These 400 five-digit random numbers have been generated by a Hewlett-Packard HP-85 microcomputer.)

	1	2	3	4	5	6	7	8	9	10
1	63780	59264	31841	65537	27808	57533	62286	76777	76732	36341
2	57436	83070	43862	05447	59025	09380	76080	24658	25265	54904
3	03531	78198	07166	28944	81387	86641	67296	17600	66072	68711
4	86360	96353	67113	53494	76398	45768	21271	16949	31547	85935
5	84825	30378	82162	54754	59021	03167	29355	27936	03125	33551
6	78202	47595	85198	80248	83648	09678	66001	97040	65486	38577
7	44386	64519	68091	42821	97959	38359	60092	58623	69100	57169
8	96459	60821	72667	46910	88184	02291	38869	77920	49828	38303
9	51474	03208	43832	45229	12941	22506	25694	72072	07076	23059
10	86982	09159	13251	67444	22479	38877	90734	66343	85081	79657
11	46247	37766	17547	66966	16309	67889	51071	39432	72149	73418
12	48567	53051	30263	92836	24091	06778	26284	01630	42262	19906
13	06681	65697	68203	16472	00870	76850	52345	21009	10065	41319
14	02338	14956	67813	52583	64112	14975	84860	18234	78916	35631
15	12755	95321	68154	61345	21857	56210	47076	27693	01058	51008
16	96129	94926	06250	32991	33483	10999	51932	09195	60128	63177
17	22018	43476	79593	30941	73833	40751	94918	92502	88842	01946
18	88273	17978	57976	18414	05198	37891	64915	54401	17298	97122
19	60922	55407	76139	71972	00564	61031	44907	73722	19387	49589
20	27437	61033	03307	38032	89919	01087	72773	15339	73405	64661
21	62498	72404	85341	70455	51852	70845	64136	76279	63837	33991
22	15259	47215	73272	53398	58548	78494	75596	95690	18488	86995
23	18699	25343	84893	25691	54059	10360	31584	98033	71209	87039
24	81401	74051	84511	37448	73843	85316	53702	60461	36664	18709
25	06614	49518	98644	50212	62415	29887	14775	12895	65180	59415
26	27658	66668	64405	63424	21637	74024	24769	54841	24412	53856
27	07342	71403	15714	67357	12568	80873	86198	26093	66289	72393
28	36927	71347	47791	86246	36882	55477	58140	93098	91752	36776
29	41567	02373	54214	70406	45151	85981	83011	65374	36315	29756
30	57551	03154	53590	06718	09511	69916	97277	38824	99576	99965

Table No. 1 (Continuation)

	1	2	3	4	5	6	7	8	9	10
31	88585	50267	25768	79425	88639	41079	43370	90274	47669	19572
32	35894	62767	90804	48437	78745	81850	29828	42789	87284	12317
33	53698	16787	96722	65441	15699	07010	82163	63659	35217	42003
34	24955	22916	34487	71958	83086	48028	57548	40775	73175	83531
35	56603	62083	53237	23930	35677	39292	78307	19002	81654	21907
36	99730	99627	06190	77329	05713	01787	85816	23341	94928	91282
37	34123	62984	22046	10745	96784	70273	96836	01865	93206	53671
38	64454	37031	21739	19581	77855	81257	31004	81530	44404	35420
39	54783	85117	69670	46872	47264	16395	73454	33115	10193	67471
40	99586	74907	47240	72611	54740	61882	40658	06489	02495	08211

Table No. 2: Binomial Coefficients $\binom{n}{j}$ (Remark: For $10 < j \leqq n$, use the fact that $\binom{n}{j} = \binom{n}{n-j}$)

n \ j	0	1	2	3	4	5	6	7	8	9	10
0	1										
1	1	1									
2	1	2	1								
3	1	3	3	1							
4	1	4	6	4	1						
5	1	5	10	10	5	1					
6	1	6	15	20	15	6	1				
7	1	7	21	35	35	21	7	1			
8	1	8	28	56	70	56	28	8	1		
9	1	9	36	84	126	126	84	36	9	1	
10	1	10	45	120	210	252	210	120	45	10	1
11	1	11	55	165	330	462	462	330	165	55	11
12	1	12	66	220	495	792	924	792	495	220	66
13	1	13	78	286	715	1287	1716	1716	1287	715	286
14	1	14	91	364	1001	2002	3003	3432	3003	2002	1001
15	1	15	105	455	1365	3003	5005	6435	6435	5005	3003
16	1	16	120	560	1820	4368	8008	11440	12870	11440	8008
17	1	17	136	680	2380	6188	12376	19448	24310	24310	19448
18	1	18	153	816	3060	8568	18564	31824	43758	48620	43758
19	1	19	171	969	3876	11628	27132	50388	75582	92378	92378
20	1	20	190	1140	4845	15504	38760	77520	125970	167960	184756

Table No. 3: Binomial Probability Distribution. Values of $\binom{n}{j} p^j (1-p)^{n-j}$

		p									
n	j	.05	.10	.15	.20	.25	.30	.35	.40	.45	.50
1	0	.9500	.9000	.8500	.8000	.7500	.7000	.6500	.6000	.5500	.5000
	1	.0500	.1000	.1500	.2000	.2500	.3000	.3500	.4000	.4500	.5000
2	0	.9025	.8100	.7225	.6400	.5625	.4900	.4225	.3600	.3025	.2500
	1	.0950	.1800	.2550	.3200	.3750	.4200	.4550	.4800	.4950	.5000
	2	.0025	.0100	.0225	.0400	.0625	.0900	.1225	.1600	.2025	.2500
3	0	.8574	.7290	.6141	.5120	.4219	.3430	.2746	.2160	.1664	.1250
	1	.1354	.2430	.3251	.3840	.4219	.4410	.4436	.4320	.4084	.3750
	2	.0071	.0270	.0574	.0960	.1406	.1890	.2389	.2880	.3341	.3750
	3	.0001	.0010	.0034	.0080	.0156	.0270	.0429	.0640	.0911	.1250
4	0	.8145	.6561	.5220	.4096	.3164	.2401	.1785	.1296	.0915	.0625
	1	.1715	.2916	.3685	.4096	.4219	.4116	.3845	.3456	.2995	.2500
	2	.0135	.0486	.0975	.1536	.2109	.2646	.3105	.3456	.3675	.3750
	3	.0005	.0036	.0115	.0256	.0469	.0756	.1115	.1536	.2005	.2500
	4	.0000	.0001	.0005	.0016	.0039	.0081	.0150	.0256	.0410	.0625
5	0	.7738	.5905	.4437	.3277	.2373	.1681	.1160	.0778	.0503	.0312
	1	.2036	.3280	.3915	.4096	.3955	.3602	.3124	.2592	.2059	.1562
	2	.0214	.0729	.1382	.2048	.2637	.3087	.3364	.3456	.3369	.3125
	3	.0011	.0081	.0244	.0512	.0879	.1323	.1811	.2304	.2757	.3125
	4	.0000	.0004	.0022	.0064	.0146	.0284	.0488	.0768	.1128	.1562
	5	.0000	.0000	.0001	.0003	.0010	.0024	.0053	.0102	.0185	.0312
6	0	.7351	.5314	.3771	.2621	.1780	.1176	.0754	.0467	.0277	.0156
	1	.2321	.3543	.3993	.3932	.3560	.3025	.2437	.1866	.1359	.0938
	2	.0305	.0984	.1762	.2458	.2966	.3241	.3280	.3110	.2780	.2344
	3	.0021	.0146	.0415	.0819	.1318	.1852	.2355	.2765	.3032	.3125
	4	.0001	.0012	.0055	.0154	.0330	.0595	.0951	.1382	.1861	.2344
	5	.0000	.0001	.0004	.0015	.0044	.0102	.0205	.0369	.0609	.0938
	6	.0000	.0000	.0000	.0001	.0002	.0007	.0018	.0041	.0083	.0516
7	0	.6983	.4783	.3206	.2097	.1335	.0824	.0490	.0280	.0152	.0078
	1	.2573	.3720	.3960	.3670	.3115	.2471	.1848	.1306	.0872	.0547
	2	.0406	.1240	.2097	.2753	.3115	.3177	.2985	.2613	.2140	.1641
	3	.0036	.0230	.0617	.1147	.1730	.2269	.2679	.2903	.2918	.2734
	4	.0002	.0026	.0109	.0287	.0577	.0972	.1442	.1935	.2388	.2734
	5	.0009	.0002	.0012	.0043	.0115	.0250	.0466	.0774	.1172	.1641
	6	.0000	.0000	.0001	.0004	.0013	.0036	.0084	.0172	.0320	.0547
	7	.0000	.0000	.0000	.0000	.0001	.0002	.0006	.0016	.0037	.0078

Table No. 3 (Continuation)

n	j	.05	.10	.15	.20	p .25	.30	.35	.40	.45	.50
8	0	.6634	.4305	.2725	.1678	.1001	.0576	.0319	.0168	.0084	.0039
	1	.2793	.3826	.3847	.3355	.2670	.1977	.1373	.0896	.0548	.0312
	2	.0515	.1488	.2376	.2936	.3115	.2965	.2587	.2090	.1569	.1094
	3	.0054	.0331	.0839	.1468	.2076	.2541	.2786	.2787	.2568	.2188
	4	.0004	.0046	.0815	.0459	.0865	.1361	.1875	.2322	.2627	.2734
	5	.0000	.0004	.0026	.0092	.0231	.0467	.0808	.1239	.1719	.2188
	6	.0000	.0000	.0002	.0011	.0038	.0100	.0217	.0413	.0703	.1094
	7	.0000	.0000	.0000	.0001	.0004	.0012	.0033	.0079	.0164	.0312
	8	.0000	.0000	.0000	.0000	.0000	.0001	.0002	.0007	.0017	.0039
9	0	.6302	.3874	.2316	.1342	.0751	.0404	.0207	.0101	.0046	.0020
	1	.2985	.3874	.3679	.3020	.2253	.1556	.1004	.0605	.0339	.0176
	2	.0629	.1722	.2597	.3020	.3003	.2668	.2162	.1612	.1110	.0703
	3	.0077	.0446	.1069	.1762	.2336	.2668	.2716	.2508	.2119	.1641
	4	.0006	.0074	.0283	.0661	.1168	.1715	.2294	.2508	.2600	.2461
	5	.0000	.0008	.0050	.0165	.0389	.0735	.1181	.1672	.2128	.2461
	6	.0000	.0001	.0006	.0028	.0087	.0210	.0424	.0743	.1160	.1641
	7	.0000	.0000	.0000	.0003	.0012	.0039	.0098	.0212	.0407	.0703
	8	.0000	.0000	.0000	.0000	.0001	.0004	.0013	.0035	.0083	.0716
	9	.0000	.0000	.0000	.0000	.0000	.0000	.0001	.0003	.0008	.0020
10	0	.5987	.2487	.1969	.1074	.0563	.0282	.0135	.0060	.0025	.0010
	1	.3151	.3874	.3474	.2684	.1877	.1211	.0725	.0403	.0207	.0098
	2	.0746	.1937	.2759	.3020	.2816	.2335	.1757	.1209	.0763	.0439
	3	.0105	.0574	.1298	.2013	.2503	.2668	.2522	.2150	.1665	.1172
	4	.0010	.0112	.0401	.0881	.1460	.2001	.2377	.2508	.2384	.2051
	5	.0001	.0015	.0085	.0264	.0584	.1029	.1536	.2007	.2340	.2461
	6	.0000	.0001	.0012	.0055	.0162	.0368	.0689	.1115	.1596	.2051
	7	.0000	.0000	.0001	.0008	.0031	.0090	.0212	.0425	.0746	.1172
	8	.0000	.0000	.0000	.0001	.0004	.0014	.0043	.0106	.0229	.0439
	9	.0000	.0000	.0000	.0000	.0000	.0001	.0005	.0016	.0042	.0098
	10	.0000	.0000	.0000	.0000	.0000	.0000	.0000	.0001	.0003	.0010
11	0	.5688	.3138	.1673	.0859	.0422	.0198	.0088	.0036	.0014	.0005
	1	.3293	.3835	.3248	.2362	.1549	.0932	.0518	.0266	.0125	.0054
	2	.0867	.2131	.2866	.2953	.2581	.1998	.1395	.0887	.0513	.0269
	3	.0137	.0710	.1517	.2215	.2581	.2568	.2254	.1774	.1259	.0806
	4	.0014	.0158	.0536	.1107	.1721	.2201	.2428	.2365	.2060	.1611
	5	.0001	.0025	.0132	.0388	.0803	.1321	.1830	.2207	.2360	.2256
	6	.0000	.0003	.0023	.0097	.0268	.0566	.0985	.1471	.1931	.2256

Table No. 3 (Continuation)

						p					
n	j	.05	.10	.15	.20	.25	.30	.35	.40	.45	.50
	7	.0000	.0000	.0003	.0017	.0064	.0173	.0379	.0701	.1128	.1611
	8	.0000	.0000	.0000	.0002	.0011	.0037	.0102	.0234	.0462	.0806
	9	.0000	.0000	.0000	.0000	.0001	.0005	.0018	.0052	.0126	.0269
	10	.0000	.0000	.0000	.0000	.0000	.0000	.0002	.0007	.0021	.0054
	11	0000	.0000	.0000	.0000	.0000	.0000	0000	.0000	.0002	.0005
12	0	.5404	.2824	.1422	.0687	.0317	.0138	.0057	.0022	.0008	.0002
	1	.3413	.3766	.3012	.2062	.1267	.0712	.0368	.0174	.0075	.0020
	2	.0988	.2301	.2924	.2835	.2323	.1678	.1088	.0639	.0339	.0161
	3	.0173	.0852	.1720	.2362	.2581	.2397	.1954	.1419	.0923	.0537
	4	.0021	.0213	.0683	.1329	.1936	.2311	.2367	.2128	.1700	.1208
	5	.0002	.0038	.0193	.0532	.1032	.1585	.2039	.2270	.2225	.1934
	6	.0000	.0005	.0040	.0155	.0401	.0792	.1281	.1766	.2124	.2256
	7	.0000	.0000	.0006	.0033	.0115	.0291	.0591	.1009	.1489	.1934
	8	.0000	.0000	.0001	.0005	.0024	.0078	.0199	.0420	.0762	.1208
	9	.0000	.0000	.0000	.0001	.0004	.0015	.0048	.0125	.0277	.0537
	10	.0000	.0000	.0000	.0000	.0000	.0002	.0008	.0025	.0068	.0161
	11	.0000	.0000	.0000	.0000	.0000	.0000	.0001	.0003	.0010	.0029
	12	.0000	.0000	.0000	.0000	.0000	.0000	.0000	.0000	.0001	.0002
13	0	.5133	.2542	.1209	.0550	.0238	.0097	.0037	.0013	.0004	.0001
	1	.3512	.3672	.2774	.1787	.1029	.0540	.0259	.0113	.0045	.0016
	2	.1109	.2448	.2937	.2680	.2059	.1388	.0836	.0453	.0220	.0095
	3	.0214	.0997	.1900	.2457	.2517	.2181	.1651	.1107	.0660	.0349
	4	.0028	.0277	.0838	.1535	.2097	.2337	.2222	.1845	.1350	.0873
	5	.0003	.0055	.0266	.0691	.1258	.1803	.2154	.2214	.1989	.1571
	6	.0000	.0008	.0063	.0230	.0559	.1030	.1546	.1968	.2169	.2095
	7	.0000	.0001	.0011	.0058	.0186	.0442	.0833	.1312	.1775	.2095
	8	.0000	.0000	.0001	.0011	.0047	.0142	.0336	.0656	.1089	.1571
	9	.0000	.0000	.0000	.0001	.0009	.0034	.0101	.0243	.0495	.0873
	10	.0000	.0000	.0000	.0000	.0001	.0006	.0022	.0065	.0162	.0349
	11	.0000	.0000	.0000	.0000	.0000	.0001	.0003	.0012	.0036	.0095
	12	.0000	.0000	.0000	.0000	.0000	.0000	.0000	.0001	.0005	.0016
	13	.0000	.0000	.0000	.0000	.0000	.0000	.0000	.0000	.0000	.0001
14	0	.4877	.2288	.1028	.0440	.0178	.0068	.0024	.0008	.0002	.0001
	1	.3593	.3559	.2539	.1539	.0832	.0407	.0181	.0073	.0027	.0009
	2	.1229	.2570	.2912	.2501	.1802	.1134	.0634	.0317	.0141	.0056
	3	.0259	.1142	.2056	.2501	.2402	.1943	.1366	.0845	.0462	.0222
	4	.0037	.0348	.0998	.1720	.2202	.2290	.2022	.1549	.1040	.0611

Table No. 3 (Continuation)

n	j	.05	.10	.15	.20	p .25	.30	.35	.40	.45	.50
	5	.0004	.0078	.0352	.0860	.1468	.1963	.2178	.2066	.1701	.1222
	6	.0000	.0013	.0093	.0322	.0734	.1262	.1759	.2066	.2088	.1833
	7	.0000	.0002	.0019	.0092	.0280	.0618	.1082	.1574	.1952	.2095
	8	.0000	.0000	.0003	.0020	.0082	.0232	.0510	.0918	.1398	.1833
	9	.0000	.0000	.0000	.0003	.0018	.0066	.0183	.0408	.0762	.1222
	10	.0000	.0000	.0000	.0000	.0003	.0014	.0049	.0136	.0312	.0611
	11	.0000	.0000	.0000	.0000	.0000	.0002	.0010	.0033	.0093	.0222
	12	.0000	.0000	.0000	.0000	.0000	.0000	.0001	.0005	.0019	.0056
	13	.0000	.0000	.0000	.0000	.0000	.0000	.0000	.0001	.0002	.0009
	14	.0000	0000	.0000	.0000	.0000	.0000	.0000	.0000	.0000	.0001
15	0	.4633	.2059	.0874	.0352	.0134	.0047	.0016	.0005	.0001	.0000
	1	.3658	.3432	.2312	.1319	.0668	.0305	.0126	.0047	.0016	.0005
	2	.1348	.2669	.2856	.2309	.1559	.0916	.0476	.0219	.0090	.0032
	3	.0307	.1285	.2184	.2501	.2252	.1700	.1110	.0634	.0318	.0139
	4	.0049	.0428	.1156	.1876	.2252	.2186	.1792	.1268	.0780	.0417
	5	.0006	.0105	.0449	.1032	.1651	.2061	.2123	.1859	.1404	.0916
	6	.0000	.0019	.0132	.0430	.0917	.1472	.1906	.2066	.1914	.1527
	7	.0000	.0003	.0030	.0138	.0393	.0811	.1319	.1771	.2013	.1964
	8	.0000	.0000	.0005	.0035	.0131	.0348	.0710	.1181	.1647	.1964
	9	.0000	.0000	.0001	.0007	.0034	.0116	.0298	.0612	.1048	.1527
	10	.0000	.0000	.0000	.0001	.0007	.0030	.0096	.0245	.0515	.0916
	11	.0000	.0000	.0000	.0000	.0001	.0006	.0024	.0074	.0191	.0417
	12	.0000	.0000	.0000	.0000	.0000	.0001	.0004	.0016	.0052	.0139
	13	.0000	.0000	.0000	.0000	.0000	.0000	.0001	.0003	.0010	.0032
	14	.0000	.0000	.0000	.0000	.0000	.0000	.0000	.0000	.0001	.0005
	15	.0000	.0000	.0000	.0000	.0000	.0000	.0000	.0000	.0000	.0000

Table No. 4: The Exponential Function

x	e^x	e^{-x}	x	e^x	e^{-x}
.00	.0000	1.00000	.06	1.0618	.94176
.01	1.0101	.99665	.07	1.0725	.93239
.02	1.0202	.98020	.08	1.0833	.92312
.03	1.0305	.97045	.09	1.0942	.91393
.04	1.0408	.96079	.10	1.1052	.90484
.05	1.0513	.95123	.11	1.1163	.89583

Table No. 4 (Continuation)

x	e^x	e^{-x}	x	e^x	e^{-x}
.12	1.1275	.88692	2.4	11.023	.090718
.13	1.1388	.87810	2.5	12.182	.082085
.14	1.1503	.86936	2.6	13.464	.074274
.15	1.1618	.86071	2.7	14.880	.067206
.16	1.1735	.85214	2.8	16.445	.060810
.17	1.1853	.84366	2.9	18.174	.055023
.18	1.1972	.83527	3.0	20.086	.049787
.19	1.2092	.82696	3.1	22.198	.045049
.20	1.2214	.81873	3.2	24.533	.040762
.25	1.2840	.77880	3.3	27.113	.036883
.30	1.3499	.74082	3.4	29.964	.033373
.35	1.4191	.70469	3.5	33.115	.030197
.40	1.4918	.67032	3.6	36.598	.027324
.45	1.5683	.63763	3.7	40.447	.024724
.50	1.6487	.60653	3.8	44.701	.022371
.55	1.7333	.57695	3.9	49.402	.020242
.60	1.8221	.54881	4.0	54.598	.018316
.65	1.9155	.52205	4.1	60.340	.016573
.70	2.0138	.49659	4.2	66.686	.014996
.75	2.1170	.47237	4.3	73.700	.013569
.80	2.2255	.44933	4.4	81.451	.012277
.85	2.3396	.42741	4.5	90.017	.011109
.90	2.4596	.40657	4.6	99.484	.010052
.95	2.5857	.38674	4.7	109.95	.0090953
1.0	2.7183	.36788	4.8	121.51	.0082297
1.1	3.0042	.33287	4.9	134.29	.0074466
1.2	3.3201	.30119	5.0	148.41	.0067379
1.3	3.6693	.27253	5.5	244.69	.0040868
1.4	4.0552	.24660	6.0	403.43	.0024788
1.5	4.4817	.22313	6.5	665.14	.0015034
1.6	4.9530	.20190	7.0	1096.6	.00091188
1.7	5.4739	.18268	7.5	1808.0	.00055308
1.8	6.0496	.16530	8.0	2981.0	.00033546
1.9	6.6859	.14957	8.5	4914.8	.00020347
2.0	7.3891	.13534	9.0	8103.1	.00012341
2.1	8.1662	.12246	9.5	13360	.000074852
2.2	9.0250	.11080	10.0	22026	.000045400
2.3	9.9742	.10026			

Table No. 5: Poisson Probability Distribution

Values of $e^{-\lambda}\frac{\lambda^x}{x!}$

x	λ .005	.01	.02	.03	.04	.05	.06	.07	.08	.09
0	.9950	.9900	.9802	.9704	.9608	.9512	.9418	.9324	.9231	.9139
1	.0050	0099	.0192	.0291	.0384	.0476	.0565	.0653	.0738	.0823
2	.0000	.0000	.0002	.0004	.0008	.0012	.0017	.0023	.0030	.0037
3	.0000	.0000	.0000	.0000	.0000	.0000	.0000	.0001	.00001	.0001

x	λ 0.1	0.2	0.3	0.4	0.5	0.6	0.7	0.8	0.9	1.0
0	.9048	.8187	.7408	.6703	.6065	.5488	.4966	.4493	.4066	.3679
1	.0905	.1637	.2222	.2681	.3033	.3293	.3476	.3595	.3659	.3679
2	.0045	.0164	.0333	.0536	.0758	.0988	.1217	.1438	.1647	.1839
3	.0002	.0011	.0033	.0072	.0126	.0198	.0284	.0383	.0494	.0613
4	.0000	.0001	.0002	.0007	.0016	.0030	.0050	.0077	.0111	.0153
5	.0000	.0000	.0000	.0001	.0002	.0004	.0007	.0012	.0020	.0031
6	.0000	.0000	.0000	.0000	.0000	.0000	.0001	.0002	.0003	.0005
7	.0000	.0000	.0000	.0000	.0000	.0000	.0000	.0000	.0000	.0001

x	λ 1.1	1.2	1.3	1.4	1.5	1.6	1.7	1.8	1.9	2.0
0	.3329	.3012	.2725	.2466	.2231	.2019	.1827	.1653	.1496	.1353
1	.3662	.3614	.3543	.3452	.3347	.3230	.3106	.2975	.2842	.2707
2	.2014	.2169	.2303	.2417	.2510	.2584	.2640	.2678	.2700	.2707
3	.0738	.0867	.0998	.1128	.1255	.1378	.1496	.1607	.1710	.1804
4	.0203	.0260	.0324	.0395	.0471	.0551	.0636	.0723	.0812	.0902
5	.0045	.0062	.0084	.0111	.0141	.0176	.0216	.0260	.0309	.0361
6	.0008	.0012	.0018	.0026	.0035	.0047	.0061	.0078	.0098	.0120
7	.0001	.0002	.0003	.0005	.0008	.0011	.0015	.0020	.0027	.0034
8	.0000	.0000	.0001	.0001	.0001	.0002	.0003	.0005	.0006	.0009
9	.0000	.0000	.0000	.0000	.0000	.0000	.0001	.0001	.0001	.0002

x	λ 2.1	2.2	2.3	2.4	2.5	2.6	2.7	2.8	2.9	3.0
0	.1225	.1108	.1003	.0907	.0821	.0743	.0672	.0608	.0550	.0498
1	.2572	.2438	.2306	.2177	.2052	.1931	.1815	.1703	.1596	.1494
2	.2700	.2681	.2652	.2613	.2565	.2510	.2450	.2384	.2314	.2240
3	.1890	.1966	.2033	.2090	.2138	.2176	.2205	.2225	.2237	.2240
4	.0992	.1082	.1169	.1254	.1336	.1414	.1488	.1557	.1622	.1680

Table No. 5 (Continuation)

x	2.1	2.2	2.3	2.4	λ 2.5	2.6	2.7	2.8	2.9	3.0
5	.0417	.0476	.0538	.0602	.0668	.0735	.0804	.0872	.0940	.1008
6	.0146	.0174	.0206	.0241	.0278	.0319	.0362	.0407	.0455	.0504
7	.0044	.0055	.0068	.0083	.0099	.0118	.0139	.0163	.0188	.0216
8	.0011	.0015	.0019	.0025	.0031	.0038	.0047	.0057	.0068	.0081
9	.0003	.0004	.0005	.0007	.0009	.0011	.0014	.0018	.0022	.0027
10	.0001	.0001	.0001	.0002	.0002	.0003	.0004	.0005	.0006	.0008
11	.0000	.0000	.0000	.0000	.0000	.0001	.0001	.0001	.0002	.0002
12	.0000	.0000	.0000	.0000	.0000	.0000	.0000	.0000	.0000	.0001

x	3.1	3.2	3.3	3.4	λ 3.5	3.6	3.7	3.8	3.9	4.0
0	.0450	.0408	.0369	.0334	.0302	.0273	.0247	.0224	.0202	.0183
1	.1397	.1304	.1217	.1135	.1057	.0984	.0915	.0850	.0789	.0733
2	.2165	.2087	.2008	.1929	.1850	.1771	.1692	.1615	.1539	.1465
3	,2237	.2226	.2209	.2186	.2158	.2125	.2087	.2046	.2001	.1954
4	.1734	.1781	.1823	.1858	.1888	.1912	.1931	.1944	.1951	.1954
5	.1075	.1140	.1203	.1264	.1322	.1377	.1429	.1477	.1522	.1563
6	.0555	.0608	.0662	.0716	.0771	.0826	.0881	.0936	.0989	.1042
7	.0246	.0278	.0312	.0348	.0385	.0425	.0466	.0508	.0551	.0595
8	.0095	.0111	.0129	.0148	.0169	.0191	.0215	.0241	.0269	.0298
9	.0033	.0040	.0047	.0056	.0066	.0076	.0089	.0102	.0116	.0132
10	.0010	.0013	.0016	.0019	.0023	.0028	.0033	.0039	.0045	.0053
11	.0003	.0004	.0005	.0006	.0007	.0009	.0011	.0013	.0016	.0019
12	.0001	.0001	.0001	.0002	.0002	.0003	.0003	.0004	.0005	.0006
13	.0000	.0000	.0000	.0000	.0001	.0001	.0001	.0001	.0002	.0002
14	.0000	.0000	.0000	.0000	.0000	.0000	.0000	.0000	.0000	.0001

x	4.1	4.2	4.3	4.4	λ 4.5	4.6	4.7	4.8	4.9	5.0
0	.0166	.0150	.0136	.0123	.0111	.0101	.0091	.0082	.0074	.0067
1	.0679	.0630	.0583	.0540	.0500	.0462	.0427	.0395	.0365	.0337
2	.1393	.1323	.1254	.1188	.1125	.1063	.1005	.0948	.0894	.0842
3	.1904	.1852	.1798	.1743	.1687	.1631	.1574	.1517	.1460	.1404
4	.1951	.1944	.1933	.1917	.1898	.1875	.1849	.1820	.1789	.1755
5	.1600	.1633	.1662	.1687	.1708	.1725	.1738	.1747	.1753	.1755
6	.1093	.1143	.1191	.1237	.1281	.1323	.1362	.1398	.1432	.1462
7	.0640	.0686	.0732	.0778	.0824	.0869	.0914	.0959	.1002	.1044
8	.0328	.0360	.0393	.0428	.0463	.0500	.0537	.0575	.0614	.0653
9	.0150	.0168	.0188	.0209	.0232	.0255	.0280	.0307	.0334	.0363

Table No. 5 (Continuation)

x	4.1	4.2	4.3	4.4	λ 4.5	4.6	4.7	4.8	4.9	5.0
10	.0061	.0071	.0081	.0092	.0104	.0118	.0132	.0147	.0164	.0181
11	.0023	.0027	.0032	.0037	.0043	.0049	.0056	.0064	.0073	.0082
12	.0008	.0009	.0011	.0014	.0016	.0019	.0022	.0026	.0030	.0034
13	.0002	.0003	.0004	.0005	.0006	.0007	.0008	.0009	.0011	.0013
14	.0001	.0001	.0001	.0001	.0002	.0002	.0003	.0003	.0004	.0005
15	.0000	.0000	.0000	.0000	.0001	.0001	.0001	.0001	.0001	.0002

x	5.1	5.2	5.3	5.4	λ 5.5	5.6	5.7	5.8	5.9	6.0
0	.0061	.0055	.0050	.0045	.0041	.0037	.0033	.0030	.0027	.0025
1	.0311	.0287	.0265	.0244	.0225	.0207	.0191	.0176	.0162	.0149
2	.0793	.0746	.0701	.0659	.0618	.0580	.0544	.0509	.0477	.0446
3	.1348	.1293	.1239	.1185	.1133	.1082	.1033	.0985	.0938	.0892
4	.1719	.1681	.1641	.1600	.1558	.1515	.1472	.1428	.1383	.1339
5	.1753	.1748	.1740	.1728	.1714	.1697	.1678	.1656	.1632	.1606
6	.1490	.1515	.1537	.1555	.1571	.1584	.1594	.1601	.1605	.1606
7	.1086	.1125	.1163	.1200	.1234	.1267	.1298	.1326	.1353	.1377
8	.0692	.0731	.0771	.0810	.0849	.0887	.0925	.0962	.0998	.1033
9	.0392	.0423	.0454	.0486	.0519	.0552	.0586	.0620	.0654	.0688
10	.0200	.0220	.0241	.0262	.0285	.0309	.0334	.0359	.0386	.0413
11	.0093	.0104	.0116	.0129	.0143	.0157	.0173	.0190	.0207	.0225
12	.0039	.0045	.0051	.0058	.0065	.0073	.0082	.0092	.0102	.0113
13	.0015	.0018	.0021	.0024	.0028	.0032	.0036	.0041	.0046	.0052
14	.0006	.0007	.0008	.0009	.0011	.0013	.0015	.0017	.0019	.0022
15	.0002	.0002	.0003	.0003	.0004	.0005	.0006	.0007	.0008	.0009
16	.0001	.0001	.0001	.0001	.0001	.0002	.0002	.0002	.0003	.0003
17	.0000	.0000	.0000	.0000	.0000	.0001	.0001	.0001	.0001	.0001

x	6.1	6.2	6.3	6.4	λ 6.5	6.6	6.7	6.8	6.9	7.0
0	.0022	.0020	.0018	.0017	.0015	.0014	.0012	.0011	.0010	.0009
1	.0137	.0126	.0116	.0106	.0098	.0090	.0082	.0076	.0070	.0064
2	.0417	.0390	.0364	.0340	.0318	.0296	.0276	.0258	.0240	.0223
3	.0848	.0806	.0765	.0726	.0688	.0652	.0617	.0584	.0552	.0521
4	.1294	.1249	.1205	.1162	.1118	.1076	.1034	.0992	.0952	.0912
5	.1579	.1549	.1519	.1487	.1454	.1420	.1385	.1349	.1314	.1277
6	.1605	.1601	.1595	.1586	.1575	.1562	.1546	.1529	.1511	.1490
7	.1399	.1418	.1435	.1450	.1462	.1472	.1480	.1486	.1489	.1490

Table No. 5 (Continuation)

x	λ 6.1	6.2	6.3	6.4	6.5	6.6	6.7	6.8	6.9	7.0
8	.1066	.1099	.1130	.1160	.1188	.1215	.1240	.1263	.1284	.1304
9	.0723	.0757	.0791	.0825	.0858	.0891	.0923	.0954	.0985	.1014
10	.0441	.0469	.0498	.0528	.0558	.0588	.0618	.0649	.0679	.0710
11	.0245	.0265	.0285	.0307	.0330	.0353	.0377	.0401	.0426	.0452
12	.0124	.0137	.0150	.0164	.0179	.0194	.0210	.0227	.0245	.0264
13	.0058	.0065	.0073	.0081	.0089	.0098	.0108	.0119	.0130	.0142
14	.0025	.0029	.0033	.0037	.0041	.0046	.0052	.0058	.0064	.0071
15	.0010	.0012	.0014	.0016	.0018	.0020	.0023	.0026	.0029	.0033
16	.0004	.0005	.0005	.0006	.0007	.0008	.0010	.0011	.0013	.0014
17	.0001	.0002	.0002	.0002	.0003	.0003	.0004	.0004	.0005	.0006
18	.0000	.0001	.0001	.0001	.0001	.0001	.0001	.0002	.0002	.0002
19	.0000	.0000	.0000	.0000	.0000	.0000	.0000	.0001	.0001	.0001

x	λ 7.1	7.2	7.3	7.4	7.5	7.6	7.7	7.8	7.9	8.0
0	.0008	.0007	.0007	.0006	.0006	.0005	.0005	.0004	.0004	.0003
1	.0059	.0054	.0049	.0045	.0041	.0038	.0035	.0032	.0029	.0027
2	.0208	.0194	.0180	.0167	.0156	.0145	.0134	.0125	.0116	.0107
3	.0492	.0464	.0438	.0413	.0389	.0366	.0345	.0324	.0305	.0286
4	.0874	.0836	.0799	.0764	.0729	.0696	.0663	.0632	.0602	.0573
5	.1241	.1204	.1167	.1130	.1094	.1057	.1021	.0986	.0951	.0916
6	.1468	.1445	.1420	.1394	.1367	.1339	.1311	.1282	.1252	.1221
7	.1489	.1486	.1481	.1474	.1465	.1454	.1442	.1428	.1413	.1396
8	.1321	.1337	.1351	.1363	.1373	.1382	.1388	.1392	.1395	.1396
9	.1042	.1070	.1096	.1121	.1144	.1167	.1187	.1207	.1224	.1241
10	.0740	.0770	.0800	.0829	.0858	.0887	.0914	.0941	.0967	.0993
11	.0478	.0504	.0531	.0558	.0585	.0613	.0640	.0667	.0695	.0722
12	.0283	.0303	.0323	.0344	.0366	.0388	.0411	.0434	.0457	.0481
13	.0154	.0168	.0181	.0196	.0211	.0227	.0243	.0260	.0278	.0296
14	.0078	.0086	.0095	.0104	.0113	.0123	.0134	.0145	.0157	.0169
15	.0037	.0041	.0046	.0051	.0057	.0062	.0069	.0075	.0083	.0090
16	.0016	.0019	.0021	.0024	.0026	.0030	.0033	.0037	.0041	.0045
17	.0007	.0008	.0009	.0010	.0012	.0013	.0015	.0017	.0019	.0021
18	.0003	.0003	.0004	.0004	.0005	.0006	.0006	.0007	.0008	.0009
19	.0001	.0001	.0001	.0002	.0002	.0002	.0003	.0003	.0003	.0004
20	.0000	.0000	.0001	.0001	.0001	.0001	.0001	.0001	.0001	.0002
21	.0000	.0000	.0000	.0000	.0000	.0000	.0000	.0000	.0001	.0001

Table No. 6: Areas under the Normal Curve

Values of $\int_0^x \frac{1}{\sqrt{2\pi}} e^{\frac{-t^2}{2}} dt$

(the shaded area)

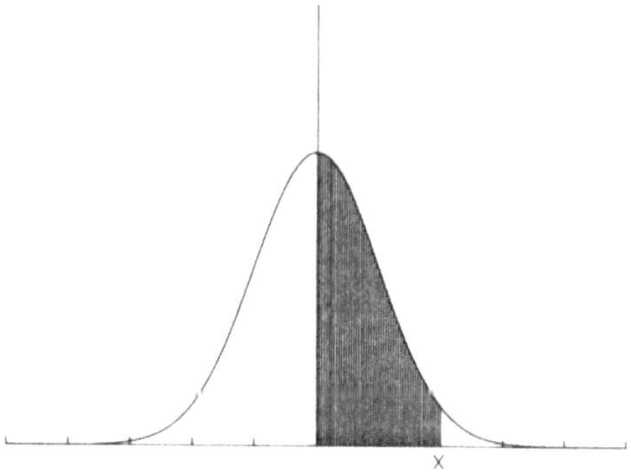

x	.00	.01	.02	.03	.04	.05	.06	.07	.08	.09
0.0	.0000	.0040	.0080	.0120	.0160	.0199	.0239	.0279	.0319	.0359
0.1	.0398	.0438	.0478	.0517	.0557	.0596	.0636	.0675	.0714	.0753
0.2	.0793	.0832	.0871	.0910	.0948	.0987	.1026	.1064	.1193	.1141
0.3	.1179	.1217	.1255	.1293	.1331	.1368	.1406	.1443	.1480	.1517
0.4	.1554	.1591	.1628	.1664	.1700	.1736	.1772	.1808	.1844	.1879
0.5	.1915	.1950	.1985	.2019	.2054	.2088	.2123	.2157	.2190	.2224
0.6	.2257	.2291	.2324	.2357	.2389	.2422	.2454	.2486	.2517	.2549
0.7	.2580	.2611	.2642	.2673	.2704	.2734	.2764	.2794	.2823	.2852
0.8	.2881	.2910	.2939	.2967	.2995	.3023	.3051	.3078	.3106	.3133
0.9	.3159	.3186	.3212	.3238	.3264	.3289	.3315	.3340	.3365	.3389
1.0	.3413	.3438	.3461	.3485	.3508	.3531	.3554	.3577	.3599	.3621
1.1	.3643	.3665	.3686	.3708	.3729	.3749	.3770	.3790	.3810	.3830
1.2	.3849	.3869	.3888	.3907	.3925	.3944	.3962	.3980	.3997	.4015
1.3	.4032	.4049	.4066	.4082	.4099	.4115	.4131	.4147	.4162	.4177
1.4	.4192	.4207	.4222	.4236	.4251	.4265	.4279	.4292	.4306	.4319
1.5	.4332	.4345	.4357	.4370	.4382	.4394	.4406	.4418	.4429	.4441
1.6	.4452	.4463	.4474	.4484	.4495	.4505	.4515	.4525	.4535	.4545
1.7	.4554	.4564	.4573	.4582	.4591	.4599	.4608	.4616	.4625	.4633
1.8	.4641	.4649	.4656	.4664	.4671	.4678	.4686	.4693	.4699	.4706
1.9	.4713	.4719	.4726	.4732	.4738	.4744	.4750	.4756	.4761	.4767
2.0	.4772	.4778	.4783	.4788	.4793	.4798	.4803	.4808	.4812	.4817
2.1	.4821	.4826	.4830	.4834	.4838	.4842	.4846	.4850	.4854	.4857
2.2	.4861	.4864	.4868	.4871	.4875	.4878	.4881	.4884	.4887	.4890
2.3	.4893	.4896	.4898	.4901	.4904	.4006	.4909	.4911	.4913	.4916
2.4	.4918	.4920	.4922	.4925	.4927	.4929	.4931	.4932	.4934	.4936
2.5	.4938	.4940	.4941	.4943	.4945	.4946	.4948	.4949	.4951	.4952

Table No. 6 (Continuation)

x	.00	.01	.02	.03	.04	.05	.06	.07	.08	.09
2.6	.4953	.4955	.4956	.4957	.4959	.4960	.4961	.4962	.4963	.4964
2.7	.4965	.4966	.4967	.4968	.4969	.4970	.4971	.4972	.4973	.4974
2.8	.4974	.4975	.4976	.4977	.4977	.4978	.4979	.4979	.4980	.4981
2.9	.4981	.4982	.4982	.4983	.4984	.4984	.4985	.4985	.4986	.4986
3.0	.4987	.4987	.4987	.4988	.4988	.4989	.4989	.4989	.4990	.4990
3.5	.499767									
4.0	.4999683									
4.5	.49999660									
5.0	.499999713									

Table No. 7: Critical Values for the Student's t Distribution (Source: This table is adapted by permission from Fisher and Yates: *Statistical Tables for Biological, Agricultural and Medical Research,* Longman Group Ltd., London; previously published by Oliver & Boyd Ltd. Edinburgh.)

Values of t such that the tail area α to the right of t equals the specified probability.

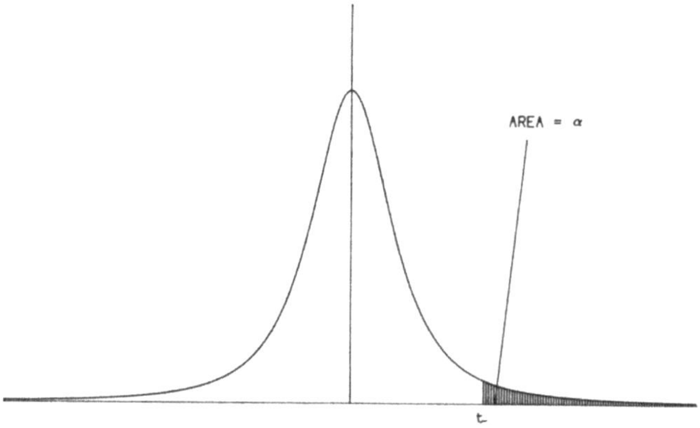

Degrees of freedom, n	Right-tail area α .10	.05	.025	.01	.005
1	3.078	6.314	12.706	31.821	63.657
2	1.886	2.920	4.303	6.965	9.925
3	1.638	2.353	3.182	4.541	5.841
4	1.533	2.132	2.776	3.747	4.604
5	1.476	2.015	2.571	3.365	4.032
6	1.440	1.943	2.447	3.143	3.707
7	1.415	1.895	2.365	2.998	3.499
8	1.397	1.860	2.306	2.896	3.355
9	1.383	1.833	2.262	2.821	3.250
10	1.372	1.812	2.228	2.764	3.169

Table No. 7 (Continuation)

Degrees of freedom, n	Right-tail area α .10	.05	.025	.01	.005
11	1.363	1.796	2.201	2.718	3.106
12	1.356	1.782	2.179	2.681	3.055
13	1.350	1.771	2.160	2.650	3.012
14	1.345	1.761	2.145	2.624	2.977
15	1.341	1.753	2.131	2.602	2.947
16	1.337	1.746	2.120	2.583	2.921
17	1.333	1.740	2.110	2.567	2.898
18	1.330	1.734	2.101	2.552	2.878
19	1.328	1.729	2.093	2.539	2.861
20	1.325	1.725	2.086	2.528	2.845
21	1.323	1.721	2.080	2.518	2.831
22	1.321	1.717	2.074	2.508	2.819
23	1.319	1.714	2.069	2.500	2.807
24	1.318	1.711	2.064	2.492	2.797
25	1.316	1.708	2.060	2.485	2.787
26	1.315	1.706	2.056	2.479	2.779
27	1.314	1.703	2.052	2.473	2.771
28	1.313	1.701	2.048	2.467	2.763
29	1.311	1.699	2.045	2.462	2.756
30	1.310	1.697	2.042	2.457	2.750
40	1.303	1.684	2.021	2.423	2.704
60	1.296	1.671	2.000	2.390	2.660
120	1.290	1.661	1.984	2.358	2.626
∞	1.282	1.645	1.960	2.326	2.576

Table No. 8: Critical Values for the Chi-square Distribution (Source: This table is adapted by permission from C. M. Thompson: *"Table of Percentage Points in the χ^2 Distribution"*, Biometrika, Vol. 32, 1942, p. 187.)

Values of χ^2 such that the tail area to the right of t equals the specified probability.

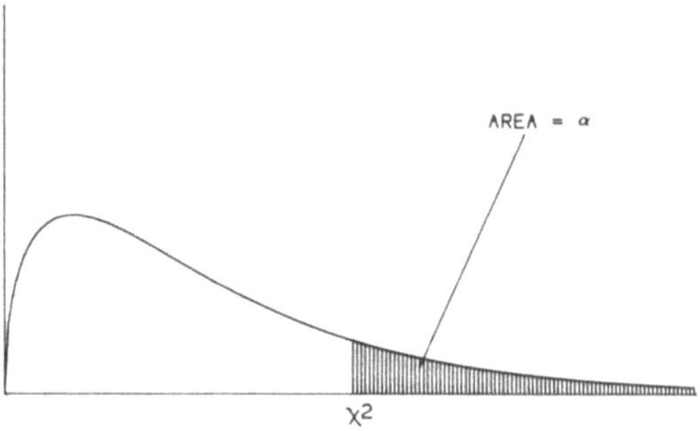

Degrees of freedom	Right-tail area α							
	.995	.990	.975	.950	.050	.025	.010	.005
1	–	–	–	.004	3.84	5.02	6.63	7.88
2	.01	.02	.05	.10	5.99	7.38	9.21	10.60
3	.07	.11	.22	.35	7.81	9.35	11.34	12.84
4	.21	.30	.48	.71	9.49	11.14	13.28	14.86
5	.41	.55	.83	1.15	11.07	12.83	15.09	16.75
6	.68	.87	1.24	1.64	12.59	14.45	16.81	18.55
7	.99	1.24	1.69	2.17	14.07	16.01	18.48	20.28
8	1.34	1.65	2.18	2.73	15.51	17.53	20.09	21.96
9	1.73	2.09	2.70	3.33	16.92	19.02	21.67	23.59
10	2.16	2.56	3.25	3.94	18.31	20.48	23.21	25.19
11	2.60	3.05	3.82	4.57	19.68	21.92	24.72	26.76
12	3.07	3.57	4.40	5.23	21.03	23.34	26.22	28.30
13	3.57	4.11	5.01	5.89	22.36	24.74	27.69	29.82
14	4.07	4.66	5.63	6.57	23.68	26.12	29.14	31.32
15	4.60	5.23	6.26	7.26	25.00	27.49	30.58	32.80
16	5.14	5.81	6.91	7.96	26.30	28.85	32.00	34.27
17	5.70	6.41	7.56	8.67	27.59	30.19	33.41	35.72
18	6.26	7.01	8.23	9.39	28.87	31.53	34.81	37.16
19	6.84	7.63	8.91	10.12	30.14	32.85	36.19	38.58
20	7.43	8.26	9.59	10.85	31.41	34.17	37.57	40.00
21	8.03	8.90	10.28	11.59	32.67	35.48	38.93	41.40
22	8.64	9.54	10.98	12.34	33.92	36.78	40.29	42.80
23	9.26	10.20	11.69	13.09	35.17	38.08	41.64	44.18
24	9.89	10.86	12.40	13.85	36.42	39.36	42.98	45.56
25	10.52	11.52	13.12	14.61	37.65	40.65	44.31	46.93
26	11.16	12.20	13.84	15.38	38.89	41.92	45.64	48.29
27	11.81	12.88	14.57	16.15	40.11	43.19	46.96	49.64

Table No. 8 (Continuation)

Degrees of freedom	Right-tail area α .995	.990	.975	.950	.050	.025	.010	.005
28	12.46	13.56	15.31	16.93	41.34	44.46	48.28	50.99
29	13.12	14.26	16.05	17.71	42.56	45.72	49.59	52.34
30	13.79	14.95	16.79	18.49	43.77	46.98	50.89	53.67
40	20.71	22.16	24.43	26.51	55.76	59.34	63.69	66.77
50	27.99	29.71	32.36	34.76	67.50	71.42	76.15	79.49
60	35.53	37.48	40.48	43.19	79.08	83.30	88.38	91.95
70	43.28	45.44	48.76	51.74	90.53	95.02	100.43	104.22
80	51.17	53.54	57.15	60.39	101.88	106.63	112.33	116.32
90	59.20	61.75	65.65	69.13	113.14	118.14	124.12	128.30
100	67.33	70.06	74.22	77.93	124.34	129.56	135.81	140.17

Table No. 9: Critical Values for the F Distribution (Source: This table is adapted by permission from Snedecor and Cochran: *Statistical Methods,* Iowa State University Press, 1967.)

Values of F such that the tail area to the right of F equals the specified probability. $F_{0.05}$ are in lightface type; $F_{0.01}$ in **boldface**.

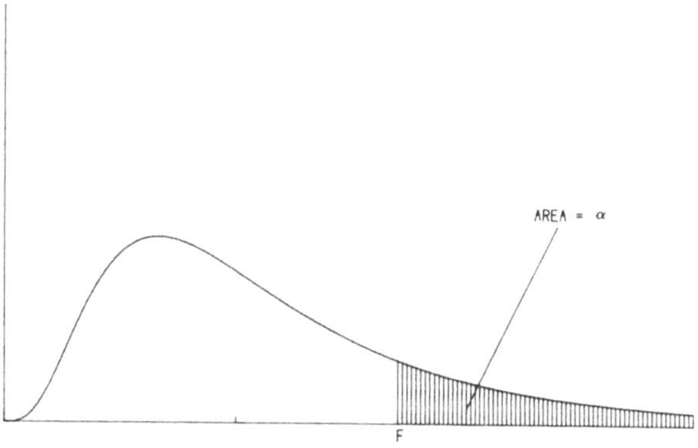

n_2 Degrees of Freedom for Denominator	n_1 Degrees of Freedom for Numerator 1	2	3	4	5	6	7	8	9	10	11	12
1	161	200	216	225	230	234	237	239	241	242	243	244
	4052	**4999**	**5403**	**5625**	**5764**	**5859**	**5928**	**5981**	**6022**	**6056**	**6082**	**6106**
2	18.51	19.00	19.16	19.25	19.30	19.33	19.36	19.37	19.38	19.39	19.40	19.41
	98.49	**99.01**	**99.17**	**99.25**	**99.30**	**99.33**	**99.34**	**99.36**	**99.38**	**99.40**	**99.41**	**99.42**
3	10.13	9.55	9.28	9.12	9.01	8.94	8.88	8.84	8.81	8.78	8.76	8.74
	34.12	**30.81**	**29.46**	**28.71**	**28.24**	**27.91**	**27.67**	**27.49**	**27.34**	**27.23**	**27.13**	**27.05**

Table No. 9 (Continuation)

n_2 Degrees of Freedom for Denominator	n_1 Degrees of Freedom for Numerator											
	i	2	3	4	5	6	7	8	9	10	11	12
4	7.71	6.94	6.59	6.39	6.26	6.16	6.09	6.04	6.00	5.96	5.93	5.91
	21.20	**18.00**	**16.69**	**15.98**	**15.52**	**15.21**	**14.98**	**14.80**	**14.66**	**14.54**	**14.45**	**14.37**
5	6.61	5.79	5.41	5.19	5.05	4.95	4.88	4.82	4.78	4.74	4.70	4.68
	16.26	**13.27**	**12.06**	**11.39**	**10.97**	**10.67**	**10.45**	**10.27**	**10.15**	**10.05**	**9.96**	**9.89**
6	5.99	5.14	4.76	4.53	4.39	4.28	4.21	4.15	4.10	4.06	4.03	4.00
	13.74	**10.92**	**9.78**	**9.15**	**8.75**	**8.47**	**8.26**	**8.10**	**7.98**	**7.87**	**7.79**	**7.72**
7	5.59	4.74	4.35	4.12	3.97	3.87	3.79	3.73	3.68	3.63	3.60	3.57
	12.25	**9.55**	**8.45**	**7.85**	**7.46**	**7.19**	**7.00**	**6.84**	**6.71**	**6.62**	**6.54**	**6.47**
8	5.32	4.46	4.07	3.84	3.69	3.58	3.50	3.44	3.39	3.34	3.31	3.28
	11.26	**8.65**	**7.59**	**7.01**	**6.63**	**6.37**	**6.19**	**6.03**	**5.91**	**5.82**	**5.74**	**5.67**
9	5.12	4.26	3.86	3.63	3.48	3.37	3.29	3.23	3.18	3.13	3.10	3.07
	10.56	**8.02**	**6.99**	**6.42**	**6.06**	**5.80**	**5.62**	**5.47**	**5.35**	**5.26**	**5.18**	**5.11**
10	4.96	4.10	3.71	3.48	3.33	3.22	3.14	3.07	3.02	2.97	2.94	2.91
	10.04	**7.56**	**6.55**	**5.99**	**5.64**	**5.39**	**5.21**	**5.06**	**4.95**	**4.85**	**4.78**	**4.71**
11	4.84	3.98	3.59	3.36	3.20	3.09	3.01	2.95	2.90	2.86	2.82	2.79
	9.65	**7.20**	**6.22**	**5.67**	**5.32**	**5.07**	**4.88**	**4.74**	**4.63**	**4.54**	**4.46**	**4.40**
12	4.75	3.88	3.49	3.26	3.11	3.00	2.92	2.85	2.80	2.76	2.72	2.69
	9.33	**6.93**	**5.95**	**5.41**	**5.06**	**4.82**	**4.65**	**4.50**	**4.39**	**4.30**	**4.22**	**4.16**
13	4.67	3.80	3.41	3.18	3.02	2.92	2.84	2.77	2.72	2.67	2.63	2.60
	9.07	**6.70**	**5.74**	**5.20**	**4.86**	**4.62**	**4.44**	**4.30**	**4.19**	**4.10**	**4.02**	**3.96**
14	4.60	3.74	3.34	3.11	2.96	2.85	2.77	2.70	2.65	2.60	2.56	2.53
	8.86	**6.51**	**5.56**	**5.03**	**4.69**	**4.46**	**4.28**	**4.14**	**4.03**	**3.94**	**3.86**	**3.80**
15	4.54	3.68	3.29	3.06	2.90	2.79	2.70	2.64	2.59	2.55	2.51	2.48
	8.68	**6.36**	**5.42**	**4.89**	**4.56**	**4.32**	**4.14**	**4.00**	**3.89**	**3.80**	**3.73**	**3.67**
16	4.49	3.63	3.24	3.01	2.85	2.74	2.66	2.59	2.54	2.49	2.45	2.42
	8.53	**6.23**	**5.29**	**4.77**	**4.44**	**4.20**	**4.03**	**3.89**	**3.78**	**3.69**	**3.61**	**3.55**
17	4.45	3.59	3.20	2.96	2.81	2.70	2.62	2.55	2.50	2.45	2.41	2.38
	8.40	**6.11**	**5.18**	**4.67**	**4.34**	**4.10**	**3.93**	**3.79**	**3.68**	**3.59**	**3.52**	**3.45**
18	4.41	3.55	3.16	2.93	2.77	6.66	2.58	2.51	2.46	2.41	2.37	2.34
	8.28	**6.01**	**5.09**	**4.58**	**4.25**	**4.01**	**3.85**	**3.71**	**3.60**	**3.51**	**3.44**	**3.37**
19	4.38	3.52	3.13	2.90	2.74	2.63	2.55	2.48	2.43	2.38	2.34	2.31
	8.18	**5.93**	**5.01**	**4.50**	**4.17**	**3.94**	**3.77**	**3.63**	**3.52**	**3.43**	**3.36**	**3.30**
20	4.35	3.49	3.10	2.87	2.71	2.60	2.52	2.45	2.40	2.35	2.31	2.28
	8.10	**5.85**	**4.94**	**4.43**	**4.10**	**3.87**	**3.71**	**3.56**	**3.45**	**3.37**	**3.30**	**3.23**
21	4.32	3.47	3.07	2.84	2.68	2.57	2.49	2.42	2.37	2.32	2.28	2.25
	8.02	**5.78**	**4.87**	**4.37**	**4.04**	**3.81**	**3.65**	**3.51**	**3.40**	**3.31**	**3.24**	**3.17**
22	4.30	3.44	3.05	2.82	2.66	2.55	2.47	2.46	2.35	2.30	2.26	2.23
	7.94	**5.72**	**4.82**	**4.31**	**3.99**	**3.76**	**3.59**	**3.45**	**3.35**	**3.26**	**3.18**	**3.12**
23	4.28	3.42	3.03	2.80	2.64	2.53	2.45	2.38	2.32	2.28	2.24	2.20
	7.88	**5.66**	**4.76**	**4.26**	**3.94**	**3.71**	**3.54**	**3.41**	**3.30**	**3.21**	**3.14**	**3.07**

Table No. 9 (Continuation)

n_2 Degrees of Freedom for Deno-minator	n_1 Degrees of Freedom for Numerator											
	1	2	3	4	5	6	7	8	9	10	11	12
24	4.26	3.40	3.01	2.78	2.62	2.61	2.43	2.36	2.30	2.26	2.22	2.18
	7.82	**5.61**	**4.72**	**4.22**	**3.96**	**3.67**	**3.50**	**3.36**	**3.25**	**3.17**	**3.09**	**3.03**
25	4.24	3.38	2.99	2.76	2.60	2.49	2.41	2.34	2.28	2.24	2.20	2.16
	7.77	**5.57**	**4.68**	**4.18**	**3.86**	**3.63**	**3.46**	**3.32**	**3.21**	**3.13**	**3.05**	**2.99**
26	4.23	3.37	2.98	2.74	2.59	2.45	2.39	2.32	2.27	2.22	2.18	2.15
	7.72	**5.53**	**4.64**	**4.14**	**3.82**	**3.59**	**3.42**	**3.29**	**3.17**	**3.09**	**3.02**	**2.96**

Table No. 10: Critical Values for the Wilcoxon Rank Sum Test (Source: This table contains material from Wilcoxon and Wilcox: *"Some Rapid Approximate Statistical Procedures"*, pp. 20–23. Copyright © 1949, 1964, Lederle Laboratories Division of American Cyanamid Company, All Rights Reserved, and Reprinted With Permission.)

Values of the rank sum for the smaller sample.

$\alpha = 0.025$ one-tail test; $\alpha = 0.05$ two-tail test

n_A	3		4		5		6		7		8		9		10	
n_B	T_L	T_U	T_L	T_U	T_L	T_U	T_L	T_U	T_L	T_U	T_L	T_U	T_L	T_U	T_L	T_U
3	5	16	6	18	6	21	7	23	7	26	8	28	8	31	9	33
4	6	18	11	25	12	28	12	32	13	35	14	38	15	41	16	44
5	6	21	12	28	18	37	19	41	20	45	21	49	22	53	24	56
6	7	23	12	32	19	41	26	52	28	56	29	61	31	65	32	70
7	7	26	13	35	20	45	28	56	37	68	39	73	41	78	43	83
8	8	28	14	38	21	49	29	61	89	73	49	87	51	93	54	98
9	8	31	15	41	22	53	31	65	41	78	51	93	63	108	66	114
10	9	33	16	44	24	56	32	70	43	83	54	98	66	114	79	131

$\alpha = 0.05$ one-tail test; $\alpha = 0.10$ two-tail test

n_A	3		4		5		6		7		8		9		10	
n_B	T_L	T_U	T_L	T_U	T_L	T_U	T_L	T_U	T_L	T_U	T_L	T_U	T_L	T_U	T_L	T_U
3	6	15	7	17	7	20	8	22	9	24	9	27	10	29	11	31
4	7	17	12	24	13	27	14	30	15	33	16	36	17	39	18	42
5	7	20	13	27	19	36	20	40	22	43	24	46	25	50	26	54
6	8	22	14	30	20	40	28	50	30	54	32	58	33	63	35	67
7	9	24	15	33	22	43	30	54	39	66	41	71	43	76	46	80
8	9	27	16	36	24	46	32	58	41	71	52	84	54	90	57	95
9	10	29	17	39	25	50	33	63	43	76	54	90	66	105	69	111
10	11	31	18	42	26	54	35	67	46	80	57	95	69	111	83	121

Table No. 11: Critical Values for the Wilcoxon Signed-Rank Test (Source: This table contains material from Wilcoxon and Wilcox: *"Some Rapid Approximate Statistical Procedures"*, p. 8. Copyright © 1949, 1964, Lederle Laboratories Division of American Cyanamid Company, All Rights Reserved, and Reprinted With Permission.)

Values of the smaller rank sum

	one-tail test			
	$\alpha = 0.05$	$\alpha = 0.025$	$\alpha = 0.010$	$\alpha = 0.005$
	two-tail test			
n	$\alpha = 0.10$	$\alpha = 0.05$	$\alpha = 0.02$	$\alpha = 0.01$
6	2	0	–	–
7	4	2	0	–
8	6	4	2	0
9	8	6	3	2
10	11	8	5	3
11	14	11	7	5
12	17	14	10	7
13	21	17	13	10
14	26	21	16	13
15	30	25	20	16
16	36	30	24	20
17	41	35	28	23
18	47	40	33	28
19	54	46	38	32
20	60	52	43	38
21	68	59	49	43
22	75	66	56	49
23	83	73	62	55
24	92	81	69	61
25	101	89	77	68

Table No. 12: Critical Values for the Kendall Correlation Test (Source: This table is adapted by permission from Kaarsemaker and van Wijngaarten: "Table for Use in Rank Correlation", *Statistica Neerlandica,* Vol. 7, 1953, pp. 41–54.)

Values of S such that the upper tail area does not exceed the specified probability

n	$\alpha = .005$	$\alpha = .010$	$\alpha = .025$	$\alpha = .050$	$\alpha = .100$
4	8	8	8	6	6
5	12	10	10	8	8
6	15	13	13	11	9
7	19	17	15	13	11
8	22	20	18	16	12
9	26	24	20	18	14
10	29	27	23	21	17
11	33	31	27	23	19
12	38	36	30	26	20
13	44	40	34	28	24
14	47	43	37	33	25
15	53	49	41	35	29
16	58	52	46	38	30
17	64	58	50	42	34
18	69	63	53	45	37
19	75	67	57	49	39
20	80	72	62	52	42
21	86	78	66	56	44
22	91	83	71	61	47
23	99	89	75	65	51
24	104	94	80	68	54
25	110	100	86	72	58
26	117	107	91	77	61
27	125	113	95	81	63
28	130	118	100	86	68
29	138	126	106	90	70
30	145	131	111	95	75

Answers to Some Exercises

3.1 a) \$9.91 billion; b) \$8.9 billion
3.3 7.83%
3.4 a) \$18,952.86; b) \$18,600; c) \$18,100
3.12 d) \$3.593 billion
4.3 a) 0.58; b) 0.63; c) 0.38; d) 0.33
4.7 a) 0.08; b) 0.94; c) 0.9118; d) 0.0082
4.18 a) 0.375; b) 0.18; c) 0.56; d) 0.67
4.24 a) 0.178; b) 0.00024; c) 0.033; d) 0.9992; e) 0.00463
4.33 a) 0.75; b) 0.0357; c) 0.25; d) 0.214
5.7 a) 0.515; b) 0.207; c) 0.050
5.27 a) 3.6; b) 0.8435; c) 0.9875; d) 0.4852; e) 0.2123
6.8 a) 0.9904; b) 0.2776; c) 0.9852
6.9 a) 0.0274; b) 1.0000; c) 0.0475
6.11 a) 2.28%; b) 6.68%; c) 1373 hours
6.20 c) 0.0358; d) 0.1353
7.22 a) 110.5; b) 0.474; c) 2.56; d) 1.599
8.1 a) 0.1868; b) 1083 families
8.6 $32.212 \leqq \mu \leqq 35.588$
8.8 a) (105.806, 119.494); b) (107.75, 117.55)
9.10 Yes
9.15 a) (38.83, 81.17); b) Yes; c) Supplier A
9.20 a) (−5.42, 1.42); b) No
9.23 a) No; b) (0.065, 0.355)
10.1 Yes
10.8 χ^2 (observed) = 19.68, $\chi^2_{0.01}(2) = 9.21$; the response rate differs.
10.12 a) $T_A = 106.5$, $T_B = 64.5$; c) Use sulfa
10.17 Reject
11.2 F(observed) = 7.85, $F_{0.05}(2, 12) = 3.89$. Reject the hypothesis that the opportunities are the same.
11.7 Yes
12.2 a) $\mu_{Y|x} = 40.072 + 1.497x$; b) 84.98
12.6 a) $y = 1.7317 + 0.4451x$; b) 0.06616; c) (0.276, 0.614)
13.3 a) $y = -2.491 + 0.099x_1 + 0.029x_2 + 0.086x_3$;
b) 78.34%; d) elevation

Index

Bei Fragen zur Produktsicherheit wenden Sie sich bitte an:
If you have any questions regarding product safety,
please contact:

Walter de Gruyter GmbH
Genthiner Straße 13
10785 Berlin
productsafety@degruyterbrill.com